ENVIRONMENTAL MOVEMENTS
Local, National and Global

Of Related Interest

A GREEN DIMENSION FOR THE EUROPEAN COMMUNITY
Political Issues and Processes
edited by David Judge

SUSTAINABLE DEVELOPMENT IN WESTERN EUROPE
Coming to Terms with Agenda 21
edited by Tim O'Riordan and Heather Voisey

RIO: UNRAVELLING THE CONSEQUENCES
edited by Caroline Thomas

NETWORKS FOR WATER POLICY
A Comparative Perspective
edited by H. Bressers, L.J. O'Toole, Jr. and J. Richardson

ECOLOGY AND DEMOCRACY
edited by Freya Mathews

DILEMMAS OF TRANSITION
The Environment, Democracy and Economic Reform in Europe
edited by Susan Baker and Petr Jehlička

ENVIRONMENTAL MOVEMENTS
Local, National and Global

edited by

CHRISTOPHER ROOTES

FRANK CASS
LONDON • PORTLAND, OR

First published in 1999 in Great Britain by
FRANK CASS PUBLISHERS
Newbury House, 900 Eastern Avenue,
London, IG2 7HH, England

and in the United States of America by
FRANK CASS PUBLISHERS
c/o ISBS
5804 N.E. Hassalo Street
Portland, Oregon 97213-3644

Website: www.frankcass.com

British Library Cataloguing in Publication Data

En vironmental movements : local, national and global
1. Environmentalism
I. Rootes, Chris, 1948–
333.7'2

ISBN 0 7146 5008 0 (cloth)
ISBN 0 7146 8066 4 (paper)

Library of Congress Cataloging in Publication Data

Environmental movements : local, national and global / edited by
Christopher Rootes.
    p.   cm.
"A special issue of the journal Environmental Politics, vol. 8,
no. 1. Spring 1999."
Includes bibliographical references and index.
ISBN 0-7146-5008-0 (cloth). – ISBN 0-7146-8066-4 (pbk.)
1. Environmentalism. I. Rootes, Chris, 1948– .
II. Environmental politics. Vol. 8, no. 1, Spring 1999.
GE195.E585   1999
363.7'05–dc21   99-21228
                                                            CIP

This group of studies first appeared in a Special Issue: 'Environmental Movements: Local,
National and Global' of *Environmental Politics* (ISSN 0964-4016) 8/1 Spring 1999
published by Frank Cass.

Printed in Great Britain by
Antony Rowe Ltd, Chippenham, Wilts.

Contents

/

Environmental Movements:
From the Local to the Global

CHRISTOPHER ROOTES

Of all the 'new' social movements which emerged from the student
movements of the late 1960s, it is environmental movements which have
had most enduring influence on politics and which have undergone the most
wide-ranging institutionalisation in terms both of the professionalisation of
their activities and of the regularisation of their access to policy-makers.
Not least as a result of pressure from environmental movements,
environment ministries are now a normal feature of western governments.
Although the emergence of green parties is only the tip of the iceberg of the
greening of the politics of industrialised societies, Green Party members
currently hold the environment portfolio in the governments of three of the
four largest western European states. Greens are established players in the
political arena of most western European states, by turns competed with and
courted by larger parties.

Green Parties have not generally grown simply or directly from
environmental movements [*Rootes, 1997c*] green parties are widely
regarded as part of a broader green movement, and the fact that greens have
entered government in an increasing number of states owes more to the
perceived strength and popularity of environmental movements than it does
to the generally marginal electoral performances of green parties
themselves.

Despite recurrent sensationalist mass media reports of the decline or
even death of the environmental movement, there is abundant evidence of
its enduring vitality. Younger people are now more likely to be members or
paying supporters of environmental movement organisations (EMOs) than
of political parties. As one generation of EMOs becomes established and
institutionalised, new, more formally organised networks of environmental
activists have emerged [*Rootes, 1997b, 1999*]. 'Eco-warriors' have become
folk heroes, not only with young people, but even with sections of a
generally conservative press [*Paterson, 1997*]. Mobilisations against new
infrastructure developments such as roads, airports, high speed railways and
waste treatment facilities have so raised the costs of such projects that they
have forced re-evaluation of policy. At a global level, NGOs which are part
of or linked to environmental movements enjoy unprecedented status as

interlocutors of the representatives of states as they attempt to grapple with the formation and implementation of policies and institutions to deal with global environmental problems.

If environmental movements have been relatively neglected in the scholarly literature by comparison with green parties, it is partly because of the sheer messiness of the phenomena so labelled. Whereas parties and individual organisations are relatively easily delimited, environmental movement? is a rather vague term and one often left deliberately vague in order to be inclusive.

The approach adopted to 'environmental movements' in this volume is an inclusive one. Thus environmental movements are conceived as broad networks of people and organisations engaged in collective action in the pursuit of environmental benefits [*Rootes, 1997c;* cf. *Diani, 1992*]. Environmental movements are understood to be very diverse and complex, their organisational forms ranging from the highly organised and formally institutionalised to the radically informal, the spatial scope of their activities ranging from the local to the almost global, the nature of their concerns ranging from single issues to the full panoply of global environmental concerns. Such an inclusive conception is consistent with the usage of the term amongst environmental activists themselves and enables us to consider the linkages between the several levels and forms of what activists call 'the environmental movement'. Parties, particularly green parties, are not in principle excluded, but the emphasis here is on the groups and organisations which generally operate through less clearly and publicly rule-governed channels and which do not seek formal political office.

The cases treated here cannot hope to be representative of environmental movements in all their diversity, but they do include countries whose environmental movements have excited particular interest and cases which well illustrate some of the most interesting issues in the development of environmental movements:

- institutionalisation and the dilemmas that attend it;

- the relationship between local environmental struggles and national and (sometimes) transnational EMOs;

- the prospects for the development of a global environmental movement.

Institutionalisation and Its Discontents

Diani and Donati lay out a framework for the analysis of organisational changes in EMOs. It is an oversimplification to say that the environmental movement has undergone a change from being a mass participatory social movement to a series of institutionalised interest groups. Like other social movement organisations, EMOs are faced with choices between professional and mass participatory forms of organisation and between conventional and unconventional forms of action. These choices are not mutually exclusive; the mix of forms and tactics varies both over time and from place to place. Whilst there is evidence that some hitherto participatory and unconventional organisations have become more professionalised and are more ready to employ conventional tactics, others which were hitherto entirely conventional now also employ less conventional tactics. Nevertheless, as society and politics are transformed by the processes we commonly refer to as 'globalisation' or 'postmodernisation', so we should expect a transformation in the character of environmental movements. Central to this is the role of mass media. More professionalised EMOs have quickly adapted to a mass mediated age but the question that now arises is whether such adaptations ultimately weaken the capacities of EMOs to effect the mass mobilisations from which the environmental movement's power initially derived and upon which it may ultimately depend.

Nowhere is concern about this more evident than in Germany. Although the German movement is widely regarded as a model of a mature and successfully institutionalised movement and as an inspiration to others, there has to date been no systematic and widely available account in English of the processes of its institutionalisation and the strategic dilemmas to which this institutionalisation has given rise. Karl-Werner Brand, in his contribution, describes the many facets of the institutionalisation of the German environmental movement and the soul-searching which that experience has provoked within the movement.

Recent, principally journalistic discussions of the German movement have suggested that it has peaked and is stagnating or even that it is in decline. In an attempt systematically to confront such assertions with empirical evidence, Dieter Rucht and Jochen Roose draw on the results of survey research and on-going analyses of press reports of environmental movement activity. The picture that emerges is much more complex than it has been generally portrayed. Certainly, the environmental movement is no longer a novelty, and environmental politics is now well entrenched in the political mainstream. The dilemmas with which this situation confronts the movement are not those of failure but of incomplete success; the question now is how best to proceed to revitalise the movement and to make further progress toward sustainability.

Although the German case is, for many reasons, *sui generis,* it can nevertheless be taken to illustrate processes of institutionalisation and its attendant dilemmas which are more general across the mature industrialised societies of northern Europe. In Britain, too, the institutionalisation of the environmental movement has proceeded apace [*Jordan and Maloney, 1997; Rawcliff, 1998*] but, even more strikingly than in Germany, it has in recent years been accompanied by a surge of less formally organised activism, particularly associated with the anti-roads movement [*Doherty, 199*], which suggests that the process of institutionalisation may be self-limiting. Partly in reaction to the consequences of the institutionalisation of older EMOs such as Friends of the Earth, new groups, characteristically organised as 'networks' rather than more formal organisations, have grown up. Derek Wall describes and analyses the process of emergence of the best known of these new groups, Earth First! (UK), and its complicated relationships with youth subcultures and other parts of the broad environmental movement 'family', including both more established EMOs and local environmental protesters. Drawing inspiration and borrowing tactics from environmental activists in other parts of the English-speaking world, even as the new groups started from a desire to 'do something' more dramatic, more radical and more immediately effective than the actions of older EMOs, those more established organisations provided the inestimable resource of a network of contacts by which the new groups could grow.

In the belatedly industrialising and newly democratic states of southern Europe, environmental movements are also becoming institutionalised, but they are doing so under conditions radically different from those of northern states. For many reasons, but especially because of the opportunities and constraints created by the efforts of successive governments to prove that the country is a fully modernised, democratised member of the EU, environmental movements in Spain have, as Manuel Jiménez demonstrates, achieved a considerable measure of access and institutionalisation even without the development of EMOs well supported by large numbers of members and supporters. Spain thus presents the curious paradox of having both the lowest level of associational membership in western Europe and an environmental movement which is practically embarrassed by the many opportunities for participation in the making and implementation of policy.

The Local and the National

Yet, if low levels of association membership are common in southern Europe, it would, as Maria Kousis demonstrates, be quite wrong to assume that there is a low level of environmental movement mobilisation in southern Europe. If one looks at the local level, then the number and duration of environmental struggles and the diversity of tactics employed by them are impressive indeed. If they are seldom linked with national EMOs, that almost certainly has as much to do with the lack of resources of those national EMOs as it does with the limitations of environmental consciousness of the protesters.[1] Indeed, when local campaigners look to better established EMOs, they often look abroad, as do their counterparts in the Third World.

Where, however, national EMOs are more resource rich and where there is a longer tradition of local environmental protest, as there is in the US, then linkages between local environmental campaigns and national EMOs are extremely important. JoAnn Carmin examines the relationship between local voluntary and national professional environmental mobilisations and finds, from an analysis of newspaper reports, that while both ebb and flow over time, there is no evidence that professionalised activity has tended to replace local voluntary action; rather, the two levels of action appear to be symbiotic. Reported action by national professional EMOs has decreased over time, whereas that of local voluntary groups has been more marked by periodic surges. However, the reported unconventional activity of local voluntary groups, despite fluctuations, has not markedly declined, and surges in unconventional action by national professional EMOs appear broadly to follow the pattern of local unconventional actions. The fact that the unconventional actions of professional EMOs continue even after those of local groups have begun to decline suggests that local groups may play a 'discovery' role in relation to environmental issues and that once an issue is securely on the national agenda, the baton of protest passes to the bigger battalions of better resourced EMOs.

The relationship Carmin detects is plausible and suggestive – and appears to be mirrored in Spain if we compare Kousis's data on local mobilisations with Jiménez's data on nationally reported protest events – but it is important to remember that all these data are based upon newspaper reports. Although, in the absence of any better evidence, these analyses deserve to be taken very seriously, it is, strictly speaking, a record of media attention to environmental movement action that they analyse rather than an unmediated record of that action. Thus, given the declining novelty value of environmental movement activity and the increasing proportion of the work of semi-institutionalised EMOs that goes on behind closed doors rather than in public, it may well be that the decline in the reported actions of national professional EMOs in the US reflects a decline in the visibility and news value of EMOs' actions rather than a real decline in their levels of activity.

If Carmin has demonstrated that the actions of local protesters and national EMOs are correlated, David Schlosberg, in his discussion of the environmental justice movement in the US, examines the networks that link local environmental protests one to another as an alternative to reliance upon centralised organisations. Increasing disillusionment with the major US EMOs, seen by many as disempowering, paternalistic and exclusive, has fuelled attempts to develop new forms of organisation sufficiently flexible to accommodate the diversity of the environmental justice movement and to respond to changing circumstances at the local level. The preference for the network over more formal and centralised organisation is something US local activists have in common with the new generation of British environmental campaigners, but Schlosberg's worry that the network is not best suited to maintaining protests over time may be misplaced in view of the extraordinary number of sustained local campaigns which Kousis finds in Greece, Spain and Portugal, countries in which for reasons of culture and resources, centralised professional EMOs are weak, and where effective networking is almost certainly more difficult than in the US. If US campaigns are rarely sustained, it perhaps has more to do with a culturally induced impatience for immediate results, with a much higher rate of spatial mobility among the population, and with the greater openness and co-optative capacities of the US political system than with the shortcomings of networks as an organisational strategy.

Toward a Global Environmental Movement?

If the diversity of conditions creates difficulties for effective environmental movement organisation in the United States, such difficulties are writ large when it comes to attempting to organise a genuinely global environmental movement. As Hein-Anton van der Heijden observes, the diversity of circumstances between the consolidated liberal democracies of the First World of western Europe, North America and Australasia, the economically and politically fragile post-socialist states of eastern Europe and the former Soviet Union, and the economically dependent and often politically unstable states of the Third World makes it improbable that ecological modernisation and sustainable development, discourses forged in the course of pragmatic compromise between contending environmental interests in the affluent and materialist First World, will be universally appropriate or accepted. Western counter-cultural activists such as those of Earth First! and Third World environmentalists alike reject these essentially modernist and anthropocentric discourses, but because resistance to such radical critique is so ingrained in the First World, it is to environmental movements in the Third World that van der Heijden looks for leadership in years to come.

Any expectation that the road to effective environmental movements in the Third World might be at all smooth is quickly dispelled by Jeff Haynes' contribution. For people in the Third World, as elsewhere, environmental concerns are combined with other economic, political and cultural grievances. If, because the inequities of power are greater in the Third World, popular movements there rarely take the form of purely environmental movements like those of the West, the determinants of their success or failure serve to emphasise the importance of wider political and economic processes to the fate of struggles to defend the environment. The lack of safeguards for democratic political activity and judicial redress of grievances and the corresponding underdevelopment of civil society more often than not conspire to defeat the most desperate efforts of the world's most impoverished people to defend their habitat. Success for their campaigns often depends upon their ability to secure the support of First World EMOs.

The past two decades have been remarkable for the speed with which new transnational agreements on environmental protection have been forged and new institutions to implement them have been developed. Informed by considerations of economic and environmental justice as well as concern for environmental protection, new institutions such as the Global Environment Facility (GEF) and, more problematically, the World Trade Organisation (WTO), have become arena for interaction between environmental NGOs and the economically dominant powers. Zoe Young explores the role of NGOs within the GEF, while Marc Williams and Lucy Ford examine the dilemmas that confront environmental activists when they contemplate the WTO.

Groups which enter negotiations with the powerful, as they do in dealing with the WTO, become domesticated both in order to enter and as a result of so doing. Yet those who remain outside do so at the expense of limiting their influence. The dilemmas which confront EMOs at the national level are thus reflected at the transnational level. Indeed, they are magnified, because the resources required to play on a global stage are so much greater than those required at national level; to a much greater extent than is true at national level, EMOs which seek to be international players are dependent upon transnational organisations, not least for the funding required to participate in international meetings.

Clearly, existing NGOs are a very imperfect approximation to the global environmental movement to which many aspire. As Young remarks, they are, as young organisations in a new institutional environment, 'adhocracies'. The possibilities of genuine democratic accountability of any kind are limited, and especially so if the public to whom they might be held accountable is a global one. There is no democratic global state and if there is a global civil society, it is one in which the possibilities of effective communication remain infinitely greater among elites than among the masses.

The problem is that it is difficult to see this lack of democratic accountability as a merely temporary stage in the development of a global environmental movement. Yet, given the accumulated evidence of the limited effectiveness of purely local or even national attempts to secure redress of environmental grievances, there is no alternative but to attempt to play the game on the global stage. Moreover, if the prospects for an effective and genuinely democratic global environmental movement appear limited today, they are likely to improve as better and cheaper means of communication make the global village ever better connected and as increasing access to higher education gives more people the personal skills and resources necessary to make common cause with their counterparts in other countries and regions.

Conclusion

It is a moot point whether the effective networking of the world's environmentalists has any prospect of outrunning the rate at which the global environment is being degraded, but there is no reason to suppose that the teeth of environmental movements have been drawn by their increasing institutionalisation. A recurring theme in these essays is the centrality to social movements of the critical moment; there is an element of social movements which is essentially and necessarily critical of established social and political relations [cf. *Eyerman and Jamison, 1991*]. Social movements cannot be wholly institutionalised and still retain the identity of social movements, and as long as there is vitality in a movement there will be those who, in the name of purity of purpose, resist the compromises entailed by institutionalisation. This is not only an irritation to established and semi-institutionalised EMOs; it is often also an invaluable asset to them for it is a reminder of the conscience of the movement, a means of keeping in touch with grass-roots opinion, and a lever which can be used in dealings with the powerful who can thus be reminded that if they too strongly resist the reasonable demands of semi-institutionalised moderates, they may fuel the altogether more disruptive campaigns of uninstitutionalised radicals. Relations between environmental radicals and the representatives of established EMOs are, as a result, often surprisingly cordial and co-operative.

Whether at local, national or global level, the dialectic of environmental movement development is an on-going process. The compelling nature of environmental issues makes it likely that there will be increasingly effective institutionalised means of addressing them, but people professionally engaged in environmental protection are well aware that the existence of a vital environmental movement greatly increases their leverage with their competitors for resources. Nor is it only moderate environmentalism whose value they appreciate; it is precisely the radical environmentalism which is most resistant to institutionalisation which is especially valued as a source of ideas.[2]

There are several reasons for thinking that radical environmentalism, however much it may in the most industrialised countries appear to have been eclipsed by the increasingly impressive edifice of institutionalised environmentalism, will be a continuing source of revitalisation of the environmental movement. For one thing, the ideas and values which inform environmental radicals are fundamentally critical not only of many of the institutions of advanced capitalism but of the ideas and values which capitalism represents. Utopian ideas which confront capitalist ideology, they cannot be completely incorporated short of a revolution which scarcely anybody believes to be imminent. Just as the highest hopes of environmental radicals are likely to remain unrealised, so even the most complete environmental protection regimes are unlikely to anticipate or to deal sufficiently quickly or effectively with every new source of environmental grievance to prevent the repeated recurrence of local campaigns of complaint and resistance. These too are a continuing source of innovation in environmental movements.

It is not merely a romantic fascination with the unconventional that justifies our continuing interest in environmental movements. Not only do they continue to be an important part of the impetus for environmental defence and improvement across the globe, but their importance as interlocutors of and constraints upon the powerful is increasingly recognised by governments, international agencies and companies alike. Their recent rapid but partial institutionalisation may have confronted environmental movements with a series of uncomfortable dilemmas, but, not least because of the dilemmas environmental movements pose for the powerful, there is every reason to suppose that they will command our attention for many years to come.

Acknowledgements

In the course of a project like this, one accumulates many debts. The European Consortium for Political Research (ECPR) deserves special thanks: the personal network which has so stimulated my own thinking about social movements was established and consolidated by a succession of ECPR workshops; the direct impetus for this collection was provided by the workshop which I directed at the 1997 ECPR Joint Sessions in Bern; and the newsletter of the ECPR Standing Group on Green Politics provided another important means of recruitment. Thanks are also due to the European Commission; the ERASMUS network on social movements initiated by Bert Klandermans helped to consolidate and extend my own environmental movement network. The EC made a further contribution through its funding of the project on the Transformation of Environmental

Activism (the TEA project – EC contract number: ENV4-CT97-0514 – see Appendix); although little in this volume is a direct product of that project, work on which commenced only in March 1998, the many exchanges of views and information during the planning stages have influenced the way several of us see the issues considered here. Lastly, but by no means least, thanks are also due to all those who acted as referees; the quality of this volume is in no small measure a product of their efforts.

NOTES

1. My own research [*Rootes, 1997a*] on local environmental campaigns surrounding the siting of waste management facilities in England suggests that the involvement of EMOs is generally very limited, principally because local groups of EMOs such as FoE are too ill-resourced to give sustained support while EMOs at the national level have too few resources to meet the many demands made upon them to do more than act as sources of basic information and network contacts. In countries such as Greece, Spain and Portugal, EMOs are much less developed and are less well resourced than their English counterparts, and the possibilities of fruitful local–national linkage are correspondingly reduced.
2. There is evidence that the institutionalisation of the environmental movement is not always seen as a positive thing by European Commission bureaucrats. As one remarked, 'My problem is that I am not waiting for lobbies, I am waiting for movements. What I hope to have is some kind of ... democratic input in my thinking' [*Ruzza, 1996: 2217–18*]. Rucht [*1997*] suggests that the environmental movement's influence at the EC level is limited by the formidable obstacles to transnational mass mobilisation; this may, however, be too pessimistic since even mobilisations restricted to the national – or even the local – level have the power to disrupt EC-favoured projects.

REFERENCES

Diani, M. (1992), 'The Concept of Social Movement', *Sociological Review*, Vol.40, No.1, pp.1–25.
Doherty, B. (1999), 'Paving the Way: The Rise of Direct Action Against Road-building and the Changing Character of British Environmentalism', *Political Studies* (forthcoming).
Eyerman, R. and A. Jamison (1991), *Social Movements: A Cognitive Approach*, Cambridge: Polity.
Jordan, G. and Maloney, W. (1997), *The Protest Business*, Manchester: Manchester University Press.
Paterson, M. (1997), 'Swampy and the Tabloids', paper presented at the conference on Direct Action and the British Environmental Movement, Keele University, 25 Oct.
Rawdiffe, P. (1998), *Environmental Pressure Groups in Transition*, Manchester: Manchester University Press.
Rootes, C.A. (1997a), 'From Resistance to Empowerment: The Struggle Over Waste Management and Its Implications for Environmental Education', pp.30–39 in Russell *et at.* [*1997*].
Rootes, C.A. (1997b), 'The Transformation of Environmental Activism', pp.40–49 in Russell *et at.* [*1997*].
Rootes, C.A. (1997c), 'Environmental Movements and Green Parties in Western and Eastern Europe', in M. Redclift and G. Woodgate (eds.), *International Handbook of Environmental Sociology*, Cheltenham and Northampton, MA: Edward Elgar, pp.319–48.
Rootes, C.A. (1999), 'The Transformation of Environmental Activism: Activists, Organisations and Policy-Making', *Innovation: The European Journal of Social Sciences*, Vol.12, No.3 (forthcoming).

Rucht, D (1997), 'Limits to Mobilization: Environmental Policy for the European Union', in 3 Smith, C. Chatfield and R. Pagnucco (eds.), *Transnational Social Movements and Global Politics: Solidarity Beyond the State,* Syracuse, NY: Syracuse University Press, pp.195–213.
Russell, N. *et al.* (eds.) (1997), *Technology the Environment and Us,* London: GSE, Imperial College.
Ruzza, C. (1996), 'Inter-Organisational Negotiations in Political Decision-Making: Brussels' EC Bureaucrats and the Environment', in C. Samson and N. South (eds.), *The Social Construction of Social Policy,* Basingstoke: Macmillan/New York: St Martin's Press, pp.210–23.

APPENDIX

THE TEA (TRANSFORMATION OF ENVIRONMENTAL ACTIVISM) PROJECT
EC contract no.: ENV4-CT97-0514

This major EC-funded project commenced in March 1998 and will be completed in March 2001. The partners in the project are:

* University of Kent at Canterbury – UK – Christopher Rootes (co-ordinator)
* Wissenschaftszentrum Berlin für Sozialforschung – DE – Dieter Rucht
* University of Aalborg – DK – Andrew Jamison
* Juan March Institute, Madrid – ES – Andrew Richards and Manuel Jiménez
* Universidad del Pais Vasco – ES – Pedro Ibarra and Iñaki Barcena
* Centre d'étude de la vie politique française (CEVIPOF), Fondation Nationale des Sciences Politiques, Paris – FR – Olivier Fillieule
* University of Crete – GR – Maria Kousis
* University of Florence – I – Donatella della Porta
* University of Strathclyde – UK — Mario Diani

The project aims to examine the various forms of environmental activism, changes in their relative incidence over the past decade and from one EU member state to another, changes in environmental movement organisations (EMOs) and their relationships with other actors within and outside the wider environmental movement, to advance explanations for the patterns of variation, and to examine their implications for policymaking at the European level.

One response to the increasing institutionalisation of established EMOs has been the proliferation of new *ad hoc* groupings which prefer the politics of direct action to those of lobbying. The apparent rise of environmental protest which is not organised by established EMOs has stimulated some EMOs to attempt to restore their credibility with the more activist elements of their constituencies by diverting part of their efforts to direct action. The result is a dilemma for policymakers who find it increasingly difficult to know whether or how far they can rely upon EMOs as mediators of environmentalist opinion.

Neither the transformation of environmental protest and EMOs nor its implications for environmental policy-making has so far been the subject of systematic social scientific investigation on a crossnationally comparative basis. In order to remedy this, the project will undertake a systematic comparison of the incidence and forms of environmental activism and its relationship with EMOs in Germany, the United Kingdom, Italy, France, Spain, Greece and Sweden as well as at the level of the EU itself.

The proposed investigation embraces three complementary strategies:

* the quantitative and qualitative study of protest events about environmental issues by means of the analysis of reports published in mass media and environmental movement publications;
* interview-based examinations of EMOs and their relations with other actors;
* observation and interviews at local level of current cases of environmental contention, and

exploration, principally by means of analysis of local media reports and informant interviews, of the incidence and forms of environmental action in selected localities.

Further information on the project will be posted on the WWW at:
http:www.ukc.ac.uklsociology/TEA.html.

Enquiries may be addressed to the project coordinator:
Chris Rootes, Centre for the Study of Social and Political Movements, Darwin College, The University, Canterbury, Kent, CT2 7NY. Tel.: (01227) 823374; email: C.A.Rootes@ukc.ac.uk

Organisational Change in Western European Environmental Groups: A Framework for Analysis

MARIO DIANI and PAOLO R. DONATI

We present a framework to analyse organisational changes among environmental groups in Western Europe since the 1980s. A more diversified range of organisational models emerges than the simple dichotomy 'grassroots protest group vs. professional lobby'. We concentrate on four organisational types, based on different organisational responses to problems of resource mobilisation and political efficacy: public interest lobby, participatory protest organisation, professional protest organisation, and the participatory pressure group. We discuss trends towards professionalisation in the context of changes to the public sphere, and point out risks that hyperprofessionalisation may entail for environmental groups.

In social movement studies, a recurring discussion focuses on the specificity of social movement organisations (SMOs) [*Edwards, 1994; Kriesi, 1996; Burstein, 1997; Jordan and Maloney, 1997*]. Do SMOs have peculiar organisational traits? Do they differ from traditional public interest groups? Should we interpret the growing inclusion of SMOs in policy networks as evidence of their institutionalisation?

We relate these broad questions to recent transformations in environmental politics. We chart organisational changes in a few Western European environmental movements since the late 1970s/early 1980s (for other, recent analyses: van der Heijden, Koopmans and Giugni [*1992*]; Dalton [*1994*]; Jamison [*1996*]; Wapner [*1996*]; Donati [*1996*]. We do not provide a thorough account of organisational transformation in terms of membership and resources. Rather, we identify a few organisational models which may guide closer empirical exploration. To date, while some have

This contribution originated in the project on the institutionalisation of environmental issues in five Western European countries, directed by Klaus Eder (European Commission-DGXII, Grant PL 210943). The authors are indebted to Klaus Eder and the other members of the research team, Karl Werner Brand, Didier Le Saout, Ger Mullally, and Bron Szerszinski, to Christopher Rootes and the anonymous reviewers of *Environmental Politics* for their comments, and especially to Sidney Tarrow for his criticism and encouragement.

focused on professionalised groups [e.g., *Jordan and Maloney, 1997*], others have concentrated on the recurrent vitality of grass-roots action [e.g., *Szasz, 1994; Lichterman, 1996; Edwards, 1995*]. However, analyses of environmental groups which account for the variety of their organisational forms are rare. So are comparative analyses of organisational changes (but see Rucht [*1993*] and Rootes [*1997*]). We provide a conceptual framework to account for the complex organisational transformations that have taken place since environmentalism emerged as a major social movement in the 1980s.

Current debates about environmental organisations are often theoretically ambiguous. Accurate reconstructions of the evolution of specific movements and/or groups are not always backed by adequate discussion of the concept of social movement organisation. We start with a typology of non-partisan political organisations,[1] based on their different responses to problems of resource mobilisation and political efficacy. We also share some of the criticism which denies the peculiarity of social movement organisations *vis-à-vis* interest groups [*Burstein, 1997: Jordan and Maloney, 1997*]. Among non-partisan political organisations we focus on those which mobilise on behalf of collective or public interests.[2]

We illustrate our typology with references to the evolution of environmental organisations in England, Ireland, Italy and, more selectively, France and Germany. SMOs which emerged in the 1980s have become increasingly bureaucratic and operate increasingly like corporations or 'protest businesses' [*Jordan and Maloney, 1997*] rather than as participatory groups [*Kriesi, 1996; Donati, 1996*]. At the same time, while impressive commonalities may be found across countries, one can also point to meaningful variation in the evolution of the different national organisations (see also Kriesi [*1996*]; Rucht [*1996*]).

We conclude by discussing the implications of the increasing relevance of professionalised organisations for environmental mobilisation capacity at the grass-roots. How might environmental organisations react to a negative change in the opportunities available to them if their organisational infrastructures at the grass roots had been completely dismantled as a result of professionalisation [*Donati, 1994*]? Even a casual glance at the evolution of environmentalist action in western Europe suggests that the trend towards professional, non-participatory forms of organisation is balanced by the recurrent vitality of local activism. However, one might also wonder whether the changing meaning of concepts such as 'national politics' and 'public sphere' might not render the model of the participatory protest group less crucial in post-industrial society than it was in industrial society.

A Typology of Non-Partisan Political Organisations

Most political organisations[3] are shaped by their response to two basic functional requirements, *resource mobilisation* and *political efficacy* [*Diani and Donati, 1996*]: on one hand, they must secure through variable combinations of money and human power (that is, voluntary action) the resources essential to organisational survival and expansion [*Wilson, 1973; Zald and McCarthy, 1987; Scott, 1985*]; on the other hand, in order to perform effectively in the political process, political organisations may select varying combinations of tactics disrupting – or at least, threatening to disrupt – routinised political procedures, and tactics reflecting in contrast their integration in institutional politics, and their compliance with the rules of the game.

Meeting these different requirements is problematic for any political organisation, whether a party, an established interest group, or a social movement challenger [*Lanzalaco, 1990; Ch.2*]. However, social movements face probably the most difficult task, given the contradiction between their marginal position in the polity and their search for political recognition.

Resource Mobilisation Strategies

SMOs face a difficult choice between two fundamental options. They may try to mobilise the largest possible support from the general public, and therefore the resources, which are essential to the maintenance of a semi- or quasi-professional group. Available strategies range from calling upon broadly supported sets of values to the provision of selective incentives to prospective members/subscribers (in the forms of services, leisure time activities, discount packages). SMOs, however, may also try to mobilise smaller, but more carefully selected, groups of committed activists. These are essential for the more demanding tasks of movement participation, including persistent organisational commitment and costly forms of collective action.

The basic alternative is between the mobilisation of 'time' (activism) or 'money' [*Oliver and Marwell, 1992*]. These options are not easily compatible. Emotional messages which provide a clear-cut definition of a movement's identity and opponents are essential to mobilise core activists [*Gamson, 1992*], but their sharpness may alienate sympathisers and prospective supporters [*Friedman and McAdam, 1992*]. It may also discourage potential supporters among established actors (public agencies or even 'concerned' private sponsors) whose contributions will be easier to attract the greater the public support for a movement.[4] The choice between mobilising time or money has important implications for SMOs: each option requires different 'mobilisation technologies' and, therefore, different organisational models [*Oliver and Marwell, 1992; Schwartz and Paul, 1992*].

Political Efficacy

SMOs' effectiveness as representatives of unvested interests may emerge out of either disruption or routinised political negotiation. Full compliance with the rules of the game may grant official recognition but depotentiate their challenge; conversely, confrontation may increase their bargaining power on some occasions, but lead ultimately to their institutional marginalisation [*Lowe and Goyder, 1983; Grant, 1989; Richardson and Watts, 1985*].

One might regard the choice of protest tactics as a tactical, ultimately contingent matter, rather than as an organisational property [*Diani, 1992; Burstein, 1997*]. Yet, despite the continuity between them, unconventional practices are far more controversial and problematic than institutionalised ones: their adoption requires distinctive organisational cultures, as activists have to regard them as an obvious choice, and be prepared to use them when needed, whether in a professionalised or a participatory form.

In sum, SMOs face at least two elementary dilemmas, having to choose between *professional vs. participatory* organisational models, and *disruptive vs. conventional* forms of pressure. By combining these two alternatives we obtain four organisational types (see Table 1):[5]

TABLE 1

A TYPOLOGY OF NON-PARTISAN POLITICAL ORGANISATIONS

| | Forms of Action | |
	Conventional Pressure	Disruption
Professional Resources	Public Interest Lobby	Professional Protest Organisation
Participatory Resources	Participatory Pressure Group	Participatory Protest Organisation

The Public Interest Lobby

A political organisation managed by professional staff, with weak participatory inclinations and emphasis on traditional pressure tactics, this comes closest to the conventional interest group.

The Participatory Protest Organisation

Emphasis on participatory action and subcultural structures combines with a strong inclination to disruptive protest. This model is closest to the classic idea of the decentralised, grassroots SMO, prepared – and equipped, given its organisational traits – to adopt confrontational strategies.

The Professional Protest Organisation

This model shares with the public interest lobby the emphasis on professional activism and the mobilisation of financial resources. However, it includes confrontational tactics among its tactical options, along with more conventional ones.

The Participatory Pressure Group

Similarly to the participatory protest organisation, rank-and-file members and sympathisers are involved in organisational life but the focus is on conventional lobbying techniques rather than protest.

Transformations in Environmental Movements Organisations[6]

From Participatory Protest Organisations to Public Interest Lobbies?

Do recent changes in environmental organisations suggest a general trend towards movement institutionalisation? Or, following our ideal-types, have we moved from *participatory protest organisation*s to *public interest lobbies*? Have conventional lobbying techniques replaced confrontational ones, and has the mobilisation of material resources grown to the detriment of grass-roots participation?

Admittedly, many environmental organisations have always approximated to public interest lobbies. Associations like Italia Nostra in Italy, the Royal Society for the Protection of Birds (RSPB) in the UK, An Taisce in Ireland, or umbrella groups like DNR (Deutscher Naturschutz Ring) in Germany have consistently preferred non-confrontational styles of action, and relied more on their members' fees than on their militancy. They have turned issues into objects of public controversy only after direct communication to policy makers proved ineffective. Remarkably, though, organisations which in the 1970s and early 1980s had a radical and participatory profile seem to have gradually evolved in the same direction.[7]

Since the late 1980s, confrontational strategies have given way to more conventional forms of pressure. In particular, political ecology organisations appear to have dropped protest mobilisations and boycotts in favour of referenda, petitioning campaigns, 'green shareholding', voluntary action in defence of the environment (for example, on coasts, rivers, lakes), lobbying, production of books, videotapes, both for the media and for direct commercial purposes, educational campaigns in schools, and even sponsorship of commercial products by 'licensing' their logos as a sort of 'eco-label' to commercial and industrial firms, in exchange for money or other forms of support on environmental initiatives [Donati, 1994: 13].

Donati refers to the most important political ecology group in Italy, Legambiente, but similar trends can be found across Europe, not only in countries like the UK [Szerszinski, 1995] where environmental protection groups have long enjoyed institutional recognition, or where environmental policy has been most dynamic like Germany [Brand, 1995], but also in countries, like Ireland, where institutional innovation in this area has been quite recent.[8]

Across Europe, major environmental groups are granted access to formal policy bodies and procedures, such as hearings, or ministerial committees, albeit to varying degree [Dalton, 1994]. They also increasingly provide institutions with expert advice – either through formal or informal channels [Donati, 1994: 39]. To be successful in these activities, environmental groups require legitimation and respectability rather than the display of strong disruptive potential. Institution-building appears gradually to be replacing confrontational politics.

One should also note the uneven success of major ecology SMOs in their attempts to launch mass protest campaigns at the national level. For example, when major Italian associations have tried to launch national campaigns (against Montedison in 1986 through the boycott of Standa, a chain of supermarket stores which was then part of the group, or against over 200 high-risk chemical plants in 1988), results have been disappointing [Donati, 1994: 43].

Even in Germany, the last decade has seen a substantial fall in confrontation, despite its relative popularity among political ecology organisations which were well integrated in the broader radical movement sector. While violent confrontation can still break out, '[violent conflicts no] longer represent the symbolic integrating focus of a system-opposing movement' [Brand, 1995: 23]. Conventional forms of campaigning tend to prevail, including voluntary work for the protection of nature sites, or educational initiatives [Brand, 1995: 25].

The mere reduction in the incidence of confrontational techniques does not necessarily imply a move towards the *public interest lobby* model. It is also compatible with the *participatory pressure group* model. Grass-roots participation has increasingly taken the form of voluntary work on specific problems rather than disruptive direct action [Diani, 1995], but comparative evidence [Eder, 1995] suggests that a transformation from participatory to non-participatory structures has also recently taken place. It has affected both the relationship between centre and periphery within environmental organisations, and that between professional campaigners and volunteers.

Environmental organisations have traditionally displayed a high division of labour among them [*Lowe and Goyder, 1983; Rucht, 1989; Diani, 1995*]. The increase in division of labour and functional differentiation *within*, rather than *between*, movement organisations seems more recent and appears to have increased headquarters' control over mobilisation campaigns, despite the fact that many issues are genuinely local.

In Italy, for example, national SMOs organise their activities around single-issue campaigns. Their central bodies consist mostly of campaign teams which share some basic resources such as press offices and legal advice, but are substantially independent [*Donati, 1994: 16–17*]. This does not merely apply to traditionally bureaucratic mass organisations like WWF, or notoriously centralised groups like Greenpeace. It also applies to Legambiente, in principle a decentralised structure, given its origins as an umbrella organisation of local groups and associations within ARCI, the cultural and leisure-time association of the Italian traditional left [*Rovelli, 1988*]. Campaign managers connect supportive experts, local groups and the central offices upon which they ultimately depend [*Donati, 1994: 17–18*].

Increasing bureaucratisation and formalisation have also characterised British groups in the late 1980s–early 1990s: WWF has moved from a structure based on eight different departments, all related to a chief executive, to five sections which are also internally fragmented, for a total of 36 central units; Friends of the Earth (FoE) have introduced a number of central coordinators; Greenpeace UK, which started in 1980 with six members of staff, counted eight working sections in 1993 [*Szerszinski, 1995: 36–7*].

Local branches maintain an important role in fund-raising. In the case of Greenpeace that is in fact the only area in which local groups of sympathisers have consistently played a role. In general, although it is run professionally from headquarters, for example, by direct mailing, fund-raising is also conducted by volunteers at the grassroots, on the occasion of demonstrations, fairs, public performances [*Donati, 1994: 20*]. Among European environmental groups, organisational survival and autonomy increasingly depend on sources of income other than membership fees or public and corporate funding [*Szerszinski, 1995: 32*].

Apart from fund-raising, however, the role of local chapters is of varying interest and concern to their headquarters. Groups like Legambiente in Italy, or WWF and RSPB in Britain, do not seem to be overly concerned with the direct involvement of their local chapters in their most visible national activities. They do differ, however, from Greenpeace in that they allow peripheral groups substantial degrees of autonomy in running their own initiatives [*Donati, 1994: 22; Szerszinski, 1995: 52*].

Formalisation and centralisation have parallelled a move from participatory to professionalised organisations. Campaign planning and coordination are increasingly controlled by professional staff. From the mid-1980s the gap between small groups of professional campaigners, focusing on lobbying strategies, and heavily media-oriented, and a supportive, but rarely mobilised, 'attentive public', has apparently increased [*Szerszinski, 1995: 11*]. Members of environmental groups are mostly involved in their organisations through mailing lists and appeals for subscription renewal. A non-participatory orientation seems to have developed [*Donati, 1994: 13; Szerszinski, 1995: 49–51*], particularly where a strong alternative movement sector never consolidated (as in Italy or France) [*Diani, 1988; Le Saout, 1995: 14; Rucht, 1996: 195–6*].

Most staff in the headquarters of ecology groups have professional training in communication and journalism [*Donati, 1994: 19*]. Many also have a background in science or law [*Lowe and Goyder, 1983; Diani, 1995 Ch.3*]. Significantly, such staff are increasingly recruited following professional criteria – regardless, in other words, of their previous experiences of environmental or other forms of political activism.

This is both a consequence and a determinant of the rising status of environmental campaigner as a distinctive professional role. This seems in turn dependent on the recent steady growth in both public concern and governmental response [*Szerszinski, 1995: 13*]. Environmentalism may offer promising professional opportunities to those combining substantive expertise with communication skills. Increasingly, top officials of environmental groups take up key positions in other groups, or join public agencies and even private corporations [*Szerszinski, 1995: 43–4*]. External experts also play a crucial role in the planning and running of national campaigns [*Donati, 1994: 21*]. While they are not part of the professional staff, their influence further reflects a trend towards non-participatory styles of action.

The move towards professional structures also results in SMOs increasingly competing to attract (scarce) financial resources from the same pool of potential supporters. While ideological conflict between SMOs is reducing, the existence of some division of labour among SMOs does not prevent market-oriented competition from developing. In turn, this discourages integration and collaboration within the movement, as it is more important for organisations to maintain and protect their specific identities [*Mullally, 1995: 48–9*]. As the German case suggests, though, privileging organisational pride may ultimately reduce the mobilisation capacity of the movement as a whole [*Brand, 1995: 29*].

The Revitalisation of Grass-roots Activism

So far we have sketched what appears to be a rather straightforward process from radicalism to institutionalisation. In particular, a *public interest lobby* model seems to be gradually prevailing over a more participatory one. But is the trend really so homogeneous? And, is there a 'trend' at all?

There are indeed some reasons for scepticism about any analysis focusing on trends from grass-roots protest to institutionalisation. First, protest groups actually represent only a small proportion of the totality of organisations active on public issues: one tenth of women's and ethnic minority groups active in the USA from 1955 to 1985 focused on protest and confrontational activities [*Minkoff, 1995: 62–3*]. Moreover, their proportional weight remained constant across the whole period, regardless of variation in the intensity of protest activities.[9]

Second, even in the most recent period of 'institutionalisation', examples of confrontational grass-roots mobilisations on environmental issues have been far from rare. In the UK since 1992 there has been a strong increase in confrontational actions promoted by, amongst others, Earth First!, the Environmental Liberation Front, and anti-road coalitions [*Doherty, 1997*].[10] The umbrella-group Alarm UK estimated that about 250 anti-road groups were active in 1994 [*Szerszinski, 1995: 15*]. In Ireland, local conflicts in the Cork area challenged development projects promoted by multinational chemical firms. In Italy, local protest actions have regularly occurred on issues ranging from dangerous industrial plants to road construction [*Donati, 1994: 41*]. Local conflicts in Germany have seen a mix of confrontation and grass-roots involvement in the policy process – as Brand [*1995: 32–3*] shows, repertoires have usually consisted of a combination of lobbying and confrontational techniques. As the position of environmental groups is one of tolerated acceptance rather than full incorporation, they persistently need to use, or to threaten to use, confrontation [*Diani and Donati, 1996*].

National networks of groups have also developed which explicitly reject professional activism in favour of voluntary, grass-roots action. Among these, organisations related to the women's movements have played a significant role. The Women's Environmental Network (WEN) in Britain and the Irish Women's Environmental Network (IWEN) have brought together independent grass-roots groups, working on issues which often exceeded environmental concerns [*Szerszinski, 1995: 52*]. WEN is run on an egalitarian and anti-professional basis, with strong collaboration between paid staff and volunteers. One of its basic principles is that of 'empowerment' – the production, through action, of individual skills which need not be restricted to specific professionals [*Szerszinski, 1995: 47–8*]. In

Germany, *Muetter gegen atomkraft* (Mothers Against Nuclear Power) was established in the aftermath of the Chernobyl accident as an informal network of women's antinuclear and alternative groups, active locally across the country [*Brand, 1995: 27*].

Thus the 1990s have also seen the creation of new participatory protest organisations, or at least, networks of groups. The spread of grass-roots groups testifies to the unease that the growing institutionalisation of major environmental actors has generated in peripheral sectors of the environmental movement.[11] One might wonder whether major national SMOs, originally close to a participatory, political ecology model, have played any role in new local conflicts; mobilisations against high-risk plants in Italy have been promoted by local coalitions in which major ecology groups like Legambiente or WWF hardly played any role [*Donati, 1994: 44–6*]. Although the latter may have represented local coalitions in front of media and institutions, thus granting local conflicts greater visibility, they did not promote the struggles in the first place. Rather, they acted as 'institutional allies' [*Tarrow, 1994; Rucht, 1996*]. Recent analyses of road protests in Britain suggest a similar pattern [*Doherty, 1997*].

Participatory Models Between Protest and Pressure

The relationship between professional and participatory trends within environmental movements is more complex than the simple 'radicalisation vs. institutionalisation' dichotomy would suggest. Many environmental activists still regard their organisations' recently achieved insider status as precarious, and argue for the preservation of organisational infrastructures which allow for grassroots participation [*Szerszinski, 1995: 45*]. On several occasions, established SMOs have been instrumental in the formation of action committees and grass-roots coalitions.[12]

Moreover, the German case suggests that when professionalisation occurs in a context where the countercultural dimension is still alive (in research institutes, alternative media, urban radical communities), it does not necessarily discourage conflictual, participatory orientations. The peculiarity of the German situation also reflects the stronger integration between ecologists and the social movement sector [*Brand, 1995: 10, 17–20*], and may be explained by the fact that in Germany protests peaked in the 1980s rather than the 1970s [*Rucht and Ohlemacher, 1992*].

Even where explicit confrontational tactics have been abandoned in favour of more conventional ones, this shift does not necessarily result in fully centralised and professionalised organisations. In Britain, in particular, major SMOs do not have a homogeneous attitude towards grass-roots action and the involvement of local branches. In the mid-1990s, while Greenpeace limited local groups to fund-raising,[13] and WWF and RSPB allowed them autonomy but did not involve them in major campaigns, CPRE and FoE allowed them substantial degrees of both autonomy and influence over the running of the organisation [*Szerszinski, 1995: 52*]. While the first three used mostly market research to keep abreast of their members' views, FoE continued to rely upon some types of grass-roots organisation.[14]

If organisational centralisation has not gone unchallenged, neither has professionalisation. Seasoned activists often regret the disappearance of the internal solidarity of the past, and are concerned that professionalisation is weakening the core values of their organisations [*Szerszinski, 1995: 46*]. Moreover, even when their focus moves away from confrontation, some bureaucratic SMOs maintain a participatory structure, which mainly promotes voluntary action. These groups often approximate a *participatory pressure group* model.

The presence of bureaucratic SMOs is not so much the result of the disappearance of mass confrontational organisations as the reflection of a long established situation. Some former protest organisations have of course changed along lines which combine elements of the public interest lobby and the participatory pressure group models – one being Legambiente.[15] Groups like WWF, however, have traditionally been hostile to confrontational activities, and emphasised education and voluntary work by their members. If they have changed at all, it has been towards more, rather than less, confrontation. For example, the Italian branch of WWF has become increasingly open to (mild) protest over the years [*Diani, 1988*]. The trend therefore is not necessarily from confrontation to (participatory) conventional pressure, but may also be reversed, as radical action repertoires spread to moderate sectors of the public.

The Professional Protest Organisation

Greenpeace comes closest to this model. It has never adopted a mass participatory model but has always been highly centralised and professional, and has depended on material resources rather than activism from its members (although available accounts somewhat differ [*Shaiko, 1993; Rucht, 1995b*]). While its repertoires often include conventional lobbying, Greenpeace has also differed from other major environmental organisations in its inclination towards spectacular confrontational strategies.

In the *professional protest organisation*, protest and confrontation are disentangled from mass, grass-roots participation. Action on behalf of the public interest is conducted by substituting for the 'logic of numbers' a particular version of the 'logic of bearing witness' [*della Porta and Diani, 1997: 202–10*]. The former regards mass involvement in collective action as the key to social movement success. The latter emphasises the role of a small minority of activists who face high personal risks to re-affirm an ethical or moral principle. However, while 'bearing witness' may be regarded as an attempt to stimulate mass action – or at least to keep dissent alive where open protest is not feasible, as in authoritarian regimes – this does not apply to a professionalised group like Greenpeace. Spectacular, risky actions by professional campaigners do not aim at mobilising sympathisers, but rather at attracting media attention and thus commanding financial resources from the general public [*Hansen, 1993*]. Unconventional disruption defines a model of 'vicarious activism' [e.g., *della Porta and Kriesi, 1999*] which is actually media-oriented rather than grassroots-oriented. The atomisation and fragmentation of the general public no longer prevents protest and contention, as the latter is managed by small professional units. The capacity of protest groups like Greenpeace to attract media attention provides them with easy access to their potential constituency, from which they may generate the resources necessary to organisational maintenance.

Conclusions: Organisational Changes and Mobilisation Potential

Contemporary environmental movements in the West display a range of organisational forms. Is diversity pronounced enough to dismiss accounts emphasising trends towards professionalisation [*Donati, 1996; Jordan and Maloney, 1997*]? On the one hand, there seems to be substantial cross-national evidence of the increasing role of professional, non participatory, and functional elements within environmental organisations. Groups which were originally close to the participatory protest model, albeit a moderate version of it (for example, FoE or Legambiente), and groups which displayed several traits of the participatory pressure group model, such as WWF, have both become increasingly professional. On the other hand, however, there are also signs that participatory protest is far from being a non-option among people committed to the environmental cause. The growth of women's and other grass-roots networks, of anti-road and other local coalitions, and of radical groups such as Earth First! all point to the persistent vitality of contentious action and cognate 'mobilisation technologies'. The emphasis on voluntary action campaigns by more established environmental associations also stresses – albeit from a different angle – the persistent relevance of members' participation.

Therefore, organisational evolution in environmental movements should not be reduced to the crude dichotomy 'movement organisation vs. interest group'. Our framework allows us to break down the broad idea of movement institutionalisation into different components. In particular, it allows us to disentangle the problem of movement professionalisation from related, still independent issues, such as the selection of the action repertoire. Rather than classifying different organisations along a continuum from 'movement organisation' to 'interest group', we can look at how traits of different models combine in different organisations.

For example, WWF seems now to combine traits of the public interest lobby and the participatory pressure group with some inclination to grassroots protest which was previously distant from its approach (although one should beware of drawing too broad conclusions about organisations with several national branches which may actually differ substantially from one another). Nor have groups like Legambiente or FoE really evolved from 'movement to institution'; they have rather gone through a more complex process of organisational change which has combined traits of both the public interest lobby and the participatory pressure group. Likewise, Greenpeace presents a peculiar blend of professional and confrontational traits which again fits badly the crude 'movement vs. institution' distinction.

The picture is similarly complex if we consider the degree of integration between core professional organisations and grass-roots activities. This is at best uneven both within and across countries (for example, stronger for FoE than Greenpeace and conservation groups, stronger in Ireland than in France or the UK). Moreover, local protest action is in general very lively and there are no signs of contraction; rather, in some countries – in particular, the UK – local protest appears to be expanding. We might indeed be simply witnessing an intermediate phase between the end of a wave of protests and the beginning of another; one of those periods when once radical, now institutionalised SMOs increasingly fail to respond to grass-roots demands, and so spur a process of self-organisation which may – under favourable conditions – lead to a challenge to established SMOs and/or to the revitalisation of their strategies and objectives.

One should also consider that local protests are not necessarily dependent on – nor are they coordinated by – central SMOs. On the contrary, a certain degree of distance between major SMOs and local groups may often prove conducive to further action [*Zald and McCarthy, 1987; Minkoff, 1995*]. It may facilitate division of labour and allow core SMOs to go ahead with their moderate and conciliatory strategies, without seeing their efforts jeopardised by their own local branches, while giving the latter a chance to play an autonomous role, more responsive to specific local circumstances (as the anti-road protests in the UK suggest [*Szerszinski, 1995; Doherty, 1997*]).

The most crucial question, however, concerns the recent lack of *national* protest activities (or, for that matter, core SMOs' failure to promote them). As a rule, the escalation of local protest activities into national, co-ordinated ones cannot rely upon merely local disconnected action groups; it requires organisational infrastructure on a national scale. Here, major environmental SMOs either have not been committed or have failed. Yet, one cannot help but wonder why one should expect environmental movements to build similar organisational structures, and thus display comparable capacities to mount national campaigns, to those of working class or nationalist movements. The very nature of environmental issues, fragmented and universalistic at the same time; the lack of a specific social basis – in particular, of a social basis which is internally connected by peculiar social networks [*Tilly, 1978*]; the open debate whether ecological change should be regarded as a political problem at all – rather than, for example, as an educational matter; the increasing difficulties central states are facing in their regulatory and policy-making functions: all these factors cast doubts over the idea that national mobilisation should be a central concern for environmental groups. Even in the recent (and more participatory) past, environmental organisations have managed to mount national campaigns only in the aftermath of emotionally charged events, like the Chernobyl accident, or when environmental issues were tightly intertwined with other social and political issues (as in the case of initiatives by the German movement sector).

The basic question is therefore whether national mobilisations are still an essential feature of contentious political conflict in a post-industrial, 'information' society. There is no question here of forgetting the persistent dominance of national political arenas in an increasingly globalised world [*Tarrow, 1996*]. It is however important to note that, as a form of collective action, the national demonstration and the national campaign rested upon a number of specific assumptions: the existence of a 'core power', embodied in the central state; the lack of opportunities for excluded social groups to have their voices heard, without directly challenging central powers and in particular their physical locations – the capital city, government buildings, etc.; the need of mass organisational infrastructure for the cultural and political socialisation of the challenging group. Individualism, increasing perception of the multiple – and largely unaccountable – sources of political power, and the expansion of the media system, have all contributed to undermine those basic tenets. As limited as the specific phenomenon can be, a full appreciation of changes in environmental organisations still requires them to be assessed against the background of broader changes in the relationship between state, civil society, and the public sphere.

A substantial body of contemporary social theory has emphasised recent fundamental changes in the public sphere, especially its individualisation [*Habermas, 1989; Melucci, 1989; Giddens, 1990; for a recent synthesis: Donati, 1997*]. In contemporary Western ('post-industrial' or 'post-modern') societies, the public sphere is no longer the locus where ideological positions and claims previously formed within semi-public social networks and communities confront each other; it is rather the locus where policy options (still mainly predetermined by either the political system or the media) are debated by individualised actors or citizens, who (ideally) participate in the determination of political choices. Such a shift, is in turn driven by two parallel transformations: the advent of the 'post-modern scene', and the development and autonomisation of the system of mass communication. The peculiar relationship between the environmental movement (and, more generally, all 'new' social movements) and the media can be best understood by reference to these phenomena.

Although no agreed meaning yet exists on such a term, the 'post-modern scene' has been described as one of de-structuration of established categories and social-cultural boundaries, and of progressive centrality of the cultural dimension in social and political processes; a scene where: 'the overproduction of signs and reproduction of images and simulations leads to a loss of stable meaning, and an aesthetisation of reality' [*Featherstone, 1991: 15; also Jameson, 1984*]. Most authors have seen the transition to postmodernism as a product of the contradictions between the rise and expansion of the welfare state and the resulting formalisation of social and political rights, a contradiction between techno-bureaucratic apparatuses and the private life-world of citizens [*Benjamin, 1980; Habermas, 1981; Melucci 1989; Offe, 1990; Beck 1992*].

The 'post-modern' condition can therefore be regarded as one of individualised social life [*Melucci, 1989; Giddens, 1990; Beck, 1992*] where the public sphere becomes populated with the politicised quest for individual autonomy and the provision of life chances, which is the essence of the new social movements [*Kitschelt, 1985; Melucci, 1989; Jamison et al., 1990; Eder, 1993*]. The new social movements are no longer concerned with the redistribution of material resources, but rather with the production of meaning which contests the 'administrative logic' of the system. Such a logic breaks the patterns of class, previously underlying the functioning and articulation of the public sphere, and pits citizens against the institutions that are supposed to be in charge of the public good. At the political level, the crisis of the party system gives way to the emergence of the 'new politics' [*Dalton and Kuechler, 1990*].

Parallel to this trend, the mass-media have, especially in Europe, and especially after the advent and liberalisation of commercial TV channels, undergone a process of increasing autonomisation from political systems and institutions [*Blumler and Gurevitch, 1995; Swanson and Mancini, 1995; Pizzorno, 1998*]. Commercialisation (the development of autonomous sources of revenue) and professionalisation (the development of autonomous 'attention and decision rules') have been crucial in these developments. They have allowed the media system to become increasingly differentiated and increasingly able to sustain its own existence and functioning, and 'have resulted in the increased dependency of both politicians and voters on the media and the messages they provide.' [*Blumler and Gurevitch, 1995: 3*]. Consequently, the relationship between the political and the media system has gone from political institutions' dominance, to 'consummated mutual adaptation' [*Blumler and Gurevitch, 1995: 189*], in which the two parties compete over the determination of the agenda, used as a means of attracting and retaining different audiences.

The changing relationship between media and politics runs parallel to the demise of 'ideological' and partisan politics:

> the very move of the media to the centre of the political process entails a degree of depoliticisation. This is because in Western democracies the press (and especially television) base their claims to legitimacy and credibility with the public on their non-political status and on their disavowals of explicitly political, particularly partisan, motives [*Blumler and Gurevitch, 1995: 213*].

One might even dare to say that the media try to become independent from the political system by posing as the specific forum for discussion of public issues, as if the media system were indeed an exhaustive representation of the public sphere. Through 'live' opinion polling, talk shows and political candidates' debates, the media have increasingly institutionalised and given real (or virtual?) substance to the concept of 'public opinion', presenting themselves, at the same time, as the real arena of political action and policy-making. This is coupled with the crisis of traditional, cleavage based partisan politics, since non-partisanship is the specific condition for media credibility as a 'vicarious' political forum. Mediated policy-making acquires, then, a specific 'populistic' tone, as the media tend to present themselves as allies for citizens' protests. This is not restricted to the 'referendum model' of media democracy, with its live polling of opinions, but also applies to recent experiments in internet democracy [*Friedland, 1996; Wheeler, 1996*], promoting public debate on political and social issues.

The two phenomena – the advent of the post-modern condition, and the autonomisation of the mass-media – converge on the ground of 'de-politicisation' or de-ideologisation. Several traits of the environmental issue render it close to a model of post-modern politics. It represents a typically universalistic and 'public good' – and therefore potentially de-politicisable – issue. It may be safely expected to attract the interest of media people [*Donati, 1989*]. The increasing resources and attention that national environmental SMOs have devoted to media work and the professionalisation of their staff are in line with a more general tendency among political organisations [*Fritz and Morris, 1991; Levine, 1994*].

Mass-mediated politics may well be a necessary form of political action in Western societies today, with the media becoming the key source of politicians' public recognition [*Pizzorno, 1998*]. The mass-media have thus acquired a new power over the political process. The more media and political actors become interested in people's recognition rather than in substantive problem-solving [*Pizzorno, 1998*], the more unstable politics and policy agendas [*Abercrombie and Urry, 1983*] and the more intense competition among policy issues are bound to become.

Changes in the political and the media system have facilitated the transformation of environmental activists into professional campaigners as well as into fully entitled members of the polity [*Donati, 1994: 40*]. Doubts arise, however, about the implications of these transformations for environmental actors' capacity to promote collective action. The remarks presented above do not imply that other, non-professional and more participatory forms of political organising would be useless. On the contrary, if variability and fragmentation are to represent the foreseeable future of political issues, then SMOs will, if they are to survive, have to organise themselves to endure such exogenously determined variations (determined, in particular, by the media) in the public attention for their issues. This entails the building of organisational infrastructures that are able to 'autonomise' and cushion themselves from the direct impact of media choices as well as – under specific circumstances – to promote and channel grass-roots participation.

In the recent past, however, major environmental groups seem consciously to have given priority to 'mobilisation technologies' [*Oliver and Marwell, 1992*] focusing on material rather than human resources [*Donati, 1994*]. Has this strategy paid off? Media coverage has undoubtedly helped to put public authorities under pressure. The greater availability of qualified expertise among environmental groups, which stems from professionalisation, may also have consolidated their lobbying position within the polity. One could also argue that, by drawing public attention to environmental issues, and thereby creating a globally favourable cultural climate, the media-oriented strategy of the major SMOs has in the last analysis fostered the emergence of local groups and grass-roots action.

At the same time, though, several drawbacks may be pointed out. First, increasing recourse to symbolic means of political pressure may well result in purely symbolic responses by policy makers. Second, major SMOs may have exchanged consensus for resources; their compliance with the rules of institutional political representation may have facilitated their access to public funds (for example, public sponsorship of their educational activities) but at the cost of reducing their potential for oppositional action. Third, the more that core SMOs target a constituency consisting of market-oriented individuals who mostly view ecology as a peculiar type of commodity, the weaker their chances become of promoting mass protest activities when needed. In the light of what is still, ultimately, a precarious institutionalisation, this seems a hazardous strategy. The sudden change in political opportunities available to German environmentalists in the early 1990s [*Brand, 1995*] has indeed exposed the limitations of hyper-professional groups when their central concerns are not as high on the public agenda as they used to be, their insider status is diminished, and they badly need grass-roots mobilisation again. Under deteriorating political conditions, highly professional environmental lobbies might well prove unable to revert to that good, old weapon of excluded interests – contentious protest.

NOTES

1. We refer to 'non-partisan political organisations' as this typology applies to a broader set of organisations than SMOs.
2. Etzioni [*1985*] distinguishes between public interests – referring to the globality of people within a given polity – and collective interests – of concern to large social groups.
3. Many of the remarks in this section might similarly apply to political parties, especially to radical, not fully institutionalised ones. However, we decided to refer to 'non-partisan' organisations because involvement in electoral competition and the opportunities attached to direct access to office render parties' responses to dilemmas of resource mobilisation and political efficacy quite different from those of interest groups and social movement organisations.
4. While rather frequent for established interest groups, the mobilisation of resources from small groups of wealthy – individual or corporate – sponsors has been traditionally rare in the case of social movements. However, in recent years cooperation between movement organisations and, for example, the business world has gradually, albeit, slowly increased in areas like environmental or consumer protection [*Donati, 1996*].
5. See Diani and Donati [*1996*, especially pp.9–14]. This typology is close to Lo's [*1992*], who differentiates between a 'market-managerial' and a 'communal' type of resource mobilisation ('professional' and 'participatory' in our terms), and the status of political organisations as polity members or challengers. Although the latter dichotomy is largely compatible with our distinction between confrontational and conventional pressure, we feel ours is preferable because being a polity member or a challenger bears only indirectly on organisational traits. See also Lofland [*1996: 139–73*].
6. Empirical evidence for this section originates largely from national studies by Brand [*1995*], Donati [*1994, 1996*], Mullally [*1995*] and Szerszinski [*1995*].
7. Johnston [*1980*] identified a similar trend for new religious sects in his analysis of the 'marketed social movement'.
8. In Ireland, the advisory committee of the Environmental Protection Agency (established only in 1993) includes two ecology organisations: Irish Women's Environmental Network (IWEN) and National Youth Environmental Organisation [*Mullally, 1995: 18*].
9. This is partially due to the short lifecycle of many protest groups, which emerge most frequently at peaks of political contention but disband very quickly with the decline of

protest waves [*Minkoff, 1995: 67–9*]. These low figures might also depend on Minkoff's data source, the *Encyclopedia of Associations* (1995, pp.131-6), which may be expected to overrepresent more formal associations. Still, the accuracy of her data in capturing both rises and falls in rates of the founding of protest organisations suggests that the portrait of the trend, if not its actual size, is quite reliable.

10. The spread of groups like Earth First! or of animal rights initiatives is not restricted to Britain [*Rucht, 1993; Jasper and Nelkin, 1992*].

11. Szerszinski [*1995: 45*]. The persistent vitality of environmental action at the grass roots is certainly not restricted to Western Europe [*Szasz, 1994; Lichterman, 1996; Yearley, 1996; Castells, 1997*].

12. For example, the Cork Environmental Alliance, a coalition of local and national groups who joined forces in 1990 to fight a proposed chemical development in County Cork [*Mullally, 1995: 28*].

13. In Ireland, however, Greenpeace seems to be expanding its links to community groups beyond mere fund-raising [*Mullally, 1995: 42*].

14. This account differs substantially from that of Jordan and Maloney's [*1997*], who regard FoE UK as a paradigmatic example of 'protest business' – in our language, 'professional protest group'.

15. Although centralisation and professionalisation have increased within Legambiente [*Donati, 1994*], significant opportunities for participation at the grass roots still persist.

REFERENCES

Abercrombie, Nicholas and John Urry (1983), *Capital, Labour and the Middle Classes*, London, Allen & Unwin.

Beck, Ulrich (1992), *Risk Society*, London: Sage.

Benjamin, Roger (1980), *The Limits of Politics*, Chicago, IL: University of Chicago Press.

Blumler, Jay G. and Michael Gurevitch (1995), *The Crisis of Public Communication*, London: Routledge.

Brand, Karl-Werner (1995), 'Entering the Stage: Strategies of Environmental Communication in Germany', in K. Eder (ed.), *Framing and Communicating Environmental Issues*, Research Report, Commission of the European Communities, DGXII, Florence: European University Institute Munich: Muenchner Projektgruppe fuer Sozialforschung.

Burstein, Paul (1997), 'Social Movement Organisations, Interest Groups, Political Parties, and the Study of Democratic Politics', in A. Costain and A. McFarland (eds.), *Social Movements and American Political Institutions*, Boulder, CO: Rowman & Littlefield.

Castells, Manuel (1997), *The Information Age: Economy, Society and Culture. Vol.II: The Power of Identity*, Oxford: Blackwell.

Dalton, Russell (1994), *The Green Rainbow*, New Haven, CT: Yale University Press.

Dalton, Russell J. and Manfred Kuechler (1990) (eds.), *Challenging the Political Order*, Cambridge: Polity Press.

della Porta, Donatella and Mario Diani (1997), *I Movimenti Sociali*, Rome: Nuova Italia Scientifica (English edition: *Social Movements*, Oxford: Blackwell, 1999).

della Porta, Donatella and Hanspeter Kriesi (1999), 'Social Movements in A Globalizing World: An Introduction', in D. della Porta, H. Kriesi and D. Rucht (eds.), *Social Movements in a Globalizing World*, London: Macmillan.

Diani, Mario (1988), *Isole nell'Arcipelago*, Bologna: il Mulino.

Diani, Mario (1992), 'The Concept of Social Movement', *Sociological Review*, Vol.40, pp.1–25.

Diani, Mario (1995), *Green Networks*, Edinburgh: Edinburgh University Press.

Diani, Mario (1998), 'Images of Sustainable Development in Italy', paper for the conference 'Environmental Movements, Discourses, and Policies in Southern Europe', 7–10 May 1998, University of Crete, Rethimno.

Diani, Mario and Paolo Donati (1996), ' 'Rappresentare' l'Interesse Pubblico: La Comunicazione dei Gruppi di Pressione e dei Movimenti', *Quaderni di Scienza Politica*, Vol.4, pp.1–42.

Doherty, Brian (1997), 'Manufactured Vulnerability', paper for the *European Sociological Association Conference*, University of Essex, Colchester.

Donati, Paolo R. (1994), 'Media Strength and Infrastructural Weakness: Recent Trends in the Italian Environmental Movement', *EUI Working Papers SPS 94/14*, Florence: European University Institute.

Donati, Paolo R. (1996), 'Building a Unified Movement: Resource Mobilisation, Media Work, and Organisational Transformation in the Italian Environmentalist Movement', in Kriesberg [*1996: 125–57*].

Donati, Paolo (1997), 'Environmentalism, Postmaterialism and Anxiety'. *Arena Journal*, Vol.8, pp.147–72.

Eder, Klaus (1993), *The New Politics of Class*, London: Sage.

Eder, Klaus (ed.) (1995), *Framing and Communicating Environmental Issues*, Research Report, Commission of the European Communities, DGXII, Florence: European University Institute.

Edwards, Bob (1994), 'Semiformal Organisational Structure Among Social Movement Organisations: An Analysis of the U.S. Peace Movement', *Nonprofit and Voluntary Sector Quarterly*, Vol.23, pp.309–33.

Edwards, Bob (1995), 'With Liberty and Environmental Justice for All: The Emergence and Challenge of Grassroots Environmentalism in the United States', in B.R. Taylor (eds.), *Ecological Resistance Movements*, NY: SUNY Press, pp.35–55.

Etzioni, Amitai (1985), 'Special Interest Groups Versus Constituency Representation', in Kriesberg [*1985: 171–95*].

Featherstone, Mike (1991), *Consumer Culture and Postmodernism*, London: Sage.

Friedland, Lewis (1996), 'Electronic Democracy and the New Citizenship', *Media, Culture and Society*, Vol.2.

Friedman, Debra and Doug McAdam (1992), 'Collective Identity and Activism', in Morris and McClurg Mueller [*1992: 156–73*].

Fritz, S. and D. Morris (1991), *Handbook of Campaign Spending: Money in the 1990 Congressional Races*. Washington, DC: Congressional Quarterly Press.

Gamson, William (1992), 'The Social Psychology of Collective Action', in Morris, and McClurg Mueller [*1992: 53–76*].

Giddens, Anthony (1990), *The Consequences of Modernity*, Cambridge/Stanford, CA: Polity Press/Stanford University Press.

Gitlin, Todd (1980), The *Whole World Is Watching: Mass Media in the Making and Unmaking of the New Left*, Berkeley, CA: University of California Press.

Grant, Wyn (1989), *Pressure Groups, Politics and Democracy in Britain*, London: Philip Allan.

Habermas, Jürgen (1981), 'New Social Movements', *Telos*, Vol.49:

Habermas, Jürgen (1989), *The Structural Transformation of the Public Sphere*, Cambridge, MA: The MIT Press.

Hansen, Anders (1993), 'Greenpeace and Press Coverage of Environmental Issues', in A. Hansen (ed.), *Mass Media and Environmental Issues*, Leicester: Leicester University Press, pp.150–78.

Hayes, M.T. (1986), 'The New Group Universe', A.J. Cigler and B.A. Loomis (eds.), in *Interest Group Politics*, Washington, DC: Congressional Quarterly Press, pp.133–45.

Hirschman, Albert O. (1982), *Shifting Involvements*, Princeton, NJ: Princeton University Press.

Jameson, Frederick (1984), 'Postmodernism, or the Cultural Logic of Late Capitalism', *New Left Review*, Vol.146, pp.53–92.

Jamison, Andrew (1996), 'The Shaping of the Global Environmental Agenda: The Role of Non-Governmental Organisations', in S. Lash, B. Szerszinski and B. Wynne (eds.), *Risk, Environment and Modernity*, London: Sage, pp.224–45.

Jamison, Andrew, Eyerman, Ron, and J. Cramer (1990), *The Making of the New Environmental Consciousness*, Edinburgh: Edinburgh University Press.

Jasper, James M. and Dorothy Nelkin (1992), *The Animal Rights Crusade: The Growth of A Moral Protest*, New York: Free Press.

Johnston, Hank (1980), 'The Marketed Social Movement', *Pacific Sociological Review* Vol.23, pp.333–54.

Jordan, Grant and William Maloney (1997), *The Protest Business*, Manchester: Manchester University Press.

Kitschelt, Herbert (1985), 'New Social Movements in West Germany and the United States', in

Maurice Zeitlin (ed.), *Political Power and Social Theory*, Vol.5. Greenwich, CT: JAI Press, pp.2273–324.

Kriesberg, L. (ed.) (1985) *Research in Social Movements, Conflict and Change*, Vol.8, Greenwich, CT: JAI Press.

Kriesberg, L. (ed.) (1996), *Research in Social Movements, Conflicts and Change*, Vol.19, Greenwich, CT: JAI Press.

Kriesi, Hanspeter (1996), 'The Organisational Structure of New Social Movements in a Political Context', in McAdam, McCarthy and Zald [*1996: 152–84*].

Lanzalaco, Luca (1990), *Dall'impresa All'associazione*, Milan: Angeli.

Le Saout, Didier (1995), 'Entering the Stage: Strategies of Environmental Communication in France', in Eder (ed.) [*1995*].

Levine, P. (1994), 'Consultants and American Political Culture', *Report from the Institute for Philosophy and Public Policy*, Vol.14, pp.1–6.

Lichterman, Paul (1996), *The Search for Political Community*, Cambridge/New York: Cambridge University Press.

Lo, Clarence (1992), 'Communities of Challengers in Social Movement Theory', in Morris and McClurg Mueller [*1992: 224–50*].

Lofland, John (1996), *Social Movement Organisations*, Hawthorne, NY: Aldine de Gruyter.

Lowe, Philip D. and Jane M. Goyder (1983), *Environmental Groups in Politics*, London: Allen & Unwin.

McAdam, D., McCarthy, J.D. and M.N. Zald (eds.) (1996), *Comparative Perspectives on Social Movements*, Cambridge/New York: Cambridge University Press.

Majone, Giandomenico (1993), 'When Does Policy Deliberation Matter?', *EUI Working Papers SPS 93/12*, Florence: European University Institute.

March, James G. and Johan P. Olsen (1989), *Rediscovering Institutions*, New York: Free Press.

Melucci, Alberto (1989), *Nomads of the Present*, London: Hutchinson.

Minkoff, Debra (1995), *Organising for Equality*, New Brunswick, NJ: Rutgers University Press.

Molotch, Harvey (1979), 'Media and Movements', in J.D. McCarthy and M.N. Zald (eds.), *Dynamics of Social Movements*, Cambridge, MA: Winthrop, pp.71–93.

Morris, A. and C McClurg Mueller (eds.) (1992), *Frontiers in Social Movement Theory*, New Haven, CT: Yale University Press.

Mullally, Ger (1995), 'Entering the Stage: Strategies of Environmental Communication in Ireland', in Eder [*1995*].

Offe, Claus (1990), 'Reflections on the Institutional Self-Transformation of Movement Politics', in R.J. Dalton and M. Kuechler (eds.), *Challenging the Political Order*, Cambridge: Polity Press, pp.232–506.

Oliver, Pamela and Gerald Marwell (1992), 'Mobilizing Technologies for Collective Action', in A. Morris and C. McClurg Mueller (eds.), *Frontiers in Social Movement Theory*, New Haven, CT: Yale University Press.

Pizzorno, Alessandro (1998), *Il potere dei giudici*, Bari: Laterza.

Richardson, Jeremy J. and Nicholas Watts (1985), 'National Policy Styles and the Environment: Britain and West Germany Compared', *Discussion Paper 85-16*, Berlin: Wissenschaftszentrum.

Rootes, Christopher (1997), 'The Transformation of Environmental Activism', Working Paper, Centre for the Study of Social and Political Movements, University of Kent at Canterbury; revised version forthcoming in *Innovation: The European Journal of Social Sciences*, Vol.12, No.3, 1999.

Rovelli, Cesare (1988), 'I Modelli Organiszativi delle Associazioni Ambientaliste', in R. Biorcio and G. Lodi (eds.), *La Sfida Verde*, Padua: Liviana, pp.73–98.

Rucht, Dieter (1989), 'Environmental Movement Organisations in West Germany and France: Structure and Interorganisational Relations', in B. Klandermans (ed.), *International Social Movement Research*, Vol.2, *Organising for Change*, Greenwich, CT: JAI Press, pp.61–94.

Rucht, Dieter (1990), 'The Strategies and Action Repertoires of New Movements', in R. Dalton and M. Kuechler (eds.), *Challenging the Political Order: New Social and Political Movements in Western Democracies*, Cambridge: Polity Press, pp.156–75.

Rucht, Dieter (1993), 'Think Globally, Act Locally'? Needs, Forms and Problems of Cross-

34   ENVIRONMENTAL MOVEMENTS: LOCAL, NATIONAL, GLOBAL

National Cooperation Among Environmental Groups', in J.D. Liefferink, P. Lowe and A.P.J. Mol (eds.), *European Integration and Environmental Policy*, London/New York: Belhaven Press/Halsted Press, pp.75–95.

Rucht, Dieter (1995a), 'Parties, Associations and Movements as Systems of Political Interest Intermediation', in J. Thesing and W. Hofmeister (eds.), *Political Parties in Democracy*, Sankt Augustin: Konrad-Adenauer-Stiftung, pp.103–25.

Rucht, Dieter (1995b), 'Ecological Protest as Calculated Law-Breaking: Greenpeace and Earth First! in Comparative Perspective', in W. Rüdig (ed.), *Green Politics III*, Edinburgh: Edinburgh University Press, pp.66–89.

Rucht, Dieter (1996), 'The Impact of National Contexts On Social Movement Structure', in McAdam, McCarthy and Zald [*1996: 185–204*].

Rucht, Dieter and Thomas Ohlemacher (1992), 'Protest Event Data: Collection, Uses, and Perspectives', in M. Diani and R. Eyerman (eds.), *Studying Collective Action*, Newbury Park, CA/London: Sage, pp.76–106.

Scott, Richard W. (1985), *Le Organiszazioni*, Bologna: il Mulino.

Shaiko, Ronald G. (1993), 'Greenpeace USA: Something Old, New, Borrowed', *The Annals of the AAPSS*, Vol.528, pp.88–100.

Schwartz, Michael and Shuva Paul (1992), 'Resource Mobilisation vs. the Mobilisation of People: Why Consensus Movements Cannot Be Instruments of Social Change', in Morris and McClurg Mueller [*1992: 205–23*].

Snow, David A., Zurcher, Louis A. and Sheldon Ekland-Olson (1980), 'Social Networks and Social Movements: A Microstructural Approach To Differential Recruitment', *American Sociological Review*, Vol.45, pp.787–801.

Strassoldo, Raimondo (1994), *Le Radici dell'Erba. Sociologia dei Movimenti Ambientali di Base*, Naples: Liguori.

Swanson, David L. and Paolo Mancini (1995) (eds.), *Politics, Media, and Modern Democracy*, New York: Praeger.

Szasz, Andrew (1994), *EcoPopulism. Toxic Waste and the Movement for Environmental Justice*, Minneapolis, MN/London: University of Minnesota Press/UCL Press.

Szerszinski, Bron (1995), 'Entering the Stage: Strategies of Environmental Communication in the UK', in Eder [*1995*].

Tarrow, Sidney (1994), *Power in Movement. Social Movements, Collective Action and Politics*, New York/Cambridge: Cambridge University Press.

Tarrow, Sidney (1996), 'Fishnets, Internets and Catnets: Globalization and Transnational Collective Action', Discussion paper, Cornell University, Ithaca, NY.

Tilly, Charles (1978), *From Mobilisation To Revolution*, Reading, MA: Addison-Wesley.

van der Heijden, Hein-Anton, Ruud Koopmans and Marco Giugni (1992), 'The West European Environmental Movement', in L. Kriesberg (ed.), *Research in Social Movements, Conflict and Change*, Supplement 2, edited by L. Kriesberg, Greenwich, CT: JAI Press.

Wapner, Paul Kevin (1996), *Environmental Activism and World Civic Politics*, Albany, NY: SUNY Press.

Wheeler, M. (1996), 'Reforming Party Structures', paper presented to the ECPR session on *New Developments in Political Communication*, Oslo.

Wilson, James Q (1973), *Political Organisations*, New York: Basic Books.

Yearley, Steven (1996), *Sociology, Environmentalism, Globalization*, London: Sage.

Zald, Mayer N. and John McCarthy (1987), *Social Movements in An Organisational Society*, New Brunswick, NJ: Transaction.

Dialectics of Institutionalisation: The Transformation of the Environmental Movement in Germany

KARL-WERNER BRAND

Environmental issues have undergone a remarkable process of institutionalisation since the early 1980s. Whereas the environmental movement became the focus of a highly confrontational, anti-systemic, left-libertarian mass movement towards the end of the 1970s, environmental concerns gained high priority with the public and on political agenda only ten years later. This had effects on the discourse as well as the organisational field of environmental actors. Big organisations became the dominant actors on the field of environmental conflict; moral protest combined with professional marketing; confrontational strategies changed to dialogical and cooperative strategies. This raised severe identity problems which increased when environmental issues were pushed into the background by economic and social problems in the 1990s. The discourse of 'sustainable development', the new master frame of the environmental debate in Germany since the mid-1990s, has triggered institutional innovations particularly at local level which provide opportunities for the environmental movement to develop a new profile as a 'glocal' (global and local) actor of civil society.

As in other Western industrial countries, the environmental movement in Germany has undergone a fundamental process of institutionalisation in the past three decades. Whereas environmental issues were still highly polarised at the end of the 1970s, they ranked high on the public agenda only ten years later; meanwhile the movement itself had become a well recognised actor in the field of national and international environmental policy. Even if clear lines of cause and effect cannot be distinguished [cf. *Midttun and Rucht, 1994; Rucht, 1996*], there can be no doubt that the environmental movement had accelerated the formation of an increasingly dense network of environmental regulation [cf. *Jänicke and Weidner, 1995*]. This sweeping institutionalisation of environmentalism is outstanding. Yet, institutionalisation may indicate rather different processes: habitualisation, professionalisation or bureaucratisation, the end of movement politics, but also the enforcement of new normative standards of behaviour, the establishment of new organisational forms of civil society, or the constitution of a new institutional terrain of environmental conflict.

The contribution deals with the particular characteristics of this process of institutionalisation in Germany and their consequences for movement mobilisation. It draws on an empirical study of changing patterns of environmental communication in Germany [cf. *Brand et al., 1997*], which has been embedded in a broader comparative analysis on 'Framing and Communicating Environmental Issues' in England, France, Germany, Ireland and Italy in the period between 1986 and 1994 [cf. *Eder, 1995*].[1] Before presenting the empirical findings, however, a short outline of the theoretical approach will be given.

The study combines a cultural, neo-institutionalist perspective with discourse theory. New institutionalism conceives institutions as rules of social interaction which meaningfully structure, sanction and stabilise social practices. However, institutions can structure social practises only so long and in so far as they are regularly reproduced through discourse. Conversely, interpretations of reality which are constructed by these discourses make sense only in so far as they also organise our lives practically. That is as valid for the reproduction of institutional structures as it is for their transformation. 'Institutional transformations are simultaneously material and symbolic transformations of the world. They involve not only shifts in the structure of power and interest but in the definition of power and interest' [*Friedland and Alford, 1991: 246*]. Thus for the analysis of the transformation of the environmental movement, developments on the discursive and symbolic level as well as on the organisational field are of major interest. Both analytical levels may be briefly illustrated.

On the one hand social movements constitute themselves in the field of symbolic struggles. They receive recognition as social actors only if they are able to lift their own competing definition of problems on to the public agenda. Within these symbolic struggles the social perception of reality is redefined, new discourse coalitions are formed, and new political cleavages emerge. This goes hand in hand with calling into question and scandalising the social practices related to the 'old' symbolic patterns. Therefore movement actors choose demonstrative, spectacular, confrontational strategies. On this level of conflict it is not power relations directly that are at issue but the power of definition. Social movements usually can shape institutions in modern, pluralist societies only indirectly: by delegitimising institutional practices, and redefining the symbolic order. Success or failure of social movements thus depends heavily on whether they are able to find strong public resonance for their arguments, critiques, and utopias. This again depends on the mediating role of the mass media. Only if movements succeed on this field of symbolic politics might they be able to break up institutional structures, networks of power, interest and domination, and to enforce new forms of institutional problem-solving.

These symbolic struggles evolve in an ever shifting discursive arena. The environmental debate is shaped by a changing sequence of issues: air- and water-pollution, limits to growth, acid rain, toxic waste, nuclear energy, Chernobyl, waste management, traffic, ozone hole or global warming. Each of these issue attention cycles gives the environmental debate a particular configuration, provides different problem links, offers a new vocabulary of motives for collective action and suggests different strategies for action.

Environmental movements do not only evolve within discursive fields of action, however, but also in a particular organisational environment. As social movement research of the past two or three decades has shown, social movements are shaped both by the political opportunity structure, and the organisational, financial, and personal resources they have at hand. On this organisational level social movements are involved in resource mobilisation, try to gain institutional influence, make efforts to form new coalitions, to enlarge the opportunities for participation, and to improve decision-making processes. Substantial changes have happened also on this level since the 1970s.

In the following five sections the restructuration of the arena of environmental conflicts and the related transformation of the environmental movement is outlined with reference to both the discursive and organisational aspects of this process. The first section provides a rough outline of the development of environmental conflict in Germany since the 1970s. The second section deals with changes in organisational structure, the third with the diversification and professionalisation of movement activities, and the fourth with the emergence of new, dialogical and co-operative forms of interaction. The fifth section, finally, discusses the restructuring of the field of environmental mobilisation by the new master frame of 'sustainable development' since the mid-1990s.

I. Development of Environmental Conflict in Germany

As in other western countries, nature conservation in Germany developed both as an organised movement and as an object of governmental regulation around the turn of the last century. Up to the 1930s practical work was based largely on honorary participation. Whereas nature conservation found support in the 'blood and soil' ideology of German fascism, it was in practice pushed into the background by the quickly growing priority of the war economy. After the Second World War, nature conservation found it hard to gain ground again, not least because fascist ideology had devalued all conservationist values, including homeland, landscape and nature. Moreover, since the war had left immense destruction, economic reconstruction became the top priority, with nature conservation concerns playing only a minor role. Even the establishment of an umbrella organisation of German nature conservation groups, the Deutscher Naturschutzring (DNR), in 1950 and its lobbying efforts did not much advance the cause.

This situation did not change until the late 1960s. Quickly rising sensitivity to environmental problems and the increased importance of planning processes at the municipal, regional and state level demanded reorganisation of nature conservation. With the Federal Nature Conservation Act (Bundesnaturschutzgesetz) of 1976 nature conservation became embedded in the idea of integrated, state-organised environmental management.

The Establishment of Modern Environmental Politics (1969–74)

The formation of the SPD–FDP coalition government in 1969 can be seen as the turning point in environmental policy. For the first time, environment-related policy tasks became integrated into a single independent policy field. Pushed by its ambitious reform claims, within a short time the government started with an 'Immediate Programme' (September 1970) followed by a detailed 'Environmental Programme' which (in its revised version of 1976) still sets the norms of environmental policy today: the principles of 'precaution', 'causation', and 'co-operation'. This implied a shift of jurisdictional competences. With a constitutional change in 1972 (Art. 74 No. 24 Basic Law), the administration of legal regulations in the fields of waste disposal, clean air, and noise abatement was transferred to the federal government. Thus, environmental policy became a policy primarily regulated at the national level, leaving only the implementation of environmental laws and its monitoring with the *Länder* (states) and the municipalities. Scientific expertise was strengthened by the establishment of the Council of Experts on the Environment (*Sachverständigenrat für Umweltfragen,* SRU) in 1972, and the Federal Environmental Office (*Umweltbundesamt,* UBA) in 1974, both serving as advisory bodies for the federal administration. This new institutional network, set up within a short time span, provided the basis for a series of legislative measures of which the Federal Air Quality Control and Noise Abatement Act (*Bundesimmissionsschutzgesetz*) of 1974 were of central and norm-setting importance.

Environmental politics during these years was based on a broad social consensus. The German Federation of Industry (BDI) welcomed the 'Environmental Programme' and the principle of 'constructive co-operation' between state and industry. Trade unions, too, engaged in environmental initiatives, of which the congress, 'Quality of Life', organised by the metal workers' union (IG Metall) in 1972 attracted the greatest public attention. Citizen groups that emerged in the early seventies primarily addressed local problems (for example, noise pollution by traffic or air pollution by nearby plants). Growing public sensitivity towards environmental problems also had repercussions on the established institutions of nature conservation, causing internal conflicts between old conservationists and new environmentalists.

Economy versus Ecology: The Polarisation on Environmental Issues (1975–82)

The oil crisis in the autumn of 1973 and the global economic recession of 1974/75 shook faith in the feasibility of progressive social change, and turned the reformist spirit into a pessimistic one. A new focus on crisis management was announced. The chancellorship passed from Willy Brandt, the 'reformer', to Helmut Schmidt, the 'doer'. With this change, the broad consensus on environmental issues was broken. In close alliance with the Federal Association of Industry and the trade unions, the government converted from being a driving force of environmental protection to being a brake upon it. Questions of energy supply gained new prominence, and, as in many other western countries, the nuclear energy programme was pushed ahead.

Against the background of broad public discussion on the 'limits to growth' and threatening ecological catastrophes, this new all-party 'growth-coalition' provoked the emergence of a strong environmental movement which had its basis in thousands of local grass-roots initiatives. The environmental movement converged on the increasingly militant conflicts about proposed construction sites of atomic power plants and sites for radioactive waste. Thus, these years resulted in a high level of polarisation concerning environmental questions. This nourished a new ecological consciousness, the rise of a new kind of environmental organisation, and a new political force – 'green' and 'alternative lists' – which first entered state (Länder) parliaments at the end of the 1970s.

Ecology Goes Mainstream (1983–90)

In the early 1980s, environmental policy found a fresh tail wind despite the decline of the anti-nuclear movement (which had been absorbed by the peace movement). First, environmental questions gained high priority in mass media coverage and public consciousness. This remained constant throughout the 1980s. Second, all established parties now had to be aware of the competition of the Greens who entered the national parliament in 1983. Third, the professionalisation and institutionalisation of 'counter-expertise' in movement organisations, in eco-institutes, in a new nation-wide, left-libertarian daily, the *'tageszeitung'* *(taz)*, and – last but not least – in the scientific staff and committees of the Green Party, gave green arguments a much better profile in the public arena.

On the side of institutional politics, many of these changes had paradoxically been speeded up by the conservative-liberal takeover of government in 1982. This political shift reversed the previous conflict constellation in parliament: whereas the progressive environmental policy of the early 1970s had been opposed by the conservative parties, the ruling conservatives of the 1980s were now confronted with an opposition (the Greens, and the Social Democrats whose ecological factions had gained the upper hand) who demanded an even more radical environmental policy. This changing context provided the government with a good opportunity to portray itself as a European protagonist in environmental protection, and its record with regard to technical environmental protection is indeed not bad. The issue of 'dying forests' *(Waldsterben)* arose in 1981/82 and dominated public discussion on environmental problems in Germany for some years. It was a good starting point for the new conservative-liberal government to demonstrate its will to take severe measures against environmental pollution. Emissions limits for power plants were drastically lowered and the introduction of catalytic converters was pushed through against the opposition of most other EC countries.

Although green ideas undoubtedly were advancing, this new institutional context raised serious problems for the environmental movement. Apart from some ongoing local conflicts, direct confrontation on the basis of mass mobilisation lost prominence. The struggle for ecological change shifted to different arenas and demanded organisational and strategic changes. Professional movement organisations like the German Alliance for Environment and Nature Conservation (BUND) and Greenpeace became, together with the Green Party, the protagonists of West German environmentalism. The growing discrepancy between the institutionalisation of environmentalism and the preserved fundamentalist self-concept of activists at the grass-roots level caused disorientation and, especially within the Green Party, fierce internal fights between 'fundamentalists' and 'realists'.

Although the Chernobyl accident in 1986 mobilised a new grass-roots movement – 'Mothers Against Nuclear Power' *(Mütter gegen Atomkraft)* – its main effects were at the institutional level. On the one hand, it pushed the public debate (and the stance of the big parties) into a critical position towards nuclear energy, dramatising the catastrophic risks perceived as inherent in modern technologies as a whole. It thus helped speed up the symbolic greening of private and public life. On the other hand, in reaction to the initially rather helpless and contradictory reaction of the *Länder* and the federal government to the Chernobyl accident, a new Federal Ministry for Environment, Nature Protection and Nuclear Safety (BMU) was established, in which formerly dispersed competences for environmental protection have been put together in one portfolio. Klaus Töpfer, who took over the ministry in 1987, symbolically represented the environmental concern of the government in an energetic and trustworthy way. By issuing a wave of new orders (for example, changes in environmental liability law, the ban on chlorine chemical products), playing a leading role in passing the Convention for the Protection of the North and Baltic Sea, and, last but not least, announcing the reduction of CO_2 emissions by 25 per cent till the year 2005, Töpfer earned the reputation of being a progressive environmentalist, especially at the international level.

Even industry began to struggle for a better environmental image. Environmental protection was firmly established in the policies of many large companies, above all, in the chemical and car industries. In addition to end-of-pipe technologies, preventive strategies increasingly gained importance (at least on the level of rhetoric). Environmental management became a central topic in industrial debates, and eco-consulting a booming industry. 'Ecological modernisation' became the central organising idea of political and economic debates.

Stagnation and Reorientation of Environmental Politics (1991–98)

The process of German unification shifted priorities rather quickly to social and economic issues. At the national level, the scope for innovative environmental policy became drastically reduced. This reflected not only growing financial restrictions but also a marked shift in the dominant frames of political discourse as a whole. Launched by the German Federation of Industry (BDI), a neo-liberal discourse on the competitiveness of Germany within the process of globalisation soon began to dominate public debate, pushing the old 'growth' frame to the fore again.

This shift of priorities is garnished with an environmental effect 'free of charge' by applying existing environmental laws on the territory of the former GDR. Environmental clean-up activities in the new eastern *Länder* (states) were not only more urgent but also appeared much more effective due to high marginal yields. There was, however, one field of environmental policy which gained high popularity in the early nineties: the field of waste policy. Because of increasing problems of waste disposal a decree was passed in 1991 which aimed at a radical reduction of packaging materials (*Verpackungsverordnung*). As a consequence the *Dual System* was established by trade and industry which demanded not only changes in individual behaviour (in separating the different sorts of waste) but also attracted public criticism due to a series of scandals. Simultaneously, the global environmental agenda entered centre stage with the preparation of the UNCED Earth Summit in Rio 1992. German environmental policy increasingly became focused at the international level, not least because it diverted attention from domestic stagnation.

The new focus on global environmental problems had unintended consequences, however. Rio and the follow-up process led to a (at first rather slow) diffusion of the concept of 'sustainable development' into German discourse on environmental questions. Whereas economic and social problems remained dominant in the public discourse during the mid-1990s, the debate on environmental politics became successively reorganised by the integrative perspective of this new 'master frame' [cf. *Semrau, 1996*]. For movement actors who had been deeply disappointed by the rapid shift of priorities in the public debate, the advancement of the concept of 'sustainable development' provided the basis for strategic reorientation and a new opportunity for public mobilisation, albeit on a different institutional terrain.

II. The Three Organisational Pillars of German Environmentalism

The rise of German environmentalism is, as in other countries, embedded in the emergence of a broader sector of 'new social movements' [cf. *Klandermans et al., 1988; Kriesi et al., 1995; Rucht 1994*]. This especially holds true for Germany where this movement sector developed a strong culturally integrating power. In no other country did these movements interweave in such densely integrated 'alternative milieux' as in Germany, thereby giving them the character of an autonomous political formation clearly distinguishable from older conflicts and movements [*Brand 1985; Brand et al., 1986*]. Only here the conflicts on the new issues gave rise to a clear polarisation between 'old' and 'new politics', 'first' and 'second culture', 'system' and 'movement'. The specific character of the environmental movement in Germany cannot be understood without reference to the dynamics of this movement sector.

Whereas the environmental movement thus acquired a predominantly left-libertarian profile, it strongly influenced the whole new social movements' sector ideologically. Though no new comprehensive ideology emerged, at the end of the decade a common criticism of technocratic society and industrial growth, and a vague 'ecotopian' vision of an alternative society, became the culturally integrating basis of oppositional, left-libertarian milieux. Nevertheless, like the women's or peace movement, the environmental movement also follows its own logic determined by the special problems involved.

As in other countries, the environmental movement is organisationally based upon three pillars: first, autonomous, loosely connected networks of local grass-root groups; second, green electoral organisations and parties; third, established nature conservation organisations and a new generation of environmental organisations. The character and the importance of each of these pillars changes over time, according both to the dynamics of the whole new social movements sector and to the internal dynamics of environmental conflict.

In the 1970s citizen action groups with their regional and issue-specific networks dominated the appearance and self-understanding of the German environmental movement. It was the clash over nuclear energy which pushed forward the development of a common collective identity of these various oppositional networks as 'movement' in the second half of the 1970s. Mass protests and militant conflicts on the planned sites for nuclear power plants or nuclear waste deposits (in Wyhl, Brokdorf, Grohnde, Kalkar and Gorleben) linked the rural resistance against 'the arrogance of power' of 'those up there' to the left-libertarian culture and protest forms of the urban 'alternative milieux'. A variety of local, regional and national magazines and newspapers – including the new national daily *die tageszeitung (taz)* founded in 1979 – created a network of communcation among these oppositional milieux. This was the breeding ground out of which at the end of the 1970s the Green Party emerged.

The election of the Greens into the Bundestag in 1983 marked the end of the fundamentalist movement phase. The polarisation into 'system' and 'movement' gave way to a new institutionalisation of movement politics [*Roth, 1994*]. The movement milieux lost much of their coherence but local grass-roots activities did not decline, at least not quantitatively. The Chernobyl accident of 1986 brought about a new nationwide surge of grass-roots activities, and the struggle against the planned nuclear reprocessing plant in Wackersdorf (Bavaria) mobilised tens of thousands of anti-nuclear activists in 1987 and 1988 till the project was finally abandoned in 1989. Again in 1996, 1997 and 1998 civil disobedience and militant protest mushroomed on a mass scale when nuclear wastes were transportet by rail (Castor Transports) to the depositories in Gorleben and Ahaus. The periodic spread of mass protest on the grass-roots level – with a comparably high militancy in the field of anti-nuclear opposition – and the more hidden activities of thousands of local environmental groups do not change the overall trend, however. With the institutionalisation of environmental concerns and public risk communication the field of environmental conflicts has irrevocably shifted to the institutional arena. It is the Greens and the professional movement organisations which, therefore, become the dominant actors in the environmental conflict of the 1980s and 1990s.

The second organisational pillar of the German environmental movement is the Green Party [cf. *Frankland and Schoonmaker, 1992; Markovits and Gorski, 1993; Raschke, 1993; Wiesenthal, 1993*]. The Greens established itself as a federal political party in 1980, building on various 'green' and 'alternative lists' which had formed at *Länder* level since 1977. These were partly made up of cadre organisations of the New Left facing a decline in importance and substance, particularly in the city states of Berlin and Hamburg, but also of more right-wing groups in states like Lower Saxony and Bavaria. By the beginning of the 1980s the party had taken on a distinctly left-libertarian ecological profile, with a political self-definition based on the idea of direct democracy. State financing of parties and electoral successes at the municipal, state and federal level – the Green party entered the Bundestag in 1983 with 5.6 per cent of the votes – gave the Greens considerable financial means which were used to speed up the extension of a green expert community within the ecological movement. Thus, until the middle of the 1980s the Green party, despite its relatively small membership, advanced to become the dominant organisation within the ecological movement.

Simultaneously, the Greens more and more lost the character of a movement party, not least due to the decline of mass mobilisation and the institutionalisation of environmental politics. The result was bitter conflict between 'realist' and 'fundamentalist' factions of the Greens in the second half of the 1980s which diminished the party's public appeal considerably. In 1990, overrun by the German unification they did not want, the Greens lost their Bundestag seats. This shock stimulated a phase of stocktaking; more 'realistic' positions began to become dominant, represented foremost by the then environment minister of Hesse, Joschka Fischer. In 1993, after lengthy negotiations, *Bündnis '90* (Alliance '90, representatives of the East-German civic movement) and the Green Party united, and this new alliance had no problems re-entering the Bundestag in 1994. However, with the diminished importance of environmental questions in public discourse, the Greens, too, lost much of their public visibility.

Whereas the Greens, in search of a new identity, ran through a less attractive phase of infighting in the second half of the 1980s, the third pillar of the environmental movement, the modernised traditional and the new environmental organisations of the 1970s and 1980s began to flourish, gaining continuously in members and financial resources [*Rucht, 1994: 266*]. This holds true, in particular, for the *Bund für Umwelt und Naturschutz Deutschland* (BUND) and *Greenpeace Germany*. The BUND (Federation for Environment and Nature Protection in Germany) was founded in 1975 as a link between traditional nature protection groups and the radical political ecology groups. Under the BUND's influence other traditional umbrella organisation of nature conservation such as the *Deutsche Naturschutzring* (DNR) or the German Association for the Protection of Birds – since 1989 under the new name *Naturschutzbund Deutschland* (NABU) (Federation of Nature Protection Germany) – also became receptive to a systematic view of environmental concerns as did the German section of World Wildlife Fund (WWF).

One of the best-known groups within the new generation of environmental movement organisations is the German branch of Greenpeace founded in 1980. As in other countries, Greenpeace is organised strongly hierarchically and focused on disruptive actions and campaigns which court high media attention. Although there exist local Greenpeace groups in nearly all bigger cities, they have no influence on the planning of campaigns. Its high numbers of individual supporters (about 500,000 in 1995) make Greenpeace financially the best equipped environmental organisation in Germany. In 1982, in the course of the debate on the 'dying of forests' and in protest against the hierarchical decision-making structures within Greenpeace, the group *Robin Wood* split off. Typical representatives of this new generation of environmental organisations also include the *Verkehrsclub Deutschland* (Transportation Club Germany), the *Allgemeine Deutsche Fahrradclub* (General German Bicycle Club), or the *Verbraucherinitative* (Consumer's Initiative). Scientific eco-institutes also play an important role in the German environmental movement. The oldest, and most renowned, is the *Öko-Institut Freiburg*. Dating back to the negative experiences of citizen action groups protesting the planned siting of an atomic power plant in Wyhl (Breisgau), it was founded in 1977 as a model of an ecologically engaged, applied approach of 'critical science'. A new step in the institutionalisation of ecologically engaged research has been the establishment of the *Wuppertal Institut für Klima, Umwelt, Energie* (Wuppertal Institute for Climate, Environment, Energy) in 1991. In contrast to the *Öko-Institut Freiburg*, it is basically state funded (by North Rhine Westphalia) and committed to the institutional promotion of energy saving, programmes of CO_2- reduction, or sustainable life-styles.

All in all, apart from the sporadic upsurge of militant anti-nuclear mass protests, environmental organisations have become the most prominent and most influencial actors within the various strands of the environmental movement in Germany. We will therefore turn now to a more detailed analysis of the organisational and ideological transformations of this movement sector since the mid-1980s.

III. Moral Protest and Professional Marketing[2]

Social movements such as environmental action groups live on their capacity to mobilise moral protest. An ideal constellation exists when conflicts can be staged as a conflict between a 'David' fighting for a just cause and a 'Goliath' who can be portrayed as the clear villain. These conditions are rarely found in Germany today. Spectacles like climbing smoke-stack chimneys no longer pay when, as a result of the relatively high standards of end-of-pipe technologies, pollution is less a matter of emissions than a product of environmentally insensitive goods. Pickets and site occupations excite conflicting reactions when they attempt to prevent the siting of high speed railway lines, ring roads or airports, things closely connected to accustomed consumption and life styles, or when alternatives (seen from an ecological perspective) are no less problematic. Environmental issues no longer have to fight in order to reach public awareness. The density of environmental regulation is relatively high. Industry outdoes itself in green marketing. The legitimacy of environmentalist concerns is no longer controversial; what is debated is how they can appropriately and efficiently be combined with economic and social concerns.

For environmental groups all this makes mobilisation more difficult. 'The simple debates are gone. Simple confrontation, simple issues, easy mobilisation – all that is gone. Everything has become much more complex' (interview, BUND/2 – 9/16/93). Environmental groups are compelled to adapt to changing circumstances. This adaptation happens at different levels: in fields of action, forms of organisation, strategies of mobilisation, and the patterns of interaction with economic and political actors.

Diversification of Fields of Action

A first striking change is the diversification of the fields of action. Established environmental organisations like BUND or NABU now take part in hearings, work in parliamentary commissions, and comment on bills. They participate at the municipal and state level in planning building projects and facilities. They have standing in court or support citizens in their legal claims. Greenpeace funds scientific studies to support issue campaigns (for example, the feasibility of an ecological tax reform). The BUND funds – together with MISEREOR – the study 'Sustainable Germany' (*Zukunftsfähiges Deutschland*) by the Wuppertal-Institute for Climate, Environment, and Energy. Greenpeace and BUND look to co-operate with firms to foster clean technologies, or to strengthen the principles of ecological management. WWF works on specific projects in more traditional areas of nature protection (for example, the protection of the mud flats on the North German coast from destruction by the building of new pipelines). Environmental organisations conceptualise alternative transportation and energy policies, and take part in their implementation at municipal and state levels. Their specialists discuss in detail the substitution of specific chemicals, or the criteria for a sustainable 'management of nature', for instance, in the forest industry. However, these environmental organisations also initiate consumer boycotts (for example, of tropical lumber or of Shell over the proposed disposal of the Brent Spar platform) and organise, if needed, confrontational protest actions, demonstrations, or spectacular pickets. Last, but not least, some of them – in particular BUND and NABU – act at the local level in the 'classical' way, protecting nature and species of wildlife by the unpaid activities of their members.

The Increasing Role of Scientific Expertise and Marketing

This differentiation of fields of action is accompanied by a continuous professionalisation of the forms of action. This trend finds expression in the increasing role of science, organisational restructuring, and in the entry of marketing methods into public relations. In the second half of the 1980s, in all major organisations, scientific experts gained importance. For large parts of the environmental movement specialised qualifications have become an essential part of their self-understanding:

> This is no longer compatible with the beginnings of Greenpeace. Our high numbers of regulars assumes that we now have to have a large number of specialists working for us, in contrast to the past. Each campaigner here who is working on issue-oriented questions is either highly qualified by training, or has high qualifications on joining due to his or her experience (interview, Greenpeace –– 14 July 1992).

The BUND also had a large increase in personnel between 1986 and 1990. Consultants with academic training, transportation experts, physicists and chemists were hired. Thus emerged the self-image of an 'organization based on skills'. As a detailed study of environmental activists in a middle-sized German city at the end of the eighties shows, issue competence is viewed as just as important at the grass-roots level [*Christmann, 1992*].

This tendency to an increasing importance of science seems to be continuing. However, for many environmental groups, in particular the Green Party, this trend at first had unintended, negative effects. Scientific arguments are harder to convey to the public than are catchy slogans. What environmental groups gain in scientific expertise they lose in public relations. Thus, marketing methods were brought in to the public relations management of the big environmental organisations. A role model for this is the PR work of Greenpeace which became the most known environmental organisation in the second half of the 1980s due to its high mass media presence. This change did not take place without a fierce fight. While Greenpeace has been planning its actions exclusively with regard to their PR efficiency since the beginning, other environmental groups refused this strategy on grounds of principle. To take up issues with a view to their resonance amongst the public seemed to be a betrayal of the moral principles of movement politics:

> I think the Greens have big trouble with that. Because ... other parties are accused of being populist. I think a little bit more populism would not hurt the Greens in gaining easier access to other parts of the population. But it is very hard to convince people in the party that a little bit more populism is not necessarily damaging to the goal of disseminating information. Or that populism necessarily means you have to water down your own positions (interview, *Die Grünen* – 18 Aug. 1992).

This conflict lost importance as a result of the progressive cooperation between political, industrial and movement actors since the end of the 1980s. Most environmental groups are now operating with marketing strategies. People coming from the movement are partially replaced by staff qualified in marketing and management. In their election campaign in 1994 the Greens hired advertising agencies for the first time. Changes also took place within the BUND. The strategy of working with experts producing comments on bills and detailed criticism gave way – not at least because of financial constraints – to 'campaign-oriented' work which was geared more towards the wider public.

Politics of Distinction

The representation to the outside, the question of 'how one presents oneself, how one is to create a consistent image of oneself' (interview, BUND/2 – 16 Sept. 1993) thus has become more and more important. Growing orientation towards marketing strategies influences the way environmental organisations interact with one another. It reinforces tendencies toward organisational patriotism and distinction. Each environmental organisation tries to forge a specific identity and image by its issue profile and styles of working. When – in rare cases at the local level – co-operation occurs, this image is defended. Thus, the BUND views itself as an organisation with profound expertise with a fundamentalist touch: 'Greenpeace is good at selling itself, the BUND has the expertise' (interview, BUND/2 – 16 Sept. 1993). Greenpeace lives on its trademark 'David versus Goliath' and its spectacular staging of public conflicts. The WWF, by contrast, avoids spectacular actions and looks for 'constructive dialogue' in order to work on 'long-term solutions' together with government, industry and unions. Groups like Robin Wood, Mothers against Nuclear Power or local initiatives cultivate (not always voluntarily) their direct democratic image of a grass-roots organisation, often delimiting themselves from the professional, efficiency-oriented style of working of the big organisations. Although co-operation among environmental organisations has improved somewhat during the economic recession of the early 1990s, the overall picture still shows pronounced rivalry, in particular between the big organisations. With the exception of meetings under the organisational umbrella of the *Deutscher Naturschutzring* (DNR) and occasional meetings of the big organisations' directors, institutionalised contacts do not exist. Despite local activists' wishes for co-operation there are, with the exception of personal contacts and networks, no regular exchanges of information, no agreements, no commonly planned campaigns, at the level of full-time management. In contrast to the hey days of ecological mass mobilisation environmental organisations have become competitors.

The New Split: Professional versus Non-Professional Organisations

The professionalisation of the environmental movement also has internal, organisational consequences. Within the big environmental organisations, management and marketing becomes more important compared to voluntary boards. Managerial categories play an increasing role. What professional working organisations are successively asking for is not any longer any kind of personal engagement but, rather, financial support. Although this is only true in its most extreme form for Greenpeace and WWF, it seems to be a rapidly generalisable tendency.

All this brings about a new differentiation within the movement. Smaller environmental organisations which cannot or do not want to keep up with this process of professionalisation face extraordinary problems of survival. 'Since all of us work on a voluntary basis and are lay-persons ... we could well do with having more professionals with paid staff. But since we run on the basis of donations of 40 Deutschmarks a year, which for that we produce a newspaper free of charge ... put another way, we scramble at the subsistence level' (interview, Mothers Against Nuclear Power – 12 Sept. 1992).

Whereas ideologically a tendency towards pragmatic environmental protection shows up among the traditional nature conservationists as well as among the radical political ecology groups since the mid-1980s, a new division now becomes significant: between, on the one hand, the big professional organisations (in particular, Greenpeace, BUND and the Green Party) which dominate environmental discourse in the public and, on the other, the smaller groups concentrating on special issues or local conflicts. This split is deepened by the growing importance of the global level of environmental politics since the UNCED conference in Rio 1992, which speeded up the international networking of the big environmental NGOs and provided them with an acknowledged status in the negotiating process on the different international regimes and the related national procedures of implementation. It is only the smaller groups that, in part, keep up the traditional style of grass-roots mobilisation, above all among anti-nuclear groups. Other 'single issue groups', such as environmental organisations in the field of transport, energy saving, or agriculture, tend to become service and lobby organisations. Many members of local action groups who have been fighting against nearby polluting plants for many years have developed high professional competence (in the questions at stake) which makes them esteemed dialogue partners for industrial representatives within the emerging discursive designs [cf. *Brand, 1997; Dreyer, 1997; Dryzek, 1997*].

Thus, doubts arise whether or not one can still speak of an environmental 'movement' at all. In the beginning of the 1990s such problems in the self-image of movement actors resulted in an intensive debate on the 'end of the environmental movement'.[3] Many of the discussants saw the end of the movement in its old form, because of the very success of its demands. The environmental movement has advanced from being a misfit and social critic to an acknowledged societal actor. Seen from this view, difficulties now arise only because of the lack of resources to meet demands. Although this 'managerial perspective' is still challenged by a more fundamentalist view of grass-roots activists who plead for a revitalisation of militant mass protest, there is little controversy about the empircal fact of a progressive professionalisation of the environmental movement. And in view of the apparently irresistable 'greening' of society, most activists welcomed this trend as a precondition for the further advancement of environmentalism:

> Shortly before unification we reached a high in the discussion about an eco-social market economy. We were all convinced by that. The two big catch-all parties started a race with regard to that question, at least in their programmes. I talked with many business managers and had the real impression that things are shifting, that they are getting on board the boat. Not as far as we do but at least with one leg. Then unification came, and environmental issues went on the backburner (interview, NABU – 28 June 1993).

It is not German unification as such, however, but its high financial and social costs, the drastic economic recession in 1992/93, and the rapidly rising unemployment rate (especially in East Germany) which generated an abrupt shift of this perception. While in politics and public discourse economic growth became first priority again, resignation gained ground among environmentalists both at grass-roots and at elite levels. The expectation that the process of ecological modernisation had already become irreversible now seems naive.

Whereas this deep disillusion gives rise to a strategic reorientation, it does not change the overall trend towards professionalisation. Rather, the shift of priorities towards economic and social problems reduces the opportunities for mass mobilisation in favour of environmental concerns still further, leaving professional organisations on their own in the attempt to give environmental questions a better standing in the public.

IV. From Confrontation to Dialogue

The organisational development of the environmental movement outlined above reflects the progressive institutionalisation of environmental conflict since the eighties. This structural trend corresponds to a general change from confrontational to dialogical and co-operative strategies. This overall trend is modified, however, by two factors. First, strategic choices depend strongly on the organisational and ideological profile of the individual group: the philosophy of Greenpeace primarily demands confrontational strategies, even if Greenpeace is also engaged in many co-operative practices; following more traditional objectives of nature conservation, WWF or NABU, by contrast, have always preferred co-operation with state agencies or industrial companies. Second, strategies of public mobilisation are very sensitive to public issue cycles and shifts in the political climate. In this section we examine both structural trends and their group-specific and cyclical variations.

Professional Environmentalism as 'Counter-Lobby' in the Political Arena

Compared to the early 1980s, relations between environmental and political actors have improved considerably. Participation in hearings or conversations with ministers pose no problems, at least for influential environmental actors. There is an obvious willingness for dialogue on the part of political actors, too. Representatives of the Federal Ministry for Environment (BMU) praise the work of environmental groups; their own influence on government policy is seen as dependent on pressure coming from 'below'. 'The power the Minister of the Environment has, he basically draws from public awareness, and when environmental protection gains political clout ... then the minister is also strong: his strongest troops are mass media, environmental organisations, and the general public' (interview, BMU/1 – 5 Aug. 1994).

52   ENVIRONMENTAL MOVEMENTS: LOCAL, NATIONAL, GLOBAL

Although Greenpeace does not take part in political lobbying and the regular hearings of interest groups in the process of policy-making, it is nevertheless praised by the administration for its 'supportive role' and its 'outstanding and competent scientists'. Thus, environmental groups (with the exception of Greenpeace) are funded by federal and state governments 'with the declared objective to create a counter-lobby'. Criticisms generally arise only when they do not meet these expectations because of 'incompetence' or 'unprofessionalism' (interview BMU/2 – 24 Sept. 1993).

There is, however, much discontent with the results of this co-operation on the part of environmental groups. This refers to procedural aspects as well as policy outcomes:

> When hearings in the ministry take place, of course, we are invited: that has become a matter of course today which was not the case 10 years ago, that is an improvement. But then there are 30 or 20 people from industry who are allowed to talk for 30 minutes or even an hour, and environmental organisations are allowed to bring in one or two people talking 5 minutes each. There you simply see the proportional representation. Industry or business and environmental organisation still do not have equal footing (interview, DNR – 28 June 1993).

The disapointment with politics grew when, after German unification and the deepening of economic crisis in the early nineties, growth politics again became first priority blocking any innovative environmental policy. Although 'the confidence dissolved that we could promote the environmental cause better *within* the parties' (interviews, NABU – 28 June 1993), the patterns of communication and interaction with political actors went on as usual albeit with a mood of resignation.

Interaction with Business Actors: The Emergence of Dialogical Patterns of Conflict Resolution

There is a striking difference in the kind of interaction with industry. Having been the clear enemy for many years, the envrionmentally sensitive parts of German industry changed towards a dialogical strategy at the end of the 1980s [*Dreyer, 1997; Dyllick, 1992; Hildebrandt et al., 1994*] and so created new opportunities for and arenas of co-operative interaction: 'We have talks on a regular basis ... with creative management representatives. And there one can see considerable open-mindedness and a thinking about how we can improve the quality of our products, improve things in the processes of supply and distribution, and this in an ecological way' (interview, NABU – 28 June 1993).

Thilo Bode, then director of Greenpeace Deutschland, also views talks with ecologically enlightened managers as 'much more exciting than all talks with politicians. A lot of things are astir. Industry approaches us, we approach them' (*Die ZEIT*, 17 June 1994, p.42). This results in consulting activities for single firms, or even in limited financial co-operation in order to facilitate the marketability of new technologies or products. A good example of such new strategies is the development of a CFC-free refrigerator in cooperation with the East German firm Foron which forced , within a year, the biggest German producers of refrigerators to develop their own CFC-free models. Another, typical example of Greenpeace's strategy to improve the economic opportunities for environmentally friendly products was the abduction of the experimental fuel-efficient Renault Vesta from a French museum and its presentation at the International Car Exhibition (IAA) in Frankfurt in 1993 to demonstrate publicly that a production car with a fuel consumtion of only 1.9 l per 100 km is technically feasible. Negotiations with representatives of VW, Opel and Mercedes-Benz followed.

BUND representatives also look out for co-operation with ecological first movers within industry. 'When we think this is a serious concern, and a firm wants to move the cause, and improve something, then we are willing to co-operate with this firm and to offer our help' (interview, BUND/1 – 24 June 1992). This position, however, was much debated. At the 1992 delegate meeting in Leipzig a list was generated which indexed industrial branches with which co-operation is denied: among them the atomic and chemical industries, as well as firms engaged in arms production or genetic engineering. Moreover, a body was established to monitor contacts. Co-operation with the department store company Hertie became a model. BUND employees examined the stock lines of Hertie for environmental soundness and made recommendations which were put into action by the company. Co-operation also resulted from BUND's waste campaign with Body-Shop which offered products packaged in an ecologically exemplary way.

Another form of co-operation which boomed in West Germany at the end of the 1980s (although it declined again when economic problems became top priority in the 1990s) is eco-sponsoring [*Bruhn and Dahlhoff, 1990; Zillessen and Rahmel, 1991*]. Particularly in the field of nature and wildlife conservation, many projects get funded thus. While Greenpeace does not employ eco-sponsoring, WWF draws most on this form of co-operation. Already in 1986 it created a marketing society which sells the use of the Panda logo for sponsoring activities.

While these are new, co-operative forms of interaction with ecologically innovative firms or companies, relations between business and environmental actors are usually rather conflictual. This is true not only for highly debated issues of nuclear energy, chlorine chemical engineering, genetic engineering and motor traffic, but also for the numerous local conflicts between citizen action groups and polluting firms. However, just as in the conflictual fields of chemical production and transportation policy, even here a simple strategy of confrontation has, in most cases, given way to a double strategy of public mobilisation and of partial co-operation in order to solve problems. Wherever serious offers of 'dialogue' exist, environmental groups usually readily take part. Consequently, one can see the emergence of interorganisational systems of negotiation at the local level in order to defuse potential conflict by dialogue, for example, between the chemical corporation *Hoechst A.G.* and the local citizen action group *Hoechster Schnüffler und Maagucker* [*Dreyer and Kesselring, 1996*]. The strategy of polarisation with its typical accompanying rituals – disclosure, moral indignation, and demonstrations on one side, and trials to ignore, discriminate against, and criminalise on the other – more and more gives way to the inclusion of protest groups in negotiations which explore the possibility of compromises. Although those offers for talks on the part of business are often tactical measures [*Dreyer, 1997*], and although the results of inclusion are often disappointing for affected citizen groups, these forms of conflict regulation set new normative standards which cannot be ignored with impunity. A series of production failures with *Hoechst* in spring of 1993 provides a good illustration. First reactions were old-style: warding off and appeasement. This generated such public indignation that the then chief executive officer was forced to resign. Moreover, *Hoechst* saw the necessity to call upon a *Gesprächskreis Höchster Nachbarn* (Round Table of Höchster Neighbours) in order to improve its massive loss of image. Up to that point, conflict mediating talks with the *Höchster Schnüffler und Maagucker* were voluntary; now they were broadened, and better access to information was institutionalised [*Kesselring, 1997*].

In general, the attitude towards industry remained ambivalent even when the belief in an irreversible process of ecological modernisation was still unbroken. There was always the suspicion that the environment is utilised as a pure marketing argument. Environmentalists feel themselves trapped in a strategic dilemma. While ecological modernisation is pushed forward by the pressure of a critical public, environmental groups can no longer control this process as soon as industry begins to work with a 'green' label. Business actors thereby gain symbolic power to define the ecological problems in question. For environmentalists it is getting more difficult to enforce their own, more radical frames in the public debate.

> Well, we do not talk for nothing, in many cases, about the 'eco-lie'. For instance, when *Opel* advertises about producing the recyclable car of the future, or the environmentally friendly car of the future. Serious

ecology, as a matter of course, has to demand that cars are used less, but not that cars are simply ecologically converted. These are the crucial points today which make it difficult for us to make clear to the public what the real conflicts are (interview, Greenpeace – 14 July 1992).

Strategic Disorientation: The Lost Faith in Ecological Modernisation

Of course, disappointment with the quickly shifting priorities of the 1990s also refers to the reaction of industry. It is not individual industrialists, however, who are blamed primarily for the blocking of ecological demands. Industry as a whole and individual companies are no longer demonised. Partly, it is acknowledged that industrial companies have to act in this way because of market necessities. This does not imply passive acceptance. Rather, it is seen as demonstrating that the assumption of a convergence of ecological and economic interests has been a naive projection of economically prosperous years. In addition, after Rio the argument has gained ground that even with economic growth unaccompanied by environmental pollution, a fundamental change is necessary in order to develop 'a model of affluence which can be reproduced by some 8 billion people without, in the long run, destroying the planet' (E.U. von Weizsäcker, *Ökologische Briefe* 3/93, p.26).

A tougher stance towards industry and politics is therefore demanded, not only by groups which have always been sceptical about a smooth strategy, but also by those who have for a long time believed in 'dialogue'. A key experience for this pragmatic, 'modern' faction of the environmental movement had been the failure of the Deutsche Umwelttag (German Environmental Congress) 1992 in Frankfurt:

> We prepared an environmental congress ... and we behaved for two years in the preparation phase like we were living before 1989. We simply didn't see that reality. It also was strongly 'dialogue'-oriented, and I still go for dialogue, but I think that environmental organisations, at the very moment when it became clear that conflicts with industry would reoccur, that is shortly after unification, that they should have more strongly shown their teeth. ... My impression is that we were too soft in a crucial phase (interview, NABU – 28 June 1993).

However, none of the established environmental organisations plead for a recourse to old strategies of confrontation. Whereas local action groups (particularly within the anti-nuclear movement) and Greenpeace have never abandoned confrontational strategies as one of their strategic options, the revitalisation of militant mass protest was no longer an available option for the environmental movement *as a whole*. Environmental groups, rather, begin to focus on questions of 'life style' demanding a radical change in the Western way of life to ensure 'sustainable development' on a global scale.

V. The New Focus on 'Sustainable Development'

While the concept of sustainable development was until the early 1990s discussed only among experts, in 1994/95 the public resonance of this discussion rose sharply. Two widely discussed publications played the role of a catalyst in this debate. The first was the report of a parliamentary Commission on questions of industrial metabolism and chemical policy (Enquete-Kommission 'Schutz des Menschen und der Umwelt' 1994). It introduced the 'three-pillars' model into the public debate. Following this model, ecological, economic, and social concerns are equally important aspects of sustainable development. On a practical level this means that any kind of environmental policy or development planning on a national, regional or local level has to integrate the interests of industry, trade unions, social and environmental groups in a balanced way. On the one hand this concept is vague enough to allow co-operation of all relevant societal groups in the (conflictual) process of definition and implementation of 'sustainable' paths of development in the various fields of politics. On the other, it suggests a participatory model of policy-making which draws heavily on the resources of civil society. Whereas this framing of sustainability promoted the rapid spread of local Agenda-21 groups in 1995/96, the study 'Zukunftsfähiges Deutschland' (Sustainable Germany) by the Wuppertal Institute for Climate, Environment and Energy (BUND and MISEREOR 1996) gave fresh tailwind to the strategic reorientation of the environmental movement on questions of 'sustainable life styles'. Within local Agenda 21 activities a lot of energy and imagination is now invested in the practical implementation of these ideas.

The new masterframe of 'sustainable development' thus provides a strong basis for new models of dialogical politics. It focuses on the recombination of social, economic and ecological aspects of development on a global as well as on a national and local scale. Sharing the optimistic bias of the 'ecological modernisation' frame of the late 1980s, it no longer shares, however, the reductionist assumption of a quasi-automatic reconciliation of economic and ecological concerns by technical innovation. Rather, it directs attention to the level of social and institutional practices, to the necessity of developing new 'sustainable' ways of everyday life and new institutional patterns of problem solving. Whereas up to the end of 1998 this conceptual reorientation, apart from a change in rhetoric, remained without serious consequences at the level of national environmental politics, it has set in motion remarkable institutional innovations at the level of local politics during the past two or three years. This is a still ongoing process with an open end. As with all master frames of the environmental debate, the concept of 'sustainable development' opens up a new discursive and practical field of conflict which creates limitations and opportunities for all sides. The prospects of the German environmental movement thus basically depend on whether it will be able to stage convincing concepts of sustainable development in the public arena and the different institutional terrains. These concepts need to provide solutions not only to environmental but also to pressing social problems. Facing the dominant neo-liberal discourse this hardly appears to be a simple task. In an age of globalisation these concepts, moreover, have to connect the local with the global level. The environmental movement has to achieve a new profile as a 'glocal' actor of civil society [cf. *Robertson, 1995*]. Co-operation through political dialogues, round tables or new forms of participatory planning can only be one strategy to gain this end. The other, equally important strategy remains symbolic mobilisation of the public, the capacity to dramatise and scandalise problems in order to delegitimise institutional practices and to enforce new definitions of problems.

NOTES

1. The study was directed by Klaus Eder and funded both by the German Research Community (DFG) and the European Commission. In the course of the study narrative interviews were conducted with nearly all environmental groups and organisations which had a significant public or media resonance on the national level [*Brand and Poferl, 1995*].
2. The interview sequences cited in the following two sections are drawn from interviews conducted with representatives of German environmental organisations in 1992 and 1993 (and from some additional interviews conducted with policy actors in 1994). For reasons of anonymity, quotations from these interviews are indicated only by the organisational label and the date.
3. Such a debate was led for instance in the *Ökologische Briefe* (Ecological letters), a monthly information bulletin on current developments in environmental policy, which was also widely acknowledged by political and business actors.

REFERENCES

Brand, K.-W. (1997), 'Die Neustrukturierung des ökologischen Kommunikations- und Interaktionsfeldes', in Brand, Eder and Poferl [*1997: 184–239*].
Brand, K.-W., Büsser, D. and D. Rucht, (1986), *Aufbruch in eine andere Gesellschaft. Neue soziale Bewegungen in der Bundesrepublik* (revised edn.), Frankfurt: Campus.
Brand, K.-W. (ed.) (1985), *Neue soziale Bewegungen in Westeuropa und den USA*, Frankfurt a.M.: Campus.
Brand, K.-W. and A. Poferl (1995), 'The German Case', in Eder [*1995*].
Brand, K.-W., Eder, E. and A. Poferl (1997), *Ökologische Kommunikation in Deutschland*, Opladen: Westdeutscher Verlag.
Bruhn, M. and H.D. Dahlhoff (1990), *Sponsoring für Umwelt und Gesellschaft. Neue Instrumente*

der *Unternehmenskommunikation*, Schloß Reichartshausen, Bonn: Gabler.

BUND and MISEREOR (eds.) (1996), *Zukunftsfähiges Deutschland. Ein Beitrag zu einer global nachhaltigen Entwicklung*, Basel: Birkhäuser.

Christmann, G. (1992), 'Wissenschaftlichkeit und Religion: Über die Janusköpfigkeit der Sinnwelt von Umwelt- und Naturschützern. Eine wissenssoziologische Betrachtung von Ökologie-Gruppen', *Zeitschrift für Soziologie*, Vol.21, pp.200–11.

Dreyer, M. (1997), 'Die Kommunikationspolitik der chemischen Industrie im Wandel', in Brand, Eder and Poferl [*1997: 240–67*].

Dreyer, M. and S. Kesselring (1996), 'Institutionelle Innovation in unsicheren Zeiten. Der "Gespächskreis Höchster Nachbarn" als Beispiel für eine Form der Standortkommunikation', *Wechselwirkung*, pp.46–53.

Dryzek, J.S. (1990), *Discursive Democracy. Politics, Policy and Political Science*, Cambridge: Cambridge University Press.

Eder, K. (1995), *Framing and Communicating Environmental Issues* (Final Report to the Commission of the European Communities, DG XII, Project No. PL 210493), Florence: European University Institute.

Enquete-Kommission 'Schutz des Menschen und der Erde' des deutschen Bundestags (ed.) (1994), *Die Industriegesellschaft gestalten. Perspektiven für einen nachhaltigen Umgang mit Stoff- und Materialströmen*, Bonn: Economica.

Frankland, E. G. and D. Schoonmaker (1992), *Between Protest and Power: The Green Party in Germany*, Boulder, CO: Westview Press.

Friedland, R. and R. Alford (1991), 'Bringing Society Back In: Symbols, Practices, and Institutional Contradictions', in W. Powell and P. DiMaggio (eds.), *The New Institutionalism in Organisational Analysis*, Chicago, IL: University of Chicago Press, pp.232–63.

Jänicke, M. and H. Weidner (eds.) (1995), *Successful Environmental Policy*, Berlin: edition Sigma.

Kesselring, S. (1997), 'Die Störfälle bei Hoechst in Frühjahr 1993. Fallstudie zur sozialen Konstruktion ökologischer Konflikte', in Brand, Eder and Poferl [*1997: 268–306*].

Klandermans, B., Kriesi, H. and S. Tarrow (1988), *From Structure to Action: Comparing Social Movement Research Across Cultures*, Greenwich, CT: JAI Press.

Kriesi, H., Koopmans, R., Duyvendak, J.W. and M.J. Giugni (1995), *New Social Movements in Western Europe. A Comparative Analysis*. Minneapolis, MN: University of Minnesota Press.

Markovits, A. and P. Gorski (1993), *The German Left: Red, Green and Beyond*, Cambridge: Polity.

Midttun, A. and D. Rucht (1994). 'Comparing Policy Outcomes of Conflicts over Nuclear Power: Description and Explanation', in Flam H. (ed.), *States and Anti-Nuclear Oppositional Movements*, Edinburgh: Edinburgh University Press, pp.371–403.

Semrau, F. (1996), *Environmental Sustainability and Institutional Innovation in the Federal Republic of Germany* (Research Report to the Commission of the European Community), Munich: MPS-Texte 9.

Raschke, J. (1993), *Die Grünen. Wie sie wurden, was sie sind*, Cologne: Bund Verlag.

Robertson, R. (1995), 'Globalisation', in M. Featherstone, S. Lash and R. Robertson (eds.), *Global Modernities*, London: Sage.

Roth, R. (1994), *Demokratie von unten. Neue soziale Bewegungen auf dem Weg zur politischen Institution*, Cologne: BUND Verlag.

Rucht, D. (1994), *Modernisierung und neue soziale Bewegungen. Deutschland, Frankreich und USA im Vergleich*, Frankfurt/New York: Campus.

Rucht, D. (1996), 'Wirkungen von Umweltbewegungen: Von den Schwierigkeiten einer Bilanz', *Forschungsjournal NSB*, Vol.9, No.4, pp.15–27.

Wiesenthal, H. (1993), *Realism in Green Politics: Social Movements and Ecological Reform in Germany*, Boulder, CO: Westview Press.

Zillessen, R. and D. Rahmel (ed.) (1991), *Umweltsponsoring. Erfahrungsberichte von Unternehmen und Verbänden*, Frankfurt/Wiesbaden: FAZ/Gabler.

The German Environmental Movement at a Crossroads?

DIETER RUCHT and JOCHEN ROOSE

To outsiders, the environmental movement in Germany is relatively strong and successful. Measured in terms of its organisational strength and protest activities, the movement is not in decline. Professionalisation and institutionalisation have allowed it to become a respectable player in established politics. Nowadays, environmentalism seems to be embraced by all social forces. Yet the movement is confronted with a number of crucial questions about its future. Although some improvements can be identified, environmental degradation continues. The institutionalisation of major parts of the movement, and few signs of further progress, give rise to problems within the movement.

The German environmental movement[1] has been relatively successful. Over the last three decades, it has grown and matured, won a number of victories and become a serious and respectable player in environmental politics. Paradoxically, however, this success and respectability tends to undermine the movement´s strength and future impact. Business as usual could even weaken the movement insofar as large parts of the wider populace may believe that support and pressure is no longer needed because improvements are already underway. Given this possibility, parts of the movement have begun to question whether they are on the right track. What are the most important goals? By which means might these be achieved? And what are the obstacles to be expected on various routes? These are probably the typical questions asked when the guidelines of the past no longer appear promising and meaningful.

Although we are mostly interested in the current problems of the movement, a considerable part of this essay is devoted to an empirically grounded analysis of the movement's course, from its beginning in the 1970s until the present time. The problems of the present can only be understood in light of past developments and experiences. To this end, we will draw heavily on quantitative data which, in some respects, may serve to confirm or correct various assumptions to be found in both the scientific literature and the internal debates of the movement. For example, some observers have identified distinct developmental stages which, in part, refer to major strategic changes.[2] Others have emphasised a growing institutionalisation and, related to this, a deradicalisation of the movement [*Wörndl and Fréchet, 1994*]. Still others have argued that the ecological movement has been in decline since the early 1980s [*Opp, 1996: 371*].

Considering these strong but weakly founded statements about the German environmental movement, we focus on the movement's structure, strategy and action repertoires, and the current strategic problems confronting it. Attention will also be paid to aspects of institutionalisation and the extent to which this process is linked to a strategic reorientation.

I. An Empirical Examination of the Transformations of the Environmental Movement

Before presenting and interpreting empirical findings, it may be useful to recap the conditions under which the modern environmental movement emerged and developed. These factors also had a strong impact on the ways in which the movement perceived and tackled environmental problems.

As in many other countries, the movement in Germany was preceded by and partially overlapped with a conservationist movement which dates back to the last decades of the nineteenth century (see Brand in this volume).[3] Unlike in the USA, where the first 'Earth Day' in 1970 set a symbolic starting point for the new movement, its counterpart in Germany initially consisted mainly of initiatives by local citizens worried about environmental degradation in their immediate neighbourhoods. At the same time, however, the 1960s debate about overpopulation, exhaustion of natural resources and environmental pollution spilled over to the policy-makers and the wider populace in the early 1970s, and also affected local citizen initiatives. The publication of 'The Limits to Growth' in 1972, the UN conference on the Environment in Stockholm in the same year, and the sudden increase in the price of oil in 1973 contributed to growing concern about the scarcity of resources and the feeling that fundamental changes were needed in the way society deals with its natural base.

Although policy-makers in West Germany reacted remarkably early in launching environmental programmes in 1970 and 1971, and passed a number of environmental laws in the following years, most environmental groups in these years were pessimistic about the future. Their discourse was dominated by doomsday scenarios and a feeling that only radical measures in policies, the economy and individual life-styles could prevent a global environmental disaster.

Many policy-makers, together with groups in industry, business and trade unions, were largely unimpressed by the warnings of environmentalists. These groups sought to discredit environmentalists by arguing that they risked blocking economic and technological progress, and thereby would cause high unemployment. Economic needs were sharply contrasted with ecological concerns, leading to a split into two camps which were unwilling to compromise. The conflict over nuclear power, which gained momentum from 1973–74 onwards, broadened this gap. On the one hand, nuclear power was perceived as a key to further progress; on the other, it was considered to be the epitome of capitalist greed for profit and power and the state´s commitment to big business rather than the needs of the citizenry. Conflicts over nuclear power increased and intensified in the second half of the 1970s, drawing in leftist radicals who had not previously been overly sensitive to environmental concerns.

Starting in the late 1970s and early 1980s, resistance against the environmental and anti-nuclear movement became less determined, and some established groups, particularly the SPD, the FDP, and the trade unions, became more receptive to the movement's critique. At the same time, large parts of the movement abandoned their fundamentalist stance. They took a more professional and pragmatic guise, and began to develop constructive proposals (for example, the use of solar and wind energy) instead of simply rejecting the status quo. More recently, several environmental organisations sought to co-operate with parts of industry, for instance in accepting offers to 'eco-sponsoring'. This trend met with mixed reactions, attracting harsh criticism from both sections within these organisations and, of course, from the more radical and more grass-roots orientated groups. The overall trend towards pragmatism is particularly visible in the large membership organisations. Even Greenpeace Germany, which tries to maintain its image of being a group of 'rainbow warriors', has begun to engage in lobbying, writing scientific reports and promoting environmentally friendly industrial products.

In some ways, the rise and development of the Green Party mirrored this overall trend. Initially, the party was created as an 'anti-party party' that in both substance and form sought to challenge established politics and to pursue a radical, if not fundamentalist, course. Very soon, this course was challenged by a 'realist' tendency which eventually became the dominant force within the party. Today, the Greens are no longer an 'alternative' party.[4] In many ways, they had to pay a price, such as accepting structural adaptations, in order to get rid of their image as outsiders or illusionists. Today the Green party is represented in several state parliaments; it was or is involved in several state governments and has become a junior partner in the new national government that came into office in the Autumn of 1998.

By and large, environmental groups are recognised as important players who were instrumental in establishing a new policy field and slowing down, or even preventing, further environmental damage. They are positively viewed by large parts of the wider populace, have gained some institutional access to the polity, and are involved in many processes of political negotiation and bargaining. At the same time, it also has to be stressed that radical groups still exist. They continue to engage, for instance, in matters of nuclear power, most notably the transport and storage of nuclear waste. Moreover, other issues, such as 'animal rights' and outdoor experiments with genetic engineering, have attracted substantial resistance and have occasionally induced violent actions.

Organisation and Resources

The movement as a whole consists of a complex network of groups and organisations with rather different components [*Rucht, 1989, 1991*]. First, there are informal and local action groups which focus on particular issues such as transport, toxic waste, or the protection of rainforests. They operate either independently from one another or form alliances from the local to the national levels. In some cases these alliances are rather loose and casual, in other cases they crystallise in more solid structures, as in the case of Robin Wood, or even in a nation-wide umbrella group such as the *Bundesverband Bürgerinitiativen Umweltschutz* (Federal Alliance of Citizen Initiatives for Environmental Protection). These groups come closest to the type of a participatory protest organisation as conceptualised by Diani and Donati (in this volume).

Second, there are more formal but relatively small organisations which produce and distribute expert knowledge. An outstanding example is the *Öko-Institut*; founded in 1977 to provide scientific and juridical support for environmental groups, it then became more independent of these groups. Most of the institutes which aim to develop some sort of 'critical expertise' co-operate in a nation-wide network, the *Arbeitsgemeinschaft ökologischer Forschungsinstitute* (working coalition of institutes of ecological research). These organisations are examples of the type Diani and Donati term 'public interest lobby'.

The third component is formed by large and usually nation-wide formal membership organisations [*Leonhard, 1986; Cornelsen, 1991; Blühdorn, 1995*]. Some of these have state-wide, regional and local chapters and a considerable membership. The two most important examples of this kind are the *Bund für Umwelt und Naturschutz Deutschland (BUND)* and the *Naturschutzbund Deutschland (NABU)*, the former German Association for the Protection of Birds (DBV). Most of the big regional and nation-wide formal organisations are members of a national umbrella organisation, the *Deutscher Naturschutzring (DNR)*, which claims to represent nearly three million members in 107 organisations. However, the DNR is less strong and powerful than it might appear because of the heterogeneity and tensions among some of its member groups. The Green Party is also a nation-wide membership organisation but, due to its status as a party, has specific features which mean it cannot be fully counted as a genuine part of the environmental movement.[5] Another sub-category of nation-wide organisations are the national sections of Greenpeace and the World Wide Fund for Nature (WWF). These organisations are special in so far as they have fairly bureaucratic headquarters with professional experts. They are mainly funded by donors who are not members and have no say in the organisation. According to rough estimates of the DNR, today the formal environmental organisations represent four million members, of whom 175,000 volunteers devote on average six hours per week to nature conservation and environmental protection.[6] Referring again to Diani and Donati´s typology, organisations such as the BUND or NABU can be classified as a mix between a public interest lobby and a participatory pressure group; Greenpeace is a clear-cut example of a professional protest organisation, whereas the WWF represents a public interest lobby.

During the communist regime in East Germany, environmentalism had a very low profile, though it was not completely absent. On the one hand, there existed the official and semi-statist *Gesellschaft für Natur und Umweltschutz* (Association for Nature and Environmental Protection). On the other hand, a limited number of small and informal initiatives tried to promote environmentalism outside state-controlled channels, criticising the ineffectiveness, if not complete absence, of environmental policy, and the lack of access to information. Not surprisingly, these groups faced many difficulties when they tried to act in public. Sometimes they were openly suppressed. Within a very short time during and after German unification, this dual structure of environmentalism in East Germany disappeared. By and large, the organisational pattern of the West German movement has been extended to the East. The large environmental groups of the West have established sections in all five Eastern states, though membership is considerably lower than in the West. Only one non-local and genuine East German organisation, the *Grüne Liga* (Green Association), founded in February 1990, could establish itself alongside West-based competitors that spread East [*Hengsbach et al., 1996: 95*].

Our own investigations try to cover the different components of the environmental movement. As well as the large organisations, which are usually at the forefront of public and scientific attention, local groups also have to be taken into account. A closer look at groups in several selected German cities and a detailed survey of local groups in Berlin provide insights into these neglected parts of the movement.

Table 1, based on different sources, provides an overview of the number of groups in selected locations over time.

TABLE 1
NUMBER OF ENVIRONMENTAL AND ANTI-NUCLEAR GROUPS
IN SELECTED LOCATIONS IN GERMANY

Year	Groups in Berlin West	Groups in Berlin East	Year	Groups in Cologne
1978	96	na		
1980	130	na	1982/83	41
1984	130	na	1984/85	52
1989	104	35	1989	46
1995	70	45	1993/94	60

Sources: Rucht, Blattert and Rink [*1997*] and counts based on local directories ('Stattbücher').

The number of environmental groups in West Berlin decreased in the most recent period of observation but increased in Cologne.[7] For other cities in the West, we have counts for single years but no trend data. When considering the size of the city, West Berlin (about 2.2 million inhabitants) certainly does not have a high density of environmental and anti-nuclear groups. For example, the local directory of alternative groups in a much smaller city such as Aachen (about 240,000 inhabitants) lists 22 environmental groups in 1988. A precise survey of environmental groups in Konstanz, again a much smaller city (245,000 inhabitants) than West Berlin, identified 62 groups in 1991 [*Christmann, 1997: 69*]. In East Germany, there are clear indications of rising numbers of groups in East Berlin, Dresden, Leipzig and Halle.[8]

Changing numbers of groups may not necessarily reflect similar trends in terms of members and adherents. Table 2 provides information on the evolution of membership of environmental and anti-nuclear groups in West Berlin.

TABLE 2
AVERAGE SIZE OF ENVIRONMENTAL AND ANTI-NUCLEAR GROUPS
IN WEST BERLIN, 1989 AND 1993

	1989	1993
Active members per group	17.8 (N=39)	17.1 (N=29)
Total members per group	267 (N=34)	141 (N=29)

Source: Rucht, Blattert and Rink [*1997*].

The average number of active group members, defined as those who participate in all or most meetings of a group, remained nearly constant from 1989 to 1993. However, the average number of all group members, including those who remain largely passive, declined considerably. This suggests that the groups were able to maintain their core but lost many of their passive members. The proportion of women in these groups – 39 per cent among the active members and 40 per cent of all members – is consistent with other studies according to which the proportion of women in environmental groups ranges between 30 and 40 per cent [*Hengsbach et al., 1996: 112*].

In addition to local groups, we also surveyed various nation-wide organisations to get information about their resources and membership. Figure 1 shows the evolution of the four largest environmental organisations in Germany during the 1980s and 1990s. Here it is important to keep in mind that numbers provided by Greenpeace and the World Wide Fund for Nature (WWF) refer to regular donors but not to formal members. Greenpeace Germany, in spite of its many donors and dozens of so-called action groups across the country, has fewer than 30 formal members.

FIGURE 1

MEMBERS OF/REGULAR DONORS TO LARGE ENVIRONMENTAL

ORGANISATIONS

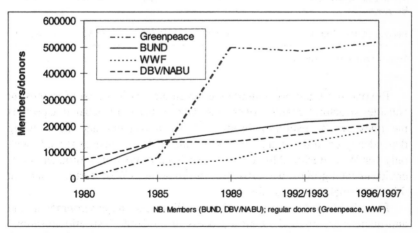

Source: Own investigations.

As can be seen, the four largest environmental groups experienced significant growth during the 1980s. More recently, however, there are signs of decreasing growth or even of stagnation. A look at medium-sized nation-wide environmental organisations confirms the impression that the period of expansion seems to have come to an end. Table 3 shows that four out of seven selected organisations, among them high-profile groups such as Robin Wood, a split-off from Greenpeace, and the *Öko-Institut*, experienced a decline in membership in the most recent period. The other three, including the Green Party, had a modest increase in members.

TABLE 3

EVOLUTION OF MEMBERSHIP OF MEDIUM-SIZED ENVIRONMENTAL
ORGANISATIONS AND THE GREEN PARTY

Organisation	1985	1989	1993	1997
Öko-Institut	4,400	5,000	5,300	4,600 (1996)
Robin Wood	750	2,400	3,000	2,000
Verbraucherinitiative	200	6,000	7,500 (1992)	9,000
Verkehrsclub Deutschland	non-existent	31,000	63,000 (1992)	70,000
Schutzgemeinschaft Deutscher Wald	21,000	25,000	40,000 (1991)	20,000
Verein zum Schutze der Bergwelt	na	5,000	4,700	4,500
Bündnis 90/Die Grünen	37,000	41,100	39,600	49,000

Source: Own investigations.

Beyond these merely quantitative developments it is also of interest to consider structural changes over time. One of the most debated aspects is the question of institutionalisation of the movement and its growing dependency upon the state. Table 4 provides data on these aspects, though only for West Berlin. Although we also have figures on a broader set of environmental groups, we restrict the information to West Berlin because in this case panel data are available.[9]

From Table 4 it can be seen that the West German environmental and anti-nuclear groups underwent a process of moderate institutionalisation[10] which, in contrast to the trend of all 'alternative groups', was reversed after 1989. When looking at the individual items on which the institutionalisation index was based, it becomes obvious that the reversal exhibited by the environmental groups is mainly a result of a lower proportion of groups that relied at least partially on paid employees and had their own office space. We assume that this is an effect of cuts in state-funding that hit some groups.

Overall, and in contrast to the development of many groups in East Germany, institutionalisation among the environmental groups in West Berlin is much lower than we, in line with most observers, would have expected (see Brand in this volume; Wörndl and Fréchet [*1994*]; Lahusen [*1998*]).

TABLE 4

INSTITUTIONALISATION AND STATE-FUNDING OF ENVIRONMENTAL
AND ANTI-NUCLEAR GROUPS IN WEST-BERLIN, 1980–93

	1980	1984	1989	1993
Institutionalisation index, average of environmental and anti-nuclear groups (range: 0–3)	1.04	1.24	1.29	1.14
N	*8*	*14*	*30*	*32*
Institutionalisation index, average of all 'alternative groups' (range: 0–3)	1.18	1.25	1.33	1.44
n	59	125	215	209
Environmental and anti-nuclear groups with financial support from the state	0%	11.8%	25%	31.3%
N (total)	*9*	*17*	*32*	*32*

Source: Rucht, Blattert and Rink [*1997*].

We see that the proportion of groups for whom money from the state is their primary or secondary source of income rose considerably during the period of observation. Whereas none of the environmental groups in our panel relied on state funds in 1980, the share of mainly state-funded groups rose to more than 30 per cent in 1993. This reflects wide use of state-funded labour programmes by environmental groups which, to our knowledge, does not apply to the subcategory of anti-nuclear groups.

Strategies and Action Repertoires

Besides the organisational aspects of the environmental movement its protest activities are also of special interest. Group structure can give only very little information about strategies and protest mobilisation. For this information we undertook a quantitative content analysis of newspaper reports.

Based on a comprehensive data-set that covers all kinds of collective protests from 1950 to 1994 in West Germany (including protests in East Germany since 1989) as reported in two nation-wide quality newspapers,[11] we are able to describe the patterns of pro-environmental and anti-nuclear protest.[12] Very few protests on these issues occurred prior to 1970, so we concentrate only on the later period. Out of the total of 8,603 protests from 1970 to 1994, 3.9 per cent were predominantly, that is in their first claim, pro-environment and another 6.6 per cent against nuclear power.[13] In terms of participants, pro-environmental events mobilised 2.9 per cent and anti-nuclear events 5.3 per cent of the participants in all protests. These proportions become higher when we use a more inclusive calculation.[14]

A second data-base derived from a different newspaper (the left-alternative *die tageszeitung*) and using a slightly different research procedure covers the period from the beginning of 1995 through June 1997.[15] Of the 1,856 protest events in that period, 7.1 per cent were pro-environment and 13.1 per cent against nuclear power. In terms of participants, 15.6 per cent were mobilised in environmental protests and another 3.4 per cent in anti-nuclear protests. To our surprise, the number of anti-nuclear protests in this most recent period by far outweighs other environmental protests which, however, mobilised many more people than the anti-nuclear protests. The reasons for this discrepancy will be discussed below.

How did pro-environmental and anti-nuclear protests, taken together, and including both first and second claims, evolve over time? Figure 2 displays the number of events and participants on a yearly basis. Data are only provided for weekend protests based on the first and larger data-set.[16]

FIGURE 2
ENVIRONMENTAL AND ANTI-NUCLEAR MOBILISATION IN
GERMANY, 1970–94

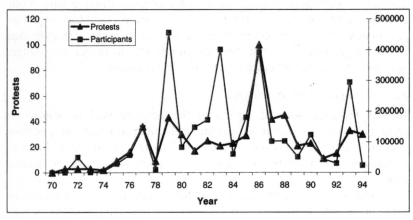

Source: Prodat: weekend protests.

By and large, the curve representing the number of protests is paralleled by the curve for the number of participants. Environmental and anti-nuclear mobilisation was still low in the first half of the 1970s, but then increased significantly and attained high levels during most of the 1980s. The peak in the number of protest events was reached in 1986, mainly due to reactions to the nuclear accident at Chernobyl and the conflicts around the construction of a nuclear reprocessing plant in Wackersdorf in Bavaria. By the end of that decade mobilisation decreased, but then grew again in the early 1990s with a moderate level of protest events and a considerable number of participants. We assume that German unification and the subsequent dominance of economic and social problems are the key factors for the lower profile of environmental protests from 1989 to 1992.[17] Our most recent data on the period from 1995 through mid-1997 indicate that environmental and anti-nuclear protests are again high on the agenda. They do not support widespread speculation about a decline of environmentalist activism.

In comparing mobilisation in West and East Germany from 1990 to 1994, we find that 20.7 per cent of all environmental protests in Germany occurred in the East. This corresponds roughly to the proportion of the population in East Germany. With a share of 12.3 per cent, anti-nuclear protests in East Germany were clearly underrepresented. Most striking, however, was the underrepresentation of East Germany in terms of participants, accounting only for 2.4 per cent of all anti-nuclear protesters from 1990 to 1994. While in the following years, 1995 to mid-1997, the share of anti-nuclear protest events in East Germany remained similar to that during the previous period, the share of participants rose strongly (13.4 per cent).

A closer and separate look at pro-environmental and anti-nuclear activism in different periods shows that the structure of mobilisation has changed over time. Table 5 demonstrates that, throughout all periods, pro-environmental protests were on average significantly larger than anti-nuclear protests. In the 1980s and between 1995 and 1997, the median but not the mean of anti-nuclear protests was higher than that of other environmental protests. This overall pattern probably reflects differences in both the mobilisation structures and the preferred kind of activities. Environmental protests are often conducted by large nation-wide membership organisations, include mass demonstrations and collections of signatures, and tend to be less radical. By contrast, anti-nuclear protests are mostly organised by small and more informal groups. They also more often involve high risk activities which relatively few people are prepared to undertake. The average size of anti-nuclear protests was particularly low in the period 1995–97, when much of the activity was geared to blocking the transport of nuclear waste [*Blowers and Lowry, 1997*], whereas in other periods mass demonstrations or collections of signatures were also an important part of the action repertoire.

TABLE 5
AVERAGE PARTICIPATION IN ENVIRONMENTAL
AND ANTI-NUCLEAR PROTESTS

Issue	1970–79	1980–89	1990–94	1995–1997/I
Environmental				
Mean	15,777	10,825	15,973	15,815
Median	1,575	400	760	100
N (valid cases)	28	165	51	69
Anti-nuclear				
Mean	4,765	5,272	6,581	2,111
Median	500	1,000	235	300
N (valid cases)	109	233	52	114

Sources: Prodat project and Rucht.

The differences in the mobilisation structure of pro-environmental and anti-nuclear protests become evident in Table 6, which displays the distribution of different types of collective actors. Anti-nuclear protests are mainly carried out by informal groups, whereas formal associations and political parties played a significant role in pro-environmental protests. Contrary to what one might expect, the proportion of informal groups in both pro-environmental and anti-nuclear protests is higher in the latest period.[18]

TABLE 6
TYPES OF COLLECTIVE ACTORS IN ENVIRONMENTAL
AND ANTI-NUCLEAR PROTESTS (PERCENTAGES)

	1970–94		1995–1997/I	
	Environmental	Anti-nuclear	Environmental	Anti-nuclear
Informal group	30.2*	65.8*	51.6	69.0
Formal association	65.5	24.4	25.8	10.5
Political party	4.4	9.8	0.0	0.8
Network/alliance	na	na	12.3	6.7
Anonymous	na	na	10.3	13.0
Total	100.0	100.0	100.0	100.0
N	252	225	155	239

*Including network/alliance.

Sources: Prodat project and Rucht.

When we group together the distinct forms of protests in four broader categories[19] and consider their proportions by period, we see that in each phase anti-nuclear protests were clearly more disruptive than the other pro-environmental protests (Table 7). Probably most striking is the high proportion of violent environmental protests in the period from 1995-97. This deviation from the overall pattern is mainly influenced by a few single issues such as activities against outdoor experiments with genetically engineered plants and against a Mercedes Benz car test site. These results clearly contradict assumptions to be found in the literature that, due to the trend towards institutionalisation, 'the protest quietened down, and environmental groups concentrated their activities within established forms of interest representation' [*Wörndl and Fréchet, 1994: 263*]. While the trend towards institutionalisation of one, probably the dominant, segment of environmental groups certainly cannot be denied, we stress the fact that this trend is paralleled by a continuation and even an increase of more radical forms of protest. Seemingly, the very fact that 'social movements tend to be absorbed by the system' [*ibid.: 264*] provides a motive for the radicalisation of other groups, as was the case with the rise of groups such as Earth First! and the Sea Shepherd Society in the US [*Scarce, 1990; Rucht, 1995*] and anti-road and animal rights groups in Great Britain [*Doherty, 1996; Doherty and Rawcliffe, 1995*].

TABLE 7
TYPES OF ACTION OF ENVIRONMENTAL AND ANTI-NUCLEAR
PROTESTS IN DIFFERENT PERIODS (PERCENTAGES)

	1970–79		1980–89		1990–94		1995–1997/I	
	Envir.	Anti-nuclear	Envir.	Anti-nuclear	Envir.	Anti-nuclear	Envir.	Anti-nuclear
Appeals/procedural	63.6	32.7	32.9	16.2	31.9	15.0	36.1	14.7
Demonstrative	29.5	47.9	44.9	51.6	49.1	45.0	34.3	43.7
Confrontational	6.8	17.0	17.4	20.6	18.1	36.3	16.6	24.9
Violent	0.0	2.4	4.8	11.5	0.9	3.8	13.0	16.7
Total	100	100	100	100	100	100	100	100
Degree of radicalism (range: 1–4)	1.43	1.90	1.94	2.27	1.88	2.29	2.07	2.44
N	44	165	207	339	116	80	169	245

Sources: Prodat project and Rucht.

As one might expect, for both environmental and anti-nuclear protests the state was the main target. It attracted 55.9 per cent of all environmental and 67.3 per cent of all anti-nuclear protests in the period from 1970 to 1994. Private enterprises were the second most important target with 29.7 per cent and 28.5 per cent, respectively.

As far as spatial mobilisation is concerned, the proportion of local and regional mobilisation for environmental protests first decreased, but then increased significantly (36.4 per cent 1970-79, 31.1 per cent from 1980 to 1989 and 46.7 per cent from 1990 to 1994). A different trend could be observed for anti-nuclear protests (49.7 per cent, 41.4 per cent and 40.5 per cent, respectively). This seems to reflect the fragmentation of environmental issues on the one hand and, after the struggles around particular nuclear power plants, the concentration of the anti-nuclear groups on the issue of nuclear transport. To our surprise, transnational and international mobilisation of protests within German territory did not increase over time as the widely discussed trend towards globalisation might suggest. When we compare the 1980s with the first half of the 1990s, the proportion of such protests actually declined for both environmental protests (from 5.2 to 3.3 percent) and anti-nuclear protests (from 9.6 to 5.1 per cent).

II. The Environmental and Anti-Nuclear Movement in Context

The environmental movement in Germany does not form a coherent body but consists of very different components that, to some extent, overlap and are only loosely connected to one another. As the analysis has shown, the anti-nuclear movement, which certainly can be considered as being part of the broader environmental movement, exhibits quite distinctive traits and therefore should be treated separately.

The pro-environmental and anti-nuclear movements underwent major qualitative and quantitative changes. Both movements were able to create a solid infrastructure, to win the support of many adherents, and to carry out a large number of protest activities. Overall, the pro-environmental movement is more diversified and fragmented, consisting of more heterogeneous organisational components when compared to the anti-nuclear movement. The former relies on small local groups, professional organisations and nation-wide membership organisations, whereas the anti-nuclear movement has a more informal and decentralised structure with no formal organisations at the national level. These contrasts are clearly mirrored by the types of mobilising collective actors and their different ideologies and strategies. As a whole, the pro-environmental movement has become pragmatic and moderate over time, although most recent data suggest that this trend has come to a halt. By contrast, the anti-nuclear movement has maintained its radical and uncompromising stance.

Both movements were successful in several ways. In terms of absolute organisational membership the movements in Germany are the largest in Europe.[20] In terms of policy impacts, though not providing comparative data, some observers claim that 'the environmental movement in Germany seems to have been more successful than anywhere else' [Blühdorn, 1995: 167]. But this does not mean that the environmental and anti-nuclear movements have achieved most of their goals. In quite a number of conflicts, the movements have lost their battles. They also continue to face strong resistance when it comes to building new highways, expanding airports, and introducing a rapid train system. Nevertheless, the movements have attracted the attention of the mass media over decades, won the support of large parts of the populace, influenced political elites and strongly shaped environmental and energy policies. Today, environmental policy in Germany is a fully-fledged policy domain [Weidner, 1995]. Environmental issues range high on the agenda of the populace and established policy arena [Wissenschaftlicher Beirat, 1996].

Environmental concerns are, at least rhetorically, endorsed by virtually all groups in the state and large parts of industry. Even considering that environmental conditions still continue to deteriorate in various areas, things are less bad than they would be without the activities of the movements. The influence of the movements is particularly salient in the field of nuclear energy where, in spite of fierce resistance and powerful adversaries, they were able to stop the further exploitation of nuclear energy. In some instances, the anti-nuclear movement even prevented large-scale and extremely costly nuclear facilities, already completed, from going into operation.[21] Today, a clear majority of the populace disapproves of nuclear energy. Besides the Green Party which took an anti-nuclear stance from its beginnings, the SPD, during its party congress in 1986, also opted to phase out nuclear energy.

The relative strength and success of the German environmental movement is certainly not only the result of high motivation and strategic abilities, but has also to be interpreted in the light of the wider political and social context in Germany. Several factors were particularly favourable to the movement. First, the movement was part of a broader social movement family, the so-called new social movements, which were particularly strong in Germany. This facilitated the creation of broad alliances and drew on a large conscience constituency beyond the immediate adherents of the movement; many groups in areas such as women's liberation, peace and disarmament, and development in the Third World were also supportive of environmental concerns and campaigns. Eurobarometer data on the mobilisation potential of new social movements show that, particularly in Germany, the sympathisers and supporters of these movements tend to perceive the latter as an integrated phenomenon [Fuchs and Rucht, 1994].

Second, the elites were or became divided over environmental issues, so that the movement gained some leverage within the realm of established politics. At a later point, the presence of the Green party in the national and several state parliaments was also instrumental in keeping environmental issues on political and public agenda.

Third, the sheer number and visibility of environmental problems in Germany was probably higher than in most other Western countries which are less populated, less urbanised and less industrialised. Unlike countries such as the USA, Canada or even France, yet very similar to countries such as Belgium or the Netherlands, Germany has hardly any spaces relatively untouched by civilisation. It is very difficult to overlook or to escape environmental damage.

Fourth, Germany is a relatively rich country that, in terms of its economic competitiveness, can 'afford' environmental protection. Many environmental regulations imply costs or restrictions that run against the logic of short-term profit-seeking. For this reason, the movement at first faced great resistance from both corporations and trade unions but this diminished when it became obvious that environmental protection can be the basis of a profitable industry, that environmentally friendly technologies and goods may provide competitive advantages on the world market, and that environmental investments may be favourable to the national economy in the long run. Such considerations then facilitated the task of environmental movements.

We have little solid data to assess whether or not the movement in Germany was, by international standards, outstanding in its mobilisation and policy impacts. From the protest event data provided by Koopmans [1995] and Kriesi et al. [1995] on four West European countries for the period from 1975 to 1989, it is clear that the environmental and anti-nuclear movements in Germany, taken together, were absolutely and relatively more important than their counterparts in Switzerland, France and the Netherlands. Relative to the size of the population, the anti-nuclear movement in Germany also mobilised more people than the movements in the three other countries, whereas the German environmental movement was second after Switzerland.[22] As for the policy impacts of the environmental movements, it is extremely difficult to make comparative assessments because of problems of causal attribution and the complexity of measuring impacts in the policy domain. A more detailed analysis presented elsewhere indicates that the German environmental movement was indeed among those which were relatively successful [Rucht, 1999].

III. The Movement at a Crossroads

In spite of their impressive gains there are signs that the anti-nuclear movement and, in particular, the environmental movement face a stalemate which one could associate with a mid-life crisis. In terms of policy impacts, it seems to be clear that no major breakthroughs can be expected. The domain of environmental politics has lost its novelty and excitement. In the last few years, it has been overshadowed by 'bread and butter issues' such as unemployment, budget deficits, and the integration of immigrants.

Other problems result from the structural changes the movement has experienced. By and large, environmental politics has become a matter of experts in a routine business. The locus of attention seems to shift to the international level, thus making it difficult for the smaller and more locally oriented groups to stay involved and to undertake meaningful local actions. No wonder that there are signs of an estrangement between the small autonomous and locally oriented groups on the one hand and the professional environmental organisations on the other. Also, within formal membership organisations a gap between the professionals and the rank and file seems to emerge. Furthermore, conflicts around strategic and tactical questions appear to increase. For instance, the BUND was shattered by several internal disputes. One was about eco-sponsoring that, in the eyes of a minority of adherents, would compromise the organisation due to too close a collaboration with industrial firms that are provided with a prestigious 'green' label in exchange for money.

Another conflict was triggered by a deal between an electricity corporation and the BUND's Thuringia section. The latter accepted seven million Deutschmarks in exchange for withdrawing from its legal action against the construction of the hydroelectric plant in Goldisthal. Although this money was completely devoted to environmental protection, many BUND members, as well as representatives from other groups, felt that this deal would undermine the credibility of the organisation.[23] Also a minority of Green Party members is increasingly suspicious about the pragmatic course of the party and, according to their view, the tendency to compromise its stances in order to become a respectable and well-established player. Whereas in its earlier days the Green Party frontally attacked the chemical industry as one of its main 'enemies', now representatives from both sides meet in workshops. During the first of these meetings in 1997, Michaele Hustedt, the environmental speaker of the Green members in the Bundestag, argued: 'A sustainable economy cannot be reached against but only with industry' (*die tageszeitung,* 24 June 1997, p.7).

Professionalisation, the complexity of environmental matters, internal contradictions and the loss of clear enemies all make it more difficult to maintain the motivation and zeal of the activists. In spite of a stable or slightly increasing membership, representatives of some large organisations complain about a lack of commitment. Also smaller local groups tend to lose their passive members. Some organisations show clear signs of bureaucratisation and oligarchisation whereas others simply fade away or radicalise. No wonder that some close observers are pessimistic about the current state and future of the movement. They worry about the 'lame environmental associations' which tend to lose their critical impetus,[24] the difficulties in finding new recruits for environmental organisations,[25] the 'sobering of environmental activists' in the light of a declining awareness of environmental concerns in the wider populace,[26] and the illusion that enough has been done for environmental protection.[27]

When environmental issues become more complicated, conflicts may also arise between environmental groups which, unlike in earlier periods, may find themselves on different sides of the barricades. For example, many environmental groups which want to reduce individual transport are supportive of the construction of new railroads, whereas other and mainly local groups oppose such plans because they involve environmental damage in particular places. A similar conflict constellation is to be found around the construction of modern windmills. Many environmental groups support windmills as a clean and sustainable form of energy production, but other groups oppose windmills because they produce noise in their immediate environment and, above all, impair the natural beauty of rural areas.

The main problem with today's environmentalism in Germany, however, is usually not a high level of conflict among and within the groups but rather a more general disillusion and insecurity about what can be done. Should one continue the path towards professionalisation or should one find means to reactivate the rank and file? Should one engage more and more in negotiations, expert committees, conventional lobbying strategies or should one rather increase the level of disruptive action? Is it advisable to focus on local activities or has one to engage more at the European level or even beyond?

Obviously, there are no easy answers to these kinds of questions. In addition, other issues such as continuing high rates of unemployment, state budget deficit, taxation and the consequences of immigration have moved to the forefront of people's minds and public attention, making it hard for environmental groups to maintain, let alone to increase, their level of activity. Even groups such as Greenpeace which, from an outsider perspective, have been extremely successful, have begun to question if they can simply continue as they did in the past. Probably a deeper sense of crisis is needed not only among environmentalists but also among the wider populace to bring about the changes that would allow for a revitalisation of the movement.

NOTES

1. In spite of the fact that the environmental movement in Germany is widely debated and quite a number of studies on various aspects of the movements have been undertaken, we still lack a comprehensive and detailed empirical study. For overviews, see Brand, Büsser and Rucht [*1986*], Rucht [*1991, 1994*], Opp [*1996*], Ehmke [*1998*] and Brand (in this volume). Only the anti-nuclear power movement, which may be perceived as part of the broader environmental movement, has been analysed in much detail [*Kitschelt, 1980; Rucht, 1980; Nelkin and Pollak, 1981; Radkau, 1983, Wagner, 1994*].

2. An early typology identified an initial period with conflicts around local issues in the late 1960s and early 1970s, a second stage of building and connecting organisations and broadening and linking issues from 1973 to 1978, and a third stage marked by the movement's institutionalisation and diversification [*Brand, Büsser and Rucht, 1986; Rucht, 1991*]. Another periodisation marks a first stage of environmental policy 'from above' (1969–74), a second stage of environmental polarisation (1974-82), and a third stage of ecology as mainstream (since 1993) [*Hengsbach et al., 1996: 78–9*]. A recent account [*Brand, 1998*; see also Brand in this volume] suggests a first period (1969–74) in which environmental policy was established as a reform policy, a second (1975–82) in which ecological and economic concerns were seen as mutually exclusive, a third period (1983–90) in which the theme of ecology was institutionalised, a fourth (1991-95) in which the repercussions of a globalising economy prevailed and overshadowed environmental issues, and a fifth period (1996+) in which ecological conflicts were framed along the lines of sustainable development.

3. By environmental movements we refer to the network of non-governmental groups and organisations that aim to prevent the exploitation and/or destruction of natural resources by means of political and social intervention, including collective protest. In their attempts at strategic intervention, the environmental movements can be distinguished from the traditional and predominantly apolitical conservationism that prevailed until the late 1960s. Whereas conservationist groups focused mainly on local and sectoral issues without embedding these into a broader approach, environmentalism tends to have a more dramatic and more coherent perception of the problem ('Save planet earth'). Even when mobilising at the local level, environmental actors perceive their mobilization as part of a worldwide movement according to the slogan 'act locally, think globally' [*Rucht, 1993*].

4. In a recent survey by Emnid, respondents were asked: 'Did the Greens, over the years, become an established party like the others, or are they still an alternative party?' Seventy-three per cent of the adherents of the Green Party perceived it as an established party, as did 51 per cent of the overall population. For the development of the Greens, see also Frankland [*1995*].

5. The party has a fully-fledged programme that goes far beyond environmental issues. Moreover, many activists and supporters are not primarily concerned with the ecological issue. Finally, since members of the party are also involved in some governments, the party´s status as a non-governmental group (see the definition in note 3) becomes questionable.

6. See documents of the *Bundestag*, BT-Drs. 13/5674.

7. The figures in Table 1 should be considered with caution; we had to rely on informed estimates or counts based on local directories which tend to underestimate the actual number of existing groups. For example, a study on citizen initiatives dealing with problems of car traffic and public transport in Berlin identified 256 groups in the period from 1973 to 1993 [*Schneider-Wilkes, 1996*]. According to the author, the number of these groups was increasing over time but their policy impacts were decreasing.

8. From 1989 to 1993, the number of environmental and anti-nuclear groups rose from 8 to 24 in Dresden, from 6 to 16 in Leipzig and from 6 to 15 in Halle [*Rucht, Blattert and Rink, 1997*].

9. These data are drawn from two larger surveys. The first (N = 473) on 'alternative groups' in West and East Berlin was conducted in 1991. All questions were asked retrospectively for the years 1978, 1980, 1984 and 1989, corresponding to the available issues of the local directory of 'alternative groups'. The second survey (N = 415) referred to the same spectrum

of groups in Berlin (West and East) and Leipzig and documented the situation of the groups at the time of the survey. A subset of the second survey are 210 groups in West Berlin already investigated in 1991. For a detailed analysis of these groups see Rucht, Blattert and Rink [*1997*].

10. Institutionalisation is measured by an index based on eight variables which were dichotomised: paid employees, members with special training relevant to their role in the group, own office space, legal status, tax exemption, formal hierarchy, formal subgroups, and division of labour between group members.

11. The *Frankfurter Rundschau* and the *Süddeutsche Zeitung*. For more information about the research design and methodology, see Rucht and Ohlemacher [*1992*], and Rucht and Neidhardt [*1998*].

12. We prefer to separate the category of anti-nuclear protests from other environmental protests because, as shown in some of our data, each exhibits quite distinct features.

13. Very few protests were directed *against* environmental protection (eight events, 0.1 per cent) or in favour of nuclear power (five events, 0.1 per cent).

14. When we combine the first and second claims and, in the case of pro-environmental protests, add those activities directed against large-scale projects such as conventional electricity plants, construction and enlargment of airports and so on, the share of pro-environmental protests is 6.1 per cent (participants 7.7 per cent) and of anti-nuclear protests 6.9 per cent (participants 5.3 per cent).

15. Unlike the first data set, the second also includes local reports for the city of Berlin.

16. When it comes to time series, we use only weekend protests because data on weekday protests from 1970 to 1974 are still missing.

17. See also Hengsbach [*1996: 103*] and Brand [*1993*].

18. It could be argued that this finding is an effect of the use of a different newspaper and different coverage which in the period from 1995 to 1997/I also included the local section of the paper. However, when only the national section is considered, the proportion of informal groups remains almost constant.

19. The original list of 21 forms of action was reduced to four broader types of action, namely appeals and procedural protests (for example, distribution of leaflets, collection of signatures, litigation), demonstrative actions (for example, marches, rallies), confrontational actions (for example, sit-ins, blockades) and violent actions (damage of property, injuries).

20. Krohberger and Hey [*1991: 4–5*]. According to more selective data on a just a few groups [*van der Heijden, Koopmans and Giugni, 1992*], the German environmental organisations range third in a four-country comparison, after the Netherlands and Switzerland, when the size of the population is taken into account.

21. According to the nuclear industry and electricity companies, investments of about 15 billion Deutschmarks were in vain and further investments of 11.3 billion are blocked or at risk due to pending litigation [*Ehmke, 1989: 147*].

22. The reported volume of participation in unconventional events of the environmental movement was 16,000 in Switzerland, 11,000 in West Germany, 5,000 in the Netherlands, and 2,000 in France. The respective figures for the anti-nuclear movement are 26,000 (Germany), 24,000 (Switzerland), 15,000 (Netherlands) and 9,000 (France) [*Kriesi et al., 1995: 22*]. For a more detailed comparison, see van der Heijden, Koopmans and Giugni [*1992*].

23. *Die tageszeitung*, 28 April 1997, p.6.

24. Jörg Bergstedt, 'Lahme Umweltverbände', *die tageszeitung*, 14 and 15 March 1998, p.8.

25. Michael Bauchmüller, Zuviel Arbeit, wenig Hilfe, *BUNDmagazin*, 1997, No.4 and Hengsbach *et al.* [*1996: 112*].

26. See our findings about declining passive members, as well as Peter Bühler, Ökologische Ernüchterung, *Die Zeit*, 28 May 1998, p.39.

27. Niels Boeing, 'Ein Volk von grünen Illusionisten', *die tageszeitung*, 4 and 5 July 1998, p.8.

REFERENCES

Blowers, A. and D. Lowry (1997), 'Nuclear Conflict in Germany: The Wider Context', *Environmental Politics*, Vol.6, No.3, pp.148–55.

Blühdorn, I. (1995), 'Campaigning for Nature: Environmental Pressure Groups in Germany and Generational Change in the Ecology Movement', in Blühdorn, Krause and Scharf [*1995; 167–222*].

Blühdorn, I., Krause, F. and T. Scharf (eds.) (1995), *The Green Agenda: Environmental Politics and Policy in Germany*, Keele: Keele University Press.

Brand, K.-W. (1993), 'Strukturveränderungen des Umweltdiskurses in Deutschland', in *Forschungsjournal Neue Soziale Bewegungen*, No.1, pp.16–24.

Brand, K.-W. (1998), 'Geschichte und Stand der Umweltbewegung', unpublished manuscript.

Brand, K.-W., Büsser, D. and D. Rucht (1986), *Aufbruch in eine andere Gesellschaft. Neue soziale Bewegungen in der Bundesrepublik Deutschland* (new edition, originally 1983) Frankfurt/M.: Campus.

Christmann, G.B. (1997), *Ökologische Moral. Zur kommunikativen Konstruktion und Rekonstruktion umweltschützerischer Moralvorstellungen*, Wiesbaden: Deutscher Universitätsverlag.

Cornelsen, D. (1991), *Anwälte der Natur. Umweltschutzverbände in Deutschland*, Munich: Beck.

Dalton, R.J. (1994), *The Green Rainbow: Environmental Groups in Western Europe*, New Haven, CT and London: Yale University Press.

Diekmann, A. and C.C. Jaeger (eds.) (1996), *Umweltsoziologie* (Special Issue 36 of *Kölner Zeitschrift für Soziologie und Sozialpsychologie*), Opladen, Westdeustcher Verlag.

Doherty, B. (1996), 'Paving the Way: The Rise of Direct Action against Road-building and the Changing Character of British Environmental Mobilisation', unpublished manuscript.

Doherty, B. and P. Rawcliffe (1995), 'British Exceptionalism? Comparing the Environmental Movement in Britain and Germany', in Blühdorn, Krause and Scharf [*1995: 235–49*].

Ehmke, W. (1998), 'Transformationen der Ökologiebewegung', *Forschungsjournal Neue Soziale Bewegungen*, Vol.11, No.1, pp.142–54.

Frankland, E.G. (1995), 'Germany: The Rise, Fall and Recovery of Die Grünen', in D. Richardson and C. Rootes (eds.), *The Green Challenge. The Development of Green Parties in Europe*, London and New York: Routledge.

Fuchs, D. and D. Rucht (1994), 'Support for New Social Movements in Five Western European Countries', in C. Rootes and H. Davis (eds.), *A New Europe? Social Change and Political Transformation*, London: UCL Press, pp.86–111.

Hengsbach, F., Bammerlin, R., Dringer, C., Emunds, B. and M. Möhring-Hesse (1996), *Die Rolle der Umweltverbände in den demokratischen und umweltethischen Lernprozessen der Gesellschaft*, Stuttgart: Metzler-Poeschel.

Kitschelt, H. (1980), *Kernenergiepolitik: Arena eines gesellschaftlichen Konflikts*, Frankfurt/M.: Campus.

Koopmans, R. (1995), *Democracy from Below: New Social Movements and the Political System in West Germany*, Boulder, CO: Westview Press.

Kriesi, H. and M. G. Giugni (1996), 'Ökologische Bewegungen im internationalen Vergleich: Zwischen Konflikt und Kooperation', in Diekmann and Jaeger [*1996: 324–49*].

Kriesi, H., Koopmans, R., Duyvendak, J.W. and M. G. Guigni (1995), *New Social Movements in Western Europe: A Comparative Analysis*, Minneapolis, MN: University of Minnesota Press.

Krohberger, K. and C. Hey (1991), *Die Beteiligungschancen der Umweltverbände auf europäischer Ebene*, Freiburg: EURES – Institute for Regional Studies in Europe.

Lahusen, C. (1998), 'Der Dritte Sektor als Lobby. Umweltverbände im Räderwerk der nationalen Politik', in R. von Strachwitz (ed.), *Dritter Sektor. Dritte Kraft. Versuch einer Standortbestimmung*, Düsseldorf: Raabe.

Leonhard, M. (1986), *Umweltverbände. Zur Organisation von Umweltschutzinteressen in der Bundesrepublik Deutschland*, Opladen: Westdeutscher Verlag.

Nelkin, D. and M. Pollak (1981), *The Atom Besieged: Antinuclear Movements in France and Germany*, Cambridge, MA and London: MIT Press.

Opp, K.-D. (1996), 'Aufstieg und Niedergang der Ökologiebewegung in der Bundesrepublik', in Diekmann and Jaeger [*1996: 350–79*].

Radkau, J. (1983), *Aufstieg und Krise der deutschen Atomwirtschaft 1945–1975*, Reinbek: Rowohlt.
Rucht, D. (1980), *Von Whyl nach Gorleben. Bürger gegen Atomprogramm und nukleare Entsorgung*, Munich: C.H. Beck.
Rucht, D. (1989), 'Environmental Movement Organizations in West Germany and France – Structure and Interorganizational Relations', in B. Klandermans (ed.), *Organizing for Change: Social Movement Organizations Across Cultures*, Greenwich, CT: JAI Press, pp.61–94.
Rucht, D. (1991), 'Von der Bewegung zur Institution? Organisationsstrukturen der Ökologiebewegung', in R. Roth and D. Rucht (eds.), *Neue soziale Bewegungen in der Bundesrepublik Deutschland* (2nd Revised Edition, originally 1987), Frankfurt/M.: Campus, pp.334–58.
Rucht, D. (1993), '"Think globally, act locally"? Needs, Forms and Problems of Cross-National Cooperation Among Environmental Groups', in J.D. Liefferink, P.D. Lowe and A.P.J. Mol (eds.), *European Integration and Environmental Policy*, London, New York: Belhaven Press.
Rucht, D. (1994), *Modernisierung und neue soziale Bewegungen. Deutschland, Frankreich und USA im Vergleich*, Frankfurt/M.: Campus.
Rucht, D. (1995), 'Ecological Protest as Calculated Law-breaking: Greenpeace and Earth First! in Comparative Perspective', in W. Rüdig (ed.), *Green Politics Three*, Edinburgh: Edinburgh University Press, pp.66–89.
Rucht, D. (1999), 'The Impact of Environmental Movements in Western Societies', in M. Giugni, D. McAdam and C. Tilly (eds.), *Do Movements Matter?* Minneapolis, MN: University of Minnesota Press (forthcoming).
Rucht, D. and F. Neidhardt (1998), 'Methodological Issues in Collecting Protest Event Data: Units of Analysis, Sources and Sampling, Coding Problems', in D. Rucht, R. Koopmans and F. Neidhardt (eds.), *Acts of Dissent: New Developments in the Study of Protest*, Berlin: Sigma, pp.65–89.
Rucht, D. and T. Ohlemacher (1992), 'Protest Event Data: Collection, Uses and Perspectives', in R. Eyerman and M. Diani (eds.), *Issues in Contemporary Social Movement Research*, Beverly Hills, CA: Sage, pp.76–106.
Rucht, D., Blattert, B. and D. Rink (1997), *Soziale Bewegungen auf dem Weg zur Institutionalisierung? Zum Strukturwandel 'alternativer Gruppen' in beiden Teilen Deutschlands*, Frankfurt/M.: Campus.
Scarce, R. (1990), *Eco-Warriors: Understanding the Radical Environmental Movement*, Chicago, IL: Noble Press.
Schneider-Wilkes R. (1996), 'Ist die Luft für Bürgerinitiativen dünner geworden? Erfolg und Mißerfolg Berliner Verkehrsbürgerinitiativen 1973–1993', *Vorgänge*, Vol.35, No.3, pp.41–8.
van der Heijden, H.-A., Koopmans, R. and M.C. Giugni (1992), 'The West European Environmental Movement', *Research in Social Movements, Conflicts and Change*, Supplement 2, pp.1–40.
Wagner, P. (1994), 'The Anti-nuclear Movements in their Social Contexts: Society and Polity in Western Europe before and after 1970', in H. Flam (ed.), *States and Anti-Nuclear Oppositional Movements*, Edinburgh: Edinburgh University Press, pp.37–69.
Weidner, H. (1995), '25 Years of Modern Environmental Policy in Germany: Treading a Well-Worn Path to the Top of the International Field', Paper FS II 95-301, Wissenschaftszentrum Berlin.
Wissenschaftlicher Beirat der Bundesregierung Globale Umweltveränderungen (1996), *Welt im Wandel: Wege zur Lösung globaler Umweltprobleme. Jahresgutachten 1995*, Berlin and Heidelberg: Springer.
Wörndl, B. and G. Fréchet (1994), 'Institutionalization Tendencies in Ecological Movements', in S. Langlois *et al.* (eds.), *Convergence and Divergence? Comparing Recent Social Trends in Industrial Societies*, Campus: Frankfurt/M., Montreal: McGill-Queen's University Press, pp.247–68.

Mobilising Earth First! in Britain

DEREK WALL

In 1991 Earth First!, a radical green network inspired initially by the US movement of the same name, mobilised in the UK and has since acted as a catalyst for direct action anti-road campaigns at sites including Twyford Down in Hampshire and the M11 in East London. Structural factors, both political and economic, have aided its emergence but structural influences 'do not march in the streets' or determine the nature of collective action; instead they provide opportunities that must be consciously exploited by key activists or political entrepreneurs. The creation of the anti roads movement of the 1990s is a clear example of how cultural resources may be invoked to activate existing green networks so as to resource accelerated mobilisation.

UK environmental politics in the 1990s has been marked by the mobilisation of Earth First! and the growth of direct action, particularly but not exclusively targeted against road construction. Earth First! was originally founded in the US in 1980 by green activists disillusioned with the approach of existing environmental social movement organisations such as the Sierra Club [*Taylor, 1991*]. Earth First! attracted controversy both because of a commitment to direct action (including sabotage) and the Malthusian views of some founding activists. In turn, the EF! (UK) mobilisation has been seen as providing evidence of an end to 'British exceptionalism'; previously, in contrast to continental Europe, the UK apparently lacked strong social movement activity [*Doherty and Rawcliffe, 1995; Rootes, 1992; Rüdig and Lowe, 1986; Rüdig, 1995*].[1] In practising and promoting environmental direct action, EF! (UK) and the wider anti-roads movement have been conceptualised as successfully increasing the visibility of green political demands and radicalising green campaigning [*Doherty and Rawcliffe, 1995: 247*]. While EF! (UK) has been understood as a 'new social movement' influenced by considerations of cultural identity [*Purkis, 1996*], this study emphasises that political and economic factors together with historical continuities have influenced its emergence. Numerous accounts place the activist at the centre of explanations of movement mobilisation [*Jenkins, 1983: 531; Schmitt, 1989: 585*], arguing that whatever the structural conditions, without the initial efforts of small numbers of innovators who 'produce and propagate ideologies' [*Schmitt, 1989: 585*] and mobilise other resources, movements are unlikely to emerge [*Eyerman and Jamison, 1991: 3; Jenkins, 1983: 533*]. The emergence of EF! (UK) suggests the utility of focusing on activist entrepreneurs and placing their accounts in historical and structural context.

Empirical Research

Personal participation in the network in 1991 and 1992 allowed privileged access to key activists including EF! co-founder Jason Torrance, Davy Garland, the founder of the second EF! group in Britain, and militants who advocated illegal repertoires of action. While participant observation is not uncommon amongst social movement or green political researchers, such early experience of an emerging mobilisation provided a perhaps unique research opportunity.

Research focussed on in-depth analysis of qualitative interviews with 29 key EF! (UK) activists who acted as political entrepreneurs, consciously mobilising resources to create a direct action network. Activist accounts can be seen as furnishing sign posts or clues to mediating factors that link individual motivation to wider social and political processes, while indicating contingent and subjective aspects of involvement that may also be influential [*Bhaskar, 1989; Wall, 1998, 1999*]. Such activist accounts allow individuals to explain their own participation and may provide hermeneutically rich data. The first cohort of 14 interviewees included individuals who had founded EF! (UK) during its first year of mobilisation between April 1991 and 1992. The second cohort, of 15 interviewees, examined for comparative purposes other key activists who had become involved in the movement after April 1992.

Triangulation was achieved by participant observation and examination of activist texts. Discussion of the controversial issue of damage to property (see below) is a useful illustration of the importance of such an approach. Research into three failed EF! (UK) mobilisations and wider UK green movement history generated useful contrasting data. Empirical research was informed by a critical realist approach as operationalised by Miles and Huberman [*1994*] so as to improve the quality of data collection and subsequent analysis [*Wall, 1998, 1999*].

Mobilising Earth First!

An enduring EF! (UK) network was created by two further education students, Jake Burbridge and Jason Torrance, from Hastings, East Sussex in the spring of 1991. Previously active in a number of green movement bodies including Friends of the Earth (FoE), the Green Party, Greenpeace and peace groups, they had become critical of existing green groups and networks and sought a new approach to environmental activism. 'In the summer to 1990 ... Jake ... got hold of a copy of *Deep Ecology* [*Devall, 1985*] and ... wrote off to the Earth First! address in the back and ... became the U.K. contact' (Torrance interview).

Both co-founders showed an enthusiasm for what they perceived to be EF! (US)'s belief in deep ecology and its repertoires of action. A friend noted:

> I remember sitting in the refectory with Jake and Jason and they [had] got this, this Earth First! newspaper from America and they were looking through it going, 'cor, this is great ... have you seen this'. And there are all these nutty people on tripods trying to stop rainforest destruction and general forest destruction. What they were doing was really powerful just getting out there and physically stopping it from happening, um, and then telling people to wake up ('Mary' interview).

The first EF! (UK) action, a blockade of Dungeness nuclear power station, replicated existing peace movement and anti-nuclear power repertoires. Torrance noted, 'we were known as the direct action people and we'd bring in our skills from the peace movement'. The action was framed from a deep ecology perspective with a press statement observing that the Dungeness area contained 'the best example of a cuspate foreland in the world ... home to over 600 species of flora and fauna, some of which are rare' (*Green Anarchist* , 1991, 28, p.24).

Burbridge and Torrance worked hard to make links with existing UK green networks, sending out letters to 'see if anybody was interested in starting an Earth First! group ... people into the old peace movement various people they knew in student networks in the Green Student Network and in the CND student network, people in the Green Party' ('Mary' Interview) . Early contact was made with George Marshall, originally active in Australia, who provided EF! (UK) with an issue focus (rainforests) and a strong ability to mobilise financial resources. During the 1980s and early 1990s images of burning rainforests had become a powerful symbol of global environmental destruction [*Hannigan, 1995: 45; Pearce, 1991: 183*] and rainforest actions were to provide EF! (UK) with campaign with which to mobilise existing green activists. The first 'mass' action occurred on 4 December 1991 when EF! (UK) attempted to prevent the M.V. Singa Wilstream from docking with a cargo of rainforest timber from Sarawak at Tilbury on the Thames Estuary. This intervention, based on an Australian model of 'ship actions', was preceded by extensive networking and a mailing to green movement contacts. Sea Shepherd, the militant splinter group from Greenpeace, resourced the event with power boats. Although the action failed to prevent the ship from docking, it was seen as helpful in building an activist base for non-violent direct action (NVDA) and in generating iconic images:

> How could stopping an international port not be big news, so FoE came in on it with their huge inflatable rubber chain saw that, of course, got in all the press photos and, you know, it was really great to sit down in a huge line of people all linked arms, blockading the gate, people there from WWF, Survival International, FoE local groups, EF! local groups, RAG local groups, Green Party, you name it. There was probably 150-200 people there ... Tilbury was really the first ambitious action we had done in this country (Torrance interview).

A second ship action was held in Liverpool in March 1992, where 400 activists occupied the docks. In May 1992 over 200 activists occupied a timber yard, Timbmet, outside Oxford, forcing it to close for the day. In June 1992 a similar EF! (UK) timber yard action occurred in Rochdale.

Increasingly, road campaigning became more important and Torrance organised a campaigns meeting to plan anti-car actions in August 1991 with

> key people in the then very thin anti-roads/traffic/car movement, people from ALARM [All London Against the Road Menace], some EF!ers from EF! groups, I think some one came from South Downs, Davy came up, a woman came up from the newly formed Littlehampton Earth First! ... Karen Noble and She has an intense hatred of the motor vehicle to a supreme level which I was very impressed with – and Angie came and we had a really, just had a really amazing brain storm on setting up a new roads campaign (Torrance interview).

The meeting focused on the need to develop 'a grassroots resistance anti-car culture' and led to the creation in April 1992 of EF! (UK)'s Reclaim the Streets (RTS) campaign, which aimed to 'do imaginative and non-violent direct actions, and to reclaim the streets of London from cars and traffic and give it back to people' [Anon, 1992: 4]. South Downs EF! 'carried out the first road blockade in the Carmageddon campaign' in Brighton, suffering one arrest (EF! Action Update, 1991, 2 p.1). Shane Collins, a Green Party activist and founder of Brixton EF!, described the first London blockade on 15 May 1992:

> We invented this carmageddon day and printed loads of flyers sort of saying 'Are you pissed off with cars. Do they get up your nose' and I

guess about seventy or eighty people turned up at Victoria Embankment and we went up to Waterloo Bridge and sat down a few times ... in the road (Collins interview).

'Critical mass', a repertoire of road occupation where cyclists block traffic was accelerated by RTS but had previously been utilised by activists in Bristol in 1990 to block the M32 motorway in Bristol [*Control, 1991*]. The concept of a street party, where pedestrians occupy and enjoy road space, developed from these early Carmageddon actions but had originally been used in the 1970s by Commitment, a radical green group established by the Young Liberals, to block London's Oxford Street and Piccadilly Circus (Anderson interview). Participants were mobilised by the promise of 'fun'. Mass participation lowered the cost of taking part by making police action less likely. Each action led to more ambitious interventions. During the largest, in July 1996, 7,000 protesters occupied and closed a London motorway, the M41 [*Honigsbaum, 1996: 28; Bellos and Vidal, 1996: 7*].

EF! (UK) condemnation of the car coincided with an upsurge in local, usually single issue, anti-roads campaigns. Such campaigns predated EF! (UK)'s mobilisation. During the mid-1970s a repertoire of disrupting public inquiries had successfully halted a number of projects [*Twinn, 1978; Tyme, 1978*] but at this stage campaigns generally rejected NVDA and favoured legal campaigning. In contrast EF! (UK) explicitly appealed for direct action to campaign against road building and sought to link road construction to global environmental problems. The EF! (UK) *Action UpDate* identified three road projects where the EC Environment Commissioner had intervened against the plans of the Department of Transport (DoT). An appeal was made for support in 'confronting the bulldozers' if construction went ahead at the East London River Crossing, an extension of the M3 at Twyford Down, and the M11 in East London (*Action Update*, 1991, 2, p.3).

Direct action in attempts physically to prevent road construction began at Twyford in the spring of 1992. Torrance claims that the Twyford Down Association (TDA), a local campaign group that had long opposed plans to build the M3 extension, had asked for NVDA training,

> Earth First! was getting a bit of a name for itself as a direct action group in this country and you know, to be honest there wasn't much to choose from, there was Earth First! direct action-wise or Earth First! so people, when, other groups, when they were considering direct action, would ... if they knew our London contact address would contact us or local groups ... so late '91 we got a phone call from the Twyford Down Association (Torrance interview).

Burbridge visited David Croker, a former Conservative councillor and leading TDA activist and attempts were also made to network with FoE by Torrance. On 18 February EF!ers carried out the first direct action at Twyford with the TDA supporters. 'Six protesters from the radical green group Earth First were arrested during a weekend of protests against plans to extend the M3 motorway ... Environmentalists and local people had occupied two Victorian bridges over the Waterloo to Weymouth line which had been due for demolition' (*The Independent*, 19 Feb. 1992, p.1). The permanent protest camp, used by peace campaigners, most notably the Greenham women, and the Australian rainforest movement, was diffused to the anti-roads movement at Twyford [*Begg, 1992: 9–10; Roseneil, 1995: 172*]. Croker had been a participant in non-violent direct action against road construction during the 1970s, so was perhaps particularly receptive to EF! (UK) [*Tyme, 1978*].

> We talked to David Croker about setting up a camp, again drawing inspiration from elsewhere, drawing from in the bush in Australia and U.S. and peace camps here, and I then thought wow, just imagine one day, fucking hell we could have all these camps over here against roads [laughs]. And there you go it happened ... so I mentioned the idea of a camp to Roger [Higman the FoE transport campaigns officer] and he said, 'No, no silly idea. You know the last thing we want is loads of people trampling on a SSSI [Site of Special Scientific Interest].' So anyway he won me around to that on some point but I was kind of still looking but not as seriously as I should have been at camps in other places (Torrance interview).

At Twyford where this tactic was first used to oppose road building, camps were variously maintained by FoE, EF! (UK) and a group of identity-oriented New Age travellers, the Dongas Tribe. The very first anti-road camp was initiated, despite Higman's reported comments, by FoE.

> FoE decided on a symbolic occupation of the threatened Water Meadows ... launched with Merrick, Jonathon Porritt, and Andrew Lees of FoE being chained across the site. The weather instantly turned cold and wet, and local people fell into the habit of taking hot coffee and breakfast down to the site [*Bryant, 1996: 189*].

FoE received an injunction from the Department of Transport [DOT] forcing them to abandon their protest. The potential fines for breaking such an injunction and maintaining an illegal encampment, made the use of this tactical adaption problematic for social movement organisations such as FoE (Freeman interview). Conversely, this repertoire was ideal for a loose, decentralised 'network' with few assets to be seized such as EF! (UK) or the

Dongas tribe. In the summer of 1992 at Twyford:

> The camp, at the time, was very much made up of groups of travellers
> who had ended up there ... first time I went down there there were
> only half a dozen people, literally a couple of travellers who had been
> involved in other stuff and looked a lot older than everybody else, a
> woman with a couple of kids on the run from social services, an ex
> army drop out, also people coming up from EF! in Brighton ('anon
> one' interview).

Thus as well as attracting more instrumentally oriented activists, camps
provided a magnet for New Age travellers, other sub-culturalists and
individuals simply seeking to escape from authority, family commitment or
urban unemployment. The linkages, sometimes conflictual, sometimes co-
operative, between EF! (UK) and other radical green activists, local
campaigners, environmental pressure groups and permanent identity
oriented campers were to be a constant feature of the anti-roads movement.

> EF! got told to leave by the Dongas tribe, well a few people because
> they were upsetting the karma of the place. This was a couple of days
> before Yellow Wednesday.
>
> [So Dongas are distinct from EF!?]
>
> No! It became so around that split because of dominant people in
> Dongas. Those sympathetic were in the background ... EF! brought
> people to Twyford, that was what really did it, that was what boosted
> EF!, they were the network who did it. Other networks wouldn't touch
> it, FoE wouldn't touch it, none of them would touch it and that is still
> the kicking power of EF! It can produce people who are willing to do
> something ('anon one' interview).

The camp was continued near the summit of Twyford Down by
travellers and EF! (UK) activists until December 1992, when they were
evicted on 'Yellow Wednesday'. The Dongas moved to a woodland 'about
fifteen miles from Winchester' over the remainder of the winter before
travelling to the West of England (Lush interview). Although some Dongas
identified themselves as EF! (UK) activists, there was friction between the
two bodies. Some Dongas were neo-tribalists with a complex mythological
commitment to the land; some believed that Twyford Down was the site of
King Arthur's Camelot, a minority practised an often exclusionary
naturalist lifestyle and were sometimes hostile to other activists (Interview
accounts).[2] Finally, a new camp was created by EF!ers in February 1993
(Lush, 'anon one' and 'Jazz' interviews).

EF! (UK) activists were instrumental in creating permanent anti-roads camps and enduring campaigns at over a dozen sites. An EF! group 'Green Man' helped initiate direct action at the M11 in East London [*Mercer, 1994: 118*]. Five members of Bath EF! started a camp on the site of the Batheaston by-pass ('Clare' interview). Torrance noted 'very often Earth First! comes together around an action or an issue like up in Wymondham in East Anglia and [an] Earth First! group really grew and blossomed around the Wymondham by-pass.'

Between 1993 and the autumn of 1995 EF! (UK) increasingly dissolved into a wider anti-roads movement. Typically EF! (UK) local groups would initiate or support an anti roads camp to the exclusion of other issues. Green Man EF!, Bath EF!, Camelot EF! merged into the respective No M11, Save our Solsbury and Friends of Twyford Down anti-road campaigns.

Biodegradation was accelerated by the politicisation of youth dance culture threatened by the then-proposed Criminal Justice Bill (1994). The anti-roads movement also began to diversify. In Glasgow, EF! remained highly visible within the campaign, emphasising their self-identity, in part due to the participation of EF! (UK) co-founder Burbridge between 1994 and 1995. Working class communities were more active in Glasgow than at other sites of road protest and a socialist political group, Militant, helped mobilise local support. Campaigners in Glasgow drew upon the long traditions of direct action, manifest, for example, during the anti-poll tax campaign of the late 1980s/early 1990s and workplace occupations of the early 1970s.

At Solsbury Hill and other southern English road protest sites, identity campaigners and local single issue activists were strongly involved. Tania de ste Croix, a Green Party and EF! (UK) activist, was instrumental in coordinating the campaign and eventually saw her family home destroyed. At the M65 near Preston, working class communities were again drawn into the protest and identity campaigners were active.

At the M11 in East London, the cultural aspects of protest were emphasised by some (but not all participants) and strong links were forged with the inhabitants of homes due to be demolished [*Anon, 1996; Jordan, 1996*]. Squatting was used as an important tactic with homes threatened with demolition being fortified. Much effort was invested in creating telephone trees and vigorous attempts were made to draw new activists into NVDA campaigning. The No M11 campaign refounded RTS in 1995 and initiated a series of ever more ambitious street parties. Similar street parties and critical masses were initiated in over a dozen urban centres during the mid 1990s.

By 1996 mass NVDA was increasingly being combined with repertoires of sabotage. In July 1996, 7,000 people occupied a stretch of motorway in London in an action initiated by RTS and supported by other EF! (UK) groups ('anon two' interview). A giant carnival figure surrounded by thousands of activists provided cover for unknown individuals using pneumatic drills to dig holes in the road surface [*Bellos and Vidal, 1996: 7*]. Arson attacks on construction machinery occurred during a rally and site occupation to mark the first anniversary of work on the Newbury bypass [*Moyes, 1997: 3*]. Increasingly dramatic tactics of tunnel digging, which deliberately placed activists at risk of injury, gave rise to formidable media interest [*Doherty, 1997*]. One tunnel digger, 'Swampy', was virtually deified by the press and became a household name in the UK.

Since 1996 EF! (UK) and the wider direct action movement have focussed less on road construction. Opposition to a new runway at Manchester airport led to protest in 1997, while genetics and housing on green field sites have become increasingly important mobilising themes.

Networks and Resources

EF! (UK)'s emergence and trajectory confirms the importance of preexisting networks in facilitating mobilisation [*Diani, 1994; Freeman, 1980; Granovetter, 1973; McAdam, McCarthy and Zald, 1988*]. EF! (UK) founding activists functioned as political entrepreneurs networking with other activists to gather other resources and promote forms of diffusion to create a new mobilisation. In doing so, EF! (UK) used existing movement networks to overcome a classic dilemma of resource mobilisation for emerging movements. Without resources, mobilisation may prove impossible, yet the cost of elite sponsorship can be 'normalisation' [*Piven and Cloward, 1977: xi*]. Office space, office equipment, boats for use in early forms of direct action and other physical resources were mobilised via the peace movement and Green Student Network (GSN). Contacts with *The Ecologist* provided finance for rainforest action.

Activists with discretionary time were drawn initially from varied green networks. Communication networks including *Green Anarchist, Green Line*, the GSN mailing and the US *Earth First! Journal* were vigorously exploited. EF! (UK) initiated protest actions and recruited supporters from existing bodies rather than seeking to create its own membership structures. This pattern of networking to create a body of protesters is apparent as EF! (UK) moved from local environmental protest in East Sussex and Kent, to national (and international) rainforest campaigning to the anti-roads activity. By 1992 this activist base was large enough to meet the relatively modest resource needs of producing the EF! (UK) newsletter, supporting direct action and holding occasional national gatherings. Student unions and local environmental centres have helped to sustain both local and national activity since 1992 (Durham interview).

Networking brought with it the influence of the ideologies, issues foci, repertoires of action, strategies and articulations of existing green networks. For example, mass NVDA repertoires were derived from the peace and Australian rainforest movements. Repertoires of sabotage, in turn, were derived from animal liberation militants and to a lesser extent EF! (US) (Foreman and Haywood 1993). Conflict within EF! (UK), at least during the initial years of mobilisation, over issues of repertoire and strategic direction can be conceptualised as conflict inherited from these preexisting networks. Tilly, from Oxford EF!, who had been active at Greenham noted, the importance of

> the peace movement's and Greenham's ideas on non violence, I wanted to bring some of those ideas into Earth First! ... we've got to say for Earth First! there will be no ecotage, this is like an accountable non violence movement ... for direct action and civil disobedience and all that stuff but it's going to be up front and in the public eye ...I felt really behind that and so when we organised the Timbmet we had this ground rule of non violence and no damage to property.[3]

In contrast a second Oxford activist, observed: 'A key model throughout the 80s was the Animal Liberation Front, of course, in terms of they were directly resolving things in a clandestine manner, etc.' ('Mix' interview).

In response to being asked whether 'violence towards human beings is something you would see as outside Earth First!', a female interviewee argued 'Or to animals of course but violence to machines is thoroughly welcomed and blessed.'[4]

None the less, NVDA actions, initially small and strikingly iconic, later larger in scale and more disruptive, accelerated early recruitment. Such actions created publicity in both mass and green media, encouraging participation on the part of potential activists.

> When Earth First! came along it did a number of things. It broke us out of the student ghetto, it gave us a powerful new tactic – direct action, it linked us into an international network and it gave a focus which made the network much more effective. The Green Student Network was never very effective because it was never very clear what it was for. With Earth First!, direct action gave the network a focus and to this day there is a huge overlap between the Green Student Network and the Earth First! network (Begg interview).

By contrast, interview accounts indicate that after 1992 activists from *outside* existing green networks were increasingly likely to become involved in the anti-roads movement.

Political Opportunities

Resource mobilisation and network approaches do not provide complete explanations of EF! (UK) mobilisation. Researchers have noted that many well resourced efforts at mobilisation have failed in the past [*Marx, 1979*]. Resources alone do not create movements, while access to finance and physical resources may discourage the use of repertoires of direct action that threaten the removal of resources via legal sanctions. It is also necessary to explain why existing green activists were attracted to EF! (UK) and why existing networks were willing to donate resources. Equally it is necessary to explain why wider network links outside of the broad green movement came to be exploited after 1992.

Some theorists have argued that such questions can be answered using the concept of political opportunity structure (POS) defined as 'consistent – but not necessarily formal, permanent or national – dimensions of the political environment which either encourage or discourage people from using collective action' [*Tarrow, 1994: 18*]. Rootes [*1997*] has challenged the indiscriminate use of POS on the grounds that, as well as genuinely structural variables, the model includes relatively contingent factors.[5] Critics have also challenged the assumption that more permanent structural conditions or shifts in such conditions can unproblematically be translated into action [*Melucci, 1992: 239*]. Thus it can be argued that as a conceptual tool the POS lacks a clear, empirically accessible mediating link to movement action and fails to show how

> structural characteristics of political systems enter the hearts and minds of movement organizers and participants … Philosophers of social science have repeatedly emphasised that theories of social behaviour should specify the mechanisms that translate social structures into individual and group actions … by linking action directly to structure, current applications of POS often fail to appreciate the complex and sometimes contradictory ways in which political structures influence movement mobilization. The resulting explanations are … incomplete … and sometimes plainly wrong [*Kriesi et al., 1995: 37*].

Thus qualitative use of activist accounts may be essential in investigating the specific influence of political factors, whether truly structural or more contingent, on activist participation and mobilisation/strategy [*Della Porta, 1995: 19; Rucht, 1990*]. Indeed, Kriesi *et al.*, while using quantitative methods, noted that POS theorists often derive 'strategies from abstract categories such as "the strength of the state" or "open input structures", which obviously have little meaning for the average movement activist'[*1995: 37*, see also *McAdam, 1982*].

Political factors identified from the analysis of activist accounts were clear but diverse. The increased salience of environmental issues in the late 1980s helped raise support for radical environmental action ('Mary' interview). Existing green movement organisations, responsive to shifts in the policy making process within the environmental domain, provided an important form of organisational mediation between the POS and EF! (UK). The apparent openness of the POS to environmental demands in the late 1980s encouraged many existing green movement family members to endorse assimilative strategies. Linked to such assimilative strategies was a resistance to activist pressures which demanded a more confrontational stance. An apparent opening in the POS helped promote politically 'realist' strategies, but when the POS remained closed, such strategies became less effective. Such continued closure ultimately increased support for differentiation/diffusion within the green movement easing the emergence of EF! (UK) .

Typically, FoE moved towards more assimilative strategies in the period 1987–92 [*Lamb, 1996; McCormick, 1991: 117*]. Porritt, its Director between 1984 and 1990, noted how the organisation had shifted 'since 1987, from campaigning and working *against* industry to working increasingly *with* industry', observing that 'FoE spent a lot of time beating at doors because people didn't want to let us in. We had to work hard to get the attention of ministers … Now we just have to nudge the door, it opens wide, and we fall flat on our faces, not really knowing what to do when we get there [*Porritt in McCormick, 1991: 117*]. The FoE Annual Report of 1989/90 argued that the organisation had moved 'from opposition to proposition' with a resulting transformation of 'campaigning tools' [*Huey, 1990: 3*].

There is also evidence that a more assimilative strategy was linked to a less libertarian organisational form. Describing his approach on behalf of the London Rainforest Action Group to FoE, Marshall noted:

> I remember going around to Friends of the Earth and saying I wonder whether I could look at your files and they just completely freaked out … [that] they would actively contact their local groups, autonomous local groups and tell them not to get involved in our stuff was disheartening and actually was a declaration of war. … this was June 1991 (Marshall interview).

Sheila Freeman, an FoE employee who became an EF! (UK) activist in 1993, also noted: 'I went on the M11 campaign that FoE also didn't get involved with at all. It was the same thing again (as Twyford), they thought it was too anarchic, … too much direct action, not enough public sympathy behind it (Freeman interview).

Such a pattern also occurred in other pressure groups and the Green Party, one commentator noted:

the turmoil within the Green Party is simply one symptom of the wider crisis. Other signs include the violent denunciation of market environmentalism ... and the haemorrhage from FoE of local members who are frustrated by the restrictions placed on them by the leadership and are attracted by the more confrontational direct approach of anarchist influenced groups [Dickson 1992: 10–11].

Ultimately, the failure of the policy process, despite the promise of the 'greening' of Mrs Thatcher around 1988/89, to open to even modest environmental demands led to increasing support for direct action.

Political closure also helped create new allies for environmental direct action. While the interplay between the green movement family and youth subcultures has been apparent, in a sporadic fashion, for perhaps a century [Paul, 1951], legislation against 'raves' clearly accelerated such links in the 1990s. Tom Fox of the Freedom Network stated 'We want to have more parties, more roads protests and more big squats. The more people they attack with the Criminal Justice Bill the more people come into our circle' [Travis, 1994: 5]. Thus a primarily hedonistic youth subculture resourced anti-roads protest with new participants and new technologies of protest. Changes in local planning controls also drew more conservative groups and individuals into direct action [Lowe and Flynn, 1989: 262]. Although some of these individuals continued to be suspicious of EF! [Bryant, 1996], many others were highly supportive, Hook [1993: 10] observed: 'It was interesting to note that many TDA members took part in the EF! protest, either bodily or by bringing food. When asked where his children were, one local, dressed in a barbour and green wellington boots, replied that they were off "tampering with some machinery; not to worry".'[6]

Alternative Movement Activity

Shifting priorities within the broad green movement family and between the green and other movements also aided EF! (UK)'s emergence:

In the late 1970s and early 1980s, the peace movement (in Britain, at least) tended to overshadow the green movement, and the liberals and radical liberals who might otherwise be campaigning against nuclear power (and other environmental issues) were campaigning against nuclear weapons.Since the peace movement went into decline, the environment movement has grown correspondingly [Anon 1994: 13].

A number of founding activists, many of whom had been highly active in the peace movement, broadly endorsed this conclusion (interviews with Torrance and 'Mary'). After the end of the Gulf War and with the thawing of the cold war, peace clearly fell down the agenda for greens; other issues of planetary survival took its place. Others had transferred energy from animal liberation campaigning or participation in other elements of the green movement (Garland, Molland and 'Mix' interviews).

Activists, from the second cohort of interviewees, who had become involved in EF! (UK) after 1992, were increasingly found to have participated in other movements. Those who might previously have supported the labour movement participating in the Labour Party, far left parties or trade unions, seemed less likely to do so in the late 1980s. One activist argued:

> The working class lost pretty much all of its power in the 80s, so people didn't get involved in the Marxist and anarchist workerist groups ... what is the point of joining a group with no power, if you are going to move something you need a lever. Power is crucial, it led young militants to reassess and look for new ways of doing things ('anon one' interview).

Several activists from the second cohort of interviewees with no previous connection with the green movement moved from labour movement participation because of rising concern with environmental grievances and a perception that green issues could act as a vehicle for a wider radical politics . In this sense activists moved, as in the title of Bahro's book, from *Red to Green* [*1984*]. Although links between the green and labour movements have been relatively limited since the decline of 'the early Green Politics' around 1905, participation that had occurred in the 1970s and early 1980s seems to have declined in the late 1980s [*Gould, 1988*]. Rootes notes the links between the Labour leadership and the Campaign for Nuclear Disarmament in the 1980s, and argued that the Party was 'a broad church' encompassing a variety of tendencies ... permeable to young radicals in a way that, say, the German SPD was not' [*Rootes, 1992: 184*]. Although agreeing that the Labour Party nationally largely rejected green concerns, Rootes also argues that the populist style of the local socialism of left-wing labour councils such as Ken Livingstone's Greater London Council promoted 'environmentalist initiatives'. The Labour Party ceased its support for CND in the late 1980s, local socialism was marginalised by local government reforms, and the Party became less sympathetic to social movement demands in general [*Heffernan and Marquesse, 1992*]. Political realism intensified with the election of Tony Blair as Labour Party leader in 1994. On the eve of the 1996 Labour Party Conference sacked Liverpool dock workers held a street party and direct action protest with RTS and other EF! (UK) groups [interview with 'anon two']. The dockers approached RTS, both as possible allies and as a source of a new repertoire of action, after RTS had attempted to occupy the offices of London Transport in support of striking tube workers. The series of joint actions between the dockers and the RTS, including a pre-election social justice march, were perhaps more a product of the weakness of the labour movement than the strength of ecosocialist/anarchist sentiments within RTS.

Economic Opportunities and Challenges

Other specifically economic factors aided mobilisation. First, accelerated road-building and other forms of large-scale construction provided grievances around which different demands could be mobilised. At cherished localities such as Twyford or Claremont in East London, roads acted both as a potent symbol of global environmental damage and a concrete threat to valued sites laden with cultural and natural significance. As Rüdig and Lowe state: 'There would be no environmental movement ... without the existence of environmental problems ... Highly visible and disruptive capital projects 'such as hydroelectric dams and new airports have been central to environmental protest movements' [*1986: 279*]. While greens may not merely seek redress of particular grievances but to create more fundamental transformation, without such concrete grievances or 'mobilisation targets' a green political critique may appear too diffuse and abstract to allow movement mobilisation [*Rüdig, 1993: 3*]. Such 'targets' act as symbols or points at which particular concerns can collect together to reach a threshold where protest may occur.

Second, increased youth unemployment and mass higher education resourced anti-roads mobilisation by accelerating biographical availability. In particular, youth unemployment resourced the DIY movement linking EF! and Rave culture.

The influence of employment was noted by Anderson who undertook direct action to protest against the effects of the car on the environmental in December 1971 in Oxford Street, London. Discussing why his group Commitment failed to create a mass environmental direct action movement, he observed:

> There was less awareness of the issues. Also I think unemployment has made a big difference Now there are a lot more people about with less to lose. At that time when people were arrested in Oxford Street their main fear about being arrested wasn't that they would get fined ... people were afraid of losing their jobs, whereas now if you have

masses of people who don't have jobs anyway they will be prepared to go further (Anderson interview).

Third, diffusion, both from outside the UK and from other UK movements, was enhanced by what Harvey has termed 'time-space' compression [*1990*]. Long-term trends of capital accumulation have both accelerated technological development and increased globalising trends, reinforcing EF! (UK) and other activists' adoption of new technologies of protest such as the mobile phone and video camera. Merrick, an anti-road campaigner at Newbury, noted, 'Mobile phones and CBs are great. God, all this would've been so much harder ten or twenty years ago' [*Merrick, 1996: 10*].[7] Improved communication on a global scale has accelerated EF! (UK) founders' ability to borrow repertoires of action and symbolic resources from their US namesake and Australian activists (Marshall interview).

Culture and Construction

Without the macro-structural factors of global environmental change, political closure and economic change, it is unlikely that EF! (UK) would have emerged as a significant mobilisation. Yet such structural factors cannot be used to explain EF! (UK) mobilisation in a deterministic way. First, structural factors clearly have contradictory effects. For example, direct action requires, as we have noted, a pool of 'biographically available' activists resourced above all with discretionary time. Equally, full employment creates a disciplinary effect discouraging participation in action that absorbs time and creates risk of injury or legal sanction (Anderson interview). Yet increasing unemployment may, conceivably, for much of society reduce the salience of environmental issues and promote demands for accumulation. Second, different structural factors interact. For example, green protest cannot be 'read off' from environmental grievances such as global warming, the 'political' reaction to environmental problems can take diverse forms including pressure group lobbying, electoral politics or lifestyle change. Third, structural influences, far from being immediately visible, are often mediated by additional institutional processes and cultural factors. For example, the apparent opening and subsequent closure of the POS to environmental demands in the late 1980s/early 1990s was strongly mediated, as noted, for EF! (UK) founders via the behaviour of more formal groups with a stronger orientation to conventional political processes, such as FoE or the Green Party.

Such observations reinforce the contention that opportunities provided by structural factors need to be *consciously* exploited if movement mobilisation is to occur. In this context, I would argue that EF! (UK) is a clear example of how instrumentally motivated political entrepreneurs constructed a movement mobilisation by exploiting structural opportunities.[8] While hostile to professional political entrepreneurs within formal social movement organisations, the initial EF! (UK) activists explicitly aimed to ferment direct action where preexisting grievances prove insufficient to create sustained collective action. Typically, Torrance noted in reference to Marshall: 'he came straight from Australia and had been banging his head up against a brick wall trying to get local grassroots direct action off the ground and again just like me and Jake ... he was really into getting things going in this country' (Torrance interview).

Marshall returned to the UK with the explicit intention of creating a direct action movement against rainforest destruction. Torrance consciously aimed to create a grassroots movement against car culture. While challenging the more conservative assumptions of formal and salaried political entrepreneurs within environmental pressure groups, the initial EF! (UK) activists invoked powerfully charged symbols, blended and borrowed repertoires, and mobilised preexisting networks. In short, while they received no salary, they took on the function of political entrepreneurs.

EF! (US), with associations of neo-Malthusian excess, state repression and controversial repertoires of sabotage [*Cohen, 1992*], provided a potent icon or symbol of fundamentalism around which co-founders Burbridge and Torrance could attract disaffected green radicals. Begg noted, 'I got a leaflet ... from Hastings Earth First! ... I knew the Earth First! name from having heard about American Earth First! and it interested me straight away'. Rather than acting as a source of distinct political assumptions or novel practices, EF! was a known 'brand name', providing a set of symbols around which activists could cohere. After the initial recruitment of green activists, wider networking became possible. Thus structural opportunities threw up potential allies including identity-oriented neo-tribalists, frustrated socialists, local communities fighting road construction, and ravers criminalised by new legislation. Building on existing green networks, repertoires and symbols, EF! (UK) political entrepreneurs have acted as a catalyst for accelerated mobilisation that has created a new generation of environmental activists who are inventing novel networks, repertoires and symbols. EF! (UK) can thus be seen as both aiding *green movement reproduction*, a process that has been sustained, according to some commentators, since the 1880s [*Gould, 1988; Veldman, 1994; Wall, 1999*] and *green movement mutation* into new fields of action and discourse.

NOTES

1. This exceptionalism may be more apparent than real if continental European and British mobilisation on peace and animal liberation issues are compared. The electoral failure of the Green Party and a far smaller anti-nuclear power movement appear more exceptional [*Wall, 1998; Ch.2*].
2. Heterogeneous and controversial beliefs combining paganism and English nationalism myths were apparently derived from a wider traveller community and a rich sense of ritual practice [*Lowe and Shaw: 112–24*].
3. Personal participation suggested that this was not entirely the case, I observed numerous acts of minor damage during the Timbmet event.
4. Such a derivation of repertoires should not be applied in an over-simplistic fashion; there was some overlap amongst interviewees between former animal liberation and peace movement activists. Equally, many animal liberation campaigns utilise conventional repertoires of pressure group lobbying rather than clandestine sabotage.
5. I have retained the concept of political opportunity structures in this text, given the established nature of the concept within social movement literature, but a deeper consideration of what constitutes a structure is clearly needed. A useful starting point might be to examine Bhaksar's critical realist ontology of social structures that tend to be hidden, relatively enduring rather than permanent, plural and ultimately open to transformation via collective action [*1989*].
6. During participation in the Golden Hill direct action campaign against supermarket construction on a greenfield site in Bristol in 1992, I found that relations between EF! (UK) activists and former Bristol West Conservatives Party workers were extremely good.
7. The reference to 'CBs' lacks strict chronological accuracy!
8. This not to say that the bulk of participants or even later key activists were so consciously motivated by strategic analysis of the value of creating and sustaining direct action or indeed that identity can ever neatly be separated from strategy, especially in green mobilisations where lifestyle is often part of political commitment.

REFERENCES

Andrews, T. (1991), 'Making headway', *Green Line*, No.87, pp.4–5.
Anon. (1992), 'Road Fury', *Wild*, No.1, p.4.
Anon. (1994),'Auto-Struggles: The Developing War Against the Road Monster', *Aufheben*, No.3, pp.3–23.
Anon. (1996), 'Review: Senseless Acts of Beauty: Cultures of Resistance since the Sixties', *Aufheben*, No.5, pp.43–4.
Begg, A. (1992), 'Witness for the world', *Green Line*, No.94, pp.9–10.
Bellos, A. and J. Vidal (1996), 'Trees Planted in Fast Lane at Protesters' Party', *The Guardian*, 15 July, p.7.
Bahro, R. (1984), *From Red to Green*, London: Verso.
Bhaskar, R. (1989), *Reclaiming Reality*, London: Verso.
Bryant, B. (1996), *Twyford Down*, London: Chapman and Hall.
Cohen, N. (1992), 'Eco-Radicals Warn of Violence', *Independent on Sunday*, 19 April, p.5.
Control, S. (1991), *Away with All Cars*, Stoke-on-Trent: Play Time for Ever Press.
Della Porta, D. (1992), 'Life Histories in the Analysis of Social Movement Activists', in M. Diani and R. Eyerman, *Studying Collective Action*, London: Sage.
Della Porta, D. (1995), *Social Movements, Political Violence and the State*, Cambridge: Cambridge University Press.
Devall, W. (1985), *Deep Ecology: Living as if Nature Mattered*, Salt Lake City, UT: Peregrine Smith.
Diani, M. (1994), *Green Networks*, Edinburgh: Edinburgh University Press.
Dickson, B. (1992), 'A Crisis of Diversity', *Green Line*, No.101, pp.10–11.

Doherty, B. (1997), 'Tactical Innovation and the Protest Repertoire in the Radical Ecology Movement in Britain', European Sociological Association Conference, Essex University 27–30 Aug.

Doherty, B. and P. Rawcliffe (1995), 'British Exceptionalism? Comparing the Environmental Movement in Britain and Germany', in I. Blühdorn, Krause, F. and T. Scharf (eds.), *The Green Agenda: Environmental politics and Policy in Germany*, Keele: Keele University Press.

Eisinger, P. (1973), 'The Conditions of Protest Behaviour in American Cities', *American Political Science Review*, Vol.67, pp.11–28.

Evans, G. (1991), 'The Green Party: An Insider Account', unpublished M.Phil. thesis.

Eyerman, R. and A. Jamison (1991), *Social Movements: A Cognitive Approach*, Cambridge: Polity Press.

Freeman, J. (1980), *Social Movements of the Sixties and Seventies*. New York, NY: Longmans.

Gould, P. (1988), *Early Green Politics*, Brighton: Harvester.

Granovetter, M. (1973), 'The Strength of Weak Ties. A Network Theory Revisited', *American Journal of Sociology*, Vol.78, pp.1360–80.

Green 2000 (1990), 'Towards a Green 2000', unpublished ms., St. Margaret's, Middlesex.

Hannigan, J. (1995), *Environmental Sociology*, London: Routledge.

Harvey, D. (1990), *The Condition of Postmodernity*, Oxford: Basil Blackwell.

Harvey, D. (1996), *Justice, Nature and the Geography of Difference*, Oxford: Basil Blackwell.

Heffernan, R. and M. Marquesse (1992), *Defeat From The Jaws of Victory*, London: Verso.

Honigsbaum, M. (1996), 'Why I Want to Block the Capital's Roads', *Evening Standard*, 16 July, p.28.

Hook, W. (1993), 'A View from the Hilltop', *Green Line*, No.104, pp.10–11.

Huey, S. (1990), *Annual Report and Accounts 1989/1990*, London: Friends of the Earth.

Lamb, R. (1996), *Promising the Earth*, London: Routledge.

Jenkins, J. (1983), 'Resource Mobilization Theory and the Study of Social Movements', *Annual Review of Sociology*, Vol.82, pp.527–53.

Jordan, J. (1996), 'M11/Claremont Road Revisited', unpublished paper, *CityStates*, Signs of the Times/New Statesman, 29 June.

Kriesi, H., Koopmans, R., Duyvendak, J. and M. Giugni (1995), *New Social, Movements in Western Europe*, London: UCL Press.

Lang, T. and H. Raven (1994), 'From Market to Hypermarket', *The Ecologist*, Vol.24, No.4, pp.124–37.

Lowe, P. and A. Flynn (1989), 'Environmental Politics and Policy in the 1980s', in J. Mohan, *The Political Geography of Contemporary Britain*, London: Macmillan.

Lowe, R. and W. Shaw (1993), *Travellers – Voices of the New Age Nomads*, London: Fourth Estate.

McAdam, D (1982), *Political Process and the Development of Black Insurgency, 1930–1970*, Chicago, IL: University of Chicago Press.

McAdam, D. (1986), 'Recruitment to High-Risk Activism: The Case of Freedom Summer', *American Journal of Sociology*, Vol 92, pp.64–90.

McAdam, D., McCarthy, J. and M. Zald (1988), 'Social Movements', in N. Smelser (ed.) *Handbook of Sociology*, Beverly Hills, CA: Sage.

McCormick, J. (1991), *British Politics and the Environment*, London: Earthscan.

Martell, L. (1994), *Ecology and Society*, London: Polity Press.

Marx, G. (1979), 'External Efforts to Damage or Facilitate Social Movements: Some Patterns, Explanations, Outcomes, and Complications', in M. Zald and J. McCarthy, *The Dynamics of Social Movements*, Cambridge, MA: Winthrop.

Melucci, A. (1989), *Nomads of the Present*, London: Radius.

Melucci, A. (1992), 'Frontier Land: Collective Action Between Actors and Systems', in M. Diani and R. Eyerman, *Studying Collective Action*, London: Sage.

Melucci, A. (1996), *Challenging Codes*, Cambridge: Cambridge University Press.

Mercer, P. (1994),*The UK Directory of Political Organisations*, London: Longmans.

Merrick (1996), *Battle for the Trees*, Leeds: Godhaven.

Miles, M. and Huberman, A. (1994), *Qualitative Data Analysis*, London: Sage.

100   ENVIRONMENTAL MOVEMENTS: LOCAL, NATIONAL, GLOBAL

Moyes, J. (1997), 'It's Not Violence That Middle England Won't Tolerate, It's Police Snooping', *The Independent*, 13 Jan., p.3.

Paul, L. (1951), *Angry Young Man*, London: Faber.

Pearce, F. (1991), *Green Warriors*, London: Bodley Head.

Piven, F. and R. Cloward (1977), *Poor People's Movements: Why They Succeed and How They Fail*, New York, NY: Pantheon.

Purkiss, J. (1996), 'Daring to Dream: Idealism in the Philosophy, Organisation and Campaigning Strategies of Earth First!', C. Barker and P. Kennedy, *To Make Another World: Studies in Collective Action*, Aldershot: Avebury.

Rootes, C. (1992), 'The New Politics and the New Social Movements: Accounting for British Exceptionalism', *European Journal of Political Research*, Vol.22, pp.171–91.

Rootes, C. (1995), 'Britain: Greens in a Cold Climate', in D. Richardson and C. Rootes (eds.), *The Green Challenge*, London: Routledge.

Rootes, C. (1997), 'Shaping Collective Action: Structure, Contingency and Knowledge', in R. Edmondson (ed.), *The Political Context of Collective Action*, London: Routledge.

Roseneil, S. (1995), *Disarming Patriarchy: Feminism and Political Action at Greenham*, Milton Keynes: Open University Press.

Rucht, D. (1990a), 'Campaigns, Skirmishes and Battles: Anti-Nuclear Movements in the USA', France and West Germany, *Industrial Crisis Quarterly*, Vol.4, pp.193–222.

Rüdig, W. (1990), *Anti-Nuclear Movements*, London: Longman.

Rüdig, W. (1993), 'Editorial', *Green Politics Two*, pp.1–8.

Rüdig, W. (1995), 'Between Modernism and Marginalisation: Environmental Radicalism in Britain', in B. Taylor (ed.), *Ecological Resistance Movements*, New York: State University of New York Press.

Rüdig, W. and P. Lowe (1986), 'The Withered "Greening" of British Politics', *Political Studies*, Vol.34, pp.262–84.

Schmitt, R. (1989), 'Organizational Interlocks Between New Social Movement and Traditional Elites: The Case of the West German Peace Movement', *European Journal of Political Research* , Vol.17, pp.583–98.

Steinmetz, G. (1994), 'Regulation Theory, Post-Marxism, and the New Social Movements', *Comparative Studies in Society and History*, Vol.36, No.1, pp.176–212.

Tarrow, S. (1994), *Power in Movement*, London: Cambridge University Press.

Taylor, B. (1991), 'The Religion and Politics of Earth First!', *The Ecologist*, Vol.21, No.6, pp.258–66.

Travis, A. (1994), 'Eco-Warriors to Step Up Battle Against Howard's Bill', *The Guardian*, 5 Aug., p .6.

Twinn, I. (1978), 'Public Involvement or Public Protest: A Case Study of the M3 at Winchester 1971–1974', Polytechnic of the South Bank.

Tyme, J. (1978), *Motorways versus Democracy*, London: Macmillan.

Veldman, M. (1994), *Fantasy, the Bomb and the Greening of Britain*, London: Cambridge University Press.

Wall, D. (1998), 'The Politics of Earth First! in the UK', unpublished Ph.D. thesis, University of the West of England.

Wall, D. (1999), *Earth First! and the Anti-Roads Movement*, London: Routledge.

Voluntary Associations, Professional Organisations and the Environmental Movement in the United States

JOANN CARMIN

This research examines the relationship between voluntary and professional environmental organisations in the United States. A content analysis of newspaper abstracts for a 15 year period suggests that the unconventional actions of voluntary groups precede similar types of activities of professional organisations by one or more years. Although their actions are interrelated, voluntary groups often identify and respond to emerging issues while professional organisations tend to focus on shaping the policy agenda and affecting policy outcomes. The combined activities of voluntary associations and professional organisations make it possible for the environmental movement to retain a presence and advance environmental policy.

Local Activism, National Organisations, and the American Environmental Movement

The policy cycle is often described as a series of events that begins with problem identification and concludes with policy enactment and implementation. Although groups ranging from local community associations to formal lobbying organisations are active in this process, most research has focused on professional organisations. The result is that the roles and strategies of different types of groups participating in the policy arena have not been fully elaborated. This research examines the repertoires of action adopted by local voluntary associations and national professional environmental organisations, the different roles that these groups play in the public policy process, and the way that each of these types of organisations contributes to the overall character of the environmental movement.

Portions of this research were supported by a John D. Rockefeller Summer Graduate Fellowship administered through the Yale University Program on Nonprofit Organisations. This controbution benefited from comments and suggestions made by Barbara Hicks, Chrstopher Rootes, and two anonymous reviwers.

Characteristics of Professional and Voluntary Movement Organisations

The relationship between professional organisations and political action has been best elaborated by resource mobilisation theory (RMT). One of the dominant frameworks used by American scholars to explain the activities associated with social movement organisations, RMT suggests that collective action is a purposeful political form of expression that occurs when sufficient resources such as funding, facilities, and labour are present [*McCarthy and Zald, 1977*]; organisations are a critical resource to both mobilisation and movement maturation. RMT suggests that movement organisations have undergone a transition. Classical movement associations were staffed by 'beneficiary' constituents, individuals directly affected by an issue and willing to volunteer their time and labour. Recent movement organisations have developed large memberships consisting of 'conscience' constituents who primarily donate funds rather than time and energy. Noting an increase in full-time leaders, routinised tasks, codified membership criteria, and hierarchical decision-making processes in social movement organisations, McCarthy and Zald [*1977*] suggested that a transition from classical voluntary to professionalised organisations was taking place and that this change could be attributed to increases in discretionary resources, patronage, and movement entrepreneurs.

In the US environmental movement there are numerous professional organisations. It is likely that the activities of these groups have been influenced by indirect controls or 'institutional channelling'. According to McCarthy, Britt, and Wolfson [*1991*], non-profit legislation is a legal and subtle means of cooptation and conflict mitigation because it provides inducements that lead radical actors to become formal organisations. Movement organisations that engage in educational activities receive exemption under Section 501(c)(3) of the United States Internal Revenue Code of 1959. While this status limits political activity, it is preferred since donors can deduct the value of any contributions that they make from their total taxable income. Organisations that receive 501(c)(4) status under the Code are authorised to conduct political activity, but the type and volume of activities are controlled; donations are not tax-deductible but organisations are exempt from paying tax on income and assets.

Registered non-profit organisations receive tax advantages not afforded to private corporations, non-registered associations, or individuals. In return, they must meet and maintain standards that limit the structural and strategic options that they can employ. To retain non-profit status, professional organisations must file tax documents and provide reports to members. For many professional organisations, membership refers to individuals who make annual donations rather than people who spend their time managing the organisation or even participating in organisational activities. In essence, members hire movement professionals to serve as a voice on their behalf. Because the political activities of non-profit organisations also are controlled, most professional nonprofit movement organisations sponsor educational and research-oriented activities. Although some engage in expressive and unconventional activities, these actions are rare among 501(c)(3) organisations and infrequent among 501(c)(4) organisations. Litigation, lobbying, and expert testimony are the main forms of political action associated with professional organisations.

Resource mobilisation theory examined organisations that had adopted the characteristics of movement interest groups [Lo, 1992]. These formal organisations were composed of paid professionals who primarily attempted to foster change by lobbying or through direct contact with elected representatives [Schwartz and Paul, 1992]. Professional movement organizations play a number of important roles such as providing visibility and stability to movements over time [Staggenborg, 1988], but while they maintain a distinct political presence, they are not the sole source of movement activity. A variety of mobilising structures, including informal networks, independent grass-roots associations, and community groups, contribute to the formation, character, and ongoing activities of social movements [McAdam, 1996; Kriesi, 1996; Rucht, 1996; Lo, 1992].

Early social movement theory suggested that protest was a form of action used by marginalised and alienated individuals to express their grievances [Kornhauser, 1959; Gurr, 1970]. The implication inherent in the increased presence of professional organisations [McCarthy and Zald, 1973] is that latent sentiments can be mobilised and movements can be formed in the absence of critical events. However, research focusing on local mobilisation suggests that critical incidents play a significant role in fostering community-based collective action: when the nuclear reactor at Three Mile Island became contaminated, residents mobilised in response; similarly, when landfills, incinerators, and other unwanted forms of land use are proposed in communities, people frequently organise and mobilise to express concern. These 'Not in My Backyard' (NIMBY) responses are common when some form of environmentally-oriented grievance is present [Walsh, Warland and Smith ,1993; Walsh, 1981; Szasz, 1994].

When opposition to a local issue arises, it rarely stems from professional groups. Residents concerned about impending issues take the initiative to form ad hoc committees, informal organisations, and loose coalitions. For many community activists this may be the first time they have participated in politics. Often, these individuals engage the system through legitimate means such as speaking with elected representatives or attending public hearings. In situations where legitimate actions fail to make a difference, more expressive and unconventional acts may follow. Many local groups acting in response to suddenly imposed grievances do not attempt to become formal non-profit organisations; many are short-lived, single focus associations but others are more formalised and enduring, community groups formed with the intent of making a long-term commitment to local issues.

Community-based activism stemming from both short-term and more enduring voluntary associations plays an important role in social movements and in the public policy process. Community members and local associations engage in a range of activities that frequently have a different focus and trajectory than the activities that stem from professional organisations. In contrast to professionals, community members typically donate their time and energy. These voluntary activists do not regard political involvement as a career choice, but as a necessary response to a problem [Walsh, 1981] or as a means of becoming involved in the ongoing development of their communities [Lichterman, 1996].

The repertoires of action that social movements adopt are linked to political institutions and political culture [Kriesi, 1996; Kriesi, Koopmans, Duyvendak and Giugni, 1995]. In the US, a variety of formal and informal structures provides a basis for social movement activity. While both professional and voluntary associations contribute to movement activities, the interrelationship between these two types of organisations has received only limited attention. In the environmental arena, it appears that professional and classical movement organisations have both remained active and that each may play a distinct role in the policy process. The remainder of this study examines the historical and contemporary activities of local voluntary and national professional environmental movement organisations and the relative influence of each in the US public policy process.

Organisations and the US Environmental Movement

Although the environmental movement is regarded as a recent phenomenon, competing philosophical and ethical perspectives on the relationship of humans to the natural environment as well as debates over what constitutes appropriate resource use and technological development have been present throughout much of American history. With an emphasis on wilderness and wildlife conservation or recreation, a number of environmental organisations were formed in the late nineteenth and early twentieth centuries: the Appalachian Mountain Club in 1876, the Boon and Crockett Club in 1885, the Sierra Club in 1892, the Audubon Society in 1905, the Izaak Walton League in 1922, and the Wilderness Society in 1935 [Nash, 1967; Sale, 1993].

Resource management and nature protection were not, however, the only issues and strands of action that shaped the contemporary movement. The emphasis on industrialisation and urbanisation prior to the Second World War placed new pressures on the natural environment and on human health. As the population in the cities swelled, so too did environmental hazards. With industrial waste being dumped into waterways and open pits, no sewers or regular trash collection, emissions from both households and factories flowing freely into the air, public health issues such as water quality, sanitation, waste, and air pollution became pressing concerns. Since no workplace regulations had been put into effect, workers were exposed to an array of chemicals and heavy metals. Although action was fragmented and sporadic, as pollution and occupational concerns mounted, numerous individuals and groups attempted to promote legislation that would ensure human health and safety [Gottlieb, 1993].

After the Second World War, rising affluence heightened demand for consumer goods as well as contributed to additional pressures to preserve scenic and recreational areas [Andrews, 1999; Gottlieb, 1993; Hays, 1987]. Concerns about quality of life and the impact of technology on human health mounted. At the same time, the emergence of the science of ecology, popularisation of scientifically-based publications (for example, Rachel Carson's Silent Spring), enhanced communications systems, and environmentally destructive accidents (for example, Cuyahoga River catching on fire, the Santa Barbara oil spill) contributed to public awareness and concern about environmental issues. By the 1960s, environmental protest began to arise on college campuses, in local communities, and in the nation's capital. The emerging focus on environmental protection that arose in the late 1960s and early 1970s was accompanied by the formation of a new generation of professional environmental organisations. The Environmental Defence Fund, National Resource Defence Council, and Friends of the Earth were among the first to be formed. These organisations, more political than their recreation-oriented ancestors, addressed issues such as air and water pollution, nuclear power, and solid waste. This rise in professional organisations occurred during an era of heightened legislative activity initiated with President Nixon signing the National Environmental Protection Act in 1970 and followed by a series of new environmental policies.

Mitchell [1989] suggests that membership in professional environmental organisations has progressed through three waves. Between 1960 and 1969, membership in established organisations increased as Americans became aware of environmental problems and as these organisations became more aggressive about preservation and pollution. While interest was raised in the years preceding the first Earth Day in 1970, a second surge of activity followed. By the mid-1970s, membership levels waned and it was suggested that environmentalism had been a fad [*Mitchell, 1989; Mitchell, Mertig and Dunlap, 1991*]. Established environmental groups such as the Sierra Club and Audubon Society as well as some newer organisations such as the Environmental Defence Fund and National Resource Defence Council endured the down turn in membership but a number of smaller organisations disappeared. A third cycle was sparked in the 1980s by Reagan's anti-environmental activities which, fostering a renewed interest in the environment, helped organisations to recruit new members and once again assert a strong presence [*Mitchell, 1989; Mitchell, Mertig and Dunlap, 1991*].

As the environmental movement grew, organisations experienced increased pressures for formalisation and professionalisation. The complexity of legislation, increasing levels of organisational membership, and constraints from funders and the government forced many organisations to hire full-time staff members. It also became necessary for these organisations to maintain offices so that they could be reached by their constituents, comply with administrative requirements, and maintain a profile that was visible enough to gain them access to politicians and to the political process [*Mitchell, Mertig and Dunlap, 1991*]. The combination of these factors forced many environmental organisations to retain a cadre of professional staff who have clearly defined roles and follow formal management procedures. Staffed by lawyers, scientists, and professional environmentalists, these groups typically participate in election activities, lobbying, and litigation. Over time, a small group of national environmental organisations has come to dominate the lobbying landscape. While several have local chapters, most are centralised in Washington, DC where they work on policy reform and enforcement [*Cable and Cable, 1995*].

In addition to national organisations, a number of coalitions and committees have formed at different points in time to address regional, state, and local environmental issues. Activism frequently is initiated by residents of local communities. In contrast to professional environmentalists, members of local groups typically are directly affected by the issue they are addressing and they tend to concentrate on taking immediate steps to remedy a problem. Many local groups are formed with the intent of coping with a specific issue rather than shaping national policy or advancing an issue onto the national policy agenda [*Freudenberg and Steinsapir, 1992*].

Similar to professional environmental activity, local opposition or NIMBY behaviour has historical roots. In the nineteenth century, debate and conflict arose over issues such as the location of railroads, slaughter houses, hospitals, and saloons [*Meyer and Brown, 1989*]. Now, as then, it is the close proximity of a threat that causes people to react [*Benford, Moore and*

Williams, 1993; Lober, 1995; Walsh, 1981]. Although communities have long been concerned to prevent locally unwanted land uses and to preserve human and ecosystem health, the specific issues have changed over time. Waste sites, effluent from factories, and contamination from military bases are some of the issues now addressed. For many years, local protest was associated with affluent individuals who had the time and financial resources to spend dealing with community problems but local protest is not merely an upper-class phenomenon. The environmental justice and environmental equity movements have been organised around the premise that sitings are likely to occur in areas where poor and ethnic minority communities reside. Members of these communities have become increasingly resistant to undesired changes in land use and have become active in preventing sitings.

Legislation that mandates citizen participation in environmental decision-making and a general belief in the efficacy of democratic process typically establish the expectation that individuals can act and can effect a desired change either directly or through their elected representatives. In many instances, the realisation that the system is not open to input and that even a large number of local residents working to advance a cause may not result in action on their behalf by elected officials [*Anderson and Midttun 1985; Freudenberg and Steinsapir, 1992; Molotch, 1970*] may establish a path to activism that is distinct from the one traversed by career environmentalists affiliated with professional organisations. Threats to personal health, property, and quality of life as well as restricted access to the political process provide continual incentives for the creation of voluntary associations [*Edwards, 1995*]. In contrast to professional organisations which primarily rely on institutionally sanctioned forms of action, local groups are generally both willing and able to employ a wide range of tactics. Protest and confrontational actions designed to capture the attention of the media as well as public officials are frequently employed. Unconventional acts that attract attention are often combined with activities that have a direct impact on outcomes such as litigation, presentations at public hearings, and lobbying of elected officials. Local groups often are less willing to compromise than are professional organisations [*Cable and Cable, 1995*] since they are dealing with problems that directly affect individual health and community well-being.

The activities of grass-roots organisations have been associated with a number of beneficial outcomes. Local actions have contributed to cleaning contaminated sites, preventing polluting facilities from being built, forcing corporations to improve production processes, providing social support to affected individuals, influencing national attitudes toward the environment and public health, and enhancing right to know legislation and citizen participation [*Freudenberg and Steinsapir, 1992*]. Once established, community-based organisations can follow a number of different trajectories. Local groups generally rely on volunteers more interested in problem resolution and community stability than non-profit status or organisational survival. As a result, many local organisations cease to exist when the problem they are confronting is resolved or adequately addressed. Fearing that problems could reemerge, other groups decide that they should continue to monitor the progress of the issue around which they were formed. Having found a voice, some groups turn their collective attention to a broader range of community issues and still others build on what they have begun by engaging in national politics.

Research Methodology

When general trends in environmental mobilisation and environmental organisations are examined, it appears that professional organisations and voluntary associations address different types of environmental issues and rely on different types of tactics. In reality, the issues and actions of these groups may be interrelated and the combined activities of professionals and volunteers may have helped to sustain the environmental movement by ensuring that relevant issues are addressed and advanced through the policy process. Most research on environmental mobilisation focuses on professional organisations and on the movement as a homogeneous entity. As a result, the dynamics between voluntary and professional organisations have been given limited attention. Using a content analysis, this research examines trends in environmental mobilisation and investigates interdependencies between local voluntary and national professional movement organisations for the 16-year period 1975 to 1990.

The coding system developed by McAdam [*1982*] for content analysing newspaper articles about the civil rights movement was modified for the environmental movement. Social movements have been defined in numerous ways, but interaction, conflict, and identity are features of most definitions [*Diani, 1992*]. While collective action can occur as an isolated event, social movements engage in sustained action [*Tilly, 1984*] and seek an enduring change in some element of the social, political, or economic structure [*McCarthy and Zald, 1977*]. In this research, the environmental movement has been defined as activities that challenge existing or proposed practices or policies on the basis that they are environmentally unsound or that advocate activities and policies that will lower pollution, promote better environmental quality, and enhance sustainability. All environmental and conservation oriented abstracts in the *New York Times Index* from 1975 through 1990 were read.[1] Information on the actor or initiating unit, the problem being addressed, and the type of movement activity were recorded for each entry that could be associated with the environmental movement.[2]

Environmental *actor* refers to the agent responsible for executing or organising an environmentally oriented activity. Non-governmental actors that made efforts to improve environmental quality, prevent environmental degradation, promote new or more stringent environmental policies, and protect undeveloped areas were classified as members of the movement. Counter-movement activities and organisations, research and policy institutes that support existing institutional arrangements, and governmental agencies were not included as movement actors. For each actor included in the study, it was necessary to determine what type of affiliation was being maintained or what group was being represented. When examining patterns in the civil rights movement, Jenkins and Eckert [*1986*] developed a classification scheme for different types of groups. They distinguished between (1) individuals who are not affiliated with a formal movement group; (2) crowds; (3) local community organisations such as church and student groups; (4) local chapters of national groups; (5) groups that are formed *ad hoc*; (6) voluntary organisations focused on an issue (classical SMOs); and (7) professional SMOs [*Jenkins and Eckert, 1986: 817*]. In this study, these seven categories of affiliation were aggregated into two groups representing professional and voluntary actors. *Professional* actors comprise national social movement organisations that identify with the goals of the environmental movement, chapters of national organisations, and coalitions that involved national organisations. *Voluntary* actors comprise unaffiliated individuals, *ad hoc* committees, crowds, voluntary community associations. In general, professional organisations consisted of the major national environmental organisations and their affiliates while voluntary associations were independent local or grass-roots groups.

Environmental *action* refers to the strategy or tactic that an actor employs within the context of the movement. Actions were classified as either conventional or unconventional. Building on Garner's [*1977*] definitions and Kitschelt's [*1986*] classifications of tactics, actions were coded as *conventional* when they used established legal mechanisms to foster change. These actions included seminars and other types of information intensive educational efforts (excluding information dissemination on how to engage in non-institutionalised action), informative speeches or articles, litigation, and lobbying. *Unconventional* actions are those activities that are more dramatic and visible to the general population than institutional activities. Therefore, unconventional actions included riots, demonstrations, blockades, street theatre, and defacing property.

The use of newspapers and newspaper indices for analysing social movement activity has been criticised [e.g., *Rucht and Ohlemacher, 1992*]. In particular, there are two major problems associated with newspaper analysis that are relevant to this research. The first issue is content bias. News reports often express the personal sentiments and political position of the author. Since only factual information was recorded from each article, bias stemming from the style of reporting should not affect the quality of the data or the data analysis. A second consideration is whether the coverage is representative of the complete range of social movement activities for any given period. It is likely that there is both under and over-reporting of events depending on factors such as novelty [*Meyer, 1993*] or the degree of public interest in an issue [*Downs, 1972*]. While newspaper reporting has become an accepted means of data collection when studying macro-processes of social movements [e.g. *Gurr, 1970; Jenkins and Eckert, 1986; Jenkins and Perrow, 1977; McAdam, 1982; Meyer, 1993; Olzak, 1992; Kriesi et al., 1995*], conventional actions are less newsworthy than unconventional actions and therefore it is likely that they will be under-reported. Additionally, it is likely that the reporting of local actions will reflect the regional interests of the readership. Since it is likely that reporting trends will be relatively consistent over time, to accommodate the reporting issues noted this analysis focuses on expressive actions and uses percentages and ratios rather than absolute numbers.

Trends in Environmental Movement Actors and Actions

Environmental action arising from both professional and voluntary actors is consistently present throughout the 15-year period investigated. As shown in Figure 1, when all types of acts are combined, although there are obvious ebbs and flows in environmental action, both types of groups maintain a presence. Relative to professional organisations, voluntary groups appear to act in more pronounced surges. Local voluntary groups exhibit a general rise in action between 1976 and 1980. Actions then taper off, but there are clear peaks of activity in 1985, 1987, and 1989. There is also some evidence that the rise and fall of activity stemming from professional organisations follows the activity patterns of voluntary groups as suggested by the lagged correlations reported in Table 1. The correlations for total action indicate that a negative relationship is present in years zero through two. This relationship suggests that as voluntary action decreases, professional activity increases within a year or two of this decline. A significant positive relationship is present at year four. While this could be interpreted to mean that professional action decreases when voluntary action increases, the four year time span is sufficiently long that the correlation could be reflecting a new cycle of action and therefore is indeterminate.

FIGURE 1
ENVIRONMENTAL ACTION AND ENVIRONMENTAL POLICY

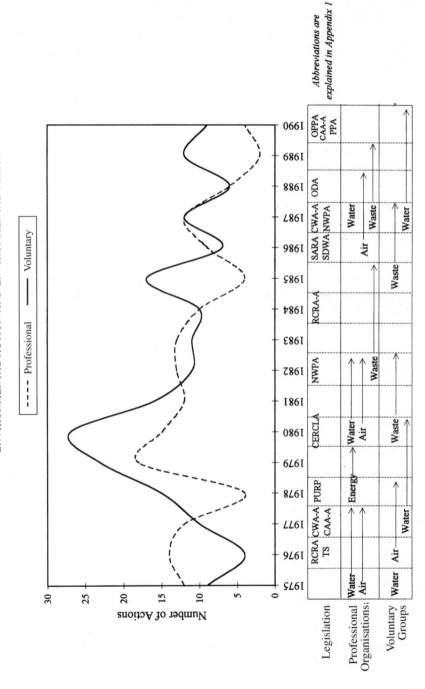

Abbreviations are explained in Appendix 1

TABLE 1

LAGGED CORRELATIONS BETWEEN PROFESSIONAL AND VOLUNTARY
ENVIRONMENTAL ACTIVISM

	#Years	Total Action	Unconventional Action
	4	-0.004	-0.237
	3	0.400	-0.046
	2	0.473	-0.200
Professional Precedes	1	0.077	-0.240
Voluntary			
	0	-0.121	0.880**
Professional Follows			
Voluntary	1	-0.200	-0.999*
	2	-0.149	-0.112
	3	0.247	-0.398
	4	0.590*	-0.180

*Significant at Alpha .05; **Significant at Alpha .0001

When unconventional action is examined in isolation, the ebbs and flows of environmental activity exhibited by voluntary and professional groups are more clearly delineated. As suggested by Figure 2, relative to total environmental action, activity by local voluntary groups has remained fairly stable while reported activity stemming from professional organisations has decreased. This change in the pattern of action reflects the differences in the types of activities that are employed by each of these organisations. On average, the news reports about professional organisations indicate that they engage in higher levels of conventional action (60 per cent) than voluntary groups (40 per cent). A higher volume of unconventional action is conducted by voluntary groups, but professional organisations consistently engage in protest and other types of noninstitutional behaviours.

The lagged correlations in Table 1 suggest that there is a significant relationship between unconventional and expressive activities staged by voluntary groups and the activities of professional organisations. The positive relationship present at year zero indicates that when the unconventional actions of voluntary groups increase, professional organisations also engage in unconventional acts. The significant relationship in year one provides further indication that the activities of professional organisations follow the patterns of action that have been exhibited by voluntary groups. The negative relationship between the activities of the two groups suggests that there is a lag in timing, with the unconventional actions of professional organisations increasing after the unconventional acts of voluntary associations begin to decline.

The highest level of reported action stemming from both professional

FIGURE 2

UNCONVENTIONAL ACTIONS OF PROFESSIONAL ORGANISATIONS AND VOLUNTARY GROUPS

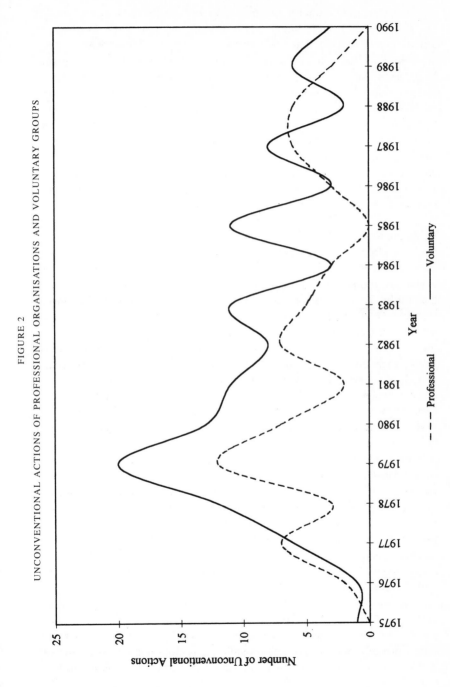

organisations and voluntary groups was in the late 1970s. This may reflect an increase in conventional action and an associated decline in environmental activity that was deemed newsworthy. While there has been an overall decline in the volume of action reported over the 15-year period being examined, it is clear that both types of groups have maintained a presence and have continued to employ a range of tactics. Although professional organisations employ unconventional behaviours, the lower proportion of this type of action is consistent with the social and legal environments in which they operate. The pattern of unconventional activity stemming from voluntary groups and the relationship between voluntary and professional action provides some indication that environmental movement activity may be stimulated and initiated by classical movement organisations such as community groups and grass-roots coalitions.

The aggregate data representing cycles of environmental action gives the impression that there is some coordination between local voluntary and national professional organisations. When actions are linked to issues, a more nuanced picture of the movement emerges, demonstrating both autonomy and integration of the two types of organisations. As suggested by Table 2, anti-nuclear activity is the most frequently reported environmental activity as well as that with the greatest relative volume of unconventional action. This is followed by action directed toward the safe disposal of solid waste and the protection of air and water quality. Professional organisations appear to have dedicated more energy toward the reduction of air and water pollution than volunteer associations. Waste disposal receives a similar amount of attention while voluntary groups focused more heavily on nuclear energy, particularly the siting of energy plants, than did their professional counterparts. An important distinction in issue orientation is wildlife preservation where almost all of the reported activity was initiated by professional organisations. All of the peaks in both professional and volunteer unconventional activity depicted in Figure 2 include heightened levels of protest against either nuclear energy plants or nuclear weapons. In addition to the anti-nuclear sentiments being expressed, the rise in professional action in 1982 reflects concerns about water protection while the increase in 1987 signifies heightened concern about water, air, and waste. The surges in voluntary activities are associated with action against air and water pollution in 1983, waste in 1985 and 1987, and both water and waste in 1989.

The substantive issues addressed by professional organisations and voluntary associations may be indicative of the types of change that each is seeking to achieve and the distinctive relationships that each has to the policy process. In general, professional organisations address issues that are national in scope (75 per cent) and voluntary associations focus on local

TABLE 2

ACTORS AND ACTIONS BY TYPE OF ENVIRONMENTAL ISSUED
ADDRESSED (%)

Issue	Total	Actor		Action	
	%	Professional	Voluntary	Conventional	Unconventional
Air Pollution	11	9	3	10	1
Energy	3	3	0.4	3	0.1
Nuclear Energy					
& Weapons	43	10	33	12	30
Pollution & Politics					
– General	8	5	2	7	0.5
Waste Disposal	17	8	9	10	6
Water Pollution	12	8	4	10	2
Wildlife Preservation	6	6	0.4	6	0.1
Total	100%	49%	52%	58%	39%

(Differences in totals are due to rounding)

level issues (67 per cent). Figure 1 positions the total actions of voluntary and professional organisations above a grid that represents the years that policies were enacted and the major issues that each of these organisations addressed during these time periods. As suggested by Figure 1, the issues being addressed by professional organisations loosely correspond to pending policy enactments. For example, professional organisations focused on air and water issues in the period leading up to the passage of Amendments to the Clean Air and the Clean Water Acts. Similarly, in 1982 there is a rise in national activity addressing waste. This corresponds to Amendments in both the Resource Conservation and Recovery Act and to Superfund. The heightened action in these periods may reflect the efforts that professional organisations make toward affecting public policy decisions. While they engage in conventional actions such as lobbying in order to promote these changes, the associated degree of unconventional action may be the way in which professional organisations sensitise the broader public to issues and enlist popular support for policy initiatives.

In contrast to professional organisations, many volunteer groups appear to be responding to sudden grievances or locally specific concerns. Local reaction to waste, for example, began to increase in 1980 and continued to be one of the main issues that communities addressed for several years. During 1981 alone, residents protested waste storage, fought to have contamination cleaned, petitioned against the siting of hazardous waste disposal and treatment plants, and worked with a university in conducting a survey to locate an unknown source of illness. These patterns of action suggest that while national professional organisations focus on affecting changes in national policy, local voluntary groups are seeking immediate action and attention to pending problems.

Voluntary and professional organisations have a different focus and scope, but the issues that they address are not completely distinct. In numerous instances there is evidence that voluntary action arising in response to emergent local issues attracts the interest of professional organisations. Recognition that the issue has national significance and the initiation of institutional efforts by one or more professional organisations may result in the issue being placed on the national agenda and advanced through the policy cycle. For example, in 1980 there is a peak in local activity that corresponds to waste disposal issues arising in communities. In the two years that follow there are ongoing community reactions to specific issues pertaining to waste. In 1982, professional organisations begin to address waste disposal. In 1984 the Resource Conservation and Recovery Act Amendments are signed into legislation and in 1986 the Superfund Amendments are enacted. Similarly, in 1985 local communities began reacting to waste that was washing up on the shores of the Atlantic Ocean. The actions of multiple communities were directed toward very specific incidents. By 1987, waste disposal returned to the agendas of some professional organisations. These actions intensified and culminated with the passage of the Ocean Dumping Act in 1988. While not every issue follows this pattern of interdependency, there is sufficient evidence to suggest that the overall action of both voluntary associations and professional organisations results in coordinated actions within the policy arena.

The Influence of Voluntary Associations and Professional Organisations

The data suggest that over the 15 years examined, the environmental movement consistently was advanced by the combined activities of voluntary associations and professional organisations. Because of their proximity and familiarity with community concerns, voluntary associations often became aware of salient local issues. As a result of their attention and efforts, these groups alert their local communities to important issues as well as sensitise the broader public to emerging problems. Professional organisations provide an ongoing presence for environmentalism. These organisations not only have the resources and capacity to endure, but also to advance issues of national concern through the policy cycle. By directing their efforts to shaping the policy agenda and to affecting policy outcomes, they foster legitimacy for the movement and promote long-term change.

The data suggest that the type of action employed by each of these

THE ENVIRONMENTAL MOVEMENT IN THE UNITED STATES   117

different types of groups is commensurate with the political environment in which they primarily participate. Since many local voluntary groups do not have access to local politicians or the legitimacy to get issues placed on local agenda, they tend to employ a broad range of tactics and frequently engage in unconventional forms of action to draw attention to issues. While professional organisations employ some unconventional tactics, they do so relatively less often than the voluntary groups. Attempting to change national policy requires interacting with elected representatives and participating in institutional procedures. Because many professional organisations have established their role as a legitimate voice for environmental causes, they can gain access to the political process. However, in order to retain non-profit status and legitimacy these organisations favour more institutionally accepted forms of behaviour.

Many of the actions initiated by the voluntary groups included in this study were a response to locally-based grievances. As previously noted, resource mobilisation theory maintains that critical events are not necessary for initiating mobilisation. The patterns of action revealed in this study suggest that sudden grievances and critical incidents often serve as catalysts for community action. An important outcome of local responses to grievances, particularly when expressive and unconventional tactics are employed, is that the general public as well as elected and appointed officials become sensitised to community concerns. A related effect is that professional movement organisations and foundations also become aware of emerging issues and the importance of working to resolve general classes of environmental problems.

In the United States, the major professional environmental movement organisations have been criticised for being out of touch with the environmental issues that affect their constituents [*Bullard, 1993; Gottlieb, 1993*]. The patterns revealed by these data provide only partial support for this observation. It appears that professional organisations address pending policy issues while local groups focus on pressing concerns within their communities. However, it also appears that a functional relationship exists between the different types of groups. Although community groups tend to focus on local issues, their actions do not occur in isolation from national politics. As the patterns revealed in this research suggest, local groups may create awareness of emerging issues. As the public becomes increasingly aware of these issues and as national groups get involved in fostering changes, discrete local concerns may ultimately lead to national policy enactments.

The patterns of action revealed in this study may be unique to the environmental movement and characteristic of the nature of environmental problems rather than indicative of trends in other movement sectors. Similar to other movements, a number of environmental issues are general in nature and cross local, state, and national boundaries. Many issues, however, are site specific and contribute to the unique qualities of the environmental movement. The location of landfills and incinerators, the presence of chemical waste, or the habitat of an endangered species are associated with particular parcels of land. The connection of environmental issues to specific locales fosters activity within local communities. At the same time, this continued emergence of local political involvement may moderate movement tendencies toward centralisation and professionalisation.

The resource mobilisation school maintains that professional movement organisations are the cornerstones of mobilisation in the US. Consistent with this thesis, professional environmental organisations appear to provide a foundation and offer stability to the movement. Although these organisations are critical to environmentalism, they do not appear to establish either the pace or the tone of the movement. The autonomy of local groups enables them to identify emerging issues and to respond using a variety of tactics. For local voluntary groups, organisational maintenance is generally less important than the resolution of the issue which prompted mobilisation. As new issues arise, these grass-roots associations respond and act as movement catalysts. Professional organisations have the capacity to work steadily to foster policy outcomes. It is this interaction between the more expressive local voluntary groups and the more conventional national professional organisations that makes it possible to identify emerging environmental issues and advance environmental policy in the political arena.

NOTES

1. The entries read were listed under the headings: Air Pollution, Animals, Atomic Energy and Weapons, Birds, Chemistry and Chemicals, Coastal Erosion, Defoliants, Energy, Environment, Fish, Forests, Herbicides, Nature, Oceans, Parks, Pesticides, Pollution, US-Environmental Problems, Waste Materials, Water Pollution, Wetlands, Whales and Whaling, Wilderness Areas, Wildlife, and Wildlife Sanctuaries. Although coding was completed for both conservation and environmentalism, the findings reported here are limited to environmentalism.
2. A pilot study was conducted in order to determine the reliability of the coding instrument and the validity of the content categories. Four raters coded five to seven page segments of the 1970 *Index* which were assigned by the primary researcher. Agreement on the initiating unit, the nature of the event, the issue, and the scope of activity was 89 per cent, 82 per cent, 86 per cent, and 93 per cent respectively. Although there was a high level of agreement, the differences that emerged between raters were discussed to further improve the coding procedures. The differences could be attributed to unfamiliarity with the environmental movement, problems of clarity in the coding terminology, or the presence of a situation for which no category was delimited. The instrument was revised based on the pre-test findings.

REFERENCES

Andrews, Richard N. L. (1999), *Managing the Environment, Managing Ourselves*. New Haven, CT: Yale University Press.

Anderson, Svein S. and Atle Midttun (1985), 'Conflict and Local Mobilization: The Alta Hydropower Project', *Acta Sociologica*, Vol.28, No.4, pp.317–35.

Benford, Robert D., Moore, Helen A. and J. Allen Williams, Jr. (1993), 'In Whose Backyard?: Concern About Siting a Nuclear Waste Facility', *Sociological Inquiry*, Vol.63, No.1, pp.30–48.

Bullard, Robert D. (1993), *Confronting Environmental Racism: Voices From the Grassroots*, Boston, MA: South End Press.

Cable, Sherry and Charles Cable (1995), *Environmental Problems Grassroots Solutions: The Politics of Grassroots Environmental Conflict*, New York: St. Martin's Press.

Diani, Mario (1992), 'The Concept of Social Movement', *The Sociological Review*, Vol.40, No.1, pp.1–25.

Downs, Anthony (1972), 'Up and Down with Ecology: The "Issue Attention Cycle"', *Public Interest*, Vol.28, pp.38–50.

Edwards, Bob (1995), 'With Liberty and Justice For All: The Emergence and Challenge of Grassroots Environmentalism in the United States', in B.R. Taylor (ed.), *Ecological Resistance Movements: The Global Emergence of Radical and Popular Environmentalism*, Albany, NY: State University of New York Press.

Freudenberg, Nicholas and Carol Steinsapir (1992), 'Not in Our Backyards: The Grassroots Environmental Movement', in R.G. Dunlap and A.G. Mertig (eds.), *American Environmentalism: The U.S. Environmental Movement, 1970-1990*, Philadelphia, PA: Taylor & Francis.

Garner, Roberta A. (1977), *Social Movements in America*, Homewood, IL: The Dorsey Press.

Gottlieb, Robert (1993*), Forcing the Spring: The Transformation of the American Environmental Movement*, Washington, DC: Island Press.

Gurr, Ted R. (1970), *Why Men Rebel*, Princeton, NJ: Princeton University Press.

Hays, Samuel P. (1987), *Beauty, Health, and Permanence: Environmental Politics in the United States 1955-1985*, Cambridge: Cambridge University Press.

Jenkins, J. Craig and Craig M. Eckert (1986), 'Channelling Black Insurgency: Elite Patronage and Professional Social Movement Organisations in the Development of the Black Movement', *American Sociological Review*, Vol.51, No.6, pp.812–29.

Jenkins, J. Craig and Charles Perrow (1977, 'Insurgency of the Powerless: Farm Workers Movements (1946–1972)', *American Sociological Review*, Vol.42, pp.249–68.

Kitschelt, Herbert P. (1986), 'Political Opportunity Structure and Political Protest: Anti-Nuclear Movement in Four Democracies', *British Journal of Political Science*, Vol.16, No.1, pp.57–85.

Kornhauser, William (1959), *The Politics of Mass Society*, Glencoe, IL: Free Press.

Kriesi, Hanspeter (1996), 'The Organizational Structure of New Social Movements in a Political Context', in McAdam, McCarthy and Zald (eds.) [*1996: 152–84*].

Kriesi, Hanspeter, Koopmans, Ruud, Duyvendak, Jan Willem and Marco G. Giugni (1995), *New Social Movement in Western Europe: A Comparative Analysis*, Minneapolis, MN: University of Minnesota Press.

Lichterman, Paul (1996), *The Search for Political Community: American Activists Reinventing Commitment*. New York: Cambridge University Press.

Lo, Clarence Y.H. (1992), 'Communities of Challengers in Social Movement Theory', in Morris and Mueller [*1992: 224–48*].

Lober, Douglas J. (1995), 'Why Protest?: Public Behavioral and Attitudinal Response to Siting a Waste Disposal Facility', *Policy Studies Journal*, Vol.23, No.3, pp.499–518.

McAdam, Doug (1982), *Political Process and the Development of Black Insurgency, 1930–1970*, Chicago, IL: University of Chicago Press.

McAdam, D., McCarthy, J.D. and M.N. Zald (eds.) (1996), *Comparative Perspectives on Social Movements: Political Opportunities, Mobilizing Structures, and Cultural Framings*, New York: Cambridge University Press.

McCarthy, John D. (1996), 'Constraints and Opportunities in Adopting, Adapting, and Inventing', in McAdam, McCarthy and Zald (eds.) [1996: 141–51].

McCarthy, John D. and Mayer N. Zald (1977), 'Resource Mobilisation and Social Movements: A Partial Theory', American Journal of Sociology, Vol.82, No.6, pp.1212–41.

McCarthy, John D., Britt, David W. and Mark Wolfson (1991), 'The Institutional Channelling of Social Movements in the Modern State', Research in Social Movements, Conflicts and Change, Vol.13, pp.45–76.

Meyer, David S. (1993), 'Institutionalizing Dissent: The United States Structure of Political Opposition and the End of the Nuclear Freeze Movement', Sociological Forum, Vol.8, No.2, pp. 157–79.

Meyer, William B. and Michael Brown (1989), 'Locational Conflict in a Nineteenth-Century City', Political Geography Quarterly, Vol.8, No.2, pp.107–22.

Mitchell, Robert C. (1989), 'From Conservation to Environmental Movement: The Development of Modern Environmental Lobbies', in M.J. Lacey (ed.), Government and Environmental Politics: Essays on Historical Developments Since World War Two, Washington, DC: Wilson Center Press, pp.81–113,

Mitchell, Robert C., Mertig, Angela G. and Riley E. Dunlap (1991), 'Twenty Years of Environmental Mobilisation: Trends Among National Environmental Organisations', Society and Natural Resources, Vol.4, pp.219–34.

Molotch, Harvey (1970), 'Oil in Santa Barbara and Power in America', Sociological Inquiry, Vol.40, Winter, pp.131–44.

Morris, A.D. and C.M. Mueller (eds.) (1992), Frontiers in Social Movement Theory, New Haven, CT: Yale University Press.

Nash, Roderick (1967), Wilderness and the American Mind, New Haven, CT: Yale University Press.

Olzak, Susan (1992), The Dynamics of Ethnic Competition and Conflict, Stanford, CA: Stanford University Press.

Rucht, Dieter (1996), 'The Impact of National Contexts on Social Movement Structures: A Cross-Movement and Cross-National Comparison', in McAdam, McCarthy and Zald (eds.) [1996: 185–204].

Rucht, Dieter and Thomas Ohlemacher (1992), 'Protest Event Data: Collection, Uses, and Perspectives', in M. Diani and J. Eyerman (eds.), Studying Collective Action, Newbury Park, CA: Sage Publications, pp.76–106.

Sale, Kirkpatrick (1993), The Green Revolution: The American Environmental Movement 1962–1992, New York: Hill & Wang.

Schwartz, Michael and Shuva Paul (1992), 'Resource Mobilization versus the Mobilization of People: Why Consensus Movements Cannot be Instruments of Social Change', in Morris and Mueller [1992: 205–23].

Staggenborg, Suzanne (1988), 'The Consequences of Professionalization and Formalization in the Pro-Choice Movement', American Sociological Review, Vol.53, No.4, pp.585–606.

Szasz, Andrew (1994), EcoPopulism: Toxic Waste and the Movement for Environmental Justice, Minneapolis, MN: University of Minnesota Press.

Tilly, Charles (1984), 'Social Movements and National Politics', in C. Bright and S. Harding (eds.), Statemaking and Social Movements: Essays in History and Theory, Ann Arbor, MI: University of Michigan Press, pp.297–317.

Vig, Norman J. and Michael E. Kraft (1994), Environmental Policy in the 1990's: Toward a New Agenda, Washington, DC: CQ Press.

Walsh, Edward J. (1981), 'Resource Mobilization and Citizen Protest in Communities Around Three Mile Island', Social Problems, Vol.29, No.1, pp.1–21.

Walsh, Edward J., Warland, Rex and D. Clayton Smith (1993), 'Backyards, NIMBY's, and Incinerator Sitings: Implications for Social Movement Theory', Social Problems, Vol.40, No.1, pp.25–38.

APPENDIX 1

ABBREVIATIONS AND ENVIRONMENTAL LEGISLATION

Adapted from Vig and Kraft [*1994: Appendix 1*]

Abbreviation	Legislation	Main Provisions
CAA-A	Clean Air Act Amendments of 1977	Postponed compliance deadlines for auto emission and air quality standards.
CAA-A	Clean Air Act Amendments of 1990	New requirements, deadlines, and standards for clean air standards.
CERCLA	Comprehensive Environmental Response, Compensation, and Liability Act of 1980 (Superfund)	Authorized the federal government to respond to to hazardous waste and to clean emergencies chemical waste sites.
CWA-A	Clean Water Act Amendments of 1977	Extended water treatment deadlines and set national standards for waste pretreatment.
CWA-A	Clean Water Act Amendments of 1987	Extended water pollution control programs, established national estuary program.
NWPA	Nuclear Waste Policy Act of 1982	Established national plan for disposal of high-evel nuclear waste.
NWPA-A	Nuclear Waste Policy Act Amendments of 1987	Specified Yucca Mountain as study site
ODA	Ocean Dumping Act of 1988	Amendments to end dumping of sewage sludge and industrial waste in the oceans by 1991, established dumping fees, permit requirements, and penalties.
OPPA	Oil Pollution Prevention, Response, Liability, and Compensation Act of 1990	Increased fees for oil spill clean-up costs, required double hulls, government direct clean-ups, and contingency planning.
PPA	Pollution Prevention Act of 1990	Established office of pollution prevention.
PURP	Public Utility Regulatory Policies Act of 1978	Regulation of electric and natural gas utilities and crude oil transport to conserve energy.
RCRA	Resource Conservation and Recovery Act of 1976	Hazardous waste treatment, storage, transport and disposal
RCRA-A	Resource Conservation and Recovery Act Amendments of 1984	Revised and strengthened EPA waste facility regulation procedures.
SARA	Superfund Amendments and Reauthorization Act of 1986	Funding to clean most dangerous chemical waste dumps.
SDWA	Safe Drinking Water Act of 1986	Reauthorised Safe Drinking Water Act of 1974; revised EPA drinking water programs.
TS	Toxic Substances Control Act of 1976	Advance market testing, allowed EPA bans, and prohibited most uses of PCB's.

Networks and Mobile Arrangements: Organisational Innovation in the US Environmental Justice Movement

DAVID SCHLOSBERG

This study examines and evaluates the political practice of networking in the US environmental justice movement. Networking is a strategy that has evolved in opposition to perceived problems with centralised organisations, and out of the inherent diversity of the movement. This form of organising not only proposes a remedy to the limitations of the conventional model, but is also more able to confront changes in the nature of power, capital, and the political oversight of environmental problems. The study concludes with an examination of some of problems that might hamper a networked movement.

Over the last decade or so in the US, many grass-roots environmental groups have become increasingly alienated from the major environmental groups and the mainstream environmental lobby.[1] Criticisms have increased of a number of aspects of the major organisations, both in their everyday actions and their organisational form. There has been anger at the lacklustre and ineffective campaigns of the mainstream, disappointment at the lack of attention to the diversity of the grassroots, distrust of the professional atmosphere of organisations, frustration with control by the major funding organisations rather than memberships, and criticism of the centralised, hierarchical, professionalised organisations that are not accountable to memberships or local communities.[2]

In addition, and more specifically, the environmental justice community has been critical of the larger organisations for what they claim is their disregard of the wide variety of environmental hazards faced by people of colour, a paternalistic attitude toward low income and minority communities and grass-roots groups, and the lack of attention to diversity in the memberships, staffs, and boards of the Big Ten groups.[3]

Increasingly, grass-roots environmental movements have developed an entirely different *form* of organising. The environmental justice community, for example, has responded by organising a movement in a manner quite distinct from the Big Ten – in its model, its structure, and its tactics. Rather than constructing large Washington-based organisations, this movement has been networking and making connections, creating solidarity out of an understanding and a respect for both similarities and differences, and working from a variety of places with a wide array of tactics.

It has become popular to talk about networks in social movements generally and the environmental justice movement specifically. Indeed Diani argues [*1995: xiii*] that it has become the rule rather than the exception to talk about social movements as networks in recent years.[4] This trend began, one could argue, with the seminal work of Gerlach and Hines [*1970*] on the loose, dispersed networks of social movements in the 1960s. More recently, Bullard describes the environmental justice movement as a network of civil rights, social justice, and environmental groups.

My purpose here is twofold. First, I examine the *processes* that make up the network that is the environmental justice movement. What does it mean, and what does it look like, to be a social movement that is structured as a network? Secondly, I examine these structures as an *alternative* to the model used by the larger, major US environmental groups, which are structured more like the interest groups of conventional pluralist thinking and design. The argument here is that the environmental justice movement has recognised the limitations of past models of organising and eschews that conventional form and strategy.

I begin by exploring the value of difference in the movement, as the base of the newly developed network structures and processes lies in an acknowledgment of plurality, varied experiences, and diverse understandings of environmental problems. I continue by examining the bases of the environmental justice movement in a number of pre-existing social and political networks. I then turn to how networks link issues and establish alliances among diverse groups, and how networks form in order to deal with environmental issues of varying dimensions. I will also examine some of the reasons why this form of organising is a tactical strength, as it mirrors and maps itself onto the changing nature of the structures and practices of capital and politics. Finally, in an initial attempt to evaluate the network form, I examine some of the difficulties in, and criticisms of, networking as a social movement strategy.

The Value of Plurality
From William James's [*1976* [*1912*]] understanding of radical empiricism to Donna Haraway's [*1988*] situated knowledges, a variety of theorists have insisted on acknowledging that diverse understandings are bred by varied experience. Such an acknowledgment, however, has had trouble making the crossover from theory to political action; numerous examiners of past social movements and attempts at democratic process have pointed this out.[5] But

environmental justice takes difference seriously, and the recognition of diversity is really at the center of the movement.

While Capek [*1993*] writes of a singular Environmental Justice 'frame', she acknowledges that many environmental justice groups and networks incorporate ideas and themes outside of the frame she defines. This inability to completely frame the movement is crucial. In the various organisations and networks that make up the environmental justice movement, there is no insistence on one singular point of view, one policy that will solve all problems, or one tactic to be used in all battles. There is no one 'environmental justice,' 'minority', or 'grassroots' view of the environment. One study of social and environmental justice organisations found varied motivations for organising and a basic belief in the heterogeneous nature of the movement [*ECO, 1992: 35, 39*]. While there are obvious themes repeated throughout the movement – health, equity, subjugation, and the inattention of governmental agencies and representatives, for example – the particular experiences of these issues, and the formulation of understandings and responses, differ according to place. Rather than one particular frame, there is a coexistence of multiple beliefs as to the causes, situation of, and possible solutions for issues of environmental justice. The movement is constructed from differences such as these, and revels in that fact.

The environmental justice movement has an understanding of perspective and culture as grounded in the experiences of individuals and their communities. Knowledge is seen as situated, and hence the diversity of perspectives that emerge are seen as points of view located solidly in a particular place. The challenge of the movement is to validate this diversity in order to bring it into a network and add to its strength. As Barbara Deutsch Lynch argues:

> If environmental discourses are culturally grounded, they will differ in content along class and ethnic lines. Where power in society is unequally distributed, not all environmental discourses will be heard equally. Thus, questions of environmental justice must address not only the effects of particular land uses or environmental policies on diverse groups in society, but the likelihood that alternative environmental discourses will be heard and valued [*1993: 110*].

Environmental justice requires an understanding of the existence and importance of multiple perspectives and the validation of that variety. The cultural pluralism that forms the base of the movement, once recognised, opens opportunities for collaboration and the innovation of common action.

The processes that were present in the First National People of Color Environmental Leadership Summit of October 1991 serve as an example of the importance placed on plurality. Resisting a political process that many saw as built on keeping people of color divided, participants emphasized that all those coming to the table would be respected, that there would be equity in participation across race, ethnicity, gender, and region. Numerous participants noted the openness to difference, the listening to others, the mutual respect, solidarity, and trust that were both expressed and affirmed at the conference (see, for example, Grossman [*1994*]; Lee [*1992*]; Miller [*1993*]). Organisers worked to make the experience, at its base, inclusive.

Participants affirmed that difference and plurality, forged with mutual respect into solidarity, add a strength to the movement. There were differences around race, gender, age, culture, and the urban/rural split, among others.[6] Dana Alston argued that the Summit brought a spirit of solidarity, and that the most important thing was the bonding that occurred across the differences [*Di Chiro, 1992: 104*]. Lee notes that the openness and inclusivity of the process showed that 'difference can be cooperative instead of competitive, that diversity can lead to higher harmony rather than deeper hostility' [*Lee, 1992: 52*]. What appeared through a respect for the many different stories, perspectives, and cultures, were some common themes. Difference was forged into unity, but a unity that kept diversity, rather than uniformity, at its base. Participants entered diverse; they left both diverse and unified.

The point here is that diversity is more than a slogan for environmental justice. There is attention paid to the many different experiences people have in their environments, the cultures that inform those experiences, and the various evaluations and reactions that emerge from them. Recognising and validating these differences is at the heart of environmental justice.

The Social Bases of Networks

The networks that make up the environmental justice movement differ from the organising of the Big Ten from the very base, and one of the key differences between the major organisations and grass-roots networks is where participants actually come from. Big Ten groups grew tremendously in the 1980s, and have become increasingly dependent on recruiting people from mailing lists – people who have no previous connections to the groups, but share basic interests. Conversely, local environmental justice and anti-toxics groups most often begin with people as real members of community social networks.

Solidarity originates in community relationships – pre-existing social networks around where people live, work, play, and worship. A number of sociologists [e.g. *Fischer, 1977: Wellman, Carrington and Hall, 1988*] have written about the importance of social and civic networks in creating community, and social movement theorists have picked up on the relationship between these networks and social action. As Tarrow [*1994: 6*] has argued, the magnitude and duration of much collective action 'depend[s] on mobilizing people through social networks and around identifiable symbols that are drawn from cultural frames of meaning'. Organisation emerges out of shared experiences and existing social networks around family, neighbourhood, school, work, religion, and racial and ethnic identity.[7]

Pre-existing relations and social networks have been crucial in the organisation of the environmental justice movement. Churches have played a major role: the United Church of Christ's Commission for Racial Justice did the first major study of the relationship between toxic wastes and race [*United Church of Christ, 1987*] and was the major organiser of the First National People of Color Environmental Leadership Summit. The United Methodist Church's Department of Environmental Justice and Survival and the National Council of Church's Eco-Justice Working Group have also helped to bring religious networks into the development of the movement. Other pre-existing social networks, such as established social justice organisations, community organising centres, and historically black colleges, have added to the movement.

Two illustrations should suffice here. In the Southwest, the establishment of the Southwest Network for Environmental and Economic Justice (SNEEJ), came out of an original meeting and 'dialogue' that built on a decade of previous organising of groups working in issues such as police repression, immigration, food and nutrition, health care, campus issues, land and water rights, and worker/community issues of plant sitings [*Moore and Head, 1994, 192*]. One member group of SNEEJ, the Mothers of East Los Angeles (MELA), is a closely knit group of Mexican American women who organised in opposition to the siting of a prison, oil pipeline, and toxic waste incinerator in their neighbourhood [*Pardo, 1990*]. The mothers already had some contact with one another through traditional roles as the caretakers of the health and schooling of their children, and it was through these networks that they disseminated information about the numerous unfortunate plans for the neighbourhood. They also used the common experience of the church: weekly Monday marches would be organised through Sunday contacts [*Schwab, 1994: 56*].[8]

The point here, and one that distinguishes the environmental justice movement from the major groups in the US, is that people become involved not through mailing lists, but from the variety of systems of pre-existing support.

> People get to build support, friendship, camaraderie, goodwill, and fellowship with people they already know. If they have to form a

coalition with others, it is not one person going cold turkey to deal with a group of unfamiliar people; it is a group of people who have already established some relationships with others whose interests might be similar, interfacing with another group [*Taylor, 1992: 43*].

At the base of networks are not simply shared interests, but more broadly shared experiences. Their origins demonstrate a politics of relations rather than a politics of isolated bodies of interest.

Linking Issues, Creating Networks

The environmental justice movement expands the notion of environment by defining it not just as external nature or the 'big outside', but as the places that people live, work, and play. Environment is community [*Di Chiro, 1995*]. The movement address 'environmental' issues as they relate to a broader agenda which includes employment, education, housing, health care, the workplace, and other issues of social, racial, and economic justice [*Austin and Schill, 1991*]. As Pulido has argued [*1996: 192–3*] environmental justice struggles are not strictly environmental. Instead, they challenge multiple lines of domination, and 'it is difficult to discern where the environmental part of the struggle begins and where it ends.' This linkage of issues is evident in surveys [*ECO, 1992: 35*], and in much of the literature of the movement itself [e.g., *Alston, 1990: 13; Cole, 1992: 641; Lee, 1993: 50; Moore and Head, 1993: 118*]. Richard Moore of SNEEJ argues, 'we see the interconnectedness between environmental issues and economic justice issues' (Moore quoted in Almeida [*1994: 22*]. Lois Gibbs, of the Citizens Clearinghouse for Hazardous Waste (CCHW),[9] notes that 'environmental justice is broader than just preserving the environment. When we fight for environmental justice we fight for our homes and families and struggle to end economic, social and political domination by the strong and greedy' [*CCHW, 1990: 2*].

This understanding of an environmentalism with diverse issues and an assertion of linkage calls for a broader movement – one that must necessarily forge a solidarity among a range of groups and movements. This type of networking across issues and groups is a key defining characteristic, and organising strategy, of the growing environmental justice movement. Examples of these issue linkages, and the concomitant networking, are numerous. Individual member organisations of SNEEJ often deal with the interrelationship of issues of race, class, and gender. Activists battling computer chip plants often have to deal not only with issues of contamination, but also with the politics of public subsidies of private corporations. Organisers working on health problems of strawberry pickers in California are inevitably brought into the contested terrain of immigration law.

While individual groups begin by working on specific issues, they often come to see not only the theoretical links between diverse problems, but usually begin to take on some of the other issues that affect them. As Peggy Newman, a past field organiser for CCHW, explains, '[i]nstead of seeing differences in our work for environmental justice and homelessness, health advocacy, worker rights, immigrant rights, community economic development, gay and lesbian rights, we must look for the common ground among the issues and be willing to assist in each others' efforts and coordinate our work' [Newman, 1994: 94]. Some see the linking of issues in the movement as a unifying phenomenon [Hofrichter, 1993: 89].

But it is important here to note that this type of unity does not emphasise uniformity. Networks and alliances in the environmental justice movement depend as much on their differences and autonomy as they do on unity. In the formation of networks of solidarity, this is an important notion: that there is not necessarily one single unifying commonality, a single glue or mortar. Instead, a network holds itself together along the common edges of its pieces – where there is similarity or solidarity. The resulting mosaic itself – the movement – becomes the major commonality. Within a network, there remains both multiplicity and commonality.

Some networks or alliances are very conscious of this issue. Groups that share environmental concerns may still have radical differences. Yet the commonality of environmental experience serves as the mortar, even when there are differences in culture, style, ideology, or tactics. Respect for differences goes hand in hand with the building of an alliance.[10] SNEEJ, for example, is constantly working to keep Asian and African-American, Latino and Native American, urban and rural, and other differences, part of the network. When the women of South Central Los Angeles were battling a city-proposed incinerator, they were joined by white, middle-class women from two slow-growth groups across the city. Hamilton notes that '[t]hese two groups of women, together, have created something previously unknown to the City of Los Angeles – unity of purpose across neighborhood and racial lines' [Hamilton, 1990: 11]. Part of the crucial task of building networks is developing co-operation across numerous gaps – geographic, cultural, gender, social, ideological – and numerous organisations have come to see part of their task as the building of bridges between diverse communities and organisations [Anthony and Cole, 1990: 16; Schwab, 1994: 415; Williams, 1993]. The resulting alliances and networks span diverse issues, individuals, and groups, connecting them while continuing to recognize the numerous foundations those bridges are based on.

Rhizomes, Locality and the Breadth of Networks

Networks, in addition, have grown beyond the bounds of these examples of working together solely on the local level. Environmental problems do not limit themselves to the imposed boundaries of neighbourhood, city, state, or nation. Neither nature on its own, nor the environmental problems we construct through our interaction with it, confine themselves to a single level. Networks have developed along a number of lines that environmental problems and issues spread.

The metaphor of the rhizome is useful here. Rhizomes are a type of root system that does not send up just one sprout or stalk; rather, they spread underground and emerge in a variety of locations. Rhizomes connect in a way that is not visible – they cross borders and reappear in distant places without necessarily showing themselves in between.[11] The rhizome metaphor may be helpful in discussing situations that may be localised, but still shared by people in different places. Rhizomatic organising is based in making the connections – recognising patterns across both distance and difference. The conditions outside an oil refinery, municipal incinerator, or silicon chip manufacturer will be similar no matter where they are located, and so those communities will share environmental problems. Networks, then, may be built not only by people and organisations with differences coalescing around a particular local or regional problem, but also as people in distant areas respond to similar circumstances – toxic waste sites, types of manufacturing, particular toxins, shared health problems.

Local groups in the growing anti-toxics and environmental justice movement rarely remain isolated and unconnected. What makes environmental justice a *movement* are the linkages formed beyond the local. Most groups make links to other groups in their own locale, but, increasingly, groups make contact with outside organisations and existing networks which can provide resources, information, and solidarity. This 'translocality', as Di Chiro [*1997*] calls it, brings together groups and communities that would not otherwise have identified or developed a sense of commonality.

The first key large-scale network to develop came directly out of Love Canal and the Love Canal Homeowners Association (LCHA). Lois Gibbs and the LCHA were inundated with requests for information as the story of Love Canal and their fight with the local, state, and federal governments spread [*Gibbs, 1982*]. Gibbs and other volunteers began the Citizen's Clearinghouse for Hazardous Waste (CCHW) with the idea of helping other communities organise for environmental justice. By 1993, they had reported assisting over 8,000 groups [*CCHW, 1993: 3*].

Networking at the CCHW happens in a number of ways. As a resource centre, the CCHW funnels information about key toxics, issues, industries, and companies to communities who are faced with these particular environmental problems. Communities share their experiences with the CCHW, enriching the resource base for other communities. The CCHW also distributes information about specific problems and issues in organising, such as fundraising, research, leadership, running meetings, legal issues, and the problems faced by women as they become increasingly involved in a political battle. They also send organisers to work with citizen groups on environmental and organisational issues. The organisation sponsors regional Leadership Development Conferences, where local leaders from various communities come together to share knowledge, experiences, and tactics. And CCHW holds a national gathering every year, which in addition to enabling networking, gives people the sense that their local battle is part of a larger, diverse movement.

In addition, the CCHW helps to bring individuals and communities together in a number of ways. Often, individuals or groups that call with a specific issue are put directly in touch with nearby groups that have had similar experiences. One of the unwritten rules of the CCHW is that if you get help, you are also expected to give it to others [*CCHW, 1989: 1*]. A local group that has been victorious, keeping a facility out of their community, will be encouraged to follow the story and see where a company is likely to try again. They then contact grassroots groups in these communities, warning them of the impending issue and offering assistance in organising.

The CCHW also focuses on the space between the local and the national, with an emphasis on 'larger than locals'. As local grassroots groups continually spring up, they need someone or group to turn to. The national group is there, but they cannot be continually everywhere and all-knowing. The larger than locals occupy the middle space. They are often state-wide organizations who know specific state laws and related battles, and are more accessible for help on a daily basis [*S. Lynch, 1993: 48–9*]. Larger than locals may develop and stay focused around specific issues, offering networking and assistance to groups dealing with these issues. Or they may expand either on the issues they deal with or on the tactics used.

One of the other most well-organised environmental justice organisations is the Southwest Network for Environmental and Economic Justice (SNEEJ). After its beginning in a dialogue of Latino, Asian American, African American, and Native American activists from over thirty community organisations in Oklahoma, Texas, New Mexico, Colorado, Arizona, Utah, Nevada, and California, the Network has become involved in campaigns around environmental justice in the EPA, the impact of high-tech industries on communities, justice on the US–Mexico border, sovereignty and toxic dumping on Native lands, and farmworker pesticide exposure. SNEEJ focuses on the importance of linkages, and has used networking to make a variety of connections.

Member groups of SNEEJ include those involved in struggles in both urban and rural communities, such as those fighting contamination from oil refineries in Richmond, CA, and those who live near the waste site in Kettleman City, CA, where toxic materials from the refinery are dumped. SNEEJ also has developed a network of communities that have dealt specifically with issues raised by the location of particular industries, such as the microelectronics industry. SNEEJ expanded this work in developing, with the Campaign for Responsible Technology (CRT), the Electronics Industry Good Neighbor Campaign (EIGNC). In its origins it tied together communities in Albuquerque, Austin, Phoenix, and San Jose; it has expanded to include groups in Portland and Eugene, Oregon, as well as groups across the border in Mexico.

The growing concern with networking and alliances, and the development of a rhizomatic movement, works against the NIMBY misnomer and the claim that local protests against environmental problems and undesirable land use comes from an 'enclave consciousness'. Plotkin [*1990: 226, 229*] argues that 'the place-bound confines of neighborhood constituted the relevant "environment" of community land-use protest ... Clearly the end result of the enclave consciousness is a policy of "beggar thy neighbor" as community groups regularly seek to export or exclude the perceived "bads" of urban life while fencing in the goods.' The only aims of these groups, he argues, are to avoid domination and be left alone [*1990: 227*]. But the development of networks and alliances expands the understanding of community and locality. Numerous neighbourhoods need protection, and the way to get that is not to be left alone, but to develop solidarity with others facing the same dangers in their neighborhoods. Activists celebrate the grass-roots links forged with other communities. As they argue, environmental justice is not about NIMBY, but rather the critical invention of new forms of coalition politics [*Avila, 1992*].

The anti-toxics movement may have begun isolated, with communities fighting companies and local governments on their own. But after Love Canal, hundreds of citizen groups began to form, and they reached out to others. The EPA's own study on public opposition to the siting of hazardous waste facilities [*US EPA, 1979*], notes that siting opposition before 1978 was done almost exclusively by groups on their own, while after 1978 more than half of the groups began to network in some way. Just as Love Canal became a focal point in 1978, resistance to PCB dumping in the majority African-American Warren County, North Carolina in 1982 became a focal point for further organising around environmental racism and environmental justice. Community groups are no longer isolated; far from

NIMBY and enclave consciousness, connections are being made with an understanding that the concern is with 'Everyone's Backyard'.[12]

Network as Organisational Structure

The concept and practice of networks applies not only to pre-existing structures that evolve into political organisations, or the formation of groups around interrelated issues in various localities, but also to the very organisational structure of many of these groups. Previous ties in the neighbourhood, such as those that aided in the development of MELA, or previous social justice networks, which came together to form SNEEJ, become the basis of more formal organisation. But these networked organisations are quite distinct from a centralised, hierarchical, formal social movement organisation – what Zald and McCarthy [*1987: 20*] call an 'SMO'.

In fact, it is a critique of the SMOs, or major environmental organisations, that has driven the environmental justice movement to a more decentralised structure. The top-down, centralised managerial style and structure of the major groups has been criticised as disempowering, paternalistic, and exclusive. Organisers of the environmental justice movement have been conscious of the need to keep ownership of the movement in the hands of everyday participants, rather than in centralised organisations.[13] The key for organisers has been to create organisational models that are sufficient for networking purposes and strong enough to confront issues, but yet are both flexible and diverse enough to respond to changing circumstances at the local level.

Documents and discussions within the movement repeatedly stress the importance of decentralisation, diversification, and democratisation, as opposed to the centralised organisation with a singular leadership. When activists gathered for the regional dialogue that led to the development of SNEEJ, there were some that wanted a national organisation – but most argued for the importance of developing the network at the grassroots and regional levels [*Almeida, 1994: 30*]. The CCHW has also eschewed centralisation, arguing that 'it is empowered communities and local group autonomy that makes us strongest' [*CCHW, 1993: 3*]. Those gathering at the First National People of Color Leadership Summit also declined the temptation to develop a centralised organisation, and emphasised the importance of organising networks. Many activists noted that one of the most promising achievements of the summit was its commitment to an organisational model that stressed diversity and non-hierarchical principles, in contrast to the technocratic managerial style of the mainstream environmental groups [*Di Chiro, 1992: 105*]. Richard Moore of SNEEJ argued that the Summit was not about building an organisation, but rather 'building a movement. As a movement gets built, it starts from the bottom up. And those movements that we have seen develop from the top down are no longer there. So what we are about here is building a network, or building a net that works' [*Lee, 1992: 19*].

Recognising, drawing on, and formalising the loose links among activists and other neighbourhood, familial, or occupational ties of solidarity, recent networks have developed a unique relationship between their center and base. As Tarrow [*1994: 146*] argues, 'the strategy of drawing on existing structures of solidarity may weaken the ties between center and base, but, when it succeeds, the resulting heterogeneity and interdependence produce more dynamic movements than the homogeneity and discipline that were aimed at in the old social-democratic model'. Brecher and Costello [*1990: 333*] note the importance of multiple organisations and levels of coordination in distinguishing between new networks and old forms of organizing. The heterogeneity and dynamism discussed by Tarrow, and multiplicity and coordination noted by Brecher and Costello, are apparent throughout the grass-roots environmental justice movement. Rather than a singular, centralised, and formal organisation, the movement has stressed a network structure – bottom-up, informal, spontaneous, and multiple. All of the qualities that supposedly destroy organisation have served, in fact, to build and sustain a movement..

Both SNEEJ and the CCHW have developed organisational and decision-making structures that take these lessons and principles seriously.[14] In SNEEJ, guidelines lay out the right of member organisations to be heard, respected, and involved in all aspects of the Network, including participation in committees and the coordinating council, in the decision-making process, and in resolutions for the annual gathering. SNEEJ guidelines insist that each individual and organisation that is part of the Network also has the right to self-control, autonomy, and self-determination [*SNEEJ, 1993*]. The ideals of the Network are based on the combination of decentralisation and solidarity.[15]

The CCHW has recently changed their organizing model to further emphasise community networking. The 'New Deal' replaced field offices with an 'Alliance of Citizen Organizers' [*Brody, 1994*]. CCHW trains local groups who volunteer to help other groups and leaders in their area. But the individual Alliance groups are responsible for organising with, and offering specific technical assistance to, groups in their region. Alliance members also participate as strategists for the CCHW, meeting in Roundtable format on specific issues such as dioxin, sludge, and economic development. This new model puts primary emphasis on direct networking between groups, further strengthening the network rather than the central CCHW office or staff.[16]

A network, then, is not simply the connection between issues and groups, but is a particular method and practice of that connection as well. Function, in this case, follows form.

Diversifying Tactics and Resources

One of the other key strengths of networking is the use of numerous, yet interlinked, strategies and tactics. Networking allows for two types of strategic diversity in the realm of tactics. First is the use of various points from which the movement addresses an issue, from the local level up through the national and international. Local groups have been involved in front line struggles at plant sites and waste dumps. Groups have coalesced regionally and statewide, bringing a number of groups into a focused attack. And the movement has addressed national issues, including government and industrial policy as well as the practices and policies of the national environmental groups.

In addition, at each of these levels the movement has used a variety of tactics and strategies, both legal and extralegal. People have circulated petitions and talked to neighbours; they have attended local government meetings and organised their own accountability sessions for local officials, candidates, agencies, and companies. There have been innumerable legal demonstrations, rallies, marches; a few picketed shareholder meetings and creative street theater actions; and a variety of organised illegal sit-ins and blockades.[17] There have also been numerous administrative complaints, citizen suits and tort actions [Cole, 1994a, 1994b, 1994c]. Finally, environmental justice groups and networks have pushed for changes in public policy, again from the local level up to the international.

All of these tactics are seen as useful to the progress and growth of the movement, and none is seen as an end in itself. Even those that focus on changing environmental policy and laws see the limitations of a focus on that singular strategy.[18] The key to the success of the networking strategy is the simultaneous use of a wide range of tactics. A movement organised as a network has an inherent organisational flexibility. Groups can use the types of tactics suited to their own local situation while coordinating these actions with others. And individual groups can themselves try a variety of tactics as their struggle continues. At the CCHW, this is understood, in part, as 'flexibility' [CCHW, 1993: 36].

But it is also the respect for the importance of cultural and ideological diversity in the CCHW's network which leads to a respect for diverse tactical approaches:

> Instead of trying to walk, talk and look the same we should celebrate
> how different cultures, ways of acting and approaches to fighting the

issues have involved many more people in our struggle and brought about change... Some communities protest in the streets and take over public meetings, while others hold prayer vigils outside public buildings and walks of concerns led by their religious leaders. It is allowing people to act in a manner in which they are comfortable, and retaining their cultural ways and values that keeps us moving forward. This diversity of people and cultures also keeps those in power from knowing what to expect and from controlling us. We should embrace our diversity as it is one of our most powerful tools [*CCHW, 1993: 3*].

In welcoming a variety of types of community participation in the movement, the CCHW demonstrates, once again, that inclusivity builds strength.

Networking also allows for a thorough and efficient pooling and mobilisation of resources. Local groups involved in a project, campaign, or action require a variety of resources. Groups need technical information, advice on, and analysis of specific issues. Assistance will be needed on organisational issues – structure, leadership, participation. Most will need either advice on finding funding or direct monetary support. More than likely groups will eventually have a need for legal advice and services. And there is always the issue of how to approach, use, and deal with the media. Networking makes for the possibility of the mobilisation of resources – both internally, by the sharing of the existing resources of the network, and externally, by linking with other groups or networks which can provide various resources.

The internal sharing of resources is one of the basic reasons for organising networks. The CCHW, for example, is seen as a 'support mechanism' that assists thousands of grass-roots groups around the country [*Newman, 1993*]. SNEEJ notes that part of its task is the provision of a broad base of support for local, state, and regional work. Both organisations provide education, technical assistance, training in leadership, assistance in obtaining funding from various sources, and help in attending and participating in actions and events from local to international. But resources flow not only from the centre of the network outward, for example, from the main offices of CCHW or SNEEJ, but from group to group within networks as well. One activist argues that the point of networking 'is that we can teach each other. And that is how you begin to pool resources, monetary, intellectual and strategy' (quoted in Lee [*1992: 45*]). Groups use networks to build on local knowledge of a particular issue, and then pass that information along to other groups. Networks also help in the exchange of ideas and the pooling of resources by helping local groups get in touch with other networks or groups (experts in law, government processes, or particular areas of environmental research) who may specialise in a particular issue area. Grass-roots groups may also link up with larger, more established environmental groups, such as Greenpeace and the National Resources Defense Council (NRDC). Many activists argue that their campaigns would not have been possible without the resources of national organisations [e.g., *Calpotura and Sen, 1994: 255; Oliver, 1994: 90–91*]. This networking greatly increases the resources available to any one group that might have worked in isolation.

Here it is important, and interesting, to note that even with the grass-roots critique of the major environmental organisations many local environmental justice groups network with, and use the resources of, those same organisations. There is a long history of this type of synergy and co-operation, going back to the Environmental Defense Fund's work with the United Farm Workers and California Rural Legal Assistance on the issue of DDT in the late 1960s. More recently, a number of national groups have assisted in the development of the national environmental justice networks even as they have been criticised for policies, or their presence in local communities has created problems. EDF, for example, has been thoroughly criticised for its well-known hijacking of the McDonald's styrofoam campaign [*Dowie, 1995: 139–40*], and has been specifically accused of environmental racism in their support of pollution trading rights in the US (which gives permission, say critics, to older facilities in poor neighborhoods and communities of color to pollute over otherwise legal limits). Yet recently EDF has been of assistance to the National Oil Refinery Action Network (NORAN), which has filed an environmental racism suit against the California Air Resources Board for an emission trading scheme in Los Angeles [*Cone, 1997*]. Greenpeace has also been criticised by local groups in the past for being outsiders who hijack issues and campaigns, but the organisation has been active in key environmental justice battles in from the founding protest of the movement in Warren County, North Carolina to key victories in both Kettleman City and Los Angeles, California.[19]

The central issue in relationships such as these is *how* the groups are to work together. Again, it is the *process* that is crucial to grassroots groups, and it is not surprising that issues of process are central to grass-roots criticisms of the major organisations. Grass-roots groups in the environmental justice network have been willing to work with the major groups (especially given their resources), but the emphasis is on the *with*. The movement has welcomed tactical alliances and meaningful partnerships, but have insisted on retaining local control over issues and campaigns. The national organisations are respected parts of a network as long as they *assist* in an issue rather than attempt to *direct* local groups. I will come back to this issue in evaluating the network form.

Confronting Changes in Capital and Politics

There are many who argue that the US environmental movement must continue its liberal organisational strategy – that differences in the movement must be smoothed over in order to present a united front as an interest group pushing for plausible legislation [e.g., *Norton, 1991*]. And there is no shortage of environmental pundits attempting to push the movement in one direction or another, with one singular ideology or another. The argument here, on the other hand, is that a political strategy of networking strengthens the movement with a mobilisation of diversity. Networking gives a movement many points of attack, positions from which to argue, and tactics to use, while helping to pool resources efficiently. Networks are also a countermeasure against changes in the understanding of power, changes in political oversight, and, most importantly, changes in the nature of production and political economy.

First, many theorists have discussed the relationship among various forms of power or control and the value of a diverse, and linked response. Foucault [*1978, 1979, 1980*] has argued that power itself is a network that needs to be examined in its extremities. Laclau and Mouffe [*1985*] have also asserted that there are numerous forms of power and antagonisms in the social realm, and networks can develop in response. Haraway [*1985, 1991: 170*] argues that an understanding of the web-like structure of power may lead to new couplings and coalitions. Networks develop, then, not just out of pre-existing social relations and responses to environmental problems, but also out of an understanding of, and alliance around, how power links issues. This is illustrated most forcefully by the fact that most local environmental justice organisations may begin with a single issue in mind, but most often begin to relate issues and various forms of domination.

Second, and perhaps most obviously, capital itself has taken on a more rhizomatic form which poses a problem for previous interest group strategies. Capital's expanding strategy includes flexibility in production systems, a geographical division of labour, a geographical dispersal of production, and an ethic of mobility which enables companies to take advantage of capital and employment conditions they judge to be most advantageous [*Harvey, 1991*]. In response, a number of recent works on grass-roots environmentalism [e.g., *Brecher and Costello, 1994b; Gould, Schnaiberg, Wienberg, 1996; Karliner, 1997*] have focused on the need to revise and update the political strategy of the environmental movement in the face of the transnationalisation of political economy. On one level, individual localities and states have less control (in terms of environmental and labor laws) over such mobile capital – and the trend is increasingly to *reduce* such controls in order to attract industry [*Gould, 1991*]. On another level, neiether national nor local organisations working alone can produce the pressure necessary to implement such controls. National environmental organisations simply do not have the political clout to impose restrictions on capital, and local groups working in isolation are up against the corporate promises of economic development (and political contributions). As Gould *et al.* [*1996*] describe, environmental protection is sacrificed in the face of the 'treadmill of production'. Increasing regimes of 'free trade' will continue this transition.

The necessary response to this treadmill, however, is the network. In that network organising makes it possible to respond in numerous areas simultaneously, it is a more formidable opponent to such structures and strategies. The response to transnational capital (and the translocal mobility of that capital) must, of necessity, be coordinated networks and coalitions.[20]

Finally, though obviously related, the third type of change that networks are suited for is the evolving nature of the political sphere, especially when it comes to environmental oversight. Political decisions are made on more than just the national level. At the state, county, and local level, decisions on issues of growth, environmental regulation, and corporate incentive packages are crucial to both industry and citizens. On the other hand, however, the globalisation of capital also minimises the decision-making realm of the nation state as the market seeks to take its place. If the major environmental groups continue their focus on the national government, then they miss a host of relevant political decisions. Citizen action is necessary on the regional and local level, because that is where much of the control remains lodged; it is necessary on the global level because the institutions of governance there are so limited (and undemocratic). And it is necessary to network across each of these levels, as political power flows through them simultaneously. In their respective analyses of grass-roots environmental organising, both Szasz [*1994*] and Gould, Schnaiberg and Weinberg [*1996*] stress the importance, and strength, of coalitions under current political-economic conditions. For the latter, this form of resistance is necessary to counter the 'transnational treadmill of production' [*1996: 196*].

Brecher and Costello [*1994a, 1994b*], have used the metaphor of Jonathan Swift's Lilliputians to describe the networking strategy. The little people used a web of hundreds of threads to capture Gulliver. Similarly, a variety of local actions, woven together, creates a network strong enough to tackle problems larger than those which any locality might be able to deal with on its own. The various threads that make up a powerful network come from numerous positions; the basis of network organising is to recognise, validate, and forge solidarity with these various positions. The emphasis is on both the importance of each and the strength in numbers of the numerous strands.

The argument here is that the environmental justice movement represents just such a Lilliputian, transnational, translocal, rhizomatic movement. It is a 'large' movement, but it is large because of the sheer number of local and small-scale groups that have interacted and intertwined as local concern with toxics, environmental inequity, and environmental racism has grown. Both the Movement, and its political success, have come with this linking.

The environmental justice movement is seen as a threat [*Waxman, 1992; USEPA, 1991*] because it merges both groups and issues. It brings environmental, economic, and democratic issues to the table, and refuses to break those issues down according to the lines of governmental authority – toxics issues to EPA, workplace issues to OSHA, participation issues to state legislators. Like the Lilliputians, the movement has worked together to combine forces, creating a network that shows numerous signs of success. The activities of the network have not only strengthened local groups and community resistance and attracted new grass-roots organisations, but they have been instrumental in identifying and addressing the larger problems that are shared, in numerous ways, across these diverse communities. In doing so, they have also affected environmental policy at both local and national levels. As Penny Newman argues [*CCHW, 1993: 21*], '[w]hen the networks of women of color and poor communities of the US and the networks from around the world merge into a cooperative network the reverberations will be felt in every corporate board room and governmental stronghold worldwide'. Ambitious, maybe, but actions and responses to date point to its plausibility.

Evaluating the Strategy

Up to this point, I have tried to lay out the motivation, design, and workings of the networked organisational structure in the environmental justice movement, as well as show its possible promise and effectiveness. But it seems suitable at this point to ask a simple question of network organizing: is it a thoroughly workable form? It is possible to list the numerous victories of the US movement – the closure of waste dumps and incinerators, the prevention of others, the establishment of an Office of Environmental Justice in the EPA, President Clinton's Executive Order on Environmental Justice, and others.[21]   But I want to evaluate the network strategy by examining three issues that may be the greatest weakness of the form: the problems of longevity, relationships over distance and difference, and the lack of an overall alternative vision.

First, networks by their very definition are mobile arrangements. Local groups often dissipate when their concern has run its course – after either victory or loss. Projects and campaigns begin and end, and individuals and groups burn out. Sustained resistance is rare. What happens when some of the Lilliputians drop their strings? The problem with this lack of staying power is that both governmental agencies and corporations are influenced by longevity; while they can often wait out sporadic protests, they have a much more difficult time ignoring community organisations and networks that have become established and coordinated.

But one strength of the network form is that the contact remains, even if informal. Groups which pull back, or even dissipate, will often be ready for new mobilisations. In one example, a local group in the Southwest US was very active in the Campaign for Responsible Technology (CRT) until it dropped out of the network in order to pursue more specific issues of the indigenous peoples of the region. One organiser of the CRT noted the sense of loss that came with this departure, and the effect of the loss of that one link in the larger network. But as the CRT developed a project on the water use of the high tech industry [*SWOP/CRT, 1997*], the group which had dropped out offered input specific to the effects on indigenous populations.

In addition (and related) to the issue of longevity, networks must constantly keep up relations across both distance and difference. Difficulties of this sort come in a number of forms. When very different communities, or groups within communities, come together some may see themselves becoming part of a larger movement, while others remain most firmly associated with their most pressing particular issues. Within networks, solidarity is understood differently by different groups. Hence, a group working on indigenous issues might not see themselves completely aligned with a network which addresses the high tech industry, even if their respective foci overlap in numerous places.

Within a varied network like SNEEJ, other difficulties arise. Activists have complained that the resources of the network go to those groups or communities which 'cry loudest', which often happen to be the groups or communities which already have some resources at their disposal. And, of course, networks or coalitions that form within specific geographical areas, like a large city, face race and gender issues. A white member of an active group in a Western city told me that all the media, government, and foundation attention is paid to groups primarily of people of colour, which were, in his mind, neither as broad nor as effective as his own group. Elsewhere, some minority activists have pressured white activists and academics to leave the articulation of issues of environmental justice solely to people of colour [*Epstein, 1995: 7*]. Obviously, these attitudes – and it is difficult to determine whether they are minor or widespread – hamper the development and longevity of environmental justice networks.

Yet another tension in the development of network relations over distance and difference is the relation between the grassroots and the major and/or mainstream environmental organisations. As noted previously, while grassroots groups are often very critical of the major groups, they have often turned to these groups – and their resources – for alliances on specific campaigns and actions. Differences certainly remain between local groups, major organisations, and all that fall in between. The major groups often continue to ignore localised issues, and refrain from participating in them even when asked by locals. But a number of the major groups have learned that, while grass-roots groups and networks are suspicious of the mainstream, they *do* appreciate their assistance, as long as it is offered within a respectful process. Hence, the mainstream groups that work most successfully with the grassroots are those that work with the local groups, listen to their concerns, and do not make major moves without consultation with, and direction from, those locals. Generally, and as discussed by Gould *et al.* [*1996: 195–6*], the most successful efforts are made when alliances are formed between grassroots and larger regional or national organisations. Conversely, local mobilisations are often short and unsuccessful if the national groups 'countermobilize' against them.

Finally, it could be argued that any political struggle or movement that took on the rhizomatic form and decentralised functions of a network would simply become an amalgamation of numerous decentered struggles, incapable of dealing with the 'big pictures' of power, political economy, or the globalisation of many environmental issues. On the contrary, the assertion here has been that multiple, localised oppositions are a tactical strength. The key is the application of diverse critiques, approaches, and styles in various places of action.[22] Environmental degradation is not simply the singular product of a lone 'mega-machine' which can easily be unplugged in one place or with one singular changed practice. The targets of the environmental movement are varied; and so the movement itself is necessarily decentred and multiple. The issues and abuses that form the motivations for political action need to be targeted at the local level, in the multiplicity of places where they emerge. The multiplicity of experiences, issues, and resistances that have developed in the environmental justice movement call for and exemplify diverse approaches to change in varied venues. The basis of the movement is this composite character, and the plurality of levels of attack.

The criticism of all of this, of course, is that the focus is on resistance, and not on large-scale visions of global alternatives. On the contrary, the argument here is that solidarity across locally-based groups creates movements that reach and connect beyond the local and particular. Obviously, there are similarities among different communities and experiences. Issues of the power of capital, the market imprisonment of policy, the exclusion of effected populations from policy-making, the desire for participation and democratisation, and a focus on political process as a way to address both a lack of equity and recognition come up time and time again in the movement. Environmental justice networks, based even as they are on resistance, have shown themselves quite capable of flexing fairly large-scale – even global – muscles. Recent cross-border movements around NAFTA and GATT, World Bank policy in the Amazon, ozone policy, and the ownership of indigenous knowledge serve as examples.

In addition, it is important to recognise the politics and process of the environmental justice movement as a form of prefigurative politics [*Epstein, 1988*]. The form of the movement itself, and its development of this form out of critiques of past social movement organising, is a living articulation of an alternative form. Networks are not simply a means to an end – and a defensive end at that. They are an example of an attempt at an alternative political structure. In this sense, the movement counters many social movement theorists and left activists who argue that only a unified movement organised around a singular agenda can accomplish significant social change.

Conclusion

Networking and alliance-building have become a major tactic in environmental organising in the US, especially among grass-roots activists and groups. This move has been in response to the limitations of past models of organising as well as the changing nature of the structures and practices of capital and politics.

Networks begin at the level of the community, with bases in everyday relationships at home, church, work and play. The organisation of networks takes these local realities seriously, and continues the recognition and validation of diverse experiences, even as it links the multiplicity of peoples and issues into alliances. While they may restrict themselves to a local alliance around a local issues, these alliances may also take on a larger, and often more rhizomatic form. Networks expand the notion of environmental locality, as they expose the similarities shared by communities in disparate places.

Networking also goes beyond organisational form; it becomes the mode of organisational function. Decentralisation, diversification, and democratisation drive networks, as opposed to the centralised and hierarchical practices of past movements and present mainstream organising. Finally, these networks display a strength and resilience one might not expect from such a decentralised organisation. The plurality of a movement, its diverse tactics, and its numerous resources are understood as strategic advantages in organising.

What the development of networking shows, especially as it has been used in the environmental justice movement, is a new form of movement organising that is based on the strength of diversity. Dismissed is the conventional organising model, which sees difference as a hindrance. Instead, these networks and alliances have recognised the reality and importance of diverse experiences, validated multiplicity, and created a solidarity that has become a dynamic and effective environmental movement in the US.

NOTES

1. Previous versions of this research have been presented at the Western Political Science Association conference in Portland, OR, March 1995; an on-line conference on Environmental Cultural Studies sponsored by the American Studies Department at Washington State University, June 1997; and *Environmental Justice: Global Ethics for the 21st Century*, University of Melbourne, Oct. 1997. The author is grateful to John Dryzek, David Carruthers, Irene Diamond, Dan Goldrich, Noel Sturgeon, Nathan Teske, and Doug Torgerson, in addition to editor Chris Rootes and two *Environmental Politics* referees, for comments on various incarnations of these ideas. An expanded version of this essay appears as a chapter in *Environmental Justice and the New Pluralism: The Challenge of Difference for Environmentalism*, Oxford University Press, 1999.
2. See Dowie [*1991, 1995*] and Gottlieb [*1990, 1993*] for discussions of these complaints. From within the movement, see Bullard (1994), Montague [*1995*], Cockburn and St. Clair [*1994*]. For a fascinating account of the limits funding organisations put on the movement, see Rozek [*1994*].
3. The Big Ten consists of Natural Resources Defense Council, Environmental Policy Institute, National Wildlife Federation, Environmental Defense Fund, Izaak Walton League, Sierra Club, National Audubon Society, National Parks and Conservation Association, Wilderness Society, and Friends of the Earth. For criticisms from an environmental justice perspective, see various essays in the collections edited by Bryant [*1995*], Bullard [*1993*], and Hofrichter [*1993*]. Numerous environmental justice organisations and activists signed two key letters to the mainstream leaders listing these complaints [*Shabecoff, 1990*].
4. Diani's work, especially his definition of social movements as networks [*1992*], has certainly aided this trend in the sociological literature.
5. See Breines [*1989*] and Miller [*1987*] on the new left, and Freeman [*1975*] and Sirianni [*1993*] on the feminist movement.
6. Ruffins's [*1992*] account of the summit includes a discussion of the effect of bringing together Native American and Hawaiian activists with more urban-based African-American activists. After years of bitter feeling about the white environmental community's focus on wilderness and animals rather than the urban environment, indigenous activists helped him to experience, for the first time, 'the moral imperative of protecting animals and trees and land' [*1992: 11*].
7. Examples abound. Much has been written of the importance of extended families and community networks in the activism of working-class and African-American women [e.g., *Haywood, 1990; Krauss, 1994; Naples, 1992*]. The emergence of individuals in social networks also played a key role in determining participation in the civil rights movement [*McAdam, 1988*]. Churches have also been a source of activism around civil rights issues in African-American and Latino communities.
8. One of my favourite examples of the use of pre-existing social networks in environmental justice organising is the transition of the Newtown Florist Club, in Gainesville, Georgia, from a group that began by collecting money to buy flowers for ill residents to one organizing to learn about and fight against toxics released in the community [*Kerr and Lee, 1993, 13*].

144   ENVIRONMENTAL MOVEMENTS: LOCAL, NATIONAL, GLOBAL

9. CCHW has recently revised its name to 'CHEJ: Center for Health, Environment, and Justice'; I will continue to refer to them as CCHW throughout this study.
10. One of the most impressive examples of such an alliance was built between Latinos and Hasidim in the Williamsburg section of Brooklyn, New York [Greider, 1993]. El Puente and United Jewish Organisations worked together against a storage facility of low-level radioactive waste and a massive garbage incinerator the city planned for the neighbourhood.
11. Deleuze and Guattari [1987] spawned the use of the rhizome metaphor. Their first three characteristics of a rhizome are the principles of connection, heterogeneity, and multiplicity [1987: 7–8]. For other discussions of the metaphor in environmental politics, see LaChapelle [1994], and Kuehls [1995].
12. Appropriately, this is the name of the newsletter of the CCHW.
13. See, for example, the discussion by SNEEJ co-ordinator Richard Moore in Almeida [1994].
14. The environmental justice movement does not hold a monopoly on this type of organizing in US environmentalism. Bron Taylor [1995] discusses this type of 'solidarity activism' in both Earth First! and the Rainforest Action Network. For a thorough picture of networked solidarity in Earth First!, see Ingalsbee [1995].
15. This is not to assert that relations in the network actually work this way all of the time. The point here is the attention to these principles in the establishment of a grassroots network. I will return to a discussion of some of the limitations of the network form.
16. The model also, not coincidentally, conserves scarce resources.
17. For specific examples, see various issues of some of the newsletters of the movement, such as Everyone's Backyard; Race, Poverty and the Environment; Crossroads; New Solutions; and Voces Unidas.
18. Mililani Trask, an attorney active in environmental justice and sovereignty issues in Hawaii, argues that the legal realm is a valid one, but warns against a singular faith in the image of legal justice: '[D]o not put your eggs in the basket of the blind white lady. We must try other approaches' [Lee, 1992: 38].
19. Greenpeace has recently imploded in the US, closing field offices, firing canvassers, and shutting down most of its active projects, including environmental justice.
20. The CCHW specifically suggests networking as a method of thwarting industry tactics. Waste companies looking for a site will choose a half-dozen or so communities that would be potentially suitable; they then sit back and watch how the communities react, moving into the one that is least resistant. In these cases, the CCHW suggests a meeting of groups from each target site to form a 'non-aggression pact' and unite around the principle of 'not in anyone's backyard' [Collette, 1993: 5].
21. See the list of general successes compiled by Freudenberg and Steinsapir [1992].
22. This mirrors, for example, Foucault [1978: 96].

REFERENCES

Almeida, Paul (1994), 'The Network for Environmental and Economic Justice in the Southwest: Interview with Richard Moore', Capitalism, Nature, Socialism, Vol.5, No.1, pp.21–54.
Alston, Dana (1990), Taking Back Our Lives: A Report to the Panos Institute on Environment, Community Development and Race in the United States, Washington, DC: The Panos Institute.
Anthony, Carl and Luke Cole (1990), 'A Statement of Purpose', Race, Poverty, and the Environment, Vol.1, No.1, pp.1–2.
Austin, Regina and Michael Schill (1991), 'Black, Brown, Red, and Poisoned: Minority Grassroots Environmentalism and the Quest for Eco-Justice', Kansas Journal of Law and Public Policy, Vol.1, pp.69–82.
Avila, Magdalena (1992), 'David vs. Goliath', Crossroads/Forward Motion, Vol.11, No.2, pp.13–15.
Brecher, Jeremy and Tim Costello (eds.) (1990), Building Bridges: The Emerging Grassroots Coalition of Labor and Community. New York: Monthly Review Press.
Brecher, Jeremy and Tim Costello (1994a), Global Village or Global Pillage: Economic Reconstruction From the Bottom Up, Boston, MA: South End Press.

Brecher, Jeremy and Tim Costello (1994b), 'The Lilliput Strategy: Taking on the Multinationals', *The Nation*, Vol.259, No.21, pp.757–60.

Breines, Wini (1989), *Community and Organization in the New Left, 1962–1968: The Great Refusal*, Second Edition, New Brunswick, NJ: Rutgers University Press.

Brody, Charlotte (1994), 'The New Deal: CCHW's New Organizing Model Takes Form', *Everyone's Backyard*, Vol.13, No.4, pp.11–13.

Bryant, Bunyan (1995), 'Issues and Potential Policies and Solutions for Environmental Justice: An Overview', in Bunyan Bryant, (ed.), *Environmental Justice: Issues, Policies, and Solutions*, Covelo, CA: Island Press.

Bullard, Robert D. (ed.) (1993), *Confronting Environmental Racism: Voices from the Grassroots*, Boston, MA: South End Press.

Bullard, Robert D. (ed.) (1994), *Unequal Protection: Environmental Justice and Communities of Color*, San Francisco, CA: Sierra Club Books.

Calpotura, Francis and Rinku Sen (1994), 'PUEBLO Fights Lead Poisoning', in Robert D. Bullard, (ed.), *Unequal Protection: Environmental Justice and Communities of Color*, San Francisco, CA: Sierra Club Books.

Capek, Sheila (1993), 'The "Environmental Justice" Frame: A Conceptual Discussion and an Application', *Social Problems*, Vol.40, No.1, pp.5–24.

Citizens Clearinghouse for Hazardous Waste (CCHW) (1989), *Everybody's Backyard*, Vol.7, No.2, p.1.

Citizens Clearinghouse for Hazardous Waste (1990), *Everybody's Backyard*, Vol.8, No.1, p.2.

Citizens Clearinghouse for Hazardous Waste (1993), *Ten Years of Triumph*, Falls Church, VA: Citizens Clearinghouse for Hazardous Waste.

Cockburn, Alexander and Jeffrey St. Clair (1994), 'After Armageddon: Death and Life for America's Greens', *The Nation*, Vol.259, No.21, pp.760–65.

Cole, Luke (1992), 'Empowerment as the Key to Environmental Protection: The Need for Environmental Poverty Law', *Ecology Law Quarterly*, Vol.19, pp.619–83.

Cole, Luke (1994a), 'Environmental Justice Litigation: Another Stone in David's Sling', *Fordham Urban Law Journal*, Vol.21, p.523.

Cole, Luke (1994b), 'The Struggle of Kettleman City for Environmental Justice: Lessons for the Movement', *Maryland Journal of Contemporary Legal Issues*, Vol.5, p.67.

Cole, Luke (1994c), 'Civil Rights, Environmental Justice and the EPA: The Brief History of Administrative Complaints Under Title VI', *Journal of Environmental Law and Litigation*, Vol.9, pp.309–98.

Collette, Will (1993), *How to Deal with a Proposed Facility*, Falls Church, VA: Citizens Clearinghouse for Hazardous Waste.

Cone, Marla (1997), 'Civil Rights Suit Attacks Trade in Pollution Credits', *Los Angeles Times*, 23 July 1997, p.A1.

Deleuze, Gilles and Felix Guattari (1987), *A Thousand Plateaus: Capitalism and Schizophrenia*, Minneapolis, MN: University of Minnesota Press.

Diani, Mario (1992), 'The Concept of Social Movement', *Sociological Review*, Vol.40, pp.1–25.

Diani, Mario (1995), *Green Networks: A Structural Analysis of the Italian Environmental Movement*, Edinburgh: Edinburgh University Press.

Di Chiro, Giovanna (1992), 'Defining Environmental Justice: Women's Voices and Grassroots Politics', *Socialist Review*, Vol.22, No.4, pp.93–130.

Di Chiro, Giovanna (1995), 'Nature as Community: The Convergence of Environment and Social Justice', In William Cronon, (ed.), *Uncommon Ground: Rethinking the Human Place in Nature*, New York: Norton.

Di Chiro, Giovanna (1997), 'Local Actions, Global Expertise: Remaking Environmental Expertise', presented in the on-line conference on 'Cultures and Environments: On Cultural Environmental Studies,' June 1997; sponsored by the Washington State University American Studies Department.

Dowie, Mark (1991), 'American Environmentalism: A Movement Courting Irrelevance', *World Policy Journal*, Vol.9, pp.67–92.

Dowie, Mark (1995), *Losing Ground: American Environmentalism at the Close of the Twentieth Century*, Cambridge: MIT Press.

Environmental Careers Organization (ECO) (1992), *Beyond the Green: Redefining and Diversifying the Environmental Movement,* Boston, MA: Environmental Careers Organization.

Epstein, Barbara (1988), 'The Politics of Prefigurative Community: The Non-Violent Direct Action Movement', in Mike Davis and Michael Sprinker (eds), *Reshaping the U.S. Left: Popular Struggles in the 1980s,* London: Verso.

Epstein, Barbara (1995), 'Grassroots Environmentalism and Strategies for Social Change', *New Political Science,* Vol.32, pp.1–24.

Fischer, Claude S. (1977), *Networks and Places: Social Relations in the Urban Setting,* New York: Free Press.

Foucault, Michel (1978), *The History of Sexuality. Vol. 1, An Introduction,* New York: Random House.

Foucault, Michel (1979), *Discipline and Punish: The Birth of the Prison,* New York: Random House.

Foucault, Michel (1980), *Power/Knowledge,* New York: Pantheon Books.

Freeman, Jo (1975), *The Politics of Women's Liberation,* New York: McKay.

Freudenberg, Nicholas and Carol Stensapir, (1992), 'Not in Our Backyards: The Grassroots Environmental Justice Movement', in Riley E. Dunlap and Angela G. Mertig (eds), *American Environmentalism,* Philadelphia, PA: Taylor & Francis.

Gerlach, Luther P., and Virginia H. Hine, (1970), *People, Power, and Change: Movements of Social Transformation,* Indianapolis, IN: Bobbs-Merrill.

Gibbs, Lois (1982), *Love Canal: My Story,* Albany, NY: State University of New York Press.

Gottlieb, Robert (1990), 'An Odd Assortment of Allies: American Environmentalism in the 1990s', *Gannett Center Journal* 4, No.3, pp.37–47.

Gottlieb, Robert (1993), *Forcing the Spring: The Transformation of the American Environmental Movement,* Washington, DC: Island Press.

Gould, Kenneth (1991), 'The Sweet Smell of Money: Economic Dependency and Local Environmental Political Mobilization', *Society and Natural Resources,* Vol.4, pp.133–50.

Gould, Kenneth, Allan Schnaiberg, and Adam Weinberg (1996), *Local Environmental Struggles: Citizen Activism in the Treadmill of Production,* Cambridge: Cambridge University Press.

Greider, Katherine (1993) 'Against All Odds', *City Limits,* Vol.18, No.7, pp.34–8.

Grossman, Karl (1994), 'The People of Color Environmental Summit', in Bullard (ed.) [*1994*].

Hamilton, Cynthia (1990), 'Women, Home and Community: The Struggle in an Urban Environment', *Race, Poverty, and the Environment,* Vol.1, No.1, p.3.

Haraway, Donna ([1985] 1991), 'A Cyborg Manifesto: Science, Technology, and Socialist-Feminism in the Late Twentieth Century', in *Simians, Cyborgs, and Women: The Reinvention of Nature,* New York: Routledge.

Haraway, Donna (1988), 'Situated Knowledges: The Science Question in Feminism as a Site of Discourse on the Privilege of Partial Perspective', *Feminist Studies,* Vol.14, No.3, pp.575–99.

Harvey, David (1991), 'Flexibility: Threat or Opportunity?', *Socialist Review,* Vol.21, No.1, pp.65–77.

Haywood, Terry (1990), 'Working Class Feminism: Creating a Politics of Community, Connection, and Concern', Ph.D. dissertation, Graduate School and University Center of the City University of New York.

Hofrichter, Richard (ed.) (1993), *Toxic Struggles: The Theory and Practice of Environmental Justice,* Philadelphia, PA: New Society.

Ingalsbee, Timothy (1995), 'Earth First!: Consciousness and Action in the Unfolding of a New-Social-Movement', Doctoral dissertation, Department of Sociology, University of Oregon.

James, William (1976 [1912]), *Essays in Radical Empiricism,* Cambridge, MA: Harvard University Press.

Karliner, Josh (1997), *The Corporate Planet: Ecology and Politics in the Age of Globalization,* San Francisco, CA: Sierra Club Books.

Kerr, Mary Lee, and Charles Lee (1993), 'From Conquistadores to Coalitions', *Southern Exposure,* Vol.21, No.4, pp.8–19.

Krauss, Celene (1994), 'Women of Color on the Front Line', in Bullard (ed.) [*1994*].

Kuehls, Thom (1995), *The Space of Eco-Politics*, Minneapolis, MN: University of Minnesota Press.

LaChapelle, Dolores (1994), 'The Rhizome Connection', in David Clarke Burks (ed.), *Place of the Wild: A Wildlands Anthology*, Covelo, CA: Island Press.

Laclau, Ernesto, and Chantal Mouffe (1985), *Hegemony and Socialist Strategy: Toward a Radical Democratic Politics*, London: Verso.

Lee, Charles (1993), 'Beyond Toxic Wastes and Race', in Bullard (ed.) [*1993*].

Lee, Charles (ed.) (1992), *Proceedings: The First National People of Color Environmental Leadership Summit*, New York: United Church of Christ Commission for Racial Justice.

Lynch, Barbara Deutsch (1993), 'The Garden and the Sea: U.S. Latino Environmental Discourses and Mainstream Environmentalism', *Social Problems*, Vol.40, No.1, pp.108–24.

Lynch, Sue Greer (1993), 'Larger than Locals: The Critical Link', in Citizens Clearinghouse for Hazardous Waste, *Ten Years of Triumph*, Falls Church, VA: Citizens Clearinghouse for Hazardous Waste.

McAdam, Doug (1988), *Freedom Summer*, Oxford: Oxford University Press.

Miller, James (1987) *Democracy is in the Streets: From Port Huron to the Siege of Chicago*, New York: Simon & Schuster.

Miller, Vernice D. (1993), 'Building on Our Past, Planning for Our Future: Communities of Color and the Quest for Environmental Justice', in Hofrichter (ed.) [*1993*].

Montague, Peter (1995), 'Big Picture Organizing, Part 5: A Movement in Disarray', *Rachel's Environment and Health Weekly*, No.425.

Moore, Richard and Louis Head (1993), 'Acknowledging the Past, Confronting the Future: Environmental Justice in the 1990s', in Hofrichter (ed.) [*1993*].

Moore, Richard and Louis Head (1994), 'Building a Net that Works: SWOP', in Bullard (ed.) [*1994*].

Naples, Nancy (1992), 'Activist Mothering: Cross-Generational Continuity in the Community Work of Women from Low-Income Urban Neighborhoods', *Gender and Society*, Vol.6, No.3, pp.441–63.

Newman, Peggy (1993), 'The Grassroots Movement for Environmental Justice: Fighting for Our Lives', *New Solutions*, Vol.3, No.4, pp.87–95.

Newman, Peggy (1994), 'Beyond the Neighborhood – Women Working for Multi-Ethnic, Multi-Issue Coalitionss', *The Workbook*, Vol.19, No.2, pp.93–5.

Norton, Bryan G. (1991), *Toward Unity among Environmentalists*, Oxford: Oxford University Press.

Oliver, Patsy Ruth (1994), 'Living on a Superfund Site in Texarkana', in Bullard (ed.) [*1994*].

Pardo, Mary (1990), 'Mexican American Women Grassroots Community Activists: "Mothers of East Los Angeles"', *Frontiers*, Vol.11, No.1, pp.1–7.

Plotkin, Sidney (1990), 'Enclave Consciousness and Neighborhood Activism', in Joseph M. Kling and Prudence S. Posner (eds), *Dilemmas of Activism: Class, Community, and the Politics of Local Mobilization*, Philadelphia, PA: Temple University Press.

Pulido, Laura (1996), *Environmentalism and Social Justice: Two Chicano Struggles in the Southwest*, Tucson, AR: University of Arizona Press.

Rozek, Victor (1994), 'A Gathering of Warlords', *Wild Forest Review*, March, pp.22–5.

Ruffins, Paul (1992), 'Defining a Movement and a Community', *Crossroads/Forward Motion*, Vol.11, No.2.

Schwab, Jim (1994), *Deeper Shades of Green: The Rise of Blue-Collar and Minority Environmentalism in America*, San Francisco, CA: Sierra Club Books.

Shabecoff, Philip (1990), 'Environmental Groups Told They Are Racists in Hiring', *New York Times*, 1 Feb. 1990.

Sirianni, Carmen (1993), 'Learning Pluralism: Democracy and Diversity in Feminist Organizations', in John W. Chapman and Ian Shapiro (eds), *Democratic Community: NOMOS XXXV*, New York: New York University Press.

Southwest Network for Environmental and Economic Justice (SNEEJ) (1993), 'Southwest Network for Environmental and Economic Justice', Albuquerque, NM: SNEEJ.

Southwest Organizing Project (SWOP) and the Campaign for Responsible Technology (CRT) (1997), *Sacred Waters*, Albuquerque, NM: Southwest Organizing Project.

Szasz, Andrew (1994), *Ecopopulism: Toxic Waste and the Movement for Environmental Justice*, Minneapolis, MN: University of Minnesota Press.

Tarrow, Sidney (1994), *Power in Movement: Social Movements, Collective Action and Politics*, Cambridge: Cambridge University Press.

Taylor, Bron (ed.) (1995), *Ecological Resistance Movements: The Global Emergence of Radical and Popular Environmentalism*, Albany, NY: State University of New York Press.

Taylor, Dorceta (1992), 'Can the Environmental Movement Attract and Maintain the Support of Minorities?', in Bunyan Bryant and Paul Mohai (eds), *Race and the Incidence of Environmental Hazards: A Time for Discourse*, Boulder, CO: Westview Press.

United Church of Christ Commission for Racial Justice (1987), *Toxic Wastes and Race in the United States: A National Study of the Racial and Socioeconomic Characteristics of Communities with Hazardous Waste Sites*, New York: United Church of Christ.

United States Environmental Protection Agency (US EPA) (1979), *Siting of Hazardous Waste Management Facilities and Public Opposition* (SW-809), Washington, DC: Government Printing Office.

United States Environmental Protection Agency (1991), 'Memorandum on Draft Environmental Equity Communication Plan'.

Waxman, Congressman Henry A. (1992), 'Environmental Equity Report is Public Relations Ploy: Internal Memoranda Reveal Report to be Misleading', Press release 24 Feb. 1992.

Wellman, Barry, Carrington, Peter J. and Alan Hall (1988), 'Networks as Personal Communities', in Barry Wellman and S.D. Berkowitz (eds), *Social Structures: A Network Approach*, Cambridge: Cambridge University Press.

Williams, Michael (1993), 'Building Bridges ... Plan the Span', *Everyone's Backyard*, Vol.12, No.4, p.18.

Zald, Mayer N. and John D. McCarthy (eds). (1987), *Social Movements in an Organizational Society*, New Brunswick, NJ: Transaction Books.

Consolidation Through Institutionalisation? Dilemmas of the Spanish Environmental Movement in the 1990s

MANUEL JIMÉNEZ

Opportunities offered by the political context have decisively influenced the evolution of the Spanish environmental movement, in relation to both changes in its political tactics and strategies and the consolidation of its organisational base. The configuration of diverse environmental policy arenas has facilitated access of environmental movement organisations (EMOs) to the decision-making sphere. Consequently, conventional forms of participation have gained relevance within the political repertoire of EMOs which have increased their level of activities, coordination and expertise. Entering the polity has not been a linear process; rather, it has been marked by fluctuations due to the limited institutionalisation of the environment and the often-politicised nature of environmental policy-making processes. The process by which movements have been consolidated has also been shaped by their limited growth and ideologies. As well as providing an account of the development of environmental movements in Spain the study attempts to contribute to a general understanding of the link between political context and the activities and organisational dynamics of environmental movements.

Structural features of the state have been much emphasised in studies of the constraints and opportunities shaping social movements' political repertoire and organisational profiles. However, in light of the criticism that analytical explanatory models such as the political opportunity structure (POS) have generated [*Rootes, 1997*], it seems that a proper utilisation of state centred approaches to the analysis of social movements should bear in mind at least four considerations: social movements organisations are reflexive actors and behave strategically – social movements are agents of political change and hence contribute to the configuration of new opportunities; the structural features of the state are not the only component of political opportunities, nor do they alone explain the activities and organisational profile of social movements – interactions of institutions with the social, economic, cultural and natural environments should be incorporated into the analysis; social movements are not homogenous actors; nor is the state a unitary or homogenous actor.

The political opportunity approach used here draws on the contributions of Kriesi *et al.* [*1992, 1995*], Kriesi [*1989, 1995*], Tarrow [*1994*], and Kitschelt [*1986*]. However, I pay special attention to the effects of the institutionalisation of environmental departments and their interaction with other state departments in opening up political opportunities for EMOs. Therefore, I do not merely focus on the system-wide attributes of the Spanish political system but, adopting a policy-level perspective, also analyse the characteristics of its environmental policy arenas.[1]

The opportunities for EMOs to participate in specific policy arenas do not depend exclusively on their resources, but also on the content of the policy issue.[2] In addition, and especially important in Spain, is the distribution of power among state agencies that influences the EMOs–authorities relationships.

This emphasises the idea of the state not as a unified body, but as 'a set of institutions which provide the parameters and the direction of public policy' [*Smith, 1993: 2*], in which policy networks vary from area to area and even from issue to issue. State-centred approaches to the study of social movements have concentrated on the autonomy of the state to develop its own administrative and rule-making capacities [*Jenkins, 1995: 23*]. From this perspective, the autonomy of the state, which is viewed as a measure of the state's strength and political effectiveness, is associated with scant permeability to new challengers. However, from the policy-level perspective adopted here, state autonomy depends also on the intra-state distribution of power and the unequal distribution of capacities to carry out public polices, dealing not only with social groups but also with the competing interests and goals of other state departments. This implies, contrary to what the POS approach might suggest, that the overall definition of the relationship between state and civil society in a particular country is not necessarily a zero-sum game and that the boundaries between state and civil society are not neat.

The power of one state agency *vis-à-vis* others is a function of its powers and budgetary and technical resources, but is also related to its capacity to create policy networks [*Smith, 1993*]. The cross-sectoral nature of environmental issues makes the dynamics of interaction between different state actors even more significant. This transversal nature of environmental policy and the profound implications that environmental regulation may have for key political issues also increases the political autonomy of the state agency.

In the case of the Spanish environmental movement, from an initial context of exclusion and repression derived from system-wide properties, the institutionalisation of environmental policy arenas has created opportunities for access through diverse issue networks, usually located at the periphery of decision-making centres. Through interaction, environmental authorities and EMOs can exchange mutual recognition (legitimising resources), information (both substantive and relative to possible attitudes behind a particular decision or a mutual sounding out), and funds in the case of groups. Issue networks reduce the organisational costs of EMOs, contribute to the configuration of movement networks, and facilitate interaction with other social sectors. However, their peripheral position makes EMOs' access highly contingent upon their ability to conflictualise the policy process. In turn this ensures that pressures towards the institutionalisation of movements fluctuate.

From the resource mobilisation perspective of McCarthy and Zald [*1977*] and the polity model of Tilly [*1978*], greater access to the polity is associated with the process of professionalisation and bureaucratisation of social movement organisations in contemporary liberal democracies [*Lo, 1992*]. Usually, the trend towards the institutionalisation of social movements is analysed as a change in the organisational base of the movements from the predominance of mass protest organisations to their replacement by movement interest groups and/or professional protest organisations [*Lo, 1992; Grant and Maloney, 1997; Diani, 1997*]. As the process of institutionalisation progresses, conventional forms of action and negotiation with authorities prevail, while the role of members shifts from activism to that of mere supporters. From this perspective, institutional-isation is the main trend propelling organisational consolidation.

In this study I prefer to see the organisational consolidation of environmental movements as the combined product of increasing social support and increasing integration into the polity. The organisational shape of a consolidated movement (including the degree of institutionalisation) is the result of responses given to organisational questions that both trends pose to the movement's organisations. The organisational shape of a consolidated movement depends on the type of relationships that its organisations establish both with those on behalf of whom they act (members, communities or society at large) and the authorities whose policies they aim to change. While institutionalisation can be considered as the main driving force of the consolidation of social movements, the influence of other factors in this process should also be taken into account: trends in social support, the conditions under which organisations gain access to the polity (formal and peripheral or central and substantial), and the biographical features of EMOs (ideology and learning from past experiences).

I. Changing Political Opportunities under Democracy

The new democratic system designed after Franco's death in 1975 reflected the desire of the political elite to maximise the chances of a peaceful and successful transition. A prior condition was a process of 'elite settlement' on the basis of the explicit recognition of the legitimacy of existing institutions, and the establishment of a model of negotiation characterised by the limited number of actors, secrecy, and ideological moderation of political parties [Gunther, 1992]. The measures to guarantee successful transition implied institutional restrictions on the new liberal democracy: strengthening the executive over the parliament; an electoral system favouring large parliamentary majorities; parliamentary election of the prime minister; and a system of public grants to political parties [Colomer, 1997].[3] The main pluralist features of the political system came from the large degree of political decentralisation achieved in the course of the 1980s and 1990s.

After the transition these formal restrictions were highlighted by the survival of leaders' autonomy and, as the politics of consensus faded away after 1979, by the 'decisionism' (limited role of the parliamentary arena) when the electoral process started to produce majority governments [Colomer, 1992, 1997]. Indeed, there have been two interrelated and mutually-reinforcing dynamics behind the limited development of Spanish civil society since the transition.

First, the continuity of administrative rules from the dictatorship maintained the closed and opaque character of the relationship between the administration and citizens, and unequal access to decision-making. Institutional reform 'did not change the basic relationship between economic structures and the state. Large private interests in the Spanish economy remained central to the apparatus of public policy-making' [Lancaster, 1989: 184].

Second, political parties started to grow through state structures rather than expanding their organisational bases in society. Initially the political parties' capacity for organisational development on the ground was conditioned not only by the fact that those more prone to be mobilised were also those ideologically motivated and less likely to agree with the elite's commitment to policy continuity and the closed decision style [Caciagli, 1984; Montero, 1981], but also because they had to compete for the votes of a majority of a depoliticised and moderate electorate [Maravall, 1982]. Following the transitional period, the political elite has lacked the will to promote the growth of party structures within society, and governments have neglected any policy promoting associational life. Public funding of political parties and peak trade union organisations granted them wide margins of autonomy from their constituencies.

In sum, the nature of the institutional reform provided very limited incentives for the development of civil society and reduced opportunities for the promotion of new demands such as those related to the environment. The dominant political discourse continued to be framed by the same notion of modernisation that instigated economic development during the last period of the dictatorship, incorporating now traditional social concerns. Growth and equality appear as two inseparable goals in relation to which environmental concerns were presented as incompatible and therefore to be subordinated, when not neglected or postponed.

This secondary importance of the environment determined the limited state intervention or incorporation of the issue, and the low level of autonomy given to environmental agencies (dispersed in, and subordinated to, different departments).This situation usually left EMOs addressing sectoral policy arenas where decisions affecting the environment were taken by closed policy communities dominated by their respective economic interest.

The legal system was hardly adapted to deal with the protection of public goods nor with their collective defense. Although the right to a healthy environment is recognised in the 1978 Constitution and the standing rights of groups defending public goods were legally sanctioned in 1985, poor environmental legislation has placed restrictions on EMOs' ability to take environmental cases to the Courts. Hence, regulatory procedures either were not developed or were closed to environmental groups. Furthermore, the efficacy of this channel was reduced by the lack of environmental awareness, ecological and technical, of prosecutors and judges.

In these circumstances, the participatory choice of environmental groups was limited to introducing conflict at the implementation stage of government decisions by means of public opinion campaigns and mobilisations, which were ignored or repressed by the authorities. The anti-nuclear mobilisations of the late 1970s and early 1980s are illustrative of the political context faced by environmental organisations. EMOs had been the main and almost the only voice criticising the first National Energy Plan (PEN) drawn up in 1975 (under the dictatorship) which contemplated a very ambitious nuclear programme. The Moncloa Pacts (1977) included the continuity of energy policy. Parliamentary discussion of the second National Energy Plan in 1979, the first under democracy, was preceded by the nuclear accident in Harrisburg and the turn of parties of the left towards anti-nuclear stances. Despite this and the large number of mass mobilisations across Spain (see p.161 – Figure 1) anti-nuclear protesters were ignored by the UCD government. The antinuclear commitment of the Socialist Party (PSOE) seemed more of a strategy to appease party militants and increase its electoral prospects than a real policy position. In fact, in 1983, when the Socialist government revised the PEN, it maintained the policy direction of the previous PENs, including the exclusion of the antinuclear opposition. The adoption of a nuclear moratorium was due to economic conditions rather than to a policy-reorientation [*Lancaster, 1989: 178*] and again disregarded movement demands. It only considered anti-nuclear protests when deciding which nuclear plants under construction would be cancelled [*Costa, 1983*]. Energy policy illustrates the limited opportunities that the new regime offered to EMOs which inherited closed policy communities dominated by vested interests, backed by political leaders' autonomy, and isolated from any parliamentary or administrative remedy.

The political context for environmental demands during this period not only affected the political tactics through which environmental demands were translated into the political sphere. It also adversely affected the organisation of the environmental movement, adding further difficulties to the initial establishment of EMOs in Spanish society, limiting their capacity to steer environmental protest or to place it in a broader framework of increasing environmental degradation.

The marginal position of Spanish EMOs is clearly related to a dominant political and cultural discourse orientated towards economic growth and a political system clearly biased in favour of financial interests [*Medhurst, 1984*]. None the less, the internal difficulties of the environmental movement should also be linked to the general conditions shaping the political context during the transition period and the first years of the democratic regime. As Diani [*1995: 15*] notes, the relationship between an actor's perception of working in an open or closed political context influences the pattern through which inter-organisational linkages crystallise. In cases of political exclusion, concerns about group identity tend to dominate, and 'movement networks may be expected to be more deeply segmented along ideological, class, or other symbolically relevant lines'.

Environmental organisations in Spain were not divorced from, but were largely a product of, broader political transformations. Their concerns were intermingled with broader political issues. This 'politicisation' was not only fostered by the priority placed on democratic values and practices opposed to those of the authoritarian regime, as seen in their internal organisation and political action (for instance, through the strict observance of internal democratic practices of *asamblearismo* or by stressing the preservation of different national identities). More so than in consolidated democracies, EMOs, like many other social movements, acted during the transition as platforms for political activists. The presence in their leadership of members of left-wing opposition parties exacerbated internal disputes on purely ideological lines and promoted organisational instability. This 'politicisation' prevented linkages between different EMOs. During this initial phase of the environmental movement all attempts to establish an inter-organisational network failed [*Varillas and Da Cruz, 1981; Varillas, 1997*].

The 1990s have tempered the formal and informal institutional closure of the democratic regime to environmental demands. The relative abatement of re-distributional conflicts and diffusion of new values have favoured the political salience of environmental issues. Consequently, although modernisation discourse still predominates, environmental awareness has spread among civil servants, a process helped by natural turnover amongst bureaucrats. This has been most noticeable in expanding environmental administration through the incorporation of new (young) personnel and the transfer of personnel, in many cases linked to the environmental movement, from the conservationist world.

The environmental movement suffered from the consequences of the high level of politicisation during the transition and the subsequent demobilisation and co-optation of civil society initiatives. In the early 1980s, its organisational base was quite weak. By the late 1980s this situation was clearly improving. The consequences of the incorporation of environmental issues into the political agenda have been decisive for the evolution of the environmental movement, but the relative significance of the environment (and of EMOs) should be considered in the broader context of the political moderation of civil society after the transition. Political changes, affecting the social framework within which social movements operate, have given the environmental movement a central (and more combative) position within the (still barren) landscape of Spanish civil society.

Changes in the operational framework of the 'Spanish social movements sector', and the position of the environmental movement within it, may be illustrated by comparing some of the organisational features of the last two waves of peace mobilisations in Spain: the anti-NATO campaign between 1981 and 1986 and the campaign against the Gulf War in 1990–91.

The peace mobilisations during the first half of the 1980s still largely reflected the particularities of social mobilisations during the transition. In the anti-NATO campaign, the initiative and organisational base of the protest was in the hands of peace organisations which were generally linked to revolutionary parties and the PSOE and the Communist party (PCE), the former increasing its presence in society rather than in the political sphere, while the latter adopted a less radical stance and more electorally-orientated opportunistic tactics. EMOs participated in various civil platforms but were overshadowed by the leadership of these political organisations. This campaign reflected two features of social mobilisation during the first decade after Franco's death: the co-optive strategy of the left-wing parties and the leadership of a generation of political activists who had their origins in the opposition to the authoritarian regime, and had been or were still members of left parties, with longstanding experience in leading protest in labour conflicts, movements for political amnesty, or nationalist movements.

By 1990, when protests against the Gulf War led to a revival of the peace movement, the initiative and organisational base corresponded to EMOs (Greenpeace at the state level, and local EMOs), which were followed by other organisations (anti-militarist, feminist, trade unions). Two factors illustrate the general change in the political landscape. On the one hand, the mid-1980s marked the demise of a generation of radical left-wing activists; according to Prevost [1993: 158], defeat in the NATO referendum was particularly devastating for this political generation, who abandoned political activity or were incorporated into the major political parties (PSOE and PCE). On the other hand, extra-parliamentary radical parties virtually disappeared.

The institutionalisation of environmental politics has been decisive. Incorporation of the issue through the institutionalisation of central and regional specialised policy arenas, although slow and incomplete, has also substantially modified the political context for environmental groups. Although it remains difficult in the 1990s to consider the environment as a consolidated policy arena, it has certainly been gaining ground within the state apparatus and policy priorities. Broadly speaking, the process of institutionalisation has been shaped, on the one hand, by the influence of EU environmental policy, the innovative nature of which has had particular influence in the context of Spain's underdeveloped environmental policy [Font, 1996], and, on the other hand, by the continuing process of decentralisation initiated in the early 1980s that has led to a quasi-federal state structure.

The increasing incorporation of environmental issues within the different levels of government has broadened opportunities for environmental demands and catalysed environmental groups' political activities. The characteristics of the policy arena seem to have modified the dominant statist approach to the issue, favouring co-operative interaction. According to Font, 'the Europeanization of the Spanish policy has favoured a redefinition of the operational framework of Spanish environmental policy' [1996: 11]. In the case of EMOs, the politicised character of environmental policies and conflicts has meant that these patterns of cooperation have alternated with more conflicting, non-cooperative relationships. Both the Europeanisation and decentralisation of environmental policy have helped to undermine the cohesion of public administration and led to vertical conflicts between autonomous communities, the state and Brussels. In general, as the policy process has become more a multi-level game, opportunities have increased for previously excluded demands such as the environment.

These two general patterns of change, the broader socio-political context in which EMOs are located and the more specific scenario of the environmental policy in which EMOs operate, have an interrelated and mutually reinforcing impact on the consolidation of the environmental movement.[4] On the one hand, EMOs have won social and political recognition as representatives of the environment (an increasingly valued good). On the other, EMOs' potential resources have increased, as have opportunities for a broader repertoire of political tactics. In all, EMOs have gained manoeuvrability when designing their strategies, either exerting their influence from the initial policy stages or negotiating directly with environmental authorities. They can exploit political conflicts between different levels of the administration; they also articulate demands at the state-level, globalise local conflicts, and create citizen platforms and networks of groups.

II. Movement Consolidation and Changes in the Political Repertoire

The new political opportunities described above have modified some of the main channels through which EMOs exert political pressure: courts; administrative channels; institutional channels; and non-conventional forms of participation. Variations over time in the forms of action deployed by the environmental movement reflect the impact of changes in political opportunities at the meso-level of the environmental policy arena more than changes in the overall system.

Courts

Spanish EMOs resort to legal action only in very crucial cases and when the probabilities of success are very high. Recourse to legal action varies according to the nature of the EMOs (ecological groups often take legal action) and, probably more significantly, their (economic) resources.

Until 1996, Spanish criminal law envisaged very few crimes against the environment. The notion of environmental crimes was first introduced in the 1983 reform of the criminal law, and basically refers to those crimes involving pollution caused by the disposal of waste products, forest fires, and security in nuclear plants. Only very low penalties were introduced. But the main factors hindering this type of activity have been the high cost of legal action (due to the need for expert witnesses and financial guarantees), as well as the lack of environmental sensitivity and technical training of public prosecutors and judges. In recent years, prosecutors specialising in environmental issues have improved this situation, but their performance has been very erratic.

Usually, the environmental movement's complaints are presented through the purely administrative channel. The EMOs interviewed consider that these are of little efficacy, since administrative courts are not prone to act unless a clear violation of procedural rules has occurred, but that they have a special value because they present opportunities to make political capital. As with legal actions, political pressure is fundamental as administrative complaints are generally accompanied by press releases and, in some cases, by symbolic direct actions. Two circumstances have favoured the use of administrative complaints: on the one hand, the creation of an environmental protection service within the Civil Guard (with which most EMOs have established a good relationship), and increasing collaboration with the different environmental departments; on the other hand, since 1986, EMOs have found in the European Commission an arena in which they may present complaints.

The Administrative Channel

Together with administrative complaints, the presentation of submissions to public inquiries has constituted the key part of EMOs' activities. Public inquiry procedures have become available through the passing of new environmental legislation pursuant to Spain's adoption of European environmental directives on Environmental Impact Assessment (EIA) in the late 1980s, and the increasing relevance of environmental departments as a result of acquiring new powers. The EIA has, at least theoretically, given EMOs access to crucial sources of information and the possibility of making submissions before any public or private intervention is authorised. However, the philosophy of these policy instruments has been undermined in the course of being adapted to the Spanish administrative system: the administration is reluctant to involve citizens in administrative decisions, and decision-makers, through legal or other mechanisms, tend to avoid applying EIA procedures. Nevertheless, disputes concerning EIA procedures have helped publicise environmental conflicts surrounding many development projects.

The Institutional Channel: Lobbying

The most straightforward institutional connection between the administration and EMOs lies in the wide range of educational and practical conservation activities financed by local, regional and state environmental departments. These activities have increased alongside the gradual incorporation of environmental issues into the policy agenda and, in most cases, they constitute the most important source of funds from the administration to the environmental movement.

But growing interactions between the authorities and EMOs exceed these 'contractual forms'. EMOs have received public recognition as social interlocutors representing the environment from a public interest perspective and their contact with government departments has increased qualitatively and quantitatively. This has had crucial repercussions. As Lowe and Goyder [1983: 65] note: 'only through close contact with government departments can groups acquire the advance intelligence and much of the information to develop their criticism of the course of official policy'.

EMOs have participated in many committees (most of them advisory, but some with policy responsibilities) with varying degrees of success Interaction in these committees is often highly politicised, but has sometimes led to specific working groups at a more technical level to elaborate legislative proposals. The most important attempts to formalise consultative interactions between the state and EMOs have been through the Advisory Committee for the Environment (CAMA) created in 1994 by the Ministry of Public Works, Transport and the Environment. However, CAMA, like most similar advisory committees, has not developed as envisaged, as an institutionalised space for EMOs' participation. Although some EMOs value the opportunity to gain information and exchange opinions, most see their participation as a waste of time (given the scant policy benefits) and resources (given the highly technical issues treated and the lack of economic means at the disposal of the Committee), and as a mere mechanism of legitimisation of government environmental policy. This led ecological groups such as Greenpeace and AEDENAT to withdraw within a year of CAMA's establishment, an action subsequently imitated by other groups.

EMOs might show more interest, either for pragmatic and/or ideological reasons, in maintaining informal contacts rather than institutionalised representation on formal advisory committees. In fact, increasing opportunities for access on specific issues may help to explain the negativity towards, and in some cases the abandonment of, advisory committees. Informal contacts with the authorities occur on a daily basis, usually regarding specific issues. Most EMO representatives interviewed described the environmental departments as most accessible and receptive to their demands and all reported a gradual improvement in their access over the last few years. However, EMO spokespersons usually see this access as a fluctuating quality of their interaction with environmental authorities. It seems that the crystallisation of this relationship has been conditioned by the political subordination of the environment to the interests of other departments. The pattern of interaction quite frequently involves conflict, which reduces the opportunities for stable alliances and ensures that EMOs remain at the periphery of decision-making. Therefore, although the creation of environmental departments has smoothed the way for the participation of EMOs in environmental policy arenas, co-operation is still highly contingent on the issue at stake. As an EMO leader states:

> the attitude of the administration toward citizens' participation is to consider it, rather than as a complement with regard to those issues where the administration does not stretch, or only gets there too late, as illegitimate interference in the realm of politicians and bureaucrats.

After a period of more intense cooperation, one EMO leader described the present more conflictual environment:

> I believe that the idea has taken root within the Government of this Autonomous Community that the environment has hindered its economic development, that the ecologist's opposition to certain projects has been a real burden ... at present those agreements are being read as defeats of the administration and victories for the ecologist.

When authorities have been closed to environmental demands, however, opportunities to publicise conflicts and to find allies have increased due to the existence of exploitable vertical cleavages within the administration. On many occasions, these administrative disputes are rooted in issues other than purely environmental questions, and constitute trials of strength between different administrations governed by different parties, or administrations governed by politicians in rival sectors of the same party. Horizontal clashes between environmental departments and other more production-oriented departments are also possible, although these may depend not only on the formal political influence of environmental institutions but also the environmental authorities' political autonomy.[5]

Non-Conventional Channels: Mass Demonstration and Symbolic Action

So-called non-conventional political tactics may be observed by examining the evolution of environmental mobilisations from 1977 to 1993.

Figure 1 shows the evolution of the number of annual mobilisations (bars) and the average number of participants (line) from 1977 to 1993. In the early years, reflecting the unfavourable political context, a low general frequency of mobilisation was punctuated by surges of mass participation. Thereafter, despite a reduced *level* of mobilisation there has, especially in recent years, been a tendency toward an increased *number* of mobilisations – evidence, perhaps, of a context relatively more favourable for advancing environmental demands, as well as of a more resourceful environmental movement.[6]

FIGURE 1
EVOLUTION OF THE NUMBER OF ENVIRONMENTAL MOBILISATIONS AND
AVERAGE NUMBER OF PROTEST PARTICIPANTS IN SPAIN, 1977–93

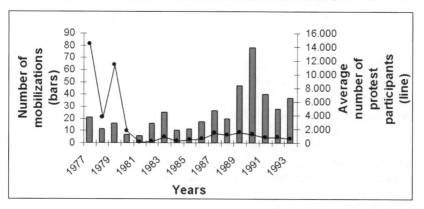

The largest number of participants corresponds to the anti-nuclear mobilisations at the end of the 1970s, coinciding with the period of mass mobilisations during the transition. During the 1980s the decline of the anti-nuclear struggle and the demobilising effects of socialist co-optation are clearly visible. Since the mid-1980s there has been a notable increase in non-conventional activities, with an inverse relation between the number of events and total number of participants.

The interpretation of the latter trend should be related to the changes in political opportunities described above, and to the wider repertoire of activities available to the environmental movement in the 1990s. With increasing resources, the relative increase in participation through administrative channels (submissions and lobbying) has not reduced the level of non-conventional activity. But we may suppose that non-conventional activities have changed their meaning and their role in the strategies deployed by EMOs. Mass mobilisations do not seek to consolidate the social and political legitimacy of EMOs in particular and environmental demands in general; rather, they seek to focus the authorities' attention on an issue. The greater media coverage that most EMOs have received has made it easier for environmental groups to promote their demands publicly without the need for mass collective actions. The increasing number of 'symbolic' direct actions, in the Greenpeace style, performed by a few core-activists aimed at capturing media attention rather than mobilising the population, explains the reduced average number of participants seen in the figures.

On the other hand, the broader repertoire of actions, increasing possibilities for working through conventional channels and for concentrating resources on lobbying activities, may also have restricted the use of mobilisation tactics to those occasions where other means have been exhausted and there are reasonable expectations of success.[7] In this context, the threat of mobilisation can be used as a weapon to guarantee the existing level of access.

As mentioned above, recent developments in Spanish environmental movements show similarities to those of their European counterparts. In his comparative study Kriesi [1996] observes, independently of the political context, a relative increase in conventional forms of action in the movements' political repertoire. Diani [1997] also points out that recent research on environmental movements has detected the increasing access of environmental groups throughout Europe, not only where environmental policy has been more dynamic and responsive but also in countries such as Ireland (and Spain) where institutional innovation in this field has been more recent. It also seems to fit Dalton's [1994] findings that EMOs in different Western countries value similarly (that is, highly) their level of access to their environmental agencies. However, the evidence in the Spanish case seems also to support Diani's doubts about the extent to which greater access is unambiguously driving environmental movements towards institutionalisation. In Spain, as in other Western countries studied by Dalton, the institutionalisation of the interactions between EMOs and environmental authorities has been rather limited.

Therefore, the incorporation of the environment into the political agenda is not so far linked to the pacification of the movement's strategies. Despite the expansion of conventional forms, their efficacy still depends on the resort to (or threat of) non-conventional forms of pressure and the socialisation of conflicts. Neither is there an appreciable trend towards the moderation of EMOs' demands in exchange for insider status, although some EMOs consider this a potential problem for the future.

III. Movement Consolidation and Organisational Transformation

Organisational transformation is ultimately linked to the type of activities and strategies used by EMOs. The expansion of the environmental movement[8] has implied an increase in conventional forms of pressure, educational and practical conservation activities, and networking activities (to maintain a higher level of internal coordination and information). In many circumstances, these activities imply considerable technical and organisational skills. Three organisational trends associated with this increasing access to the polity should be examined in order to assess the extent to which such trends indicate a process of institutionalisation: the movement's network cohesion; the specialisation/professionalisation of EMOs; increases in economic resources.

Network Cohesion

Contacts with environmental authorities have helped to establish patterns of interactions between different EMOs (both at the state and autonomous community level). On the one hand, the representation of the environmental movement in the policy process has intensified the exchange of resources (and meanings) within the different environmental networks of EMOs with similar attributes (in goals and/or identity profile), and/or geographic sphere of influence. On the other hand, it has also contributed to the cohesion of the different strands of the environmental movement as a whole. In both cases, the need to deal with specific issues and the advantages of adopting common strategies have orientated EMOs' interactions towards pragmatism in which a minimum consensus can be reached over a given issue in a context in which the movement's agenda is dictated by the agenda of environmental policy. Increasing activity in the policy process has reduced the space for ideology that previously characterised EMOs' interaction. This is consistent with the expected pattern of movement actors' interactions within an open political context, in which,

> opportunities for issue-specific action will require a more limited recourse to ideology as a mobilisation means, nor will major differences between activists be emphasized. It may also be expected that, in principle at least, the criteria whereby movement actors select their allies will be more relaxed and inclusive than in the previous, closed situations [*Diani, 1995: 15*].

However, integration into issue networks is not the only variable linked to the increasing integration of EMOs (and networks); nor should this process be interpreted as uni-directional. Rather, these two dynamics are mutually reinforcing. I have already mentioned the decline of the 'politicisation' effect of the transition period and the gradual generational replacement of the first environmental leaders, which contributed to the de-ideologisation of EMOs' relationships. The social learning process of that initial period may also have contributed to the more pragmatic approach to interactions. It has been precisely the experience of disagreement during the transition and the highly valued principle of decentralisation that has generated a movement culture very sensitive to local autonomy and pragmatic when coping with differences of opinion among organisations. According to EMOs themselves, this explains why the process of coordination, which began in 1970s, is still continuing.

Other relevant factors include the gradual rapprochement between the conservationist and ecological paradigms (clear from the adoption by the largest conservationist Spanish EMOs, ADENA-WWF, of a global view of the environment) and the greater involvement of Greenpeace with native environmental EMOs, largely due to its successful implantation in Spain, and its improved capacity to adapt international campaigns to Spanish conditions as well as to design specific campaigns for the country.

EMOs' Specialisation and Professionalisation

Increasing opportunities to exert political leverage through lobbying activities, to use new policy instruments of control such as EIA, and the organisational ability to deal with mass media, all require expertise and organisational efficiency. EMOs have increasingly professionalised their staff and organised their activities through working groups which operate with relative autonomy. This has, in some cases, led to the specialisation of EMOs around a limited number of issues. All EMO leaders are conscious of the need to become more professional, and also the price of doing so:

> We have quite a lot of access, which we have obtained during the last ten years. I do not want you to think I am self-satisfied, but this access is due to our weight as a pressure group ... This access is something that we have had to win by exerting pressure by using our capacity to reach public opinion through the press, our capacity to respond and denounce, etc. Unfortunately I always have to tell new ecologists that, these days, paperwork is crucial, even if we like going out to the countryside.

> The environment has become a technical question, during the mid-1970s we were driven more by our heart, now the issues are more specialised and require technical skills.

This view seems to suggest a trend towards an increasing division of labour and functional differentiation within Spanish EMOs and campaigning groups that now share a central infrastructure (for example, press office and legal advice) and act autonomously; they also have greater central control over campaigns despite their genuinely local character. As Donati points out in reference to the Italian case, 'campaign managers act as bridges between supportive experts, local groups and a central secretariat on whom in the last instances they depend' (Donati [*1994: 17–18*], cited in

Diani [*1997*]). However this trend is, so far, counterbalanced in the Spanish case by the importance attached to the autonomy of local branches by many ecologists, as well as by the still predominantly voluntary nature of the organisations' staff.

Increasing Economic Resources

The trend towards professionalisation has not resulted in a generalised shift from voluntary to paid staff. There are exceptions; at the state-level, Greenpeace and Adena-WWF employ paid staff to carry out their technical work, and at the autonomous community level those that have memberships of thousands usually rely on paid staff for administrative and technical work. But membership levels are still rather low, and the main source of income (except for Greenpeace), especially in the 1990s, has been grants from the states. Therefore the general trend towards the organisational model represented by Greenpeace – the protest business as described by Jordan and Maloney [*1997*] – is not the only trend, although membership growth is almost exclusive to this type of organisation.[9] EMOs' difficulties in expanding potential social support in the form of activists or supporters is at the heart of the organisational dilemma faced by the Spanish environmental movement.

In sum, I have stressed the links between the process of institutionalisation of environmental policy arenas and the strengthening of the organisational resources of EMOs, the cohesion of movements' networks, and the broadening of their political tactics and strategies. This process involves a certain trend toward movement institutionalisation (increasing conventional activities; professionalisation, increasing coordination at national level). This trend has been shaped, on the one hand, by the conditions under which they have gained access to the polity. The formal rather than substantive institutionalisation of the environment as an area of decision-making made EMOs' access contingent upon their capacity to socialise conflicts as a means of generating diverse points of access. Therefore, and so far, the resort to conventional modes of actions is not replacing confrontational modes but, rather, has become complementary. On the other hand, the features of the environmental movement, especially their sensitivity to centralisation, has reduced tendencies to centralisation.

IV. Consolidation Through Institutionalisation? Dilemmas for the Future

So far I have concentrated on the impact of access upon movement consolidation without taking into account the evolution of movement interaction with society. As stated in the introduction, organisational consolidation is seen as the combined product of increasing social support and increasing access to the polity. The peculiarity of the Spanish environmental movement resides precisely in the limited role played by this second dynamic of organisational transformation. The scant capacity to mobilise resources from society (in terms of money/membership or activists) and the trade-off between their actual level of influence and their opportunities to expand their social base gives a particular meaning and relevance to the organisational dilemmas usually linked to processes of environmental movements' consolidation:

Policy Benefits versus Membership Benefits?

The increasing political relevance of the environmental movement has not been associated with an increase in membership.[10] The ability of many EMOs to spread their social support is conditioned by the circumstances under which they have obtained political access; thus the goals of achieving policy benefits and expanding their membership are incompatible. Most activities that EMOs undertake create little social echo. Lobbying produces few benefits in terms of social recognition of their activities. Their commitment to making official complaints and lobbying activities leaves few resources for recruitment campaigns.[11] Additionally, the flow of public funds towards EMOs is still rather modest and orientated to specific projects or activities, and so has little effect on their infrastructural and social consolidation.

Professionalisation versus Participation?

The highly technical nature of these activities limits the involvement of members in EMOs' activities. The lack of time and resources with which to organise voluntary work means that participation (whether through membership or voluntary work) is always in short supply. A leader of a local EMO identified the trade-off between professionalisation and participation:

> We stress the importance of participation, we are an organisation with quite high levels of activism. However, in spite of the effort that we make (all the information is easily accessible, all the regular meetings are open), it is very difficult for those who are in charge of the issues, to keep to the rhythm of the rest of the association, i.e., for there to be participation, … we cannot stop, there is no time for training members, the desire for participation is limited by our capacity to train.

Membership problems have increased the financial constraints of many EMOs, which have also seen their (usually rather modest) budgets depend increasingly on public grants. Public money was a major source of income for all but one of the EMOs consulted.

Public Financing versus Organisational Autonomy?

Through public grants, EMOs risk acting as agents of the government, performing certain tasks and diverting their attention from other activities. EMOs, especially ecological groups, seem to have mitigated these possible effects by integrating publicly financed projects into the framework of their own activities. Another consequence of depending on public grants is the limits that this imposes when designing long-term strategies. EMOs' uncertainty about their budgets in the short-term hampers planning and increases the risks of investing in their organisational base (paid staff and infrastructure). Another typical trade-off with which public grants are associated is the moderation of their criticism of the administration. Although some EMOs identify some trends towards institutional co-optation, only one sees the threat of the withdrawal of public funding as the cause of this.

Conflictual versus Co-operative?

The 'moderation' of EMOs' antagonistic stance in relation to environmental authorities may not derive from their dependence on public funding, but rather from the 'political manners' associated with lobbying activities. In many cases, interaction with the authorities may imply reducing demands to a number of exchangeable items as a means of achieving consensus. Conflictual interactions are still predominant, and even if some groups tend towards stable co-operative relations, the presence of radical groups has limited this process. However, it has increased the possibilities of inter-organisational conflicts and a weakening of the internal cohesion of the environmental movement. In this sense, another dilemma faced by EMOs concerns the compatibility of their political status as institutional representatives of environmental interests and the political tactics they employ. The dilemma faced here by EMOs arises from the need to retain both political legitimacy and the support of local organisations and citizens in general. The radicalisation of some environmental conflicts, leading to high levels of violence, may undermine the political recognition of EMOs and their legitimacy as political interlocutors.

These dilemmas are not unique to the Spanish environmental movement, but their consequences are, nevertheless, particularly acute in Spain. The way in which the POS has evolved means that the environmental movement, paradoxically, has been able to gain access to, and exert influence in, the policy arena, despite a relatively weak presence in civil society. In contrast to the environmental movement in Northern European countries, trends towards institutionalisation have not been linked to or preceded by a period of membership growth. In the Spanish context, therefore, the crucial question is not so much how to maintain grass-roots participation and achieve policy benefits, but how to preserve (and extend) political leverage and spread support in society. Given the increasing salience of environmental policy in Spain, the critical question is whether EMOs will be able to combine their presence in policy arenas with the development of their social base. In other words, will their consolidation have as its only driving-force their institutionalisation or will they also be able to combine this with an increased social presence?

Conclusions

The evolution of the environmental movement in Spain suggests the inadequacy of an analysis of formal political opportunities based on a simplistic conceptualisation of the state as a (closed/strong or open/weak) unitary actor. Where the environment has been institutionalised in laws and public agencies, and environmental NGOs' access to the state is formally granted, it is important to focus on the conditions defining the quality of this access. It is useful to consider the autonomy of environmental agencies (their power *vis-à-vis* other state agencies) to analyse the structural dimension in the configuration of political opportunities to access to (and influence on) policy processes faced by EMOs. It is also necessary to consider EMOs as strategic actors whose decisions are based, not only on the resources they enjoy and the opportunities they perceive but also on ideology and evaluation of past experiences. Taking into account such factors enables us to understand the quality of the interactions between environmental authorities and EMOs, and in this sense some of the dynamics explaining 'the conjunctural dimension of the insider/outsider status of environmental groups in the polity' [*Rucht, 1996*].

A more refined understanding of those factors explaining EMOs' access to the polity is also needed to analyse organisational transformation in the environmental movement. In the Spanish case institutionalisation is different from that suggested by the policy model and the literature of resource mobilisation theory. Institutionalisation is not a linear and inescapable trend in the consolidation of social movements, the above analysis suggests the 'back and forth' nature of institutionalisation pressures, as well as the way in which certain features of EMOs (their ideology, diversity and learning from past experiences of movement coordination or interaction with state elites) shape this process. The pattern of consolidation depends not only on the degree of institutionalisation but also on the patterns of social support that characterise each case. In the Spanish case, some symptoms of institutionalisation have been observed in recent developments in the environmental movement, a trend best explained by the degree of institutionalisation (formal and substantive) of environmental policy arenas rather than by system-wide features defining the degree of openness of the polity; such a trend is influenced by specific features of Spanish environmental organisations (the importance attached to local autonomy and the learning from past experiences of movement coordination), as well as by the limited increase in their ability to extract resources from society in the form of activism or financial support.

NOTES

1. The empirical arguments presented here form part of my ongoing research on the Spanish environmental movement. This comprises interviews with leaders of national (including Spanish branches of Greenpeace and WWF) and regional environmental groups, and data on environmental protest obtained from a selection of events registered in the annual indexes of *El País* from 1977 to 1983 under the classification 'environment'.

2. See Kriesi *et al.* [*1995: Ch.4*], on the importance of the evaluation of issues by established authorities and the influence of this on social movements' mobilisation.

3. The autonomous role of parliament was also limited by strict party discipline. The judicial sphere has not escaped the influence of the distribution of political power [*Aparicio, 1989: 131–6*]. Moreover, the mechanisms established for direct democracy were very restrictive.

4. Although I concentrate on general features or regularities attributable to the environmental movement across Spain, the decentralised character of the state (and of environmental powers) and the specific socio-political context in each autonomous community makes it possible to identify distinctive features of the environmental movement (and different exposure to institutionalisation trends) in the seventeen Spanish Autonomous Communities. None the less, it is difficult to understand each of these movements other than as part of a state level movement. In some cases the more significant variance derives from specificity of the socio-political context, for instance in the Basque Country where extreme nationalists have followed a strategy of movement co-optation. This has contributed to both the weakening of the organisational base of the movement (causing internal divisions) and to the radicalisation of certain environmental conflicts (as a way to obtain public visibility for nationalist issues) which, in turn, has contributed to the marginalisation of the movement, limiting their capacity to gain policy benefits [*Tejerina et al., 1995*]; for an alternative, more positive, account of the interaction between radical nationalism and the environmental movement in the Basque Country see Barcena, *et al.* [*1995*]. But usually differences concerning the formal and substantive incorporation of the environment into the regional administration represent the main factor of variance.

5. Only a few EMOs recognised these horizontal cleavages; therefore although they may exist, so far the EMOs have scarcely benefited from them. We may expect that the gradual consolidation of the environment as an autonomous political arena will increase the probability and visibility of such conflicts.

6. In empirical studies linking mobilisation and the features of the POS, full exclusion contexts are characterised by low levels of mobilisation with periods of protest followed by periods of almost no activity; while in contexts with middling opportunities for inclusion, the expected tendency is of a more constant level of activity [*Kriesi et al., 1995*] The period covered is too short to conclusively identify changes in the patterns of mobilisation. However, the results obtained allow an interpretation coherent with changes in the POS.

7. In this sense, environmental organisations have broadened their non-conventional repertoire to campaigns that are not (only) targeted at the state but (also) at the market. Greenpeace's ongoing campaign to boycott firms bottling mineral water in PVC has already obtained the commitment of 25 firms (including the largest) to stop using this plastic (*El País*, 22 Aug. 1998, p.19).

8. Varillas [*1997*] reckoned that around 300 EMOs were currently operating (in contrast to 30 in the 1970s).
9. Diani [*1997*] points out that in those countries lacking a strong counter-cultural movement, as in Italy or France, movement organisational growth has predominantly taken this form.
10. EMO affiliation levels in Spain are rather low (around one per cent of the adult population), even though 40 per cent of Spaniards are in favour of EMOs and a similar percentage do not reject the idea of being a member [*García Ferrando, 1991: 181*].
11. Greenpeace's recruitment campaigns have been quite remarkable; it grew from 1,500 supporters in 1984 to 72,000 in 1996; although the marketable nature of the name is a clear factor, it also shows the existence of a social cluster of sympathisers with the environmental movement.

REFERENCES

Aparicio, Miguel Angel (1989), *Introducción al Sistema Político y Constitucional Español*, Barcelona: Ariel.
Barcena, Iñaki, Ibarra, Pedro and Mario Zubiaga (1995), *Nacionalismo y Ecología: Conflicto e Insitutucionalización en el Movimiento Ecologista Vasco*, Madrid: Los Libros de la Catarata.
Caciagli, Marco (1984), 'Spain: Parties and the Party System in the Transition', in G. Pridham (ed.), *The New Mediterranean Democracies: Regime Transition in Spain, Greece and Portugal*, London: Frank Cass.
Colomer, Josep M. (1992), 'Development Policy Decision-Making in Democratic Spain', Manuscript.
Colomer, Josep M. (1997), 'Las Instituciones de la Crispación Política', *Claves*, No.74, pp.44–7.
Costa, Pedro (1983), *Hacia la Destrucción Ecológica de España*, Madrid: Grijalbo.
Dalton, Russell J. (1994), *The Green Rainbow*, New Haven, CT: Yale University Press.
Diani, Mario (1995), *Green Networks*, Edinburgh: Edinburgh University Press.
Diani, Mario (1997), 'Organizational Change and Communication Styles in Western European Environmental Organizations', paper presented at the twenty-fifth ECPR Joint sessions of Workshops, Bern, Switzerland, 27 Feb. to 4 March 1997.
Font, Nuria (1996), 'La Europeización de la Política Ambiental en España. Un Estudio de Implementación de la Directiva de Evaluación de Impacto Ambiental', Ph.D. dissertation, Universitat Autònoma de Barcelona.
Garcia Ferrando, M. (1991), 'Opinion Publica y Medio Ambiente', *Sistema*, No.104–5, pp.175–89.
Grant, Jordan and William Maloney (1997), *The Protest Business? Mobilizing Campaign Groups*, Manchester: Manchester University Press.
Gunther, Richard (1992), 'Spain. The Very Model of a Modern Elite Settlement', in Higley, John and Richard Gunther (eds.), *Elites and Democratic Consolidation in Latin America and Southern Europe*, Cambridge: Cambridge University Press.
Jenkins, J. Craig and Bert Klandermans (1995), 'The Politics of Social Protest', in Jenkins, and Klandermans (eds.) [*1995*].
Jenkins, J. Craig (1995), 'Social Movements, Political Representation, and the State: An Agenda and Comparative Framework', in Jenkins and Klandermans (eds.) [*1995*].
Jenkins, J. Craig and Bert Klandermans (eds.) (1995), *The Politics of Social Protest: Comparative Perspectives on States and Social Movements*, Minneapolis, MN: University of Minnesota Press.
Kitschelt, Herbert P (1986), 'Political Opportunity Structures and Political Protest: Anti-Nuclear Movements in Four Democracies', *British Journal of Political Science*, Vol.16, No.1, pp.58–85.
Kriesi, Hanspeter (1989), 'The Political Opportunity Structure of the Dutch Peace Movement', *West European Politics*, Vol.12, No.3, pp.295–312.
Kriesi, Hanspeter (1995), 'The Political Opportunity Structure of New Social Movements: Its Impact on Their Mobilization', in Jenkins and Klandermans [*1995*].
Kriesi, Hanspeter (1996) 'The Organizational Structure of New Social Movements in a Political Context', in McAdam, McCarthy and Zald [*1996*].

Kriesi, Hanspeter, Ruud Koopmans, Jan Willem Duyvendak and Marco G. Giugni (1992), 'New Social Movements and Political Opportunities in Europe', *European Journal of Political Research*, Vol.22, No.2, pp.219–44.

Kriesi, Hanspeter *et al.* (1995), *New Social Movements in Western Europe*, Minneapolis, MN: University of Minnesota Press.

Lancaster, Thomas D. (1989), *Policy Stability and Democratic Change: Energy in Spain's Transition*, University Park, PA and London: Pennsylvania State University Press.

Lo, Clarence Y.H. (1992), 'Communities of Challengers in Social Movement Theory', in Aldon D. Morris and Carol McClurg Mueller (eds.), *Frontiers in Social Movement Theory*, New Haven, CT and London: Yale University Press.

Lowe, Philip, and Jane Goyder (1983), *Environmental Groups in Politics*, London: George Allen & Unwin.

McAdam, Doug, McCarthy, John D. and Mayer N. Zald (eds.) (1996), *Comparative Perspectives on Social Movements*, Cambridge and New York: Cambridge University Press.

McCarthy, John D. and Mayer N. Zald (1977), 'Resource Mobilization and Social Movements: A Partial Theory', *American Journal of Sociology*, Vol.82, No.6, pp.1212–39.

Maravall, José (1982), *The Transition to Democracy in Spain*, New York: St. Martin's Press.

Medhurst, Kenneth (1984), 'Spain's Evolutionary Pathway from Dictatorship to Democracy', in Geoffrey Pridham (ed.), *The New Mediterranean Democracies: Regime Transition in Spain, Greece and Portugal*, London: Frank Cass.

Montero, José Ramón (1981), 'Partidos y Participación Política: Algunas Notas sobre la Afiliación Política en la Etapa Inicial de la Transición Española', *Revista de Estudios Políticos*, No.23, pp.33–72.

Prevost, Gary (1993), 'The Spanish Peace Movement in a European Context', *West European Politics*, Vol.16, No.2, pp.144–64.

Rootes, C. (1997), 'Shaping Collective Active', in R. Edmondson (ed.), *The Political Context of Collective Action*, London and New York: Routledge.

Rucht, Dieter (1996), 'The Impact of National Contexts on Social Movements' Structures: A Cross-Movement and Cross-National Comparison', in McAdam, McCarthy and Zald [1996].

Smith, Martin J. (1993), *Pressure, Power and Policy*, Hemel Hempstead, Hertfordshire: Harvester Wheatsheaf.

Tarrow, Sidney (1994), *Power in Movement*, Cambridge: Cambridge University Press.

Tarrow, Sidney (1995), 'Mass Mobilization and Regime Change: Pacts, Reform, and Popular Power in Italy (1918–1922) and Spain (1975–1978)', in Richard Gunther, P. Nikiforos Diamandouros and Hans-Jürgen Puhle (eds.), *The Politics of Democratic Consolidation: Southern Europe in Comparative Perspective*, Baltimore, MD: Johns Hopkins University Press.

Tejerina, Benjamín., José Manuel Fdz. Sobrado, and Xabier Aierdi (1995), *Sociedad Civil, Protesta y Movimientos Sociales en el Pais Vasco. Los Límites de la Teoría de la Movilización de Recursos*, Gasteiz: Eusko Jaurlaritza.

Tilly, Charles (1978), *From Mobilization to Revolution*, Reading, MA: Addison-Wesley.

Varilllas, Benigno (1997), 'El Movimiento Asociativo Ecologista', *Temas para el Debate*, No.27, pp.44–9.

Varillas, Benigno and Humberto Da Cruz (1981), *Para una Historia del Movimiento Ecologista en España*, Madrid: Miraguano.

Sustaining Local Environmental Mobilisations: Groups, Actions and Claims in Southern Europe

MARIA KOUSIS

Using Tilly's definition of 'ad hoc social movements', this study employs protest-case analysis in order to bring to the surface the differences and similarities between grassroots environmental activism and community-based environmental movements as they appear in post-dictatorial Greece, Portugal and Spain. The analysis centres on community-group profiles, networks, action and claim repertoires concerning the source of environmental degradation, the damage created, and the wider socio-economic and environmental impacts. Implications are drawn for the debates regarding environmental movements in Southern Europe and the future of the environmental movement.

Characteristics of Local Environmental Mobilisations

During the past two decades, research conducted on the environmental movement has led to a debate about how the movement is defined and visualised, and what its future might be. Some studies, focusing on the institutionalisation of the larger and more active organisations, their subsequent involvement in policy-making circles, and their support for ecological modernisation initiatives, argue that we are experiencing the 'end of ecologism' [van der Heijden et al., 1992; Jamison, 1996; Blühdorn, 1997]. Others maintain that 'environmentalism' is emerging in the form of popular resistance movements with direct challenges and implications for democracy and the conventional political arena [Szasz, 1994; Taylor, 1995]. A third group of studies concludes that hope lies in the possible collaboration between grassroots mobilisers and environmental social

The author wishes to thank Chris Rootes, Dieter Rucht, Charles Tilly and two anonymous reviewers for their useful comments on earlier drafts, as well as all 'Grassroots environmental Action and Sustainable Development in Southern Europe' project partners and research assistants for their invaluable collaboration. Any remaining errors are solely mine. This work was supported by the European Commission, DG XII for Science, Research and Development, RTD Programme 'Environment & Culture', contract no. EV5V-CT94-0393.

movement organisations (ESMOs) inside or across national borders with the aim of exercising pressure on state and supra-state bodies to protect the environment [*Gould et al., 1993, 1996; Princen and Finger, 1994*].

What constitutes a grass-roots environmental movement? Have grass-roots mobilisations been increasing? Is there co-operation between specific types of grass-roots mobilisers and larger organisations? These questions are addressed using evidence from Greece, Spain and Portugal.

Local Environmental Mobilisations: Groups, Links, Actions and Protest Duration

Local environmental mobilisations are very difficult to estimate in terms of numbers [*Diani, 1995*]. Yet an abundance of recent literature provides information on case studies or protest events associated with environmental problems affecting the local level. Tilly [*1994*] classifies social movements into three types: the professional, the 'ad hoc' community-based, and the communitarian. By comparison with professional and communitarian movements, community-based movements are more temporary but richer mobilisations which are sustained through time.[1] Thus, one very important criterion is duration over time. Aiming to distinguish between the different types of grass-roots[2] environmental mobilisations, this work begins with a review of the related literature on groups, actions and claims, considering as well the effects of duration.

Although the development of environmental movements is heavily shaped by their own actions, movements may largely be born out of 'environmental opportunities' [*McAdam et al., 1996a*]. For many students of this area it is clear that the severity of ecological disorganisation does not correlate highly with environmental mobilisations. Nevertheless, certain critical environmental preconditions are essential [*Walsh, 1988; van der Heijden et al, 1992; Gould et al., 1996; Wolfson and Butenko, 1992*]. Some argue that as the ecological 'crisis' continues, grass-roots movements appear to grow stronger [*Hofrichter, 1993; Princen and Finger, 1994*]. Others point out the process which entails the take-over of local natural resources by powerful private, state or supra-state interests and the gradual or immediate ecosystem disorganisation that results [*Schnaiberg, 1994; Gedicks, 1995*]. These critical environmental preconditions which are necessary for the existence of local environmental mobilisations are not considered as the 'ecological crisis', but are envisaged as parts of the process of ecological marginalisation [*Kousis, 1998a*]. This process stems from the intervention of social actors on ecosystems in a way that alters their functional integrity, and normally leads to the disorganisation of biological processes, the locals' loss of their resource base, and the generation of a wide range of socio-economic, political and public health risks. Counteracting the impression created by opposition to plant siting and the increasing salience of the external environment, many students of local environmental mobilisation point out that it is related to exposure effects with immediate health impacts [*Szasz, 1994; Edelstein, 1988; Bullard, 1993; Hofrichter, 1993; Kousis, 1993*]. Thus this literature suggests that the more pervasive the ecological marginalisation, the more likely the increase in local environmental mobilisations, especially those cases of sustained resistance.

The study of local contentious politics also necessitates an examination of the forms of organisation and networking (informal as well as formal) available to protesters, as well as their collective action and claim repertoires [*McAdam, et al., 1996b; McAdam, et al., 1996a; Diani, 1995; Weinberg, 1997*]. Researchers of grass-roots environmental resistance view such mobilisations as intimately tied to the community level [*Freudenberg and Steinsapir, 1991; Szasz, 1994*].³ The movement against toxics concerns contaminated communities [*Edelstein, 1988; Bullard, 1993; Hofrichter, 1993; Gottlieb, 1993; Szasz, 1994; Cable and Cable, 1995*]. NIMBY, NIOBY or NIABY⁴ groups engaged in popular resistance to unwanted landuse refer to candidate communities [*Freudenberg and Steinsapir, 1991; Rudig, 1995; Taylor, 1995*]. Finally, citizen-workers' environmental struggles are associated with community-level groups [*Gould et al., 1996; Weinberg, 1997*]. Recent community sociology also points out the intrinsic relationship between grass-roots environmental activism and the community [*Chekki, 1997*]. This ranges from the negative social and psychological impacts of toxic exposure [*Couch et al., 1997*] to the importance of municipal boundaries in framing environmental issues [*Michelson, 1997*].

The types of participating groups mentioned in such studies represent a wide spectrum of community-based or popular groups: residents, neighbours, citizens, indigenous people, natives, workers, local environmental associations, school or church affiliated groups, mothers, or other women's groups, and, to a lesser extent, local government, local professionals, and local political party representatives. Literature in this area suggests that a considerable proportion of environmental activism by these volunteer groups is not sustained. It is argued that the capacity of sustainable local environmental mobilisations is partly determined by their access to scientific and political resources from national and regional environmental organisations [*Gould and Weinberg, 1991; Weinberg, 1997*]. When local ties are transcended, and the links between the 'global' and local are made, this ensures more effective environmental protection [*Rucht, 1993; Princen and Finger, 1994; Gould et al., 1996*]. Nevertheless, the relationship between environmental NGOs and local environmental contenders has not always been very encouraging [*Gould et al., 1993*].

Thus, networks that extend beyond grass-roots environmental activism at the community level appear limited. Most such networking is autonomous [*Freudenberg and Steinsapir, 1991; Bullard,-1993; Taylor, 1995*].

Sustained local environmental resistance has been characterised by an escalation and intensification of protest activities as the demands of the mobilisers remain unanswered [*Freudenberg and Steinsapir, 1991; Kousis, 1993, 1997a; Aguilar et al., 1995; Cable and Cable, 1995; Bullard, 1993*]. This normally begins with attempts to convince public officials or the offender to stop creating and/or to clean up the problem. Negative or neutral reactions lead to the filing of law suits, publicity in the media, lobbying, and other institutional means of resolving the issues. Simultaneously, or at a later stage, depending on the responses of the challenged groups, more contentious actions are taken, such as demonstrations, site occupation, site blocking, and strikes. Thus, the duration of the environmental mobilisation is intimately tied to the number and variety of actions involved.

The importance of framing environmental issues has been stressed by most students of local environmental activism [*Weinberg, 1997; Szasz, 1994; Bullard, 1993; Gerhards and Rucht, 1992*].[5] In cases of sustained resistance, claims intensify and may change dramatically in response to the antagonist's reactions. This contrasts with the focus of the claims in unsustained cases. Such cases are usually less intense and more low key in their pervasiveness and impact. They may, for example, aim at an end-of-pipe solution [*Kousis, 1993; Gedicks, 1995*]. Issue expansion is also characteristic of the sustained resistance cases, since sometimes the reforms they advocate would lead to major alterations in the economy and society [*Szasz, 1994; Kousis, 1997a*].

On the basis of the above and for present purposes, a comprehensive way of addressing grassroots environmental activism would be to distinguish between what some [*Cable and Cable, 1995*] have labelled grievances appearing as a form of environmental activism, and community-based environmental movements. Using duration as a major criterion, *local environmental mobilisation* may be classified as (a) short-duration *grass-roots environmental activism* and (b) long duration *community-based environmental movements*. Sustained mobilisations which are identified with community-based/local environmental movements may be labelled as '*ad hoc*', not exclusively in terms of time, but because usually they initially rise as a response to a single urgent issue. In contrast to local environmental activism, they are characterised by an intensification of network building, action escalation, and claim framing.

Research Approaches

Research on grass-roots environmental action has followed two different approaches: the qualitative and the quantitative. Researchers following a qualitative or *case study* approach focus on one or a few case/s of local contention [*Kemp, 1990; Connell, 1991; Kousis, 1991, 1993; Welsh, 1993; Collin and Harris Sr., 1993; Aguilar et al., 1995; Walsh and Warland, 1997*]. These researchers adopt a regional [*Gould, 1991; Gould et al., 1996; Rangan, 1996*], a national [*Freudenberg and Steinsapir, 1991; Bullard, 1993; Hase, 1992; Szasz, 1994; Cable and Cable, 1995*], or a cross-national orientation [*Taylor, 1995; Gedicks, 1995*]. As the number of studies increases, the orientation switches from in-depth analysis of the issues of one case to analysis for many cases of one issue, or a selective set of issues, such as environmental justice, eco-populism, toxic colonialism, or popular resistance. As a result, given the nature of the case study approach, the range of coverage of the types of grassroots mobilisers, environmental problems, as well as the groups they challenge, remains limited. A more general treatment of local environmental contenders is provided by qualitative works that address the environmental movement as a whole [*Jamison et al., 1990; Yanitsky, 1996; Viola, 1997*].

Researchers following the quantitative approach examine environmental activism by both grassroots and environmental organisations, at a regional, national or cross-national level, thus addressing a wider range of environmental problems and activist issues. *Protest event* analysis [*Kriesi et al., 1995; Rucht and Neidhardt, 1998; Rucht et al., 1992*] is one strategy which has been employed. Others have collected data by means of interviews with activists and members of a wide range of groups and organisations [*Diani, 1995*].

Scope and Research Method

This work is focused upon the effects of duration on the sustainability of local environmental mobilisations in Greece, Spain and Portugal, using data derived from protest-case analysis – an alternative content analysis approach. Its aim is threefold. First, it exposes the differences and similarities between short-term grass-roots environmental activism and community-based environmental movements as regards their community-group profiles, their networks, their actions and their claim repertoires concerning the source of environmental degradation, the damage created, and the wider socio-economic and environmental impacts (related to their views on ecological marginalisation). In so doing it addresses questions such as: Are there proportionally more cases of unsustained environmental activism than of local environmental movements through time? Do participants in sustained cases reflect deeper concerns about their external environment than those protesting for a limited time? Are they exposed to more pervasive impacts? Are network extension and intensive protest activity more characteristic of sustained local environmental movements? Is exclusive community group participation more characteristic of unsustained local environmental activism?

Secondly, the study provides data on local environmental mobilisations and comparisons between local environmental activism and movements across the three countries, discussing their implications for the debate regarding environmental movements in Southern Europe. Are environmentalist concerns in Greece, Spain, and Portugal more likely to be expressed in a contentious manner at the community, rather than the associational, level? Are there clear national differences in terms of characteristics or cross-temporal changes and which are the factors determining them?

Finally, the present work links back to the wider debate about the future of the environmental movement in order to show exactly how sustained and unsustained local environmental mobilisations are situated within this debate. It also lays out the implications for other European and nonEuropean countries and regions where local environmental mobilisations have not been systematically studied so far.

The research method combines elements from both the qualitative and quantitative approaches to environmental protest. Its unit of analysis is *the protest case*. Unlike the protest-event approach, protest case analysis compiles information over five series of data: location, events, groups, time, and issue-claim linkages. Each case represents collective incident/s in which five[6] or more persons from a specific geographic area, excluding members of the national government, express criticism, protest or resistance, making a visible claim for their health, physical environment or economic status, which, if realised, would affect the interests of some person(s) or group(s) outside their own numbers during a given time period.

Tilly's [*1978*] definition of contentious gatherings is extended to include those who file procedural complaints to authority, but who may not necessarily proceed with other forms of public protest. Cases involve contentious local initiatives in which local groups either act independently or in collaboration with political party representatives, non-local environmental organisations or local authorities (for a full methodological description see Kousis [*1998b*]). Under this definition, those mobilising against a specific threat belong to a local setting, usually a community (village, town, or urban neighbourhood) or a set of communities (villages, island, or set of urban neighbourhoods), urban or rural; they may mobilise one or more times. Such contentious gatherings include formal claim-making, petitions, meetings, demonstrations, boycotts, strikes, threats, collective violence, and other forms of action. They are linked via a set of claims which, although subject to change over time, is directly related to a specific source of contention and its related antagonists.

The content analysis data refer to grassroots environmental action and sustainable development in Greece, Portugal and Spain, from the end of their dictatorial periods to 1994, inclusive. Articles were located by reading every issue of the major national newspapers *Eleftherotypia* (GR), *El Pais* (ES), *Jornal de Noticias* (PT), and *Publico* (PT),[7] as well as the ecology magazines, *Oikologia* and *Perivallon* (GR), *Nea Oikologia* (GR), *Integral* (ES), *Quercus* (ES), and *AAVV-Forum Ambiente* (PT)[8] for the same period. About 80 per cent of the articles come from national newspapers. Besides all sections of the main (including Sunday) editions, all supplements to the main edition of the newspapers were also read.[9] Once copies of all mentions were gathered they were collated into location files and subsequently into cases comprised of events, before the final selection criteria[10] were applied – a total of 1,813 articles were excluded for the three countries. Approximately 4,500 cases of local environmental mobilisations were organised from a pool of 15,032 articles [*Kousis, 1998b*]. The 1,322 Greek cases were organised using 2,940 articles, the 2,447 Spanish using 10,874 articles, and the 550 Portuguese using 1,992 articles. For present purposes, 2,704 protest cases are analysed, representing the population of the Greek and Portuguese cases, and a stratified sample of the Spanish cases.[11]

Environmental Movements in Greece, Portugal and Spain

There is increasing evidence that citizens of non-core nations are more concerned about their environment than are citizens in core nations, particularly as regards health issues [*Adeola, 1998*]. Especially in the 1990s, concern over environmental issues grew among citizens as well as environmental organisations in Mediterranean Europe [*Pridham and Konstadakopoulos, 1997*].

Since the 1960s, Mediterranean countries have been transformed from traditional to consumer-oriented and modern societies. During the past decade, studies have documented the existence and severity of various forms of pollution and related public health impacts for Southern European countries [*Lallas, 1992; Sunyer and Anto, 1992; Navarro et al., 1992; Kalandidi, 1992; Ferraz, 1992*]. Yet, although Southern European environmental experiences reflect topics and issues familiar in Northern Europe, their paths are quite distinct. Given the historical, political, socio-economic and cultural circumstances of Mediterranean Europe, environment-related movements attest to a different set of characteristics, problems and theoretical issues. For Spain, Portugal, and Greece, the end of long dictatorial regimes was followed by socialist party dominance in the

1970s and 1980s and the consolidation of democracies [*Gunther et al., 1995*].

Even though Greek and Spanish, and to a lesser extent, Portuguese societies have been characterised by intense unconventional political participation during the last two decades [*Vitsilaki, 1992; Barcena and Ibarra, forthcoming; Tejerina et al., 1995; Koopmans 1996*] the growth in research on social movements as parts of their political culture has only recently been undertaken. New social movements such as the women's and environmental movements which have risen especially with the end of the dictatorships, have only been researched since the late 1980s [*Louloudis, 1987; Diani, 1995; Aguilar et al., 1995; Demertzis, 1995; della Porta et al., 1996*].

No systematic comparison has been made of environmental movements in Greece, Portugal, and Spain. None the less, an examination of the studies appearing during the last decade does reveal some similarities and differences amongst the three countries. Especially for Greece and Spain, and to a lesser extent for Portugal, the environmental movement is seen as being comprised of both environmental organisations and local environmental groups. Most students, in a limited manner, emphasise the weak features and late appearance of the former, and the intensive yet limited character of the latter. None examines closely the different types of local environmental mobilisations.

Environmental Organisations

In the second half of the 1990s, environment-related organisations numbered 1,394 in Spain [*Holliday, 1997*], 195 in Greece [*Tsakiris and Sakellaropoulos, 1998*], and 140 in Portugal [*Ribeiro and Rodrigues, 1997*]. Yet, although there has been a well noted increase in the number of organisations during the post-dictatorial period, these movements are seen as weak by comparison with their counterparts in other European countries. In a systematic comparison of new social movements in four northern European countries and one southern, Spain is shown to have the highest levels of *all* unconventional mobilisations, the lowest per capita rate of associational membership, and the lowest number of participants in the 'ecology movement' [*Koopmans, 1996*]. It is posited that the weak associational cultures related to the limited political opportunities under the military juntas, and the wider historical context, prevented the emergence of a stronger movement in Greece [*Pridham et al., 1995; Spanou, 1995a*], Spain [*Koopmans, 1996; Holliday, 1997; Aguilar, forthcoming*] and Portugal [*Ribeiro and Rodrigues, 1997; Fidelis-Nogueira, 1996*]. An additional obstacle is the weak organisational base [*Aguilar, 1996; Holliday, 1997; Fousekis and Lekakis, 1997*] which some attribute to limited funding [*Ribeiro and Rodriguez, 1997*].

The weakness of Southern European environmental movements has also been attributed to other non-structural characteristics of the political culture, such as environmental awareness or concern, and environmental commitment. Some observers stress that although higher levels of concern do now exist, they are not followed by high levels of environmental commitment [*Holliday, 1997; Barcena and Ibarra, 1998*]. Others emphasise the overall low levels of environmental consciousness which characterise the post-dictatorial period as well as the individualistic, materialist, 'statist', and clientelistic values of the people [*Aguilar, 1994; Demertzis, 1995; Pridham et al., 1995; Ribeiro and Rodriguez, 1997*].

Factors related to the economic context have also been stressed by some, albeit more for Greece and Portugal. It is argued that less intensive and later industrialisation and urbanisation and greater demand for economic development did not provide the conditions necessary for the establishment of a strong movement [*Dede, 1993; Demertzis, 1995; Fidelis-Nogueira, 1996*]. The presence of nuclear power installations in Spain led to a much stronger anti-nuclear movement there.

Other important factors in the development of the movement are changes in the international political opportunity structure apparent in the Europeanisation of these societies, as well as the strong presence of Northern-based environmental organisations [*Aguilar, forthcoming; Fidelis-Nogueira, 1996; Valaora, 1995*].

Local Environmental Mobilisation

Of the few works on local environmental mobilisation in Southern Europe, some refer to cases of resistance even under the military dictatorships. These include those during the early 1970s which were part of the Neighbourhood Movement in Spanish cities, seeking solutions to urbanisation problems such as water pollution, sewage, waste, and the preservation of parks and tree-lined streets as well as general environmental protection [*Castells, 1983*]. Others examine cases of local resistance against environmentally damaging government-promoted industrial projects [*Louloudis, 1987; Spanou, 1995b*].

After the fall of the military regimes, local environmental mobilisations, characterised as 'single issue', are portrayed as making a much stronger but sporadic appearance in different parts of Greece [*Kousis, 1991; Pridham et al., 1995*], Spain [*Barcena and Ibarra, 1998; Aguilar, 1994*] and Portugal (Aguilar *et al.*, 1995; Fidelis-Nogueira *et al.*, 1996). Since they have been mainly presented as single case studies it is not clear what the overall profile of the majority of these has been and how widespread they are; consequently, a lot of room is left for speculation. Such mobilisations have been viewed as community-based and contentious by some, network-dependent and interest-oriented by others. The seriousness and intensity of particular conflicts have been shown especially by the early nineties, when various state projects were cancelled due to local resistance (Kousis, 1994; Fidelis-Nogueira *et al.*, 1996).

In contrast to other forms of activism, environmental grassroots resistance is *not* directly linked to political parties [*Barcena and Ibarra, forthcoming; Kousis, 1997a*]. It is expressed strongly via more informal (but not necessarily associational) structures already available in these countries, that is, via community-based groups [*Kousis, 1991, 1993; Fidelis et al., 1996; Aguilar, 1996*].

Time Trends of Actions in Local Environmental Mobilisations in Greece, Spain and Portugal

Using only one national newspaper for each country, Figure 1 provides standardised national level data across two decades of both sustained and unsustained grass-roots environmental mobilisations reported in *Eleftherotypia* (GR), *El Pais* (ES) and *Jornal de Noticias* (PT).[12] After taking into account the number of inhabitants in each country, the data show similarities as well as differences among them. The interpretation of these requires at least an examination of political, economic and methodological factors. To begin with, an overall increase is clearly visible through the 20- year period. This increase is more visible for Portugal and Spain than for Greece, especially since the late 1980s–early 1990s. In addition, the peaks and the amount of protest actions in environmental mobilisations are different for the three countries, with Greece leading, followed by Spain and Portugal until 1990, when Portugal surpasses Spain continually to 1994.

As regards the different peaks of environmental actions across the three countries, if we disregard the first election in each country (and also the second in Portugal), the number of grass-roots environmental mobilisations increases – sharply in the case of Greece – immediately before election years.[13] This occurs more often for Spain and Greece (in five out of five election years for both) than for Portugal (in five out of seven), showing part of the effects of the political opportunity structure in each country.

Although the above may provide insight into the ups and downs of environmental actions, it does not offer an adequate explanation for the marked increase of actions from the 1970s to the 1990s. This may be attributed to a general increase in environmental awareness as well as to an increase in environmental reporting across the three countries. It may also be attributed to effects of the external environment, such as the increase in ecosystem interventions during the two decades by various social actors which lead to a variety of negative impacts felt at the local level. Such

FIGURE 1

ACTIONS PER 100,000 PEOPLE, 1974–94

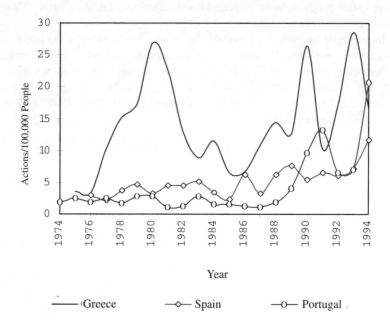

Year

——— ꞌGreece   —◇— Spain   —○— Portugal

ecological marginalisation effects, given their immediate health, ecosystem and economic impacts, are especially important for local communities.

During the first part of the post-dictatorial period the increase in actions of major environmental protest cases in the three countries included those against nuclear installations/activities, military base/activities, sewage problems, and industrial pollution. Yet, although roughly similar in their orientation, the number of actions is considerably higher for Greece. This may be largely attributed to better coverage by the selected national newspaper. *Eleftherotypia* has been reporting on environmental issues better than any other Greek newspaper during the post-dictatorial period, while it covers a considerably smaller country than *El Pais* does. Although comparable in terms of reported issues, given the size of its country, *El Pais* could not adequately cover the grass-roots environmental actions in Spain as well as *Eleftherotypia* could in Greece. In order better to comprehend the magnitude of dynamism behind these actions the number of participants engaged in them must be examined. It is expected that those numbers would be higher for Spain, followed by Greece and Portugal.

Jornal de Noticias has not provided as inclusive a coverage for Portugal as *Eleftherotypia* has for Greece. Yet, it is essential that factors other than the newspaper be examined in order to interpret the different curves for the two countries. Although similar in terms of population and size, Greece and Portugal appear sharply different as regards the related actions taken in each country. Differences also appear in general environmental awareness for the period covered. One indication of this is that whereas the first environment-related magazine in Greece appeared in 1982 followed by a second in 1984, in Portugal the first such magazine appeared in 1994. The increase in Portuguese actions since the late 1980s came close to the high peaks of Greek actions. None the less, factors explaining the variation of environmental actions between the two countries across the 20-year period must focus upon structural as well as cultural determinants.

Figure 1 also depicts a decrease of environmental actions during the mid-1980s in the three countries, especially for Greece. An appropriate explanation of this could relate to the economic situations of the countries. It is at this time that the Greek economy was most problematic, especially when compared to other EC countries, and when Spain was trying to recover from the transitional problems of the previous years [*Pridham, 1995*]. Until the mid-1980s, government instability in Portugal was an obstacle to the improvement of the economy, which nevertheless occurred later with the assistance of a strict International Monetary Fund adjustment programme (1983–85) and a flood of investments [*Pridham, 1995*].

Sustained and Unsustained Local Environmental Mobilisations

Following Tilly's [*1994*] definition, *local environmental mobilisation* which is sustained through time and characterised by an intensification of network building, action escalation, and claim framing qualifies as a *community-based environmental movement*. Mobilisations which are not sustained through time and do not have these characteristics are considered as *environmental activism* and may, but usually do not, lead to sustained resistance.

Case duration is the primary criterion used here to determine whether an environmental protest case may be characterised as a community-based movement. Grass-roots environmental protest cases that endure for one year or more are considered here as cases of sustained resistance.[14] This distinction is considered as most appropriate since mobilisers in such cases had enough time to proceed to an intensification of their actions, networking, and claim making. One third of the 2,704 cases fulfil this criterion. Sustained resistance implies as well better coverage by the press.[15]

Figure 2 portrays the actions of sustained and unsustained local environmental mobilisations compiled over the three countries for the

FIGURE 2

SUM OF ACTIONS BY DURATION OF CASE 1974–1994

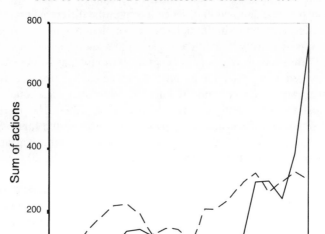

— — <1 year   ——— ⩾ 1 year

20-year period.[16] With the exception of a down-cycle in the mid-1980s, both types of protest increased until 1994 when long duration actions increased sharply, implying a growing mobilisation intensity. The amount of mobilising actions differed for the two types of cases. During the post-dictatorial period and until the early 1990s, grass-roots environmental activism made a stronger appearance than did community-based environmental movements. The actions in 1994 suggest that this pattern may not hold in the future. The finding may be interpreted as providing support for studies of environmental concern and organisations in Southern Europe that document the increase in pro-environment attitudes and behaviour. Nevertheless more research is required to address the increases in these trends, which are mostly linked to structural as well as cultural factors. The tables below provide an overall picture of the group, action and claim characteristics related to these trends.

Mobilisers' Characteristics, Links and Actions

One important set of characteristics of participants is that related to the community. Differences appear with reference to the number of communities involved in each type of protest case. Cases involving participants from more than one community appear in one-third of the sustained protest cases, and 16 per cent of the unsustained ones. Communities were coded in relation to participants' municipal boundaries,[17] neighbourhoods, or combinations of residential pockets of adjacent municipalities,[18] especially in urban areas. In both sustained and unsustained resistance cases, urban populations take the lead (about half in both), followed by rural ones (less than one third in both). Relationships[19] to other protest cases are much more apparent in the former (22 per cent) than in the latter (nine per cent). This implies possible collaborations, or by contrast, clashes, in intense local conflict situations which take place between participating groups at a sub-regional, regional, or national level.

The most prevalent types of groups which participated in or supported local environmental activism are shown in Table 1. Although the inhabitants of the area were the most frequently reported participants or supporters in both types of cases, for the sustained cases' residents, local environmental groups and political party representatives were more often engaged. Other local participating or supporting groups, which did not involve themselves as strongly include trade unions, hunters, local professionals, local activities clubs, co-operatives, local courts, parent/teacher associations, students, women, church affiliated groups, artists, and others. This finding is consistent with those of similar research [*Freudenberg and Steinsapir, 1991; Cable and Cable, 1995; Michelson, 1997; Gould et al., 1996*] in other regions across the globe which show strong community-based environmentally active volunteer groups, most of which spring up from informal networks which are often intimately linked to municipal or neighbourhood boundaries. Sustained cases, characterised by stronger local network extension, received more support from non-local environmental movement organisations (15.2 per cent of cases, versus 5.8 per cent of unsustained ones).

TABLE 1

LOCAL AND NON-LOCAL PARTICIPATING AND SUPPORTING GROUPS
BY DURATION OF CASE (%)*

Group	<1year	≥1 year	Total
Local residents/citizens/neighbours	67.2	80.2	71.5
Local representatives of political parties	8.4	23.4	13.4
Local environmental groups	24.9	32.3	27.2
Non-local ENGOs	5.8	15.2	8.9
Total	(1812)	(892)	(2704)

* Percentages calculated within duration of case for each category which was coded as a dichotomous, yes/no variable; thus percentages do not add to 100.

Table 2 provides information on ENGOs supporting, or being asked to assist local participants. According to the printed media, only in 97 cases (out of 2,704) was the assistance of ENGOs sought by the mobilisers. About two-thirds of these were cases of sustained resistance and one-third unsustained. National organisations were approached more often in short-term cases (93.6 per cent of cases, versus 69.4 per cent of long term ones). International ENGOs were approached in 30.4 per cent of the sustained cases. This pattern is also reflected in the co-ordination of actions (for example, deliberate timing or synchronisation) which local mobilisers accomplished with these organisations. There was co-ordinated action in over half of sustained cases, but in only ten per cent of unsustained cases. Thus, for a small proportion of cases, these findings provide evidence of the important relationship between community-based and professional organisations stressed in recent works [*Rucht, 1993; Princen and Finger, 1994; Gould et al., 1996*].

TABLE 2

CHARACTERISTICS OF APPROACHED ENGOs BY DURATION OF CASE (%)

Characteristics	<1 year	≥ 1 year	Total
Country of origin			
No information	-	1.5	1.0
Greece	12.9	13.6	13.4
Spain	38.7	42.4	41.2
Portugal	41.9	12.1	21.6
Northern Europe, US and Canada	**6.4**	**30.3**	22.7
Total**	(31)	(66)	(97)
(% within case duration)	100.0	100.0	100.0
Action coordination + *	**9.7**	**51.5**	38.1
Total**	(31)	(66)	(97)
% within case duration	100.0	100.0	100.0
ENGOs responses*			
no specified information	21.9	13.0	16.3
'recognition' of mobilisers	31.3	35.2	33.7
technical aid	**15.6**	**25.9**	22.1
organisational aid	**25.0**	**16.7**	19.8
publicity aid	3.1	1.9	2.3
Total number **	(32)	(54)	(86)
Total %	100.0	100.0	100.0

*   Percentages of cases responding positively were calculated within duration of case for each category which was coded as a dichotomous yes/no variable; thus percentages do not add to 100.

**   In Table 1 earlier, 240 nonlocal ENGOs (8.9% of 2,704) participated or supported local protesters. Table 2 presents ENGOs that were approached by local participants for help and were mentioned by name, i.e. 97 out of the 240. The number decreases from 97 to 86 when information is sought on the involved ENGOs' responses.

+   Referring to cases where participants coordinated their actions (e.g. deliberate timing or other synchronisation efforts) with the large ENGOs whose country of origin is shown above.

Recognition of the mobilisers occurred equally in both types of cases. Yet some moderate differences are noted in their provision of aid. More technical aid went to the sustained groups, and more organisational help to the unsustained ones.

The different action forms used in the two types of cases are depicted in Table 3, which illustrates the variety of forms from the least intrusive to the most violent. As expected, the frequencies of each action form were higher for the sustained cases, with marked differences in the most intense protest activities. The most prevalent forms for these cases were: complaints to authority, demonstrations, press conferences, petitions, the legal route, and blocking actions. By contrast, the most prominent actions of the unsustained cases were less intense: general demands via the press, complaints to authority, press conferences, demonstrations, and petitions. Consequently, duration was strongly linked to intensity in contentious actions by which mobilisers attempted to make their demands public, as well as to create pressure to achieve their goals. Yet it should be noted that the data in this table reveal that even temporary resistance peaked with unconventional political mobilisations such as demonstrations and blockades, albeit only in a small number of cases.

TABLE 3

ACTIONS TAKEN BY DURATION OF CASE (%)*

Action form	<1 year	≥ 1 year	Total
Demanding/claiming	**71.7**	**78.5**	74.0
Complaints to authority	**56.8**	**78.0**	63.7
Press conference	**26.3**	**37.7**	30.0
Signatures	**17.6**	**33.2**	22.7
Court route	**7.6**	**22.9**	12.7
Public referendum	0.5	2.2	1.1
Demonstration /public protest	**20.2**	**39.2**	26.5
Public building occupation	1.7	7.8	3.8
Strikes/closing of shops	1.4	4.6	2.5
Activity/source blockage	**8.1**	**15.9**	10.7
Road blockades/Sit-ins	**4.7**	**12.7**	7.3
Hunger strike	0.3	1.8	0.8
Threat to use arms	1.4	3.1	1.9
Damage to property	1.3	5.6	2.7
Throw things	1.0	3.1	1.7
Unintended injuries	0.2	2.9	1.1
Intended injuries	0.4	1.2	0.7
Deaths	0.1	0.6	0.2
Violence	5.5	13.0	8.0
Total	(1812)	(892)	(2704)

* Percentages were calculated within duration of case for each category which was coded as a dichotomous yes/no variable; thus percentages do not add to 100.

Although Table 3 does not depict the actions taken for each case across time, in general it was found that participants of sustained cases first attempted to convince public officials and offenders to address the problem. When confronted with indifference or negative responses, mobilisers took more radical and direct actions. Despite these, the occurrence of violence was rare in both, significantly so for the later cases. These trends are consistent with findings of similar studies [*Bullard, 1993; Aguilar et al., 1995; Freudenberg and Steinsapir, 1991; Szasz, 1994*].

Mobilisers' Claims

Local contenders organise their actions and make their claims with specific reference to the process of ecological marginalisation as regards the users of the ecosystem, the sources controlled by these users, the offences created thereby, and the impacts due to these offences. For example, locals may blame a source and its operator (factory owner) or an inactivity (failure of implementation), or alternatively, they may only make claims about ecosystem offences (air pollution in the city) without necessarily relating the problem directly to specific environmental offenders [*Kousis, 1998b*].

The mobilisers' view of the primary source or (in)activity which led to their environmental problems is provided in Table 4.[20] Although information is available for 84 categories of sources of environmental problems, Table 4 shows those with the highest frequencies, compared by case duration. Thus, in the first half of the table the sources presented were more prevalent for the short-in-duration cases. In the second half of Table 4, appear sources/(in)activities which were more often associated with cases of sustained resistance. The data show that different types of significant sources were important in each of the two types of case.

Building construction, land transport, construction in green areas, water supply infrastructure, and failure to implement environmental protection laws were the most important sources identified by the mobilisers of short-duration cases. By contrast, the disposal/storage of untreated waste, military installations, agricultural infrastructure, petrochemical production facilities, nuclear and fossil fuel energy installations, as well as the lack of environmental protection laws and policies, were identified as the more intrusive sources by the mobilisers of sustained cases. Hence, there is evidence of a clearly different concern which is related to qualitatively different types of important sources and therefore to different experiences of ecological marginalisation. There is a clear difference in subsequent framing of these experiences, as shown in the claims in short-duration cases that the inactivity leading to the problem is the failure of implementation, while in sustained cases activists more radically claim that it is the lack of environmental protection policies.

TABLE 4

SELECTED PRIMARY SOURCE (IN)ACTIVITY AFFECTING THE ENVIRONMENT
BY DURATION OF CASE(%)*

Sources prevalent in '<1 year cases	<1 year	≥ 1 year	Total
Hunting	2.2	1.0	1.8
Water extraction	1.6	.8	1.4
Land transport. traffic	3.1	1.2	2.4
Building construction	**7.9**	**4.5**	**6.8**
Parks, green area construction	**3.2**	**2.2**	**2.9**
Lack of/improper planning	2.1	1.3	1.8
Water supply infrastructure	**2.9**	**1.6**	**2.4**
Other construction	**2.5**	**1.7**	**2.3**
Non-implementation of laws	**2.3**	**1.2**	**2.0**
Sources prevalent in '≥1 year cases			
Agricultural infrastructure	**1.4**	**3.3**	2.0
Chemicals and allied products	1.6	**2.9**	2.1
Cement & other products	1.2	1.7	1.4
Military installations and activities	**2.4**	**3.3**	**2.7**
Untreated toxic waste disposal	1.3	**2.5**	1.7
Toxic/Industrial waste storage	1.2	2.0	1.4
Untreated non-toxic waste disposal	**3.1**	**4.2**	**3.4**
Nuclear energy installations	**1.6**	**2.8**	**2.0**
Fossil fuel energy installations	**1.4**	**2.7**	**1.8**
Lack of environmental policy/laws	**1.9**	**2.5**	**2.1**
Total	(1799)	(890)	(2689)

* Percentages were calculated within duration of case for each category which was coded as a dichotomous. yes/no variable; thus percentages do not add to 100.

Note: The source/(in)activity. which according to the mobilisers caused ecosystem disturbance. was coded using 84 dichotomous variables acting as categories. This table shows only those out of the 84 which are of considerable size and for which there are apparent differences between sustained and unsustained cases. Hence percentages do not come close to 100.

In both types of cases the mobilisers saw the source as being directly or indirectly controlled by various state agencies, entrepreneurial and local government groups, which they challenged more often than others. Almost no differences existed with regard to the type of primary source. In more than half of both sustained and unsustained cases, claims related to exposure factors were made. Resistance to the siting of projects was mounted in less than one-third of cases – something not revealed by the case study approach to grass-roots environmentalism. Local environmental activism has often been associated either with NIMBY actions against siting plans or toxic exposure. According to these findings, contenders mounted a, for the most part, defensive resistance against experienced, expected or suspected effects of exposure in their communities.

The offences created by the identified sources are presented in Table 5.

TABLE 5

IDENTIFIED ENVIRONMENTAL OFFENCES BY DURATION OF CASE (%)*

Offences	<1 year	≥ 1 year	Total
Noise pollution	11.0	18.3	13.4
Atmospheric pollution	**30.1**	**43.0**	34.3
Water scarcity/shortage	7.3	10.4	8.3
Water pollution	**20.5**	**34.8**	25.2
Coastal pollution	5.5	8.4	6.5
Sea pollution	5.4	9.4	6.7
Soil pollution	**11.8**	**22.6**	15.3
Soil erosion	4.4	9.0	5.9
Local eco-destruction	**66.5**	**64.6**	65.7
Total	(1812)	(892)	(2704)

* Percentages were calculated within duration of case for each category which wa coded as a dichotomous yes/no variable; thus percentages do not add to 100.

Once more, their overall intensity, according to the mobilisers, was higher in the sustained resistance cases. A very commonly mentioned offence for both was the destruction of the local ecosystem. Nonetheless, mobilisers of the sustained cases more often identified atmospheric, water and soil pollution offences. These mobilisers were seemingly more informed, and were faced with problems of longer duration, while the sources they identified also tended to have a more pervasive effect on local ecosystems.

The wide array of impacts produced by these offences is presented in Table 6. Mobilisers of both types of cases identified a closely intertwined set of ecosystem, health and economic effects which impinged upon their daily lives. Following the pattern traced in the offences, however, collective claims in sustained resistance cases were much more frequent regarding ecosystem, health, economic, and psychological impacts. The most serious impact – that 'life itself is threatened or seriously endangered' – was much more likely to be claimed in cases where resistance was sustained.

Conclusion

This investigation of local environmental mobilisation has addressed its sustainability (in terms of case duration), its Southern European character, its claims about the physical environment, basic methodological concerns, and the wider debate about the future of the environmental movement.

The protest-case approach has highlighted and differentiated community-related mobilisations into local environmental activism and local environmental movements. On the basis of case duration, it showed their similarities and differences in terms of participating groups (including

TABLE 6

IDENTIFIED IMPACTS BY DURATION OF CASE (%)*

Impacts	<1 year	≥ 1 year	Total
Negative aesthetic	**26.4**	**23.9**	25.5
Negative recreational	**17.9**	**17.8**	17.8
Negative built-environment	3.8	5.8	4.4
Negative economic	5.4	9.0	6.5
decreasing incomes	**11.9**	**20.5**	14.7
threat to economic subsistence	**9.5**	**20.1**	13.0
animal/crop destruction	**9.9**	**20.0**	13.2
Negative ecosystem: forest	11.5	13.1	12.0
wetland	3.8	6.3	4.7
land	**14.6**	**27.7**	18.9
fresh waters	**24.1**	**37.8**	28.6
coastal zones	9.1	11.9	10.0
marine ecosystems	6.6	10.1	7.7
air-shed/s	**27.2**	**41.0**	31.6
local ecosystem in general	**3.7**	**25.7**	30.9
threat to flora and fauna	**7.6**	**29.1**	21.4
green areas in the city	12.0	9.4	11.2
Negative psychological	8.9	17.0	11.6
Health: realised few incidents	4.2	7.1	5.2
Health: expected/ suspected	**29.0**	**34.8**	30.8
Health: realised many incidents	2.3	8.6	4.2
Life: threatened/seriously endangered	**15.6**	**25.4**	18.8
Total	(1812)	(892)	(2704)

*   Percentages were calculated within duration of case for each category which was coded as
    a dichotomous, yes/no variable; thus percentages do not add to 100.

their ties to external networks), applied actions and claim repertoires
concerning the source of environmental degradation, the damage created,
and the wider socio-economic and environmental impacts which were
traced for the life of the related conflicts. It documented that although there
are proportionally more cases of environmental activism, there is a clear
overall increase in local environmental mobilisations across the three
countries. On the basis of the findings, local environmental movements are
sustained community-based mobilisations characterised by network
extension, intensive protest activity and, being exposed to more pervasive
impacts, deeper concerns about their external environment. Thus the data
provided support for Tilly's taxonomy of community-based movements and
for the part of the environmental sociology literature which provided similar
findings on these issues using the case-study approach.

    For Greece, Spain and Portugal, protest-case analysis offered evidence
that leads to a reconsideration of the current debate about Southern
European environmental movements. First, although the associational
culture in the three countries tends to be 'weak', strong community and

resistance cultures do exist. Thus, the environmental movement should not only be identified with formal environmental NGOs but should also be considered at the grass-roots level. The present work attempts to point out the significance of grass-roots mobilisations, not only in terms of their stronger than expected presence, but in terms of their commitment and level of consciousness as well. In spite of the fact that these vary, especially as regards the duration of the case, the evidence attests to their increase during the post-dictatorial period. It also depicts the defensive and exposure-related character of both types of cases, something which has hitherto been neglected. Although further research is warranted, the economic factors and the related ecological marginalisation effects which led to the late development of the movements in the three countries also appear to hinder local environmental protest during hard economic times, as in the mid-1980s. Thus, in addition to the political opportunity structure, the importance of which is evident in the post-dictatorial rise of the movement and the peaking of protest before national election years, the economic opportunity structure must also be considered. One last factor, the cultural one, must also be examined in order to shed more light as to why there appear distinct country differences. There was also evidence of Europeanisation effects in links to Northern based ENGOs, and the importance of these external ties, especially for the sustained cases.

This work showed through the mobilisers' claims that although the 'ecological *crisis*' has not come, ecological marginalisation appears to have steadily increased during the 20-year period in the three countries. Ecological marginalisation provides a background of indirect effects, which has in part contributed to the rise in the number of community-based environmental movements associated with more pervasive environmental problems, as compared to those of the earlier period.

As regards the wider debate on the definition and future of the environmental movement, the findings at hand appeal to those [e.g., *Blühdorn, 1997*] who identify the environmental movement with professional environmental organisations to consider the diversity of the movement instead of implying that the role of less professional action is insignificant. Grass-roots resistance is not institutionalised. It targets powerful groups in a very direct and confrontational manner about serious problems which have immediate effects on the activists and their communities.

Yet it is not so easy to be optimistic about the aftermath of these confrontations as some [e.g., *Szasz, 1994*] suggest. The data at hand poses critical questions needing further research: why are two thirds of environmental mobilisations not sustained? Which of the sustained actions achieve their goals? What leads to a successful environmental mobilisation?

The successes of popular resistance movements can only be cautiously counted. The evidence provides support for those [e.g., *Gould et al., 1996; Rucht, 1993*] who argue that when links are made from the local level to the global, and vice versa, then there is more hope for effective environmental protection. This remains a broad challenge for the different environmental movements in our time.

NOTES

1. These three types of social movements are well reflected in the environmental movement across national cultures. Professional environmental social movement organisations with their millions of donating, but weakly committed supporters, have had a longer history than the other types and sometimes do not resemble a social movement given their highly bureaucratised styles. Typical examples would be the conservation/preservation societies. Communitarian environmentalists are those ideologically committed green activists aiming to contribute to the construction of green collective identities, for example, deep ecologists or political ecologists. Movement participants, whether they take direct or indirect action, in general call for power holders to take measures to solve the problem. This definition coincides with similar classifications of the different types of environmental movements presented by environmental sociologists [e.g. *Humphrey and Buttel, 1982; Gould, Weinberg and Schnaiberg, 1993; Dunlap and Mertig, 1992*]. Electoral competitions are excluded under this definition since parties do not challenge the system, but work from within.
2. Grass-roots, local, and community-based, are used interchangeably throughout the study.
3. According to Freudenberg and Steinsapir [*1991*] local community groups comprise the base of grassroots environmentalism which has developed into three overlapping but different levels of organisation in the US: community-based groups, regional or state-wide coalitions, and national organisations.
4. NIMBY = Not In My Back Yard; NIOBY = Not In Our Back Yard; NIABY = Not In Anyone's Back Yard.
5. Mesomobilisation actors provide master frames interpreting events in order to achieve the cultural integration of various local groups.
6. If the number was not mentioned explicitly in the articles, the coders applied rules estimating the number of participants.
7. The Portuguese team headed by Teresa Fidelis, chose «Jornal de Noticias» the oldest, independent and reliable newspaper covering such events, but given its main focus on the northern and central regions of Portugal it was supplemented by «Publico,» first appearing in 1990, which covers both national and regional events via two regions' dossiers.
8. The Portuguese environmental magazine first appears in 1994.
9. For Spain, the 'Valencia', 'Andalusia', 'Catalonia' and 'Ciudades' supplements begin in 1986. For Portugal, *Publico*'s two regional supplements were also read. For Catalonia only the years 1982-85 were excluded due to lack of time and funding.
10. The following selection criteria were applied in the three countries uniformly:
    (1) Local groups of more than or equal to five persons (or their representative/s) mobilising for local problems.
    (2) Local problems dealing with economic or health issues that were related to environmental issues, or just environmental issues.
    (3) Initiatives taken by local groups who are not directly involved in conventional politics but may collaborate with political parties.
    (4) Action forms ranging from the minimal: making general demands or public accusations towards the challenged group on the problem, to the maximal: violent episodes.

194   ENVIRONMENTAL MOVEMENTS: LOCAL, NATIONAL, GLOBAL

(5) Local groups collaborating with various nonlocal groups on local problems.

(6) Local groups collaborating with local authorities on local problems.

(7) Local or/and national group/s mobilising for national problems that affect them directly at the local level.

11. The Spanish sample was selected by examining all cases. The sample of 856 cases included all large cases, and a selection of small and medium cases. These were selected according to the importance of their size (in terms of numbers of participants), salience of environmental issues, and action repertoires. This selection procedure was carefully applied by examining all cases that were traced for every month of the whole period, by Ilse Borehard.

12. An estimate of the population of actions pertaining to protest cases was calculated and used for Spain on the basis of the specific sampling procedures that were followed by the Spanish team. In addition, the use of the regional supplements which were used in Spain (not existent in *Eleftherotypia* and *Jornal de Noticias*) was calculated and subtracted for the related periods. Thus, Figure 2 presents standardised data relying only on one national newspaper, without the use of regional supplements for all three countries.

13. National election years for Greece were: 1974, 1981, 1985, 1989 (twice), 1990, 1993; for Spain: 1977, 1979, 1982, 1986, 1989, 1993; and for Portugal: 1975, 1976, 1979, 1980, 1983, 1985, 1987, 1991.

14. Coding of the case duration variable was done using 13 categories, from '1-3 days,' to 'more than 20 years'. For present purposes these categories were re-coded into two, that is, less than 1 year, and 1 year or more. Resistance in this context is equivalent to mobilisations.

15. When looking at the number of articles employed as sources of information for each case, it is found that more articles are used in the sustained resistance cases, in a good number of cases reaching as high as more than 50 articles per case. Specifically, whereas for the majority (80 per cent) of protest cases of less than one year, one article is used, for a considerable majority (64.3 per cent) of cases lasting over a year, between 2–30 articles are used; unlike in the former, in the later set in 5.4 per cent of the cases the number of articles reaches as high as between 31 and 236.

16. Using the year of the last or only article on each case as a proxy for the ending year.

17. For Portugal the freguesia level was used, being the closest to the Spanish and Greek municipality level.

18. Although information is recorded with the names of the neighborhoods, data entries at this specific level are not yet processed.

19. Coded direct relationships to other protest cases of this data set, may be of various types. For example, mobilisers may protest in different localities for the same source, with similar claims, or the mobilisers in the same locality may make different claims on the same source, etc.

20. Usually there was more than one entry for the 84 source/(in)activity categories. The coders were instructed to identify the one emphasised by the mobilisers as the primary one.

REFERENCES

Adeola, F. O. (1998), 'Cross-National Environmentalism Differentials: Empirical Evidence from Core and Noncore Nations', *Society and Natural Resources*, Vol.11, pp.339–64.

Aguilar, S. (1996), 'Grassroots Environmental Action and Sustainable Development in Spain', in Kousis, Aguilar and Fidelis-Nogueira.

Aguilar-Fernandez, S. (1994), 'The Greens in the 1993 Spanish General Election: A Chronicle of Defeat Foretold', *Environmental Politics*, Vol.3, No.1, pp.153–8.

Aguilar, S. (forthcoming), 'Is Spanish Environmental Policy Moving Towards a More Participatory Approach? Institution-Building versus Experiences of Participation', in Eder and Kousis [*forthcoming*].

Aguilar-Fernandez, S., Fidelis-Nogueira, T. and M. Kousis (1995), 'Encounters between Social Movements and the State: Examples from Waste Facility Siting in Greece, Portugal and Spain', in Alternative Futures and Popular Protest, Conference Papers, Vol.II, 4–6 April, Faculty of Humanities and Social Sciences, Manchester Metropolitan University.

Baker, S., Kousis, M., Richardson, D. and S. Young (eds.) (1997), *The Politics of Sustainable*

Development: Theory, Policy and Practice Within the EU, London: Routledge.

Barcena, I. and P. Ibarra (forthcoming), 'Evolution of the Ecologist Movement in the Basque Country', paper presented at the international conference on 'Environmental Movements, Discourses, and Policies in Southern Europe', in Eder and Kousis [*forthcoming: 194*].

Blühdorn, I. (1997), 'A Theory of Post-Ecologist Politics', paper presented at the international conference of ISA's 'Environment and Society' section, on 'Sociological Theory and the Environment', Woudschoten, 20–23 March.

Bullard, R. D. (1993), *Confronting Environmental Racism: Voices from the Grassroots*, Boston, MA: South End Press.

Cable, S. and C. Cable (1995), *Environmental Problems, Grassroots Solutions: The Politics of Grassroots Environmental Conflict*, New York: St. Martin's Press.

Castells, M. (1983), *The City and the Grassroots: A Cross-Cultural Theory of Urban Social Movements*, London: Edward Arnold.

Chekki, D.A. (ed.) (1997), *Environment and Community Empowerment*, Research in Community Sociology, Vol.7, London: JAI Press.

Collin, R.W. and W. Harris, Sr. (1993), 'Race and Waste in Two Virginia Communities', in Bullard [*1993*].

Commission of the European Communities, DGXII (1992), *Air Pollution and Health in the Mediterranean Countries of Europe* (Air Pollution Epidemiology Report No.5), Proceedings of a workshop held in Athens, 8–10 Oct.

Connell, J. (1991), 'Compensation and Conflict: The Bougainville Copper Mine, Papua, New Guinea', in J. Connell and R. Howitt (eds.), *Mining and Indigenous Peoples in Australasia*, Sydney: Sydney University Press.

Couch, S.R., Kroll-Smith, S. and J.P. Wilson (1997), 'Toxic Contamination and Alienation: Community Disorder and the Individual', in Chekki [*1997*].

Dede, I. (1993), *Oikologiebewegung in Griechenland und in der Bundesrepublik Deutschland*, Frankfurt am Main: Peter Lang.

della Porta, D., Valiente, C. and M. Kousis (1996), 'Women and Politics in Southern Europe: Paths to Women's Rights in Italy, Greece, Spain and Portugal', revised paper presented at the fifth conference of the SSRC Subcommittee on 'Democracy and Cultural Change in the New Southern Europe', held in Crete, 7–8 July.

Demertzis, N. (1995) ,'Greece: Greens at the Periphery', in D. Richardson and C. Rootes (eds.), *The Green Challenge: The Development of Green Parties in Europe*, London: Routledge.

Diani, M. (1995), *Green Networks: A Structural Analysis of the Italian Environmental Movement*, Edinburgh: Edinburgh University Press.

Dunlap, R.E. and A.G. Mertig (1992), 'The Evolution of the U.S. Environmental Movement from 1970 to 1990: An Overview', in R.E. Dunlap and A.G. Mertig (eds.), *American Environmentalism: The U.S. Environmental Movement, 1970–1900*, Philadelphia, PA: Taylor & Francis.

Edelstein, M.R. (1988), *Contaminated Communities: The Social and Psychological Impacts of Residential Toxic Exposure*, London: Westview Press.

Eder, K. and M. Kousis (eds.) (forthcoming), *The Europeanisation of Environmental Politics*, Dordrecht: Kluwer.

Ferraz, A. (1992), 'The Health Effects of Air Pollution in Portugal', in Commission of the European Communities, [*1992*].

Fidelis Nogueira, T. *et al.* (1996), 'Grassroots Environmental Action and Sustainable Development in Portugal', in Kousis, Aguilar and Fidelis-Nogueira [*1996*].

Fousekis, P. and J.N. Lekakis (1997), 'Greece's Institutional Response to Sustainable Development', *Environmental Politics*, Vol.6, No.1, pp.131–52.

Freudenberg, N. and C. Steinsapir (1991), 'Not in Our Backyards: The Grassroots Environmental Movement', *Society and Natural Resources*, Vol.4, No.3, pp.235–45.

Gedicks, A. (1995), 'International Native Resistance to the New Resource Wars', in B.R Taylor (ed.) *Ecological Resistance Movements: The Global Emergence of Radical and Popular Environmentalism*, Albany, NY: SUNY Press.

Gerhards, J. and D. Rucht, (1992), 'Mesomobilisation: Organizing and Framing in West Germany', *American Journal of Sociology*, Vol.98, No.3, pp.555–95.

196   ENVIRONMENTAL MOVEMENTS: LOCAL, NATIONAL, GLOBAL

Gottlieb, R. (1993), *Forcing the Spring: The transformation of the American Environmental Movement*, Washington, DC: Island Press.

Gould, K.A., A. Schnaiberg and A.S. Weinberg (1996), *Local Environmental Struggles: Citizen Activism in the Treadmill of Production*, Cambridge: Cambridge University Press.

Gould, K. and A.S. Weinberg (1991), 'Who Mobilizes Whom: The Role of National and Regional Social Movement Organizations in Local Environmental Political Mobilization', paper presented at the meetings of ASA, Cincinatti, OH, Aug.

Gould, K.A. (1991), 'The Sweet Smell of Money: Economic Dependency and Local Environmental Political Mobilization', *Society and Natural Resources*, Vol.4, pp.133–50.

Gould, K.A., Weinberg, A.S. and A. Schnaiberg (1993) ,'Legitimating Impotence: Pyrrhic Victories of the Modern Environmental Movement', *Qualitative Sociology*, Vol.16, No.3, pp.207–46.

Gunther, R., Diamantouros, P.N. and H.-J. Puhle (eds.) (1995), *The Politics of Democratic Consolidation: Southern Europe In Comparative Perspective*, Baltimore, MD: Johns Hopkins University Press.

Hase, T. (1992), 'The Green Movement in Japan', in M. Finger (ed.), *The Green Movement Worldwide*, London: JAI Press.

Hofrichter, R. (ed.) (1993), *Toxic Struggles: The Theory and Practice of Environmental Justice*, Philadelphia, PA: New Society Publishers.

Holliday, I. (1997), 'Living on the Edge: Spanish Greens in the mid-1990s', *Environmental Politics*, Vol. 6, No. 3, pp.168–75.

Humphrey, C.R. and F.H. Buttel (1982), *Environment, Energy, and Society*, Belmont, CA: Wadsworth.

Jamison, A. (1996), 'The Shaping of the Global Environmental Agenda: The Role of Non-Governmental Organizations', in S. Lash, B. Szerszynski and B. Wynne (eds.) *Risk, Environment and Modernity*, London: Sage.

Jamison, A., Eyerman, R. and J. Cramer (1990), *The Making of the New Environmental Consciousness: A Comparative Study of the Environmental Movement in Sweden, Denmark and The Netherlands*, Edinburgh: Edinburgh University Press.

Kalandidi, A. (1992), 'Effects of Air Pollution on Mortality in Athens', in Commission of the European Communities [*1992*].

Kemp, R. (1990), 'Why Not in my Backyard? A Radical Interpretation of Public Opposition to the Deep Disposal of Radioactive Waste in the United Kingdom', *Environment and Planning A*, Vol.22, pp.1239–58.

Koopmans, R. (1996), 'New Social Movements and Changes in Political Participation in Western Europe', *West European Politics*, Vol.19, No.1, pp.28–50.

Kousis, M. (1991) ,'Development, Environment, and Social Mobilisation: A Micro Level Analysis', *Greek Review of Social Research*, Vol.80, pp.96–109 (in Greek).

Kousis, M. (1993), 'Collective Resistance and Sustainable Development in the Rural Greece: The Case of Geothermal Energy on the Island of Milos', *Sociologia Ruralis*, Vol.33, No.1, pp.3–24.

Kousis, M. (1994), 'Environment and the State in the EU Periphery: The Case of Greece', *Regional Politics and Policy*, Vol.4, No.1, pp.118–35.

Kousis, M. (1997a), 'Grassroots Environmental Movements in Rural Greece: Effectiveness, Success and the Quest for Sustainable Development', in Baker *et al.* [*1997*].

Kousis, M. (1997b), 'Unravelling Environmental Claim-Making at the Roots: Evidence from a Southern European County', *Humanity and Society*, Vol.21, No.3, pp.257–83.

Kousis, M. (1998a), 'Ecological Marginalization: Actors, Impacts, Responses', *Sociologia Ruralis*, Vol.38, No.1, pp.86–108.

Kousis, M. (1998b), 'Protest Case Analysis: A Methodological Approach to the Study of Local Environmental Mobilizations', Working Paper No.570, Center for Research on Social Organization, Department of Sociology, University of Michigan, May.

Kousis, M., Aguilar, S. and T. Fidelis-Nogueira (1996), 'Grassroots Environmental Action and Sustainable Development in Southern European Union', Final Report, European Commission, DGXII, contract no. EV5V-CT94-0393.

Kriesi, H., Koopmans, R., Duyvendak, J.W. and M.G. Giugni, (1995), *New Social Movements in Western Europe: A Comparative Analysis*, Minneapolis, MN: University of Minnesota Press.

Lallas, D. (1992), 'Climate, Geography and Air Pollution in the Mediterranean Area', in Commission of the European Communities [1992].

Louloudis, L. (1987), 'Social Demands: From Environmental Protection to Political Ecology', in C. Orfanidis, The Ecological Movement in Greece, Athens: 'After the Rain' Publications (in Greek).

McAdam, D., Tarrow, S. and C. Tilly (1996b) , 'To Map Contentious Politics', Mobilization, Vol.1, No.1, pp.17–34.

McAdam, D., McCarthy, J.D. and M.N. Zald (eds.), (1996), Comparative Perspectives on Social Movements: Political Opportunities, Mobilizing Structures and Cultural Framings, Cambridge: Cambridge University Press.

Michelson, W. (1997), 'Municipal boundaries and prospective LULU impacts', in Chekki [1997].

Navarro, C., Marin, A. and A. Garcia-Benavides (1992), 'Cancer Incidence in Cartagena (Spain) and air pollution', in Commission of the European Communities, DGXII [1992].

Peet, R. and M. Watts (eds.) (1996), Liberation Ecologies: Environment, Development, and Social Movements, London: Routledge.

Pridham G. (1995), 'The International Context of Democratic Consolidation: Southern Europe in Comparative Perspective', in Gunther, Diamantouros and Puhle [1995].

Pridham, G. and D. Konstadakopoulos (1997), 'Sustainable Development in Mediterranean Europe? Interactions Between European, National and Sub-National Levels', in Baker, Kousis, Richardson and Young [1997].

Pridham, G., Verney, S. and D. Konstadakopoulos (1995), 'Environmental Policy in Greece: Evolution, Structures and Process', Environmental Politics, Vol.4, No.2, pp.244–70.

Princen, T. and M. Finger (1994), Environmental NGOs in World Politics: Linking the Local and the Global, London: Routledge.

Rangan, H. (1996), 'From Chipko to Uttaranchal: Development, Environment and Social Protest in the Garhwal Himalayas, India', in R. Peet and M. Watts (eds.), Liberation Ecologies: Environment, Development, and Social Movements, London: Routledge.

Regan, R. and M. Legerton (1990) , 'Economic Slavery or Hazardous Wastes? Robeson County's Economic Menu', in J. Gaventa, B.E. Smith and A. Willingham (eds.), Communities in Economic Crisis: Appalachia and the South, Philadelphia, PA: Temple University Press, pp.146–57).

Ribeiro, T. and V. Rodrigues, (1997), 'The Evolution of Sustainable Development Policy in Portugal', Environmental Politics, Vol.6, No.1, pp.108–30.

Rucht, D. (1993), 'Think Globally, Act Locally?' in J.D. Liefferink, P. Lowe and A. Mol (eds), European Integration and Environmental Policy, London: Belhaven.

Rucht, D. (1994), 'The Antinuclear Power Movement and the State in France', in H. Flam (ed), States and Anti-Nuclear Movements, Edinburgh: Edinburgh University Press.

Rucht, D. and F. Neidhart (1998), 'Methodological Issues in Collecting Protest Event Data: Units of Analysis, Sources, and Sampling, Coding Problems', in D. Rucht, R. Koopmans and F. Neidhardt (eds.), Acts of Dissent: New Developments in the Study of Protest. Berlin: Sigma Press, pp.65–89.

Rucht, D., Hocke, P. and T. Ohlemacher (1992), 'Documentation and Analysis of Protest Events in the Federal Republic of Germany (Prodat) Code Book', Wissenschaftzentrum, Berlin, June.

Rüdig, W. (1995), 'Between Moderation and Marginalization: Environmental Radicalism in Britain', in Taylor [1995].

Schnaiberg, A. (1994), 'The Political Economy of Environmental Problems and Policies: Consciousness, Conflict, and Control Capacity', Advances in Human Ecology, Vol.3, pp.23–64.

Spanou, K. (1995a), 'Public Administration and the Environment: The Greek Experience', in M. Skourtos and K. Sofoulis (eds.) Environmental Policies in Greece, Athens: Tipothito-Dardanos (in Greek).

Spanou, K. (1995b), 'The Beginning of Environmental Policies in Greece: The Dynamics of the Political-administrative Agenda During the Dictatorship', in Spanou [1992].

Spanou, K. (ed.) (1995), Social Demands and State Policies, Athens: Sakkoulas (in Greek).

Sunyer, J. and J.M. Anto (1992),' The Health Effects of Air Pollution in Barcelona', in Commission of the European Communities [1992].

Szasz, A. (1994), *Ecopopulism: Toxic Waste and the Movement for Environmental Justice*, Minneapolis, MN: University of Minnesota Press.

Taylor, B.R. (ed.) (1995), *Ecological Resistance Movements: The Global Emergence of Radical and Popular Environmentalism*. Albany, NY: SUNY Press.

Tejerina, B., Sobrado, J.M. Fdz. and X. Aierdi (1995*), Sociedad Civil, Protesta y Movimientos Sociales en el Pais Vasco*, Vitoria-Gasteiz: Servicio Central de Publicaciones del Gobierno Vasco.

Tilly, C. (1978), *From Mobilization to Revolution*, Reading, MA: Addison-Wesley.

Tilly, C. (1994) , 'Social Movements as Historically Specific Clusters of Political Performances', *Berkeley Journal of Sociology*, Vol. 38, pp. 1-30.

Tsakiris, K. and K. Sakellaropoulos (1998), 'The Social Profile, Policies and Action of Non-Governmental Nature and Environmental Organizations in Greece', paper presented at the international conference on 'Environmental Movements, Discourses, and Policies in Southern Europe', Department of Sociology, University of Crete, Rethimno, 8–10 May.

Valaora, T. (1995), 'The Social Role of Environmental NGOs: Action and Examples from the Environmental Area', in Spanou (ed.) [*1995*].

van der Heijden, H.-A., Koopmans, R. and M. Giugni (1992), 'The West European Environmental Movement', *Research in Social Movements, Conflicts and Change*, Supplement 2, JAI Press, pp.1–40.

Vasquez Barquero, A. (1991), *Local Development: A Strategy for the Creation of Employment*, Athens: Papazisis Publishers (in Greek, translated by V. Horafa).

Viola, E.J. (1997), 'The Environmental Movement in Brazil: Institutionalization, Sustainable Development, and Crisis of Governance Since 1987', in G.J. MacDonald, D.L. Nielson, and M.A. Stern (eds.), *Latin American Environmental Policy in International Perspective*, Boulder, CO: Westview Press, pp.88–112.

Vitsilaki, H. (1992), 'The Labor Movement in Contemporary Greece', unpublished Ph.D. dissertation, Department of Sociology, University of Chicago.

Walsh, E.J. (1988) , *Democracy in the Shadows: Citizen Mobilization in the Wake of the Accident at the Three Mile Island*, New York: Greenwood Press.

Walsh, E.J. and R.H. Warland (1997),'Social Movement Involvement in the wake of a nuclear accident: activists and free riders in the TMI Area', in D. McAdam and D.A. Snow (eds.) *Social Movements*. Los Angeles, CA: Roxbury, Publ. Co.

Weinberg, A. (1997), 'Local Organizing for Environmental Conflict: Explaining Differences between Case of Participation and Nonparticipation', *Organization & Environment*, Vol.10, No.2, pp.194–16.

Welsh, I (1993), 'The Nimby Syndrome: Its Significance in the History of the Nuclear Debate in Britain', *British Journal of Historical Sociology*, Vol.26, pp.15–32.

Wolfson, Z and V. Butenko (1992) ,'The Green Movement in the USSR and Eastern Europe', in M. Finger and L. Kriesberg (eds) *Research in Social Movements, Conflicts and Change: The Green Movement Worldwide*, Supplement 2, London: JAI Press.

Yanitsky, O. (1996), 'The Ecological Movement in Post-Totalitarian Russia: Some Conceptual Issues', *Society and Natural Resources*, Vol.9, pp.65–76.

Environmental Movements, Ecological Modernisation and Political Opportunity Structures

HEIN-ANTON VAN DER HEIJDEN

During recent decades, environmental movements in First, Second and Third World countries have undergone far reaching changes. In western Europe and the United States they changed from radical grass-roots groups striving for structural social reforms into highly institutionalised mass membership organisations, working within the neo-liberal social order. In Eastern Europe and the former USSR, environmentalism flourished during the 1980s due to its articulation with national sovereignty claims but after 1989 the movement collapsed and now it lacks an institutional basis. In Third World countries, environmental groups are often torn between adaptation to western-style patterns of development and resistance against the global neo-liberal discourse. Ecological modernisation and sustainable development are both ways of dealing with environmental problems without fundamentally challenging the existing social order. Their applicability for environmental movements, however, is largely determined by political opportunity structures in individual countries.

With the approach of the millennium, in the social sciences a strong need can be observed to draw up balancesheets on all kind of topics. Inextricably bound up with this is the need to look forward, deep into the twenty-first century while preferably covering the whole globe. Postmodern criticism of grand narratives, of scientific truth claims and of the predictability of the future, all seem to be forgotten.

One subject which demands such scrutiny is the environmental movement. Established 30 years ago as one of the new social movements, it is almost impossible to imagine contemporary political discourse without it. However, at least in the West, the movement has become highly institutionalised and has lost many of its radical and utopian features [*van der Heijden, 1997*]. In several western countries, especially in those with

The author would like to thank Ineke Overtoom and two anonymous referees for their helpful comments on an earlier version of this contribution.

the most advanced environmental policy, a tendency to ecological modernisation – to environmental measures which in the long run do not hamper but boost industrialism and capitalist economy – can be observed. Important parts of the western environmental movement have acknowledged this strategy as the most promising one for the future. Due to globalisation and to the articulation of sustainable development with ecological modernisation, it could even become a catchword, not only for western, but also for Second and Third World environmental movements.

It is my contention that ecological modernisation as another grand narrative fails to be convincing. It will be argued that the articulation of sustainable development with ecological modernisation can be conceived of as an appropriate strategy for the environmental movement in some parts of the world, but not in others, the extent of its appropriateness being dependent on different political contexts.

Although I am convinced of the validity of most of the postmodern critique, I shall hazard a (relatively) grand narrative on the current state of the environmental movement and environmental discourse at a global level. However, I shall distinguish between environmental movements in First, Second and Third World countries, and I shall emphasise the impact of political contexts on the organisational structure, action repertoire, hegemonic discourse and the chances of success of environmental movements in each.[1] The developments I describe are trends, applying more to one country than to another.

In the first section I give an overview of the current state of the environmental movement in the First, Second and Third Worlds. Which developments did environmental movements pass through during the last three decades, with what results, and what is their present condition? In the second section focus shifts from environmental movements to environmental discourse. Under which conditions and in which political contexts is ecological modernisation a productive strategy for environmental movements? In the discourse of ecological modernisation capitalist economic growth and sustainable development are conceived of as a positive sum game. In many cases, however, it can be argued that ecological modernisation hampers a really sustainable development.

I. The State of the Environmental Movement at the Turn of the Century

The West

In the West, primarily the West European countries and the United States, the recent history of the environmental movement can be summarised as follows:

(1) The movement has grown from a new social movement into a network of professionalised mass membership organisations at the national level: In many Western countries the environmental movement took off as a new social movement, characterised by unconventional actions at the local level, active participation of many people concerned, and an overrepresentation of the 'new middle class'. This new social movement culminated in campaigns against nuclear energy during the 1970s and early 1980s [*Flam, 1994; Kitschelt, 1986; Rüdig, 1990*]. Thereafter, a process of deradicalisation, oligarchisation, institutionalisation and professionalisation began, manifesting itself in a tremendous growth of membership numbers in organisations at the national level, as well as in a change from active participation to 'chequebook activism'.

In the United States, the membership numbers of the ten largest conservation and environmental protection organisations rose from less than two million in 1979 to almost seven million in 1990.[2]

TABLE 1
DEVELOPMENT IN MEMBERSHIP NUMBERS (THOUSANDS) OF THE TEN LARGEST US CONSERVATION AND ENVIRONMENTAL PROTECTION ORGANISATIONS 1979 – MID-1990s

Organisation	Year founded	1979	1983	1990	mid-90s
Sierra Club	1892	181	346	560	550
National Audubon Society	1905	300	498	600	560
Nat. Parks and Conserv. Ass.	1919	31	83	100	(100)
Wilderness Society	1935	48	100	370	300
National Wildlife Federation	1936	784	758	975	(975)
Nature Conservancy	1951	(150)	(400)	600	828
World Wildlife Fund	1961	(200)	(600)	940	1.000
Environmental Defence Fund	1967	45	50	150	250
Nat. Resources Defence Council	1970	42	45	168	170
Greenpeace	1971	(150)	(320)	2.300	1.700
Total		1.931	3.200	6.763	6.453

During the mid-1990s total growth seems to have reached saturation point; some groups, for instance the Nature Conservancy, continue to grow, but others such as Greenpeace USA experienced severe losses. As in the US, mass membership organisations in Western Europe experienced enormous growth between 1980 and 1995. Four (kinds of) organisations took the lion's share: traditional, long standing conservation associations, and three transnational environmental organisations: Greenpeace, World Wildlife Fund (WWF) and Friends of the Earth (FoE). Both Greenpeace and WWF have national branches in about thirty countries (both with a total membership of about five million). FoE has national branches in more than fifty countries, many of them Third World countries, but its total constituency is much smaller (less than one million).[3]

Membership growth enabled organisations to hire professional staff. This led to a shift in the action repertoire from largely unconventional to more conventional actions and methods of influencing politics. Grass-roots activism still exists, but it has lost its leading role.

(2) Emphasis has shifted from local pollution issues to global environmental problems: In the first period of its existence the environmental movement mainly dealt with *visible* environmental problems at the local level. With respect to those problems, visible results could be achieved: cleaner rivers, less air pollution, the closing down of a nuclear plant or a polluting factory. Besides, a substantive body of environmental legislation could be introduced. In the United States between 1970 and 1980 23 federal environmental acts were signed into law [*Dowie, 1996; 33*].

From the 1980s onward, important parts of the environmental movement increasingly shifted their focus to less visible, transboundary or even global environmental problems like the extinction of species, the greenhouse effect and the depletion of the ozone layer. The platform on which these issues were articulated increasingly shifted from the individual nation-state to the international political arena. This reduced the visibility of the environmental movement at the national level.

(3) Impacts are increasingly sensitising and procedural and less substantive and structural: Four kinds of external impacts of a social movement can be distinguished: procedural, substantive, structural and sensitising [cf. *Giugni, 1995: 212 ff.*].[4] Procedural impacts refer to the access to decision-making bodies a social movement or (some of) its organisations manage to achieve. Substantive impacts refer to the material results, for instance the closing down of a nuclear plant. Structural impacts refer to changes in institutional or alliance structures, for instance the creation of a Department for the Environment or a Green Party. Sensitising impacts refer to changes of the political agenda and in public attitudes. At the most general level, the environmental movement in Western countries has effected many sensitising and procedural impacts, but fewer structural and substantive impacts.

In many countries the environment has achieved a solid place on the political agenda and public support for environmental protection in most countries, not only Western ones, is high (*sensitising impact*) [*Inglehart, 1995*]. The environmental movement has also achieved *procedural impacts*. In countries like Germany and the Netherlands, as well as on the level of the

European Union and some international bodies (UNEP), it has become part of the (inter)governmental consultation structure.[5] In the United States, the number of registered environmental lobbyists grew from two in 1969 to almost a hundred in 1990 [*Dowie, 1996: 192*].

With respect to *structural impacts* the picture is confusing. Partly due to the environmental movement, in many countries Departments for the Environment were established and environmental legislation was introduced, but the newly founded Departments appeared to lack power and the implementation and enforcement of environmental laws remained problematic. In many countries Green parties were founded but, thus far, only in a few cases, notably in Germany, have they really changed the political system.

Each national environmental movement can point to a number of *substantive impacts*: closure or replacement of polluting factories, successful opposition to the construction of new motorways, preservation of important nature reserves, reductions in pollution of air, water and soil. Nevertheless, overall, one cannot say that environmental movements have been very successful on a substantive level. The worst consequences of capitalist industrialism have been countered, but the structural causes of pollution remain intact: capitalist industrialism with its emphasis on unlimited growth, mobility, consumerism and anthropocentrism. Nowadays the environment could be conceived of as a component of almost every act and product, and environmental degradation is involved in such routine habits as driving a car, eating meat or visiting a supermarket. All these activities are taken for granted nowadays, but were hotly debated in the early 1970s, the period in which the modern environmental movement took off. Environmental degradation has become one of the routine consequences of modern life.

(4) Environmental discourse has developed from radical social change to ecological modernisation: Thirty years ago it was difficult to conceive of environmental discourse as being separated from new social movement discourse in general. Womens' rights, democratisation, the Third World, human rights and environmental protection all were part of one and the same countercultural discourse. To achieve these goals, radical structural reforms were considered necessary. From the mid 1970s onward, however, new social movements increasingly went their separate ways, and Green parties were the only integrating platforms which remained.

Along with the global hegemony of neo-liberal discourse from the 1980s onward, as well as with postmodern criticism of grand narratives, the course of the environmental movement became more pragmatic, culminating in a massive surrender to ecological modernisation. In the United States, this surrender manifested itself in the so-called 'third wave' of environmentalism, a wave in which the boardroom rather than the courtroom became the most important arena for environmental groups [*Dowie, 1996: 106*]. From then on, in Western Europe the means considered most appropriate to bring about environmental protection were not the changing *of* capitalist industrial society but changes within it.

(5) The emergence of a radical countercurrent: The recent emergence of a radical countercurrent manifests itself in at least three different ways. First, contrasting to the tendency to institutionalisation, in many Western countries radical non-institutionalised groups have emerged, ranging from Earth First!, the Sea Shepherd Society and the Earth Liberation Front to the environmental justice movement in the United States and the anti-roads movement in Britain.

Secondly, at the cognitive level, the hegemony of the neo-liberal ecological modernisation discourse is increasingly challenged by a counter-discourse. The content of this counter-discourse (or set of discourses) is very heterogeneous and varies from ecocentrism, bioregionalism and feminist ecology to eco-socialism and alternative lifestyles. What these discourses have in common is their resistance against the neo-liberal environmentalism of the mainstream movement [*Dowie, 1996: 205 ff.*].

The third way in which the radical countercurrent manifests itself is in the articulation of environmentalism with other new social movement issues such as human rights [*Dowie, 1996: 245*], the position of women [*Braidotti et al., 1994; Plant, 1989; Plumwood, 1993*], green democracy [*Doherty and de Geus, 1996*], critique of science [*Jamison et al.,1990*] and Third World development [*Braidotti et al., 1994; Saurin, 1993*].

Eastern Europe and the Former Soviet Union[6]

In the East European countries and the former Soviet Union - the Second World - the most important trends in environmentalism can be summarised as follows.

(1) In the 1980s the environmental movement flourished because of the articulation of environmental demands with national sovereignty claims: Up to the early 1980s, in most East European countries only an 'official', state-licensed environmental movement existed. In the former Soviet Union, for instance, the largest organisation was the Pan-Russian Society for the Protection of Nature with a constituency of not less than 30 million. From the early 1980s onward, the legitimacy of East European regimes crumbled, but political freedom did not yet exist. Environmental protection

was seized as a vehicle for the striving for autonomy or national independence, especially in Bulgaria, Hungary and Czechoslovakia [*Fischer, 1993: 99*].[7]

In Bulgaria, Ecoglasnost, a network of ninety local groups, became the umbrella organisation of the whole Bulgarian opposition. In 1989 it managed to use the environmental Conference on Security and Cooperation in Europe (CSCE) as a platform to articulate its demands: environmental and conservation issues, but also freedom of information, the right of association, and radical social change. The movement proved highly succesful: one day after the close of the Conference, mass demonstrations took off; one week later Todor Zhikov resigned [*Fischer, 1993: 100–101*].

In Hungary in the mid-1980s protest emerged against the construction of two hydroelectric power stations on the Danube river, one at Gabcikovo in Slovakia and one at Nagymaros-Visegrad in Hungary, 24 kilometres north of Budapest, in one of the most scenic historic areas of the country [*Persanyi, 1993: 145*]. The struggle over the dams brought many disparate groups temporarily together under the same banner: reform-minded communists, socialists, social-democrats, liberals, christian-democrats, nationalists and environmentalists. In October 1988 40,000 people in Budapest marched against the dam [*Jancar-Webster, 1993: 193*], and the anti-Dam movement made a substantial contribution to undermining the legitimacy of the regime.

In the former Soviet Union, the anti-nuclear movements in Lithuania and Armenia performed the same function.[8] Their objective was not only to close nuclear plants, but also the national independence of the two republics [*Dawson, 1995*].

(2) Strong emphasis on local pollution of air, water and soil; articulation of environmental demands with public health claims: As one or two decades earlier in the West, environmental protest in East European countries during the 1980s strongly emphasised the directly tangible pollution of air, water and soil and the consequences for public health. Environmentalism in Bulgaria took off in 1987 in response to intense chlorine pollution floating across the Danube from Romania into the town of Ruse and leading to very severe health problems. In central Europe, the areas of greatest environmental concern are the notorious region where northern Bohemia, the south-east of the ex-GDR and the south-west of Poland meet, and an area to the east of this where Czechoslovak industry around Ostrava lies adjacent to Polish Silesia, with its massive Nova Huta steelworks and associated industries. Apart from this, air pollution was also caused by the burning of highly sulphurous lignite (brown coal) [*Waller and Millard, 1992: 162*].

On 11 November 1989, just a week before student demonstrations in Prague ended the old regime, a protest march took place against living conditions in the North Bohemian town of Teplice, where coal mining had turned the land into craters and where, due to the unbreathable air, people had frequently been advised to wear masks. In the weeks preceding the revolution, a group of women, the Group of Czech Mothers, staged demonstrations in the streets of the capital against the poor quality of water [*Jancar-Webster, 1993: 193*].

It is generally agreed that such environmental problems were products of intrinsic features of decaying communist political regimes (centralisation, growth-oriented planning system, lack of democratic control, lack of information and participation) [*Fischer, 1993; Jancar-Webster, 1993; Waller and Millard, 1992*].

(3) Collapse of the environmental movements after 1989 and their weak institutional basis: After the revolutions of 1989, the situation for environmental NGOs in eastern Europe completely changed. The distinction between officially sponsored NGOs on the one hand and independent NGOs on the other hand evaporated, and in almost all eastern Europe countries Green parties were established. Some were successful. The Green Party of Slovenia won nine per cent of the votes and gained eight seats in the Socio-Political Chamber (80 seats), eight seats in the Chamber of Municipalities (80 seats) and four positions in the government. In Bulgaria, Ecoglasnost and the Green Party together obtained 39 out of 400 seats [*Fischer, 1993: 106*].

In all other countries, however, Green parties performed substantially less well. Many analysts sketch a gloomy picture of the future of environmentalism in Eastern Europe. The long tradition throughout the region of state dominance and weak society, reinforced by the experience of the past 40 years, militates against the rapid development of a strong environmental movement, as does the lack of resources, heightened by political and economic instability.[9] New NGOs in the West almost always make extensive use of the resources provided by existing organisations. No such basis yet exists in Central and Eastern Europe. Furthermore, there is little tradition of raising money through membership subscriptions and little knowledge of the techniques western NGOs have developed to mobilise public opinion and maintain public support [*Fischer, 1993: 107–8*]. In Hungary, including the green sections of the political parties, there are fewer than forty environmental groups. Only two or three have over one thousand members. Six to eight have more than one hundred, but most have only some dozen, sometimes only a couple of members [*Persanyi, 1993: 150*].

The backlash against environmentalism also has repercussions. In the

Czech Republic and in Hungary, the moratorium on the construction of the Gabcikovo-Nagymaros Dam is being reconsidered. In the four former USSR republics with nuclear plants – Armenia, Lithuania, Ukraine and Russia – the early successes of anti-nuclear activists began to unravel in the face of public apathy. In Armenia, the government decided to reopen the country's sole nuclear power station (closed in 1988), and in Lithuania steps were taken to ensure the continued operation of the Ignalina facility. In both Russia and Ukraine, moratoria on the construction of new nuclear facilities, adopted in 1990, were overturned and construction reinitiated on a number of projects. Finally, the original decision of the Ukrainian parliament to close the Chernobyl nuclear power station has now been made contingent on an immense foreign aid package [*Dawson, 1995: 443*].

A new development was the founding in 1991 of the Regional Environmental Center for Central and Eastern Europe (REC), located in Budapest. This center, generously sponsored by US, Japanese and West European governments, was (among other things) given the task to develop an effective environmental NGO-network. The result was a hesitant revitalisation of environmentalism. The new environmental NGOs, however, differed from their predecessors; 'constructive' lobbying replaced protest and grassroots activism gave way to professionalism [*Jancar-Webster, 1998*].

Third World Countries

The main trends in environmentalism in Third World countries may be summarised as follows:

(1) The articulation of environmental demands with developmental demands: Unlike western environmental organisations, Third World groups rarely campaign on the 'greenness' of an environmental issue alone. Many Third World-based environmental NGOs (ENGOs)[10] are mainly concerned with development issues, notably the promotion of social justice. Yet what often distinguishes them from 'regular' development NGOs is their emphasis on the need to pursue such objectives via the mechanisms of environmental conservation. Social justice and equity is attained by ensuring that the poor gain access to local environmental resources (that is, timber, fuel, clean water) [*Bryant and Bailey, 1997: 130*]. In India, for instance, the Chipko movement to protect trees in the hills and the anti-Narmada Dam campaign are both tied to the issue of the protection of poor people and their access to resources, embedding the environment within the argument about what kind of development is possible and desirable [*Chapman et al., 1997: 87*].

(2) A strong emhasis on forests and trees (especially in Asia), on urban pollution of air, water and soil (especially in Latin America) and on desertification (especially in Africa): The green movement in many Asian countries, unlike in Europe or the United States, began with marginalised communities of forest-dwellers and peasants. It trickled up to touch the middle classes, who formed new voluntary agencies to support grass-roots communities. If the notion of 'environment' in India has a concrete form, it is trees. Urban environments may have blocked drains, corrupt administration, air pollution, but nationally deforestation and reforestation are seen as the major issues; not global warming, not biodiversity per se, not ozone holes [*Chapman et al., 1997: 86*]. As Vandana Shiva [*1992: 195*] puts it: "For the cultures of Asia, the forest has always been a teacher, and the message of the forest has been the message of interconnectedness and diversity, renewability and sustainability, integrity and pluralism".

In Latin America, the situation more resembles the western one. The heart of the Brazilian environmental movement consists of the hundreds of mostly small, local organisations, with largely middle-class and professional memberships, that have sprung up since the early 1970s. Most have addressed local issues such as the protection of trees and parks, pollution from nearby factories, and construction projects that threatened the quality of local life. Many have also sought to educate the public about larger questions such as protecting the Amazon or using chemicals in agriculture [*Goldstein, 1992: 123*].

With the severe drought in the Sahel region during the early 1970s and the 1980s, the issue of desertification in Africa was brought into international focus. The concerns were that a steadily deteriorating situation was caused by local mismanagement (overgrazing, overcropping), exacerbated by a decline in rainfall and rapid increases in population. In preparing a proposal for a Desertification Convention, a UN Resolution invited contributions from all relevant NGOs, especially those from developing countries [*Carr and Mpande, 1996: 145, 153*]. The Desertification Convention is one of only two international environmental regimes established at the initiative of developing countries despite the resistance of industrialised countries. For many African countries, there is a strong link indeed between alleviating poverty and controlling desertification [*Porter and Welsh Brown, 1996: 101*].

(3) The local character of many environmental actions and the cooperation of local groups in national umbrella organisations: The rise of ENGOs in most Third World countries since the late 1970s can be seen to reflect the growing power and assertiveness of 'civil society' *vis-à-vis* the state (Bryant and Bailey, 1997: 130). Throughout Asia communities are fighting

against megadams which threaten to displace them and submerge forests [*Shiva, 1992: 206*]. In Thailand, people have resisted the destruction of forests since the mid-1970s [*Shiva, 1992: 205*].

Although most Third World ENGOs are community-based grassroots organisations dedicated to the direct protection of local livelihoods, the number of advocacy or grassroots support organisations is growing rapidly. There are thousands of professional ENGOs in the Third World, but their geographical distribution is uneven. India has a high number of ENGOs (500), as do the Philippines (1000) and Latin America (6000), but there are few indigenous professional ENGOs in Africa [*Bryant and Bailey, 1997: 144*].

The dismal experience of ENGOs in such countries as Vietnam or Burma still ruled by authoritarian regimes suggests the existence of a link between democratisation, the development of a middle class and the rise of ENGOs.[11] Many states make it a regular practice to support 'moderate' factions within ENGOs.[12] ENGO campaigns in many parts of the Third World are based on cooperation with the state. In Brazil their importance is recognised in legislation which stipulates that the National Environmental Council (ONAMA) must include ENGO representatives [*Bryant and Bailey, 1997: 150–51*].

A recent development in many Third World countries has been the creation of national ENGOs or national coalitions of ENGOs to develop an indigenous nationwide response to environmental problems. Examples are the Fundación Nature in Ecuador, the Green Forum Philippines, the Project for Ecological Recovery in Thailand, the Kenyan Environmental Non-Governmental Organisation KENGO (including 68 environmental groups) [*Porter and Welsh Brown, 1996: 53*], and WALHI in Indonesia, with over 500 members in 1992 [*Princen and Finger, 1994: 2*]. A further step to cooperation was the joining together of national ENGOs to form regional fora. 21 African ENGOs formed the African NGOs Environmental Network (ANEN) in 1982. By 1990, the membership had increased to 530 NGOs, located in 45 countries [*Princen and Finger, 1994: 2*].[13]

(4) The radical tendency in environmental discourse in Third World countries: Despite the inclusion of many ENGOs in governmental consultation structures, important parts of the Third World environmental movement do not accept the hegemonic global discourse of capitalism, neo-liberalism, modernism, scientism and anthropocentrism. All over the Third World, environmental groups remain to articulate their struggle against environmental degradation with the struggle against capitalist economic structures and western political and cultural imperialism.

In India, there have always been dissenting critics of the whole modernist project, some of them decidedly Gandhian in outlook, who object to big cities and industrialisation as avoidable evils [*Chapman et al., 1997: 7*]. The Gandhian dream is always honoured in India, but honoured more in the breach than the observance. The idea is kept alive as a kind of national conscience: utopian communities supported by private donations operate in all parts of India but they show no sign of becoming the dominant paradigm [*Chapman et al., 1997: 7*].

Among Indian intellectuals, however, as in many other Third World countries, there is a widely shared view that the North tries to have the final decision in issues like nuclear non-proliferation, gene patenting, trade-liberalisation, terms and costs of the transfer of technology [*Chapman et al., 1997: 8*]. Their criticism sometimes takes the form of a massive, but highly sophisticated attack, against the 'violence of Western reductionist science' [*Shiva, 1987*].[14] According to Saurin, modernisation and global environmental degradation have coincided historically. Globalised modernity can be seen to generate particular modes of knowledge, and simultaneously to displace, marginalise and destroy others. The different forms of agricultural knowledge are a case in point. Specific forms of large scale environmental degradation occur as one of the routine consequences of modernity [*Saurin, 1993: 46*].

II. Ecological Modernisation and Political Opportunity Structures

In *The Consequences of Modernity* (1990), Giddens makes the distinction between the four institutional dimensions of modernity: capitalism, industrialism, military power and 'surveillance'. It can be argued that all those four dimensions, as well as their global counterparts (world capitalist economy, international division of labour, world military order and the nation-state system respectively) contribute to environmental degradation: capitalism with its inherent tendency to growth and waste; the global separation between production and consumption and the agricultural monocultures in many Southern countries; the Gulf War, as well as the French and Indian nuclear tests are examples.

In the contemporary western debate on the relationship between modernity and the environment, two periods can be distinguished. During the period of the 'Limits to growth'-debate in the early 1970s, *de-modernisation theories* dominated. The influential *Blueprint for Survival*, published by the British branch of Friends of the Earth, sketched a model of society in which de-industrialisation, community, naturalness and small-scale production played important roles. In this period the environmental movement critically analysed the prevailing mentality. Militarism, economic growth, state monopoly capitalism, competition and consumption were criticised sharply as they were considered the most important causes of environmental problems.

With the Brundtland report, *sustainable development* and its Western elaboration *ecological modernisation* took over to become the dominant paradigm from the mid-1980s onward [*Hajer, 1995, 1996; Huber, 1982; Jänicke, 1986; Spaargaren, 1996; Weale, 1992*]. Ecological modernisation may be defined as the discourse that recognises the structural character of environmental problems but nonetheless assumes that existing political, economic and social institutions can internalise care for the environment [*Hajer, 1995*]. This perspective not only changed prevailing views of the relationship between environment and economic growth, but also those of the roles of science and technology and of both governmental and non-governmental actors, environmental organisations among them.

According to Huber [*1982: 12*], the quintessence of ecological modernisation is the twin process of the 'ecologising of economy' and the 'economising of ecology'. The dynamics of capitalism can be used to realise sustainable production and consumption ('green capitalism'), while the role of the state is just one element among a variety of initiatives and strategies developed in modern society to bring about environmental reform. The environmental movement did not need the state to realise its goals and, consequently, during the 1980s several forms of 'direct negotiations' between the environmental movement and circumscribed segments of industry, sometimes even separate firms, gained popularity [*Spaargaren, 1996: 15*].

For Jänicke, however, the greening of production and consumption without state intervention is not possible. Ecological modernisation must be actively supported by the state in the form of a green industrial policy and new forms of political intervention such as the *target group approach*. In this approach civil actors and the state enter into negotiations, trying to agree on norms and measures which are contextually relevant and which are accepted on a voluntary basis by all parties concerned. In the Netherlands, during the past 15 years the target group approach has led to the conclusion of over 50 so-called covenants between government and organised industry [*Spaargaren, 1996: 123*]. Typical of such covenants are those on phosphates in detergents, on packing materials and on cadmium in synthetic beer crates.

A more complex analysis of ecological modernisation has been presented by Hajer [*1995*]. Ecological modernisation could be conceived of as a *discourse coalition* between business, important sectors of science (natural and social), reformist progressive politicians, and large parts of the environmental movement. The different partners in the discourse coalition have introduced concepts that make issues of environmental degradation calculable and quantifiable. Ecological modernisation follows a utilitarian logic and is portrayed as a positive sum game; economic growth and the solution of ecological problems do not have to be contradictory.

How should ecological modernisation be assessed? Is it an advanced way to reconcile economic growth and environmental protection, a sophisticated and potentially global form of capitalist exploitation, or both? How should environmental movements in the First, Second and Third Worlds deal with it? Ecological modernisation can be seen as a result of institutional learning, as a technocratic project, and as a form of cultural politics [*Hajer, 1996: 251–60*].[15] From an institutional learning perspective, government and business have learned from the environmental movement that with environmental degradation something very serious is at stake. Environmental movements, on the other hand, have learned that it is possible to tackle environmental problems without fundamentally changing existing social and political structures.

The interpretation of ecological modernisation as a technocratic project maintains that ecological modernisation fails to address those immanent features of capitalism that make waste, instability and insecurity inherent aspects of modern development, that the sciences have largely been incorporated in this technocratic project and that, consequently, they are a part of the problem rather than of the solution.[16]

An interpretation of ecological modernisation as cultural politics starts from the view that debates on pollution are essentially debates about the preferred social order. In the definition of what the environmental problem 'really' is, in defining 'nature' and in defining specific solutions, one seeks either to maintain or change the social order. The structuring principle in this third interpretation is that there is no coherent ecological crisis as such, there are only *story lines*, problematising various aspects of a changing physical and social reality. Ecological modernisation is understood as the routinisation of a new set of story lines (problems, solutions, images, causal understandings, priorities) that provide the cognitive maps and incentives for social action. Coherence is necessarily artificial and discursive realities are moments in which cultural politics are being made. Hence the central concern of this interpretation is with cognitive reflexivity, argumentation and negotiated social choice.

Although Hajer's treatment of ecological modernisation is more sophisticated than other conceptualisations, it too has shortcomings. Most importantly, it pays little attention to the different political contexts in which ecological modernisation politics is being attempted. For environmental movements, however, political opportunity structures are of crucial importance; in some contexts it may be fruitful or even necessary to participate in ecological modernisation politics, in others it is a waste of time.

In our conceptualisation of political opportunity structures [*van der Heijden, 1997; Kriesi et al., 1995*], the degree of access to the political system is of central importance for the environmental movement. In a society where 'old' political conflicts (e.g. conflicts between capital and labour) have been accommodated politically, the political agenda offers more room for 'new' topics (for example, the environment) than in a society where old conflicts are still paramount. Another important distinction is that between the formal institutional structure of a state (open or closed) on the one hand, and the informal strategies of political elites towards challengers (integrative or exclusive) on the other hand. Open states are characterised by a large degree of vertical decentralisation; a reasonable division of state power between legislature, executive and judiciary; an open electoral system (examples: Germany, Switzerland). The result is a large number of 'points of access' for the environmental movement. For closed states (France) the opposite applies. The capacity of political systems to actually implement policies (strong states) is determined by a high degree of centralisation of the state and of government control over market participants (France, the Netherlands) [cf. *Kitschelt, 1986: 63–4*].

With respect to elite strategies, integrative strategies (for example, with respect to environmental organisations) are characterised by assimilation, facilitation and cooptation. In such countries (the Netherlands, Switzerland) patterns of interaction between interest groups and the executive branch are highly developed, as are mechanisms that aggregate social demands. Exclusive elite strategies are characterised by repression, polarisation and confrontation (France, Germany). Seen from an institutional learning perspective, we could conclude that ecological modernisation would not work equally in all political contexts. What conclusions may be drawn about the usefullness of ecological modernisation as a strategy for First, Second and Third World environmental movements?

First World Countries

Ecological modernisation requires a discourse coalition between business, important sectors of science, reformist progressive politicians and the environmental movement. In western Europe, the dominant view of ecological modernisation is the institutional learning perspective. The impacts of ecological modernisation, however, diverge widely, both at the EU-level as well as between individual countries. With respect to individual West European countries, on the basis of previous research into the relationship between political opportunity structures (POS) and environmental movements [*Jamison et al., 1990; Flam, 1994; Kitschelt, 1986; Kriesi et al., 1995*], one could hypothesise a list of countries whose POS is appropriate for an ecological modernisation discourse coalition, and countries whose POS is not.[17] Countries like Sweden, the Netherlands, Austria and probably Finland fulfil most of the requirements: the accommodation of old political conflicts, an open input structure, a strong implementation capacity and integrative elite strategies. On the other hand, in countries like France, Italy, Britain and Germany, the political context is not very favourable to the emergence of such a discourse coalition because, for examples, old political conflicts prevail (France) or the capacity for policy implementation is weak (Germany), both combined with highly repressive elite strategies. Political systems which are intermediate include Denmark and Switzerland, which meet three of the four requirements, but lack a strong policy implementation capacity.

Ecological modernisation policy does not as yet have a long history, and empirical research results into the effects of this policy are still scarce, but the available evidence is consistent with the propositions aforementioned. According to Neale, much in the Dutch covenant system, for instance, is consistent with a political culture which has, throughout the post-war period, emphasised corporatist values. In Denmark, on the other hand, where industry has been able to negotiate targets as well as their implementation, and legal sanctions for non-compliance are less well developed, the result has been the adoption of 'easy' targets, and a widespread failure, particularly by small firms, to meet them. Elsewhere in Europe, where state–industry co-operation on environmental policy has been less well established, national voluntary agreements have been even less effective in stimulating environmental change [Neale, 1997: 12].

Even at the EU level, the benefits of ecological modernisation can be doubted. As Neale observes, the emphasis on 'dialogue' and 'shared responsability' in the Fifth EU Environmental Action Program may seem to create new opportunities for environmental groups to increase their influence on policy. Yet many of the implementation mechanisms exclude them; voluntary agreements are negotiated by industry groups and governments, bypassing the consultative element of established legislative procedures, and environmental management systems encourage organisations to develop their own environmental targets without consulting any outsiders other than certifiers [Neale, 1997: 18].

In the United States, third wave environmentalism, the American equivalent of ecological modernisation, shows the same picture. The institutional features of the American state are not very favourable to ecological modernisation: absence of mechanisms that aggregate demands, weak policy implementation capacity, low degree of government control over market participants. In practice third wave environmentalism has taken the form of *laissez-faire* politics in which 'market based incentive', 'demand side management', 'technological optimism', 'non-adversarial dialogue' and 'regulatory flexibility' have become the buzzwords [*Dowie, 1996: 106*].

From an institutional learning perspective, ecological modernisation as universalising grand narrative fails to be convincing. It is plausible that it will work in *some* political contexts (strong, politically accommodated states with open input structures and assimilative elite strategies), with respect to *some* environmental problems (relatively simple ones), but *not* in other contexts (for example, weak states), and *not, or only to a limited extent* with respect to other environmental problems (more complex or basic ones such as limitless car driving, air traffic or meat consumption). After all, a discourse coalition between science, business, government and the environmental movement presupposes a common problem definition and a common view on solution strategies. However, the fundamental undermining of basic achievements of highly developed anthropocentric societies (limitless car driving, air traffic, meat consumption) are not likely to become part of these common problem definitions or solution strategies. For that reason, even in countries with the most favourable political opportunity structures, environmental movements should not focus exclusively on ecological modernisation as an institutional learning process. Instead, by emphasising anthropocentrism and other institutional features of modernity routinely leading to environmental degradation, they would be dealing with ecological modernisation as cultural politics.

Second and Third World Countries

In a globalising world, four fundamental aspects of the modern nation-state are compromised: its competence, its form, its autonomy and, ultimately, its authority or legitimacy [*McGrew, 1992: 87*]. Many of the most important environmental policy decisions are not taken by states, but emerge out of the production, technological and trading strategies of a relatively small number of powerful transnational companies [*Hurrell, 1994: 154*].

Increasing doubts about the viability of the technocratic (state) strategy, especially in Third World countries, have given rise to the alternative 'community approach' favoured by many NGOs. According to this approach, grassroots and peoples organisations need to play a predominant role in the transition towards a more sustainable society. This view has a strong anti-statist slant, arguing that the state is so much involved in the creation of environmental problems that it is unlikely to serve as the vehicle for their solution. However, NGOs cannot themselves fullfil the core functions of the state. On closer inspection, many of the anti-statist arguments of the environmental movement turn out to be calls for reformed and more democratic states [*Hurrell, 1994: 154*]. Here the concept of Political Opportunity Structure enters the scene again. Until now, Third

World environmentalism (especially in Asia and Africa) has mainly been rural. With the growth of the number of megacities, however, it is plausible to expect that in the twenty-first century environmental problems in the Third World will increasingly have a metropolitan character.[18] They will be linked to urban problems such as housing, traffic, sanitation and employment. With respect to these problems, decentralisation of government control (or no government control at all) are now widely seen as part of the solution [*Badshah, 1996*].

The concept of ecological modernisation is not part of the environmental discourse in Second and Third World countries; in these countries sustainable development is the keyword. Sustainable development is a less univocal term than ecological modernisation; it refers to many significantly differing perspectives: from neoliberal continuous wealth creation via stewardship (trusteeship for the planet and future generations) to empowerment of the poor and 'revelation' (the idea of capturing the spirit of communal obligation and citizenship) [*O'Riordan and Voisey, 1997: 6–8*]. All dimensions in their turn differ from each other with respect to conceptualisations of nature, social values, policy orientation and so on [*O'Riordan and Voisey, 1997: 10*]. In political practice, however, many Third World countries are not able to implement the strategy, due to their weak state structures.

Generally, the most fruitful strategy for environmental and other social movements seems to be one that sees development as nurtured by empowering people so that they can create their own identities and their own institutions. In daily practice in many cases this would imply remaining aloof from the dominant neoliberal conceptualisation of sustainable development.

Conclusion

In contemporary political debate, the environment is one of the few remaining issues on which the parameters of modernity can be fundamentally discussed. It can be argued that all four dimensions of modernity and globalisation (capitalism, industrialism, military power and surveillance) contribute to environmental degradation.

On a general level, the acceptance or rejection of this argument implies the acceptance or rejection of ecological modernisation as a potentially fruitful long-term strategy for environmental movements. After all, ecological modernisation assumes that the existing political, economic and social institutions can adequately deal with environmental problems. Consequently, it focuses exclusively on industrialism, not on capitalism, military power and surveillance, or the nation-state system.

Environmental discourse in the First World during recent decades has developed from a discourse of radical social change into a pragmatic acceptance of the *status quo*. Despite the emergence of a radical countercurrent, there are no signs of reversal of the tendency towards institutionalised mainstream environmentalism.

In the Second World environmental movements lack an institutional basis and for their survival they are largely dependent on support from the West. If the policy implementation capacities of the states were strong enough, however, environmental movements could still achieve important results in campaigning for more efficient use of energy, less pollution of air, water and soil, and so on.

The situation in the Third World partly resembles that in the Second (dependency on the West), but in many countries the Western way of life and Western economic and cultural imperialism are criticised fundamentally. (Some) Third World countries are among the few remaining places where Western-style modernisation has not yet gained absolute dominance and where environmental and other social movements have the opportunity to present alternatives.

The world-view of ecological modernisation is a thoroughly modernist and anthropocentric one. However, in the cultural politics perspective, ecological modernisation is a statement about the preferred social order, the result of a specific configuration of power in a specific period of time. As Eyerman and Jamison [*1991*] and Tarrow [*1994*] maintain, a social movement is only a movement in the true sense of the word if it challenges hegemonic worldviews, if it presents alternatives to dominant ways of interpreting reality. In this respect, the emerging radical environmental countercurrent in the West, and those parts of the environmental movements in the Third World that do not accept dominant definitions of modernisation and development, have much in common. Both criticise ecological modernisation/sustainable development at the level of cultural politics. As most states in the industrialised world are more immune to change at an institutional level, in a new, global wave of environmentalism, it is environmental and other social movements from the Third World which will play a leading role.

NOTES

1. The distinction between First, Second and Third Worlds is highly artificial. Nevertheless, it can be maintained that the differences between the three Worlds are, and will long remain, fundamental.
2. Figures in this table are extracted from Dowie [*1996: 266*]; from Mitchell *et al.* [*1992: 13, 18*]; and from own research findings. Figures in brackets are estimates. In the literature on American environmentalism a distinction is often made between lobbying and non-lobbying

218 ENVIRONMENTAL MOVEMENTS: LOCAL, NATIONAL, GLOBAL

organisations. Of the ten largest organisations mentioned in Table 1, seven are lobbying organisations while three (World Wildlife Fund, Greenpeace and the Nature Conservancy) are non-lobbying. According to Dowie, until the mid-1980s there was some noticeable variety among the large national groups. One could distinguish a Sierra Club hiker from a National Wildlife Federation hunter, an Audubon bird watcher from an NRDC biochemist. Each organisation had its own priorities and its own projects. By the mid-1980s, however, the distinctions had blurred and groups began to look and sound alike. Staffs, direct mail campaigns, rhetorics and policies – even wardrobes – became homogenised [*Dowie, 1996: 60*].

3. In a 1992 Eurobarometer survey, 20 per cent of the Dutch, eight per cent of the British, seven per cent of the German and five per cent of the French adult population claimed to be members of an environmental organisation. The percentages for other EC member countries are: Belgium ten per cent, Denmark 16 per cent, Greece two per cent, Ireland five per cent, Italy six per cent, Luxemburg 18 per cent, Portugal two per cent, Spain four per cent.

   At the European level, the activities of about 140 environmental NGOs from the EU member countries are coordinated by the European Environmental Bureau. The EEB basically is the lobbying branch of the West European environmental movement at the EU level. It has direct access to the European Commission, represents European NGOs in many international fora, and receives significant amounts of EU funding to hold sessions and round tables on specific issues.

4. Apart from external impacts, social movements also have internal impacts: impacts on the identity of a group or its individual members, and impacts on the organisational structure (for example, institutionalisation).

5. A more elaborated description of this intergovernmental consultation structure is presented in Porter and Welsh Brown [*1996*]; Princen and Finger [*1994*].

6. An overview of environmentalism in the former USSR and East European countries is given in Jancar-Webster [*1993*]; Waller and Millard [*1992*]; Wolfson and Butenko [*1992*]. Studies of environmentalism in individual East European countries include Hicks [*1996*] on Poland and Dawson [*1995*] on anti-nuclear activism in the USSR and its successor states.

7. In Poland, the significance of Solidarity in the history of environmental affairs is paramount. One of its most important offshoots is the Polish Ecological Club (PKE) which spread across the country and constituted a network of active local action groups composed of citizens, scientists and local municipal officials [*Kabala, 1993: 124*]. The task for activist groups like the PKE was to challenge the country's dominant paradigm of development. Before the events of 1989, this meant challenging Poland's heavy industry lobby [*Kabala, 1993: 126*]. By 1987 it was estimated that Poland had almost 2,000 local environmental groups [*Waller and Millard, 1992: 167*].

8. In the USSR, after the impetus to democracy and *glasnost* brought about by the Chernobyl disaster, the first informal environmental organisations started to emerge in autumn 1986. In the years thereafter several hundred groups emerged in large cities all over the country. Their main activity was to protest by means of demonstrations, road blocks, press releases and letters to government departments. In many cases, a demonstration or roadblock at the entrance to the offending facility succeeded. Between 100 and 240 plants, including paper factories and fertilizer, medicine and toy plants, were shut down in 1988 and 1989 because of ecological protests. In late 1988 the number of environmental associations amounted to about 7,500 [*Wolfson and Butenko, 1992: 43, 46*]. Around that time the first steps were taken to coordinate the various Soviet green groups and movements. Several major ecological associations were founded: the Social and Ecological Union, the Ecological Union and the USSR Ecological Foundation.

9. Poland seems to be an exception. After 1989, there existed: 70 environmental NGOs such as the League for the Protection of Nature and the Polish Ecological Club; 60 organisations that list environmental problems on their agenda, such as political, tourist and religious organisations; 35 environmental groups such as the Silesian Ecological Movement; 20 groups that include environmental concerns in their activities, such as the Zen Buddhist Association in Poland; a dozen-odd environmental foundations [*Szacki et al., 1993: 17*].

10. For an assessment of the concept of NGO and its relationship to government see Potter [*1996*] and Bryant and Bailey [*1997: Ch.6*].

11. For a counterargument see Potter (ed.) [*1996*].
12. A similar role is played by the many GRINGOs (Government Run/Initiated NGOs), for instance in the Philippines [*Bryant and Bailey, 1997: 151*].
13. Environmental NGOs at the national level increasingly have become part of global fora such as the Climate Action Network, the Antarctic and Southern Ocean Coalition (ASOC) and the Rainforest Action Network.
14. For an assessment of Shiva's position see Saurin [*1993*].
15. In this respect it could be useful to be aware of the distinction between ecological modernisation as a program, a perspective, a belief system, a program of political reform and a social theory [*Spaargaren, 1996: 21*].
16. The perspective of ecological modernisation can be seen as directly opposing Beck's idea of the 'risk society' [*Beck, 1986*], because it offers a constructive approach to deal with the environmental crisis in some well-circumscribed respects and because it assigns a positive role to modern science and technology in overcoming the environmental crisis.
17. What follows is not a strict empirical test of a set of fully worked-out hypotheses, but rather a discussion of plausible relationships between the possibilities of ecological modernisation and institutional features of the state.
18. Of the 26 urban agglomerations expected to have more than ten million inhabitants by the year 2010, 21 will be in developing countries [*Badshah, 1996: 2*].

REFERENCES

Badshah, A. (1996), *Our Urban Future: New Paradigms for Equity and Sustainability*, London: Zed Books.
Beck, U. (1986), *Risikogesellschaft. Auf dem Weg in eine andere Moderne*, Frankfurt: Suhrkamp.
Braidotti, R. *et al.* (1994), *Women, the Environment and Sustainable Development*, London: Zed Books.
Bryant, L. and S. Bailey (1997), *Third World Political Ecology*, London: Routledge.
Carr, S. and R. Mpande (1996), 'Does the Definition of the Issue Matter? NGO Influence and the International Convention to Combat Desertification in Africa', in D. Potter [*1996: 143–66*].
Chapman, G., Kumar, K., Fraser, C. and I. Gaber (1997), *Environmentalism and the Mass Media; the North-South Divide*, London: Routledge.
Dawson, J. (1995), 'Anti-Nuclear Activism in the USSR and its Successor States: A Surrogate for Nationalism?', *Environmental Politics*, Vol.4, No.3, pp.441–66.
Diani, M. and H.-A. van der Heijden (1994), 'Anti-Nuclear Movements across Nations: Explaining Patterns of Development', in: Flam [*1994: 355–82*].
Doherty, B. and M. de Geus (eds.) (1996), *Democracy and Green Political Thought. Sustainability, Rights and Citizenships*, London: Routledge.
Dowie, M. (1996), *Losing Ground. American Environmentalism at the Close of the Twentieth Century*, Cambridge, MA: MIT Press.
Dunlap, R. and A. Mertig (1992), 'The Evolution of the U.S. Environmental Movement from 1970 to 1990: An Overview', in Dunlap and Mertig (eds.) [*1992: 1–10*].
Dunlap, R. and A. Mertig (eds.) (1992), *American Environmentalism: The U.S. Environmental Movement 1970–1990*, Bristol, PA: Taylor & Francis.
Eyerman, R. and A. Jamison (1991), *Social Movements; a Cognitive Approach*, Cambridge: Polity Press.
Finger, M. (ed.) (1992), *The Green Movement Worldwide* (Research in Social Movements, Conflict and Change), Greenwich, CT: JAI Press.
Fischer, D. (1993), 'The Emergence of the Environmental Movement in Eastern Europe and its Role in the Revolutions of 1989', in Jancar- Webster [*1993: 89–113*].
Flam, H. (ed.) (1994), *States and Anti-Nuclear Movements*, Edinburgh: Edinburgh University Press.
Giugni, M. (1995), 'Outcomes of New Social Movements', in Kriesi *et al.* [*1995: 207–37*].
Goldstein, K. (1992), 'The Green Movement in Brazil', in Finger [*1992: 119–93*].
Hajer, M. (1995), *The Politics of Environmental Discourse. Ecological Modernisation and the Policy Process*, Oxford: Clarendon.

Hajer, M. (1996), 'Ecological Modernisation and Cultural Politics', in S. Lash, B. Szerszynski and B. Wynne (eds.), *Risk, Environment and Modernity; Towards a New Ecology*, London: Sage, pp.246–68.

Hicks, B. (1996), *Environmental Politics in Poland. A Social Movement between Regime and Opposition*, New York: Columbia University Press.

Huber, J. (1982), *Die verlorene Unschuld der Oecologie. Neue Technologien und superindustrielle Entwicklung*, Frankfurt: Fischer.

Hurrell, A. (1994), 'A Crisis of Ecological Viability? Global Environmental Change and the Nation-State', *Political Studies*, Vol.42, pp.146–65.

Inglehart, R. (1995), 'Public Support for Environmental Protection: Objective Problems and Subjective Values in 43 Societies', *Political Science and Politics*, Vol.28, pp.57–72.

Jamison, A., Eyerman, R. and J. Cramer (1990), *The Making of the New Environmental Consciousness. A Comparative Study of the Environmental Movements in Sweden, Denmark and the Netherlands*, Edinburgh: Edinburgh University Press.

Jancar-Webster, B. (1993), 'The East European Environmental Movement and the Transformation of East European Society', in Jancar-Webster (ed.) *[1993: 192–221]*.

Jancar-Webster, B. (1998), 'Environmental Movement and Social Change in the Transition Countries', *Environmental Politics*, Vol.7, No.1, pp.69–90.

Jancar-Webster, B. (ed.) (1993), *Environmental Action in Eastern Europe: Responses to Crisis*, Armonk, NY: Sharpe.

Jänicke, M. (1986), *Staatsversagen. Die Ohnmacht der Politik in der Industriegesellschaft*, Munich: Piper.

Kabala, S. (1993), 'The History of Environmental Protection in Poland and the Growth of Awareness and Activism', in Jancar-Webster (ed.) *[1993: 114–33]*.

Kitschelt, H. (1986), 'Political Opportunity Structures and Political Protest: Anti-Nuclear Movements in Four Democracies', in *British Journal of Political Science*, Vol.16, pp.57–85.

Kriesi, H. *et al.* (1995), *Social Movements in Western Europe: A Comparative Analysis*. Minneapolis, MN: University of Minnesota Press.

McGrew, A. (1992), 'A Global Society?' in S. Hall, D. Held and T. McGrew, *Modernity and its Futures*, Cambridge: Polity Press.

Mitchell, R. *et al.* (1992), 'Twenty Years of Environmental Mobilization: Trends Among National Environmental Organizations', in Dunlap and Mertig (eds.) *[1992: 11–26]*.

Neale, A. (1997), 'Organising Environmental Self-Regulation: Liberal Governmentality and the Pursuit of Ecological Modernisation in Europe', *Environmental Politics*, Vol.6, No.4, pp.1–24.

O' Riordan, T. and H. Voisey (1997), 'The Political Economy of Sustainable Development', *Environmental Politics*, Vol.6, No.1, pp.1–23.

Persanyi, M. (1993), 'Red Pollution, Green Evolution, Revolution in Hungary. Environmentalists and Societal Transition', in Jancar-Webster (ed.) *[1993: 134–57]*.

Plant, J. (ed.) (1989), *Healing the Wounds: The Promise of Ecofeminism*, London: Green Press.

Plumwood, V. (1993), *Feminism and the Mastery of Nature*, London: Routledge.

Potter, D. (ed.) (1996), *NGOs and Environmental Politics. Asia and Africa*, London and Portland, OR: Frank Cass.

Porter, G. and J. Welsh Brown (1996), *Global Environmental Politics*, Boulder, CO: Westview Press.

Princen, T. and M. Finger (1994), *NGOs in World Politics: Linking the Local and the Global*, London: Routledge.

Rüdig, W. (1990), *Anti-Nuclear Movements: A World Survey of Opposition to Nuclear Energy*, Harlow: Longman.

Saurin, J. (1993), 'Global Environmental Degradation, Modernity and Environmental Knowledge', *Environmental Politics*, Vol.4, No.4, pp.46–64.

Shiva, V. (1987), 'The Violence of Reductionist Science', *Alternatives*, Vol.12, pp.243–4.

Shiva, V. (1992), 'The Green Movement in Asia', in Finger (ed.) *[1992: 195–215]*.

Spaargaren, G. (1996), 'The Ecological Modernisation of Production and Consumption. Essays in Environmental Sociology', Ph.D. thesis, Wageningen.

Szacki, J., Glowaka, I., Liro, A. and B. Szulczewska (1993), 'Political and Social Changes in Poland', in Jancar-Webster (ed.) *[1993: 11–27]*.

Tarrow, S. (1994), *Power in Movement. Social Movements, Collective Action and Politics*, Cambridge: Cambridge University Press.
van der Heijden, H.-A. (1997), 'Political Opportunity Structure and the Institutionalisation of the Environmental Movement', *Environmental Politics*, Vol.6, No.4, pp.25–50.
van der Heijden, H.-A., Koopmans, R. and M. Giugni (1992), 'The West European Environmental Movement', in Finger [*1992: 1–40*].
Waller, M. and F. Millard (1992), 'Environmental Politics in Eastern Europe', *Environmental Politics*, Vol.1, No.2, pp.159–85.
Weale, A. (1992), *The New Politics of Pollution*, Manchester: Manchester University Press.
Wolfson, Z. and A. Butenko (1992), 'The Green Movement in the USSR and Eastern Europe', in Finger [*1992: 41–82*].

Power, Politics and Environmental Movements in the Third World

JEFF HAYNES

Environmental movements in the Third World are a relatively recent phenomenon. They should be seen, not as concerned purely with environmental issues, but as manifestations of wider, usually, political concerns. Such movements tend to attract the unempowered – those without the means to address their concerns in more conventional ways. Movements in India, Kenya, Indonesia, Tahiti and Nigeria are examined in the search for factors that explain their success or failure. If most were not, in the short term, successful, they have nevertheless helped to place environmental concerns on the political agenda of many countries in the Third World.

> Power ... is Brazilian rubber tappers struggling to preserve the forests upon which their livelihoods depend. Power is Indian peasants resisting hydroelectric projects that will flood their land. ... Around the world, ecology movements are demanding and creating the power to shape their own environments
>
> *[Breyman, 1993: 129, 124]*

> The state's claim to defend threatened resources and its exclusive right to the legitimate use of violence combine to facilitate its apparatus-building and attempts at social control. State threats or use of violence in the name of resource control helps them to control people, especially unruly regional groups, marginal groups, or minority groups who challenge its authority
>
> *[Peluso, 1993: 47]*

The environment has emerged as an important focus of state-society conflict in many parts of the Third World[1] over the last quarter century, very often accompanying wider demands for socio-political and economic reforms. Environmental goals are nearly always factors in wider campaigns for greater political and economic clout.

The issue is not one of 'goodies' versus 'baddies'; it would be simplistic to claim that environmental groups always want to protect their local ecology while nasty business interests invariably wish to destroy it. However, most environmental groups realise that if their local environment is seriously degraded or destroyed, it is they who will lose out. The issue may simply be *who* has the 'right' to destroy the natural environment: local people or outside interests? But the central point is that environmental protection is always highly political.

Over the last quarter century tens of thousands of environmental groups have emerged in the Third World [*Fisher, 1993: 209*], with the majority located in Latin America or Asia, fewer in sub-Saharan Africa and hardly any in the Middle East. Such a distribution is not unexpected given the comparative development of civil societies in these regions.

Despite their vast numbers, it is possible to generalise to an extent about environmental groups in the Third World. First, they aim to mobilise local people in defence of the local environment against outside interests – usually the state or big business. Second, environmental action groups are usually rurally-based. Third, women often form the core of their memberships. Fourth, while some groups have a narrow conservation focus, many others have wider socio-economic and political concerns. Fifth, environmental groups are more likely to succeed in their goals when they can exploit democratic and legal avenues. Sixth, it helps to enlist important foreign allies, such as Greenpeace International, athough this does not ensure success. Finally, environmental groups often do not win their struggles; failures outweigh successes.

Environmental groups in the Third World often attract members of subordinate groups who may share a perception that the *status quo* is inimical to their interests [*Fals Borda, 1992: 311*].[2] Women – especially educated women – and young people no longer automatically submit passively to the dictates of those with power. Fals Borda [*1992: 311*] argues that these 'two oppressed, marginal groups' strive to 'bring about a new ethos, a better kind of society and social relations in which unity may coexist with diversity'. In sum, Third World environmental groups often attract young people and women who see them as appropriate vehicles to express more general discontent with the *status quo*. The striking increase in Third World environmental groups not only signals serious trends in ecosystem decline but also the 'social stress that results from and feeds into that decline' [*Princen and Finger, 1994: 10*].

Third World environment groups always have political goals, moulded in part by a perception that political systems are not geared to deal with such concerns [*Escobar and Alvarez, 1992a: 327; Fisher, 1993; Haynes, 1997*]. Few are exclusively interested in the environment; they also tend to have a wide range of concerns, including human rights, employment and development issues [*Sethi, 1993: 125–6*]. Such groups often serve to challenge 'conventional culture and economic models of development to advance their politics. The creation of political facts by the environmental movement ... takes place through the generation of spaces wherein new meanings are forged ...' [*Escobar and Alvarez, 1992b: 15*]. In both Venezuela and Brazil, for example, 'ecological tendencies ... [with goals] beyond the primary issues of environmental destruction [led] to a search for social alternatives' [*Mainwaring and Viola, 1984: 29–30*] .

State policies in the Third World are influenced by a variety of factors, especially the nature of domestic political structures and distributions of wealth and income. Agricultural pricing policies, investment incentives, tax provisions, and credit and land concessions are designed to further elite interests at the expense of those of 'ordinary' people. Political elites are very likely to be major wealth holders with interests in a variety of activities, some of them environmentally damaging, including commercial logging, mineral and oil exploitation, plantation cropping, and large-scale irrigated farming. Relatively powerless, usually rural peoples – especially if they belong to national minorities – suffer socio-economic and environmental costs of such schemes, sometimes losing homes, farms and fishing grounds; rarely, if ever, are they compensated adequately for their losses [*Miller, 1995: 42*]. It is hardly surprising that environmental activists belonging to such groups feel that key decisions affecting their lives and environments are beyond their control. They may link human rights to environmental rights, arguing that the natural environment cannot be protected without sustaining its human communities.

Substantive measures to protect the environment are likely to attract the commitment of state officials and policy makers only if they – or their allies – will benefit. For example, the governments of both Kenya and Zambia only supported a global ban on the ivory trade when their countries' elephant herds declined to an alarming degree. It is perhaps unnecessary to mention that those benefiting from the ivory trade included senior state figures, such as politicians and military personnel [*Ellis, 1994: 62*]. For them, the prime purpose in implementing a ban on trading in ivory was that elephant stocks could recover, perhaps allowing later resumption of the trade.

The exploitation of elephants for ivory is one example of a wider pattern of elite domination with ramifications for environmental protection. Extraction of valuable natural resources is a highly significant revenue-generating strategy, embraced in pursuit of the goal of allocating assets for 'society's greater good'. What this usually amounts to is that those with power and those close to power-holders have most interest in preserving or gaining jurisdiction over natural resources; redistribution comes far down the list of priorities. Holders of state power generally interpret the value of a natural resource in relation to three factors: (a) the world market price of a product – does the going rate make it worthwhile to trade it? (b) by what strategies can it best be exploited? and (c) for what purpose(s) can resulting monetary benefits be allocated?

When the state's view of what is the correct procedure and weight of the distribution of the benefits fails to meet the expectation of local communities the result will frequently be political conflict, often involving violence [*Peluso, 1993: 52*]. The ability of power-holders to enforce the state's policies differs from country to country. But it is very common in African and Asian countries, nearly always forged from diverse cultures and forms of social organisation, for the state to find itself to some degree unable fully to implement its policies [*Jesudason, 1995: 353*]. In such an 'environment of conflict', the ability of the state to impose its will can be judged through 'its capacities to penetrate society, regulate social relationships, extract resources, and appropriate or use resources in determined ways' [*Migdal, 1988: 22*]. Such an environment of conflict will frequently result in conflict over the environment and its resources.

Strategies utilized by societal groups and the state help determine the extent of the latter's power. This is the case not only in relation to the state's ability to get people to behave in certain ways, but also its success in mobilising resources for its own ends. Groups in society may (theoretically) use the ballot box (when it is available) to vote for the government they want; however, the less-than-powerful usually find that even when elections result in a change of government few – if any – beneficial changes occur. As a consequence, subordinate groups may choose instead to use other methods – usually involving direct action – to contest the state. Increasingly, the hegemony of the state is challenged by subordinate groups in Third World countries. Often central to the struggle is the belief that states do not have the will or ability to govern for the benefit of the 'have nots'. One of the most important – although least tangible – forces destabilising governments is the 'bubbling diversity of change' taking place within numerous Third World societies as a consequence of modernisation [*Giddens, 1995*].

Another reason Third World environmental groups are burgeoning is that they often build links with transnational organisations – such as Greenpeace – helping them to grow and focus their efforts [*Haynes, 1996*]. Growing awareness of the relatedness of socio-economic and political issues leads to environmental concerns serving as a focus for wider problems; transnational links may help not only to broaden a Third World group's horizons, but also help support their struggles by supplying welcome publicity. But the key issue is that growing numbers of people in the Third World seem to believe their governments do little for them.

Struggles against sources of environmental degradation, especially deforestation and accompanying loss of livelihood, are emerging as important rallying points for popular organisation, including such groups as India's Chipko movement, Kenya's Green Belt Movement and the late Chico Mendes's National Council of Rubber Tappers (NCRT) of Brazil [*Ekins, 1992: 160–76*]. Others, such as the anti-nuclear testing movement in Tahiti and that of the identity-protection movement of the Ogonis in Nigeria are concerned with environmental issues as an aspect of political campaigns. These groups have all attained a high degree of international repute for the tenacity of their campaigns against governments widely seen as having little concern for the environment.

They also tend to emphasise the educational importance of links between environmental and socio-political concerns. For example, the NCRT's main initiative, Projeto Seringueiro, strives to inform those working and living in Brazil's forests, particularly rubber tappers, that it is appropriate to identify closely with the forests so they will understand the necessity of defending them from excessive felling. Chico Mendes, murdered leader of the NCRT, argued that 'the strengthening of our movement has coincided with the development of the education programme … all our advances, the fight against the destruction of the forest, the organizing of the cooperative and the strengthening of the union, were all possible thanks to the education programme' (Mendes quoted in Breyman [*1993: 129*]). Other coordinating bodies in various parts of the Third World also realize the interconnectness of environmental, human rights and political issues. For example, the Coordinating Council for Human Rights in Bangladesh, providing legal aid to environment ally threatened local communities, has coordinated a network of human rights and environmental organisations since 1986 [*Fisher, 1993: 31, 105, 148*].

The desirability for central organisations to co-ordinate environmental struggles – in order to focus efforts and prevent marginalisation – becomes clear when we bear in mind that many Third World governments endorse rather one-dimensional modernisation ideologies. In such worldviews – where growth and consumption at virtually any cost often seem paramount – protection of the environment is seen as a luxury only rich Western governments, under pressure from predominantly middle-class electorates, can seriously afford to entertain [*Sethi, 1993; Miller, 1995: 43–6*]. The outcome is that environmental concerns are often regarded as subversive, evidence of environmentalists' alleged 'anti-development', 'anti-nation' or 'anti-people' bias.

A series of case studies illustrates these contentions: India, where there is both democracy and a strong civil society; Kenya and Indonesia, where there is neither much democracy nor strong civil societies, but where there are signs that both may be improving; and Tahiti and Nigeria, where both civil society and democracy are underdeveloped. The point is that it helps to have a robust civil society to defend the environment because the state is forced to respond to concerted campaigns. But when environment groups are isolated and forced to act on their own they will be unlikely to succeed.

Environmental Groups and Politics in India

The Chipko Movement

India's forests — covering about one-tenth of the land area — are an essential resource for the livelihoods of rural and indigenous peoples, providing food, fuel and fodder [*Sethi, 1993: 124*]. The Chipko movement is the result of hundreds of decentralised and locally autonomous initiatives. The movement's slogan – 'ecology is permanent economy' – epitomises its chief concern to save forest resources from commercial exploitation by outside contractors. 'In effect the Chipko people are working a socio-economic revolution by winning control of their forest resources from the hands of a distant bureaucracy which is concerned with selling the forest for making urban-oriented products' (United Nations Environment Programme quoted by Ekins [*1992: 144*]).

The Chipko movement is that rare thing among Third World environmental groups: a success. Founded in 1973 in Uttar Pradesh, over the next five years it spread to many other districts of the Himalayas [*Sethi, 1993: 127*]. Its name comes from a local word meaning 'embrace'. People – usually women, the bedrock of the movement – have stopped the felling of trees by standing between them and the loggers, literally embracing them. Chipko protests in Uttar Pradesh achieved a major victory in 1980 with a 15-year ban on green felling in the Himalayan forests of the state. During the 1980s, the movement spread through India to Himachal Pradesh in the north, Karnataka in the south, Rajasthan in the west, and Bihar in the east. 'In addition, the movement stopped clear felling in the Western Ghats and the Vindhyas and generated pressure for a natural resource policy more sensitive to people's needs and ecological requirements' [*Ekins, 1992: 143*].

The Chipko movement is an example of how non-violent resistance and struggle by thousands of ordinary people, without the guidance and control of any centralised apparatus, recognised leadership or full-time cadre, can succeed under certain circumstances. More generally, Chipko helped to shift attention to the centrality of renewable resources – soil, air, water, trees – at a time of swift industrialisation in India. Chipko is a voice from the margins of Indian civil society that managed to demonstrate 'that the crucial environmental conflicts are not just city-based [such as pollution] or related to the depletion of non-renewable resources useful for industry, but arise directly from the philosophical premises embedded in the modern western and capitalist vision ...' [*Sethi, 1993: 127*].

The Narmada Valley Project

A second successful Indian example of an environmental campaign is the stopping of the Narmada Valley project (NVP), a huge hydro-electric dam and irrigation project. The Narmada, 1,312 kilometres long, is India's largest western-flowing river. More than 20 million people – including many minority tribal peoples – live in its basins, using it as an important economic and ecological resource. According to the World Bank, however, the Narmada river 'is one of [India's] least used – water utilisation is currently about four per cent and tons of water effectively are wasted every day when it could be put to use for the benefit of the region' (quoted in Elkins [*1992: 89*]). The NVP was perceived as the solution to this alleged underuse. It was to comprise two very large dams – the Sardar Sarovar Project (SSP) and the Narmada Sagar Project (NSP) – and 28 small dams and 3,000 other water projects. The planned benefits included irrigation of 2.27 million hectares of land in Madhya Pradesh, Gujarat and Rajasthan states, pisciculture, drinking water and electric power. The two main dams would also be designed to moderate floods.The Bank agreed a $450 million loan for SSP and was considering support for NSP until its backing for the entire project came to an end in 1994 [*Tran, 1994*].

Until recently, big dams had been widely regarded in India as prestige symbols of industrialisation and development. India's first post-independence Prime Minister, Nehru, called large dams the new 'temples' of modernising India [*Ekins, 1992: 88*]. Large-scale dams were planned to supply an adequate supply of cheap electricity for industrialisation. Because of this benefit hydro-electric dams were thought to justify huge capital investments and the forced removal of local people.

The successful anti-NVP campaign exemplifies the 'dwindling acceptance and militant resistance' large dams now often encounter in the Third World [*Stiefel and Wolfe, 1994: 180*]. The importance of the Narmada issue is that it struck directly at one of the fundamental development tenets: big is beautiful. It also shows that ordinary people – if they organise – can defeat both state and business interests. Despite the expected benefits, a vociferous grassroots campaign against the NVP developed when it became clear that the dams would entail massive displacement of local people. But it originated initially, not as anti-dam campaigns *per se*, but as groups of activists aiming to ensure that the environment would be protected and that people displaced by the dams were properly financially compensated. Soon, however, the separate groups joined together in common cause against the dams, forming what Elkins [*1992: 90*] describes as 'one of the most powerful social movements ever to emerge in post-independence India'. Anti-dam activists – including about one million potential 'oustees' from more than 150,000 families, voluntary social groups, and local and foreign environmentalist groups – were pitted against an opposing coalition made up of the state governments of Madhya Pradesh, Gujarat and Rajasthan, the World Bank, and big local landowners. The latter saw potential in the scheme for a major boost to irrigation and supply of electricity; local construction firms foresaw a bonanza, while many ordinary citizens believed that the benefits of the scheme would lead to all-round growth in prosperity 'through flood control, increased drinking-water supply, new jobs through a spurt in industry and allied activities' [*Sethi, 1993: 133*].

Struggles at several levels – grassroots, provincial, national and global – focused not only on the pros and cons of the NVP itself but also expanded to include the benefits and disbenefits of large 'development' projects more generally. The anti-NVP campaign won because it managed to build a powerful anti-dam coalition, involving a coalition of local peasant, women's, youth and environmental groups and transnational groups, including Greenpeace International, Friends of the Earth and the US-based Environmental Defense Fund. The anti-dam campaign forced the World Bank – because of adverse publicity – to withdraw its funding in 1994. As a result, the project has, in the absence of alternative funding, been put on 'hold'. As Lori Udall of the Washington-based International Rivers Network explained, the cancellation 'sends a strong signal to international donors that large dams are risky, expensive and destructive investments and that they should support smaller, more flexible projects' [*Vidal, 1995a*].

Two conclusions emerge from the accounts of the Chipko movement and the Narmada anti-dam campaign. The first is that it not only takes a high degree of popular organisation and mobilisation to achieve success, but also a responsive government prepared to react favourably to such efforts. Second, it helps to have influential external allies, although this in itself is no guarantee of success. When such conditions are absent it is very difficult for environmental action groups to achieve similar successes. In the next two case studies – those of environment groups in Kenya and Indonesia – partial success was achieved in the latter because activists managed to build a powerful local coalition to exploit legal avenues to challenge the government. In Kenya, however, the clout of local environment protection groups was undermined not only by their inablity to amend government policy but also by their failure to attract powerful external allies.

Politics and the Environment in Kenya and Indonesia

Kenya

The Green Belt Movement, led by Professor Wangari Maathai, emerged in the 1970s devoting itself initially to tree planting [*Fisher, 1993: 102–3*]. Initially, the Kenyan government lauded it for its efforts in seeking to hold back desertification. But, later, in 1989, Maathai became prominent in opposition to the government's scheme to build a 'world media centre' in Nairobi. The scheduled building was planned to be the tallest construction in Africa, with a giant sculpture of Kenya's president in pride of place. But the proposed site was in the middle of one of the few public parks in the capital.

Maathai sought to mobilise both domestic and international opposition to the plan. As a result, 'she was vilified and placed under virtual house arrest ... In November 1990, [she] was prevented from returning to Kenya after a trip to the USA' [*Ekins, 1992: 151–2*]. The absence of the charismatic Maathai meant the collapse both of opposition to the world media centre and, temporarily, the Green Belt Movement itself. In sum, the Maathai story is a good example of a connection between human rights abuses, 'prestige project' development, and the unsustainability of environmentally destructive policies in the name of development.

The second example from Kenya indicates that it is not only urban land space which is under threat. Kenya developed a robust policy of wildlife conservation and eco-tourism under the leadership of the archaeologist-turned-politician, Richard Leakey, from the late 1980s. [3] Leakey, who stood down from his post as director of Kenya's Wildlife Service in 1994 following a plane crash in which he lost both legs at the knee, was successful in attracting $300 million from foreign donors for his highly effective conservation campaigns.

The parks and reserves Leakey managed were once the lands of nomads and hunters and gatherers, people such as the Masai, Turkana, and Ndorobo. The policy of displacing them from land they had used for centuries began during the colonial era. Kenya's colonial conservationists had claimed not only that African hunters were cruel and wasteful but also their livestock over-grazed the land, out-competing wild animals. However, many contemporary conservationists believe that over-grazing was the exception rather than the rule; people and wildlife normally lived in equanimity. The only way to protect the region's wildlife, the colonialists believed, was to keep it apart from people – in effect, to create animal-only theme parks where the natives were unwelcome. Consequently, the country's national parks were created and people were excluded. But the locations for the parks were not 'empty' land; the homes of local people, unsurprisingly in the most fertile areas where wildlife also congregated, were unceremoniously razed.

Leakey sought, in effect, to revive colonial policy, arguing that successful animal conservation was only possible if humans were excluded. This dovetailed neatly with the ambitions of Kenya's political elite. The issue was largely to do with what foreign tourists wish to see on their holidays in 'exotic' Kenya; if they do not see plenty of big game they will go to other places – perhaps Zimbabwe or South Africa – where they can. By the early 1990s, foreign tourists, mostly from Europe, were spending 'around $50 million each year to view the elephants and other wildlife' [*Peluso, 1993: 55*].[4] Leakey argues, probably correctly, that tourists do not want to see people in the parks and, in any case, the natives want 'development' (roads, piped water, medical and educational facilities), incompatible with conservation.

Whatever the rights and wrongs of Leakey's policy, the fact is that local people were ousted from their ancestral lands without compensation and Kenya's political elites benefited financially from the policy. The Masai protested that they lost most of their dry season grazing to the parks and reserves and that 'the misinformed expectations of tourists have become more important than the lives of local people' [*Peluso, 1993*]. Before resigning from his post in 1994, Leakey was the target of attempts by certain politicians – self-declared champions of the Masai and other tribal groups – to oust him in an attempt to control the tourism industry themselves. But the issue was not 'only' about the rights and wrongs of ousting local people from land traditionally in their control. There was a further human cost. In the two years following Richard Leakey's appointment as director of Kenya's Wildlife Service in April 1989 over 100 poachers were shot and killed, many of them 'with no chance for discussion or trial; the [wildlife] rangers are licensed, like military in a state of emergency, to shoot-to-kill' [*Peluso, 1993: 57*].

The recent story of nature conservation in Kenya also involves an important role for foreign environmental organisations. The policy of shoot-to-kill poachers was, according to Peluso, actively encouraged by various foreign groups, including the Worldwide Fund for Nature (WWF), the African Wildlife Foundation, World Conservation International, the International Union for the Conservation of Nature, Conservation International, and the National Geographic Society. Declaring unequivocally that local tribal people were 'poachers', WWF argued that the Masai's 'increasing population was a major threat to the survival of elephants and other wildlife' [*Peluso, 1993: 57*].

The Kenyan government uses its power to protect and manage resources and to assert its authority where local people resist state controls. The political implications of this trend in conserving Kenyan wildlife are clear. Although equipment and funds are ostensibly allocated to protect nature, they are also used by the state to serve its own political ends. In this way, the commitment to preservation of wildlife for tourism and research serves both the economic and political interests of the Kenyan government, while its effectiveness in preserving wildlife is questionable.

Indonesia

Contention over Indonesia's forest reserves' management policies is more nuanced. Organs of the state on the island of Java interact differently with international conservation interests than in Kenya. While international conservation groups do not arm the Indonesian government in an effort to help protect tropical forest habitats as they do in Kenya, they none the less play a significant role in legitimating the state's use of violence to protect its clams to the nation's natural resources. By lobbying for sustainable forestry and defining sustainable forestry in the terms traditionally used by Western foresters or ecologists (who generally neither acknowledge nor consider the role of people in creating so-called natural environments), international conservation groups emphasise the formal, scientific, planning aspects of forest management.

In Indonesia the state's nature conservation policies are challenged by groups in civil society. In October 1994, local environmentalists began a court case against the government to spark a broad inquiry into the government's Reforestation Fund. The lawsuit, brought by the Indonesian Forum on the Environment, Wanana Lingkungan Hidap Indonesia (WALHI), an umbrella group with board members from local business and from multinationals such as IBM, helped focus attention on environmental issues in the country [*Fisher, 1993: 149*].

WALHI's lawsuit challenged President Suharto's decision to funnel $185 million from the Reforestation Fund into the coffers of the nation's aircraft industry. According to WALHI, the decision violated the government's conservationist commitment to refurbish Indonesia's vanishing rain forests [*Cohen, 1994: 44*]. But the government's defence lawyers maintained that WALHI had no legal standing to bring the suit, as the 'non-government organisation does not represent the interests of the general public', while, in addition, 'the reforestation issue should be aired in parliament, not in the courts' [*Cohen, 1994*]. A confidential Asian Development Bank report commissioned by the Ministry of Forestry pointed out that just one-sixth (16 per cent) of the reforestation funds was spent in the four years to March 1993, while direct funding of natural forest rehabilitation and conservation activity formed only three per cent of allocated funding. In other words, less than *half of one per cent* of funds allocated for reforestation in Indonesia was spent on that purpose in the 1989–93 period!

The report noted delicately that 'there is evidence of considerable and increasing flexibility on how funds are spent,' although no details were given. Moreover, 'many plantations have been situated in logged-over forest, prompting the clear-cutting of remaining trees so as to create a homogeneous forest suitable for Indonesia's rapidly expanding pulp and paper industry' [Cohen, 1994]. Nevertheless, the conservation message championed by WALHI appears to be gradually getting through. Indonesia's forestry minister, Djamaloedin Soeryohadikoesoemo, announced in late 1994 that Indonesia would reduce its timber output by 30 per cent between 1995 and 1999 in the interests of 'sustainable development'. Djamaloedin also expressed interest in pilot projects in community forestry, now in operation in Kalimantan and other areas, allowing villagers more responsibility in protecting resources.[5]

The above account of attempts at environmental protection in Indonesia illustrates well Grove's contention that, 'if there is one single historical lesson to be drawn [in relation to the environment] ... it is that states can be persuaded to act to prevent environmental degradation only when their economic interests are shown to be directly threatened' (quoted in Camilleri and Falk [1992: 175]). Once environmental groups start to campaign against deforestation they find themselves up against not only the state but also large farmers and business interests. The ability of anti-deforestation groups – and of environmental groups more widely – to succeed in their objectives is due to two main factors: (a) it is crucial that groups do not remain autonomous but link together into a wider – regional or national – alliance, while (b) a campaign is more likely to succeed if the alliance can pursue its goals through democratic and legal channels. In other words, the effectiveness of environmental endeavours is partially dependent upon the political circumstances. Two case studies from Tahiti and Nigeria illustrate these contentions.

Nuclear Testing at Mururoa: The Catalyst for Tahiti's Cultural Revolution

The decision by the French government to detonate eight – later reduced to six – nuclear explosions at Mururoa atoll in late 1995 and early 1996 was followed by a wave of global condemnation [Ghazi, 1995]. On Bastille Day, 14 July 1995, French products were boycotted, the country's embassy compounds around the world were stormed by Greenpeace protestors, and demonstrations of various kinds took place in Western and Third World countries alike [Zinn and Bowcott, 1995]. Despite these protests, the French detonated the first nuclear explosion in September, and others followed.

The tests not only stimulated global anger; they also encouraged the Tahiti independence movement, Tavini Huira-atira, to greater efforts. While global environmentalists saw the tests as contrary to the 1990s spirit of conservation, many Tahitians saw them as an example of French arrogance, further indication that the colonial power cared little for the views of its 'subjects'.

There is a long history of nuclear tests in French Polynesia. Following the Partial Test-Ban Treaty of 1963, France established its *Centre d'Experiments du Pacifique*, carrying out 41 atmospheric tests at Mururoa over the next decade before announcing a 20-year moratorium on further testing [*Fry, 1993: 228, 237*].

For South Pacific societies, the cold war moulded the way in which regional security was conceptualised; it also helped to foster regional pan-nationalism. While this originally affected 'only relations among states, it increasingly affected' social and political forces within them' [*Fry, 1993: 234*]. In both American-controlled Palau and French New Caledonia, cold war imperatives were used to justify opposition to moves for self-determination [*Danielsson and Danielsson, 1986*]. Later, campaigns for autonomy and independence gained in strength, stimulated by perceptions that the end of the cold war would lead to less bargaining power and a more stringent economic climate for the South Pacific as attention was focused elsewhere [*Callick, 1991*]. For France, however, Polynesia retained its importance as a nuclear testing site, while the remaining colonial possessions, including Tahiti, gave reason for continued involvement in an important region [*Wollacott, 1995*].

Until recent upheavals, France successfully contained dissent by the assiduous use of money, spending close to $2 billion dollars annually on its South Pacific possession [*The Economist, 1995b*]. In French Polynesia per capita GDP in 1993 was estimated by the World Bank in the 'high-income' category, that is, greater than $8,626 per annum, four times that of independent Fiji ($2,130), and many times greater than those of other independent island states in the region. Tahiti 'lives off a French military arsenal.' The economy is 'both prosperous and protected, without the worry of international competition' [*The Economist, 1995a*].

French policy is to retain its role in the region, despite the withdrawal by the other erstwhile colonial powers, maintaining that its Pacific possessions are an integral part of France and that '[a] Tahitian has the same citizen's rights as a Parisian' [*The Economist, 1995a*]. Nearly 40 years ago, the people of France's Pacific possessions, asked if they wanted independence, which would have meant a complete cessation of French aid, voted to remain a part of the French 'family'. By the 1980s, however, it was clear that the mood was changing; in New Caledonia a vociferous pro-independence movement clashed with the governing administration [*Fry, 1993: 234*].

A background of growing anti-French feeling underpinned the 1995 riots in Tahiti. The island particularly benefits as a supply base for Mururoa atoll, 1,400 kilometres to the south east. Many Tahitians work there, mostly in menial jobs, although many earn salaries allegedly in excess of $40,000 dollars a year [*The Economist, 1995a*]. These jobs are highly valued in Tahiti itself where between 25 and 40 percent of the young are without work [*Vidal, 1995b*]. Every year about 1,000 young people cannot find jobs when they leave school; the young provide many of the cadres for the pro-independence movement.

The French decision to resume nuclear testing at Mururoa was the catalyst for an eruption of anger against the French colonial presence. The riots grew from an explosion of anger, especially by the young, to become a broader-based demonstration of anti-French feeling. Vaihere Bordes, leader of a women's group, claimed that 'everyone here is united against France and the nuclear testing [yet] local government does not listen' [*Vidal, 1995b*]. For three days in September 1995, coinciding with the first nuclear test, demonstrators took to the streets destroying, burning and looting. By the end, Tahiti's capital, Papeete, was badly damaged.

The anti-France struggle focused the attention of the main groups in Tahiti's emerging civil society – particularly Hiti Tau, an environmental, development, women's, youth and cultural umbrella group, the pro-independence party, Tavini Huira-atira, and the Atia I Mua labour union – on nuclear testing, a symbolic issue focusing attention on independence [*Rood, James and Sakamati, 1995: 17; Vidal, 1995b*]. Calls for social justice and an end to environmental destruction in French Polynesia were part of the same demand: key decisions affecting people's lives must be brought back under their control. Tahitians felt divorced both from their culture and from the ability to decide their own futures. Denied self-determination, many Tahitans were no longer prepared meekly to submit to the dictates of France. Having attempted to persuade the French for two months by peaceful demonstrations and petitions, it was perhaps understandable that protests would turn violent when the French disregarded both local and global calls for restraint.

The Tahitian outburst should also be seen against the background of global demonstrations against the decision to resume nuclear testing. Tahitians were well aware of this because with access to television and radio, they were able to see the worldwide protests at first hand. As Bordes noted, '[m]inds have changed. If you go back just 30 years our parents didn't realize what nuclear power meant. In 1966 we didn't have radio, TV or an airport. Now we're in contact with the world, and we see the catastrophe' [*Vidal, 1995b*]. Tahitians also perceived, no doubt, that their own anti-French demonstrations would have the eye of the world and that the anti-colonial campaign would, as a result, be galvanised.

Environmental Activism in Ogoniland, Nigeria

Half a million Ogoni people – one half of one per cent of Nigeria's population – live on the Niger delta. The Ogoni are by tradition farmers and fishers, in the past producing food not only for local people but also for much of Rivers State. Large quantities of oil were discovered in Ogoniland in the late 1950s. Since then, oil has come to dominate both the Nigerian economy and the Ogoni people's lives. Yet, despite repeated promises from the federal government, local people have enjoyed only very limited benefits from their oil. As Naanen [*1995: 46–7*] remarks, what has happened instead is that '[t]he patterns of power distribution between central government and the component units, on the one hand, and between the various ethnic groups, on the other, have politically emasculated the Ogoni people, causing them to lose control of their resources and their environment'.

From an environmental point of view, perhaps most disastrous has been a succession of oil spills from ruptured pipelines which were driven – above ground – through farms and villages. Ogonis have had to live with the continuous noise and pollution of numerous gas flares; Ogoniland has two of Nigeria's four oil refineries, the country's only major fertiliser plant, a large petrochemical factory, and its fourth largest ocean port – all located within a few kilometres of each other [*Osaghae, 1995: 330*]. The impact of industrialisation and oil exploitation is especially serious because of the high population density – 500,000 Ogoni crammed into 404 square miles, that is, 1238 people per square mile – coupled with the fact that the vast majority depend on farming and fishing for their livelihoods. Neither the Nigerian government nor Shell is over-anxious to publicise the Ogonis' plight. An attempt by an INGO, the Unrepresented Nations and Peoples Organisation (UNPO), to send a fact-finding mission to Ogoniland was frustrated by the Nigerian government. A visa to the area was also denied to representatives of Body Shop [*Body Shop: n/d*].

Poor environmental conditions, lack of development in the area, and the unwillingness of the government to listen to Ogoni demands were the catalysts driving them to rebel. The trigger came in October 1990 when villagers at Umuechen attacked Shell production workers. Shell called in the Mobile Police (known locally as 'kill-and-go') who shot 80 villagers dead and burned down around 500 houses, some with the inhabitants trapped inside [*Africa Confidential, 1995*].

The uprising was led and coordinated by the Movement for the Survival of the Ogoni People (MOSOP), run by a steering committee drawn from various community groups, including those of women, young people – organised in National Youth Council of Ogoni People (NYCOP) – and professionals. MOSOP was led, until his execution in November 1995, by the writer Ken Saro-Wiwa. Not all Ogoni support MOSOP's aims; there is strong opposition from some Ogoni traditional leaders who are, as a result, accused of being state agents. Anti-MOSOP individuals suffered: their houses and other property were destroyed by members of NYCOP [Osaghae, 1995: 334]. Many traditional leaders' opposed MOSOP because the broadly based community group threatened to diminish their own power by encouraging previously subordinate groups to challenge them. It is clear, however, that the great majority of the Ogoni were sympathetic to MOSOP; a banned march involving 300,000 black-wearing Ogoni took place on 4 January 1996 to commemorate 'Ogoni Day' and to mourn the death of Saro-Wiwa and his eight comrades. Six marchers were killed by federal soldiers [Duodu, 1996].

Attempts to organise and mobilise the Ogoni had begun in 1989. Saro-Wiwa presented the Ogoni case before the United Nations Commission on Human Rights in Geneva in 1992. This 'marked an important turning point in bolstering people's confidence', led directly to demonstrations involving 300,000 Ogoni in January 1993 and to a subsequent appearance by an Ogoni delegation at the UN Human Rights Conference in Vienna in August of that year [Naanen, 1995: 69]. From this time, environmental and human rights organisations including UNPO, the World Rain Forest Action Group, Amnesty International, Body Shop, and Greenpeace, helped to publicise the Ogoni plight. Pressure was also brought to bear on both Shell and the Nigerian government by the British Parliamentary Human Rights Group. The government's response had elements of both 'carrot and stick', encouraging dialogue with MOSOP while nevertheless jailing Saro-Wiwa and several other Ogoni leaders on what many regarded as trumped up charges. In early 1995, Saro-Wiwa received $30,000 from the Goldman foundation, an American organisation, in 'recognition of his struggle for human and environmental justice' [Africa Confidential, 1995].

The recent struggle against the federal government and the oil companies is but the most recent manifestation of the Ogonis' desire for control over their own affairs. During the colonial era the Ogoni, along with other Delta groups, demanded a separate administrative division. This was finally achieved in 1967, after independence, with the creation of Rivers State [Naanen, 1995: 63]. In 1974, following allegations of domination by the more numerous Ijaw people, the Ogoni unsuccessfully petitioned for the creation of a separate Port Harcourt state. Demands for a separate state increasingly dovetailed with a number of other problems: economic decline, oil-based ecological degradation, and the undermining of traditional smallholder agriculture and fishing [*Saro Wiwa, 1992*].

Ogoni discontent at their position as a powerless national minority was increased by the contribution of the oil resources on their land to Nigeria's economic development. Six oilfields produced 200,000 barrels a day by 1972, yet Ogonis are denied material benefits, including piped water, electricity, medical facilities and roads [*Naanen, 1995: 65*].

While Ogoni demands were not successful in the short-term there were a number of concrete achievements, especially the raising of national and international awareness about their predicament, while the case has become a *cause célèbre*, a test of the Nigerian government's attitude towards the country's minorities and their demands for control of their lands. The hanging of Saro-Wiwa and eight other Ogoni activists in November 1995 for allegedly encouraging members of MOSOP to murder four pro-government Ogoni chiefs was met by an international outcry. Following the 'judicial murders' of Saro-Wiwa and his comrades, more than 20 other Ogoni leaders and activists, including Ledum Mitee, MOSOP deputy president, were arrested. There was a massive federal troop presence in Ogoniland [*Ogoni Community Association, 1995; Black, Bowcott and Vidal, 1995*].

The Ogonis' struggle against central government illustrates two factors in contemporary relations between the state and local minority groups in Africa: the importance of land and the concern with which states view challenges to their power from putative separatist groups. Saro-Wiwa's execution was not because he led the campaign for environmental justice, but rather because the Ogoni struggle crystallised for many other minority groups in Nigeria the stranglehold which the country's three dominant ethnic groups have on power.

Three conclusions emerge from the Ogoni and Tahiti case studies. First, groups in both polities were fighting, not only against perceived environmental injustices, but also for autonomy or independence from central control. In other words, the environmental objective was part of a wider political goal of empowerment. Second, the leading figures in both campaigns were largely young men and women, subordinate groups with little to gain from the status quo. Third, both case studies illustrate once again that, in the absence of a co-ordinated society-wide campaign against powerful state or foreign interests, environmental groups find it very difficult to ahieve their goals.

Conclusion

Bottom-up pressure on Third World governments from environmental groups has grown in recent years, often a facet of wider demands for more general political and economic reforms. Environmental activists tend to come from subordinate strata, especially from among the poor, women, the young and national minorities. The case studies – from India, Kenya, Nigeria, Indonesia and Tahiti – gave examples of why environment-oriented campaigns frequently form aspects of wider protests against states and their policies. However, environmental campaigns are only likely to succeed under certain conditions. First, it is essential – although not necessarily sufficient – that there are democratic and legal avenues to pursue environmental goals. Second, it is crucial to build a relatively wide-ranging coalition of groups and organisations, large and representative enough to take on the state and its allies, such as large landowners, senior military figures or important business interests. However, such struggles are only likely to be successful in democratic environments where strong civil societies have leverage *vis-à-vis* the state. Of the countries discussed in this article, only India falls into this category. The partial success of WALHI Indonesia underlines how, like Chipko, if environmental groups are linked together in a coalition, are well organised and tenaciousness, then they may successfully challenge the state.

A growing number of environmental groups challenges governmental and corporate practices in relation to sustainable development strategies, with modest but perhaps growing success. Underpinning such organisations' agenda is the belief that people at and near the bottom of the socio-economic pile should have the unequivocal right and opportunity to participate in shaping their own destinies when it comes to the environment. Because most Third World communities are collectively poor they tend not to be consulted on development projects that affect them. Lacking political and economic power, development policies are often simply imposed on them, as we saw with the Narmada Valley project.

The Ogonis' and the Tahitians' struggles exemplify what happens when leaders of minority or marginal ethnic and social organisations feel dissatisfied with the structure of power-sharing and resource allocation in their polities: they seek to restructure the configuration of power in a manner more acceptable to them and their followers. Yet the failure of both campaigns to achieve their goals – at least in the short term – underlines how important it is for civil society to be powerful enough to take on the state and achieve its goals in such struggles. Both the Ogonis and the Tahitians were successful in gaining foreign support but were incapable of putting together a domestic coalition of interest groups of sufficient strength to achieve their goals. The Ogonis found that neighbouring ethnic groups – with some of which they had a history of tension – were encouraged by the state to attack them. In Tahiti the situation was complicated because France is an important employer paying salaries far above the local average. People may well have warmed to the notion of greater autonomy or even independence from colonial rule, yet such aspirations may well have been offset for many by concern at what would happen to their incomes if the French departed.

NOTES

1. The term, 'Third World', was invented in the 1950s to refer, on the one hand, to the large group of economically underdeveloped, then decolonising countries in Africa, Asia and the Middle East and, on the other, to Latin American states, mostly independent since the early nineteenth century, but still economically weak. Despite a shared history of colonisation, there are important differences between Third World states. The United Arab Emirates (1993 GNP per capita $21,430), South Korea ($7,660) and Mozambique ($90), or politically singular polities such as Cuba (one-party communist state), Nigeria (military dictatorship), and India (multi-party democracy), are all considered Third World States. While the blanket term 'Third World' obscures cultural, economic, social and political differences between states, it has advantages over alternatives like 'the South' or 'developing' countries. The expression 'the South', is essentially a geographic expression which ignores the fact that some 'western' countries – Australia, New Zealand – are in the geographical south. The 'South' does, however, have the advantage of getting away from the connotation of developing towards some preordained end state or goal which is explicit in the idea of 'developing' countries (GNP figures from *World Development Report 1995*, Oxford: Oxford University Press for the World Bank, 1995, Table 1, pp.162–3).
2. It is important not to overstress the significance of environmental groups for all subordinate people. Some do not have an interest in joining or supporting environmental groups for the simple reason that they derive their incomes from working in polluting industries or are impelled by land hunger towards anti-ecological methods of farming. I am indebted for this point to an anonymous reviewer of an earlier version of this article.
3. Leakey is now a leading figure in an opposition political party, Sarafina.
4. Tourism is Kenya's most profitable industry, bringing in 20 per cent of the country's total foreign exchange.
5. This may or may not be a sign of the emergence of a primary environmental care policy in Indonesia. An emerging scheme for eco-labelling promises to add conservation safeguards; in order to sell tropical timber in developed country markets like Sweden, Australia, Canada and the US it is increasingly necessarily to demonstrate that timber comes from sustainable sources.

REFERENCES

Africa Confidential (1995) 'Ken and the Soja Boys', 17 March, pp.3–4.
Black, I., Bowcott, O. and J. Vidal (1995) 'Nigeria Defies World with Writer's "Judicial Murder"', *The Guardian*, 11 Nov.
Body Shop. n/d. (c. mid-November 1995), 'Ken Saro-Wiwa and the Ogoni. Fact Sheet'.
Breyman, S. (1993), 'Knowledge as Power: Ecology Movements and Global Environmental Problems', in R. Lipschutz and K. Conca (eds.), *The State and Social Power in Global Environmental Politics*, New York: Columbia University Press, pp.124–57.

Callick, R. (1991), 'No Blue Skies Yet in the South Pacific', *Pacific Economic Bulletin*, Vol.6, No.2, pp.1–19.
Camilleri, J. and J. Falk (1992), *The End of Sovereignty? The Politics of a Shrinking and Fragmented World*, Aldershot: Edward Elgar.
Cohen, M. (1994), 'Culture of Awareness', *Far Eastern Economic Review*, 17 Nov. 1994, p.44.
Danielsson, B. and M.-T. Danielsson (1986), *Poisoned Reign French Nuclear Colonialism*, 2nd rev. edn., Ringwood: Penguin.
Duodu, C. (1996), 'Nigerian Troops Shoot Six Dead as Ogoni Mourn Saro-Wiwa', *The Observer*, 7 Jan.1996.
The Economist (1995a), 'A Kept Woman', 15 July, p.61.
The Economist (1995b), 'France's Other Blast', 16 Sept., p.88.
Ekins, P. (1992), *A New World Order. Grassroots Movements for Global Change*, London: Routledge.
Ellis, S. (1994), 'Politics and Nature Conservation in South Africa', *Journal of Southern African Studies*, Vol.20, No.1, pp.53–69.
Escobar, A. and S. Alvarez (1992a), 'Introduction Theory and Protest in Latin America Today', in Escobar and Alvarez (eds.) [*1992: 1–15*].
Escobar, A. and S. Alvarez (1992b), 'Conclusion: Theoretical and Political Horizons of Change in Contemporary Latin American Social Movements', in Escobar and Alvarez (eds.) [*1992: 317–30*].
Escobar, A. and S. Alvarez (eds.) (1992), *The Making of Social Movements in Latin America: Identity, Strategy and Democracy*, Boulder, CO: Westview.
Fals Borda, O. (1992) 'Social Movements and Political Power in Latin America', in Escobar and Alvarez (eds.) [*1992: 303–16*].
Fisher, J. (1993), *The Road from Rio. Sustainable Development and Nongovernmental Movement in the Third World*, Westport, CT: Praeger.
Fry, G. (1993), 'At the Margin: The South Pacific and Changing World Order', in R. Leaver and J. Richardson (eds.), *Charting the Post-Cold War Order*, Boulder, CO: Westview, pp.224–42.
Ghazi, P. (1995), 'Rainbow Warriors Defy French Guns', *The Observer*, 9 July.
Giddens, A. (1995), 'Government's Last Gasp?', *The Observer*, 9 July.
Haynes, J. (1996), 'Politics of the Natural Environment in the Third World', *Contemporary Politics*, Vol.2, No.2, pp.19–42.
Haynes, J. (1997), *Democracy and Civil Society in the Third World*, Cambridge: Polity Press.
Jesudason, J. (1995), 'Statist Democracy and the Limits to Civil Society in Malaysia', *Journal of Commonwealth and Comparative Politics*, Vol.33, No.3, pp.335–56.
Mainwaring, S. and E. Viola (1984), 'New Social Movements, Political Culture and Democracy Brazil and Argentina in the 1980s', *Telos*, No.61, pp.17–54.
Migdal, J. (1988), *Strong Societies and Weak States: State-Society Relations and State Capabilities in the Third World*, Princeton, NJ: Princeton University Press.
Miller, M. (1995), *The Third World in Global Environmental Politics*, Buckingham: Open University Press.
Naanen, B. (1995), 'Oil-Producing Minorities and the Restructuring of Nigerian Federalism: The Case of the Ogoni People', *Journal of Commonwealth and Comparative Politics*, Vol.33, No.1, pp.46–78.
Ogoni Community Association UK (1995), 'Press Release: "Ogoni Campaign Builds Internationally"', 13 Nov.
Osaghae, E. (1995), 'The Ogoni Uprising: Oil Politics, Minority Agitation and the Future of the Nigerian State', *African Affairs*, 94, 376, pp.325–44.
Peluso, N. L. (1993), 'Coercing Conservation the Politics of State Resource Control', in R. Lipschutz and K. Conca (eds.), *The State and Social Power in Global Environmental Politic*, New York: Columbia University Press, pp.46–70.
Princen, T. and M. Finger (1994), *Environmental NGOs in World Politics: Linking the Local and the Global*, London, Routledge.
Rood, D., James, C. and S. Sakamati (1995), 'Collateral Damage', *Far Eastern Economic Review*, 21 Sept., pp.16–17.

Saro-Wiwa, K. (1992) *Genocide in Nigeria: The Ogoni Tragedy*, London: Saros International Publishers.
Sethi, H. (1993), 'Survival and Democracy Ecological Struggles in India', in P. Wignaraja (ed.), *New Social Movements in the South*, London: Zed Books, pp.122–48.
Stiefel, M and M. Wolfe (1994), *A Voice for the Excluded: Popular Participation in Development. Utopia or Necessity?*, London/Geneva: Zed/UNRISD.
Tran, M. (1994), 'World Bank Sees Nepal Project as Test of Credibility', *The Guardian*, 17 Nov.
Vidal, J. (1995a), 'Localism *vs* Globalism', *The Guardian*, 15 Nov.
Vidal, J. (1995b), 'Rats of the Rubbish Society Fight Back', *The Guardian*, 9 Sept.
Wollacott, M. (1995), 'A Rage for Peace and Power', *The Guardian*, 9 Sept.
World Bank. (1995), *World Development Report 1995*, Oxford: Oxford University Press for the World Bank.
Zinn, C. and O. Bowcott (1995), 'Storm of Anti-Nuclear Protests Mark Bastille Day', *The Guardian*, 15 July.

NGOs and the Global Environmental Facility: Friendly Foes?

ZOE YOUNG

The Global Environment Facility (GEF) exists to fund global environmental benefits through international development projects. Interim financial mechanism to the United Nations conventions on climate change and biodiversity, it is also hoped that it will green its parent, the World Bank, and help reform the UN. Some NGO commentators castigate GEF as greenwash for a sick system; others – part of the tacit coalition that created it – prefer to render the facility more transparent, participatory and thereby effective. The environmental movement's responses to GEF's need for legitimation in 'civil society' may begin to transcend a quandary faced in many movements for social change: whether to enter, adjust and utilise the institutional structures within which problems arise, or to avoid co-option by challenging the system from outside.

A novel multilateral aid fund for conservation, the Global Environment Facility (GEF) was replenished in 1998 with $2.75 billion to finance 'global environmental benefits' through World Bank and UN development projects. Administrators of GEF aim to embody the rhetoric and fulfil the desires of reformist, globalising sections of the environmental movement. Sometimes they disempower grass-roots environmental action in the process; they may also aid some indirectly.

The pattern of interaction between diverse NGOs claiming to represent 'civil society' and the GEF may write large a million local stories of co-operation, co-option and competition: NGOs 'inside' with GEF engage directly with a politically, economically and scientifically globalising system that those 'outside' ignore or confront directly. While governments and inter-governmental institutions (IGOs) are the main beneficiaries of

This work is based on research financed by the ESRC Global Environmental Change Programme. Thanks are due to Sonja Boehmer-Christiansen, Lucy Ford and the author's parents for encouragement and detailed comments; Chris Rootes and two anonymous referees for constructive advice; also unnamed GEF and NGO people for interviews and feedback. All mistakes and omissions remain the author's responsibility.

GEF, the productive niches it provides to some in the environmental NGO community may be unique in the political ecology of global governance.

Why and through what channels do NGOs access GEF policy and funds? How are they used, and by whom? Do they provide green expertise and credibility to elite decision-making, or do they enter and subvert the dominant discourses to support more radical allies in the broader movement? How do people in the global environmental epistemic community sustain the GEF as a development of shared value? Whether GEF contributes to 'sustainable development' – however understood – is not tackled here. Nor do I examine closely how environmental activists implement or campaign against GEF projects; the study centres on relations between groups clustering around new global flows of subsidy.

While telling a tale of GEF, I introduce NGOs involved in its creation and critique. Discussing how some have so far engaged with GEF, I link their objectives, uses and achievements. To help fulfil GEF's potential, 'civil society stakeholders' in whose name and with whose money it operates might be enabled to draw their own conclusions about how – or even whether – their self-selected representatives are working for the public good. In conclusion, I discuss developments in civil society responses to the impact of institutional globalisation on the environment. As long as globalisation is presented as immutable, details of how people do shape global institutions must be useful.[1]

NGOs Constructing the GEF

This story begins not with *Silent Spring* but with links between organised environmentalism and the structures of government. Soon before the UN Conference on the Human Environment in Stockholm, 1972, International Parliamentary Conferences (IPCE) on the Environment[2] were founded to build awareness and pressure for governmental action around the world. Western politicians thereby strengthened links with the establishment end of the environment movement: WWF, IUCN and the Sierra Club. IPCE meetings continued until 1978 when the money ran out and governmental commitment faded, and some in the environmental movement grew more politically radical.

Consequently, in the early 1980s a 'group of 10' US-based environmental NGOs[3] decided that economic growth was not only compatible with environmental protection, but necessary to finance it [*Devall, 1990*]. This distinguished 'reformers', accepting capitalist credo, from 'deeper' green groups demanding fundamental restructuring of human organisation. A report [*Cahn, 1985*] never reached the boards of the group of 10, yet summarises a sort of consensus [*Devall, 1990*]. Managerial in tone, key principles were that: sustained economic growth is good for environmental quality; regulation is good for both the economy and the environment; and NGOs should sustain rhetorically radical but practically conciliatory strategies.

Indicating acquiescence in most of the *status quo*, mainstream environmentalists formed a basis for conciliation between big NGOs (BINGOs) and western governments. Shedding radical green associations, reformers stepped up constructive discussion with OECD governments and inter-governmental organisations (IGOs) who had rejected their agenda as anti-growth. Perhaps in reaction, confrontational groupings like Earth First! emerged to raise the stakes.

By the late 1980s, the World Bank faced environmentalist demands from the US Congress. As 'parliament' of the Bank's major shareholder, Congress has more control over foreign policy than other donor countries and is sensitive to local lobbies. Under pressure from environmentalists about the World Bank's record – sometimes in 'unholy alliances' with right-wingers opposed to aid [*Rich, 1994*] – Congress tightened conditions on Bank replenishments [*Wade, 1997*]. NGOs meeting with civil servants in search of political accommodation found shared interest in financing conservation, the former gaining access to large-scale public finance, and the latter improving image and effects with the help of their best critics. Exploring the possibilities of 'sustainable development' as defined in the Brundtland report of 1987, an intricate dance between professionals in environment and development began in the corridors of power.

While 'Brundtland seeks a cooptation of the very groups that are creating a new dance of politics ... the experts of the global state ... turning them into a secondary, second rate bunch of consultants' (Visvanathan [*1991*], quoted in Escobar [*1996: 54*]), the United Nations system was already more open to 'civil society' than the Bretton Woods institutions [*Weiss and Gordenker, 1996*] and some NGOs had learned how to use it. One consequence was the International Conservation Financing Program (ICFP), initiated by UNDP through the efforts of an ex-banker with an International Wilderness Leadership Foundation [*Sjöberg, 1994*]. The World Resources Institute (WRI) was commissioned to produce a report on strategies for multi-laterally financing conservation [*WRI, 1989*]. The WRI team met with experts, banks, NGOs and development institutions in the US and ran workshops around the world before setting out options including an International Environmental Facility.

In the event, the UNDP Administrator was 'not happy' [*Sjöberg, 1994*], and claiming the report ran 'counter to the integrated vision of development and environment', tried to remove UNDP's name. This left Gus Speth (later head of UNDP) at WRI to take forward an idea rejected by its official sponsor for being insufficiently holistic and neglecting complex relations between poverty and ecology. While the formal ICFP process fizzled out, the only real difference from its recommendation is that GEF is 'global' rather than 'international', and the only regret heard from the WRI was that GEF is a fund in itself rather than a project preparation facility for existing institutions to move money through certifiably greener channels (interviews, Nov. 1997).

What is the GEF?

Some say GEF's task of 'mainstreaming' the environment internationally resembles the remit given UNEP in the early 1970s (interviews, 1997–98). Both institutions are rife with environmental expertise, neither may be able to fulfil the 'hopeless mandate' of co-ordinating institutional change, given the low status of the environment in governments. However GEF is richer than UNEP, treasury-driven, US-based, with World Bank-style 'efficiency', and designed for an age of globalisation.

GEF pays the 'agreed incremental costs' of creating 'global environmental benefits' in four 'focal areas': biodiversity, climate change, international waters and ozone depletion [*Werksman, 1996; Pernetta, 1998*]. Created in 1991 as a pilot facility in the World Bank to multilaterally finance globally valuable conservation [*Shiva, 1993; Gupta, 1995*], GEF's 'additional' trust fund is now described as the 'only game in town' by concessional aid professionals (personal communications, 1997–98). As interim 'financial mechanism' to UN conventions on climate change (FCCC) and biodiversity (CBD), GEF subsidises required activities in signatory countries not classified as sufficiently 'developed' to pay the costs themselves [*Young and Boehmer-Christiansen, 1998*]. To 'leverage' other finance into more environmentally benevolent investments, GEF might add biodiversity components to forestry projects, or shift an energy investment from fossil fuels to renewables. The aid 'sweetens' internalisation of selected environmental costs to global economic activities.

European donor government representatives initiated GEF in their trusted World Bank to pre-empt alternatives threatened for UNCED the following year [*Chatterjee and Finger, 1994*]. Lacking independent legal personality, GEF is administered through an experimental inter-institutional arrangement, but has a governing council and secretariat inside the World Bank. Yet policies are described in language [*GEF, 1994b, 1996*] – partnership and participation, stakeholder ownership and learning by doing – straight from discourses of non-linear emancipatory development [*Chambers, 1997*]. Claiming scientific and economic rationale to pursue radical alternatives, GEF presents as the culmination of committed work by diverse environmentalists.

Yet NGOs as well as G77 governments protested at Rio that GEF was a rushed fait accompli, created back to front with strategy trailing finance. After complex, sometimes heated negotiations the facility was restructured in the name of transparency and accountability before refinancing with US$2 billion in 1994. The council gained a double majority[4] voting system, and the World Bank was joined by the UN Environment Program (UNEP) and Development Program (UNDP) as 'equal' implementing agencies (IAs).

There is little documentation of how GEF staff privately see their role. From observation and interviews it appears that GEF institutions accommodate diverse opinion, some more radical than found in NGOs.[5] Yet whatever their take on environmentalism, GEF people working 'professionally' in hierarchical structures may change 'business as usual' only at the edges [Gupta, 1995]. They may be negotiating and sustaining conservation infrastructure – for example, computerised resource databases – valued by financial, scientific, governmental and increasingly, environmental elites.[6]

In the face of government conservatism, business risk aversion and bureaucracies' embedded practices, individuals in GEF value outside expertise for the work of reaching 'agreement'. We have seen how NGOs helped bring GEF into being; now it fosters NGO involvement in a 'spirit of partnership' [GEF, 1998a]. Primarily meeting the needs of governments, GEF also responds to key individuals in NGOs, to the extent that in negotiations for the establishment of the pilot GEF, some participants 'complained privately that the US position practically replicated that of Washington-based environmental advocacy groups' [Sjöberg, 1994].

Who are the NGOs?

The World Bank classifies NGOs as: (i) independent from governments and ii) having humanitarian or co-operative rather than commercial objectives.[7] In most cases academic institutions and business are not classed as NGOs. However, in the case of GEF's unique openness to 'outsiders',[8] all interested parties are grouped together and allowed access if by GEF's definition they have global environmental goals.

Motivation of NGOs may primarily be 'non-economic' in pursuit of 'public purposes', but even when seeking to 'serve, not to supply', they sell services [Harrison, 1993]. The 'neo-liberal lurch' [Sklair, 1998] towards privatisation and de-skilling of government functions in the 1980s allowed NGOs into the international aid sector [Edwards and Hulme, 1992]. Filling gaps in governance and public service left by state asset-stripping, some are active at the global level and are welcomed – not least by the United Nations (Boutros Ghali, introducing Weiss and Gordenker [1996]). Though now accessing World Bank global subsidy through GEF, even NGOs find sustainable institutionalisation of grass-roots initiatives difficult in a policy context of privatising benefits and externalising costs.

In the current ideological climate, neo-liberal economics remains the language in which 'costs', 'benefits', 'efficiency' and 'effectiveness' are expressed. Given the flexibility of tools available for environmental economics, professionals in this discourse[9] try to translate between the environmental, economic and diplomatic ministries brought together in GEF. Hence the shift towards environmental economic expertise by some NGOs (notably IUCN); and the GEF's prioritisation of 'pricing' nature to calculate incremental costs.

Rejecting the values embodied in this discourse, many ecology campaigners ignore GEF work as a side issue to globalising popular resistance to the structural roots of environmental destruction. Those allied in, for example, the emerging Peoples' Global Action (PGA) network 'for humanity and against neo-liberalism'[10] challenge directly the exploitation of communities both ecological and social. Provoked by accounts like those of Rich [1994] and the 50 Years is Enough campaign,[11] US activists disrupted the building of the World Bank's new headquarters in Washington, DC in 1995 (personal communication, Nov. 1997), and popular protest continues around the world [Walton and Seddon, 1994, SchNEWS to date]. When GEF states that 'IAs may make arrangements for GEF project preparation and execution by … NGOs … taking into account their comparative advantages in efficient and cost-effective project execution … in accordance with national priorities' [GEF, 1994b], is the organisation merely 'casting the net widely'[12] for new ideas to defuse hostile sections of civil society by co-opting them with cash?

NGO Relations with the GEF

If GEF seeks practical innovations and systemic public relations, it finds both in NGOs. Following the purposive approach of Wapner [1996], I characterise environmentalists' strategies towards GEF as 'insider' or 'outsider'. Crudely, where outsiders (for example, Greenpeace, TWN) challenge the structures in which GEF is the latest cog or branch, insiders (for example, WWF, IUCN) participate in the system as a given, seeking to use and improve it.[13]

From the point of view of a World Bank task manager for GEF projects, NGOs sometimes 'terrifically' fill an 'interesting and challenging' niche, yet rest at various points on a 'huge spectrum of input' between the technically 'competent' (and therefore useful) and the politically obstreperous (and therefore a 'hindrance') (interview, Nov. 1997). The latter, suspecting that while the World Bank 'deals the cards and calls the shots' [*Sahgal, 1998*] GEF 'has no ear to hear' objections to an enclosing, agenda, state that 'if David ever did tame Goliath, it was by using a sling shot ... not by sitting with him to discuss reform at workshops whose content was first cleared at 1818 H Street, Washington'.[14] Thus BiNGOs and others are deemed to have been co-opted by – if not before – the UNCED process [*Chatterjee and Finger, 1994; EF!, 1998*]. Yet despite disagreement elsewhere, there seems to be consensus in the 'complex, multi-faceted and often divided community' [*Conca, 1996*] of NGOs that those unwilling to 'play the game' in GEF should leave the field clear for 'constructive' critique.

The list of NGOs provided in Annex 1 is neither exhaustive nor balanced, but illustrates prominent insiders – notably those with offices in Washington, DC. Increasingly, poorer NGOs pool resources in issue-based networks whose public faces may not reflect the diversity of all involved. NGOs addressing themselves to GEF have shifted from advocacy campaigns for improvements in global finance arrangements and the World Bank in particular, towards opening GEF further. Some do both: advocacy for transparency and participation in GEF can reflect desire for these goods for advocates, for their allies and for the 'public good'.

NGO Critique of GEF

Few NGOs were keen on GEF's form and governance, even after restructuring in 1994. When the G77 grouping of countries held out token resistance in favour of a 'green fund' at Rio, they had environmental NGOs' support. NGO judgements of the Pilot Phase GEF are summarised by Bowles and Prickett [*1994*]: decision-making was neither transparent nor scientific, participation of NGOs, local people and scientists was limited, and many grants were too large for recipient institutions usefully to absorb. GEF could be counter-productive if 'additionality' reduced support for biodiversity elsewhere, so the authors suggested replacing 'incremental costs' with a 'flexible' test so that global does not undermine local conservation.

Pointedly, they suggest the World Bank's project-based approach is ill-suited to assist multiple-sourced innovations in biodiversity conservation and energy efficiency. They recommended broadening the range of institutions eligible for proposing and executing projects: GEF should become a 'marketplace of ideas'. This proposal, oft-repeated, implies that regional multilateral development banks, UN agencies, governments, academic departments and NGOs should deal direct with the secretariat instead of the IAs – rivals for GEF's honeypot.

Allegations from 'outside' were harsher: GEF is 'greenwash' [*Greenpeace, 1992*]. Bruce Rich [*1994*] of EDF cites a biodiversity project in the Congo, 'tacked on' to 'grease the skids' of a much larger World Bank loan for road-building and logging of old growth forest, intended – according to a World Bank project document – to 'breathe new life into forest exploitation'. In this context, Greenpeace and Southern NGOs have supported ongoing G77 resistance to designating GEF as permanent financial mechanism to the CBD [*Arts, 1998*].

To some critics, GEF is a product of the new world order's rhetorical renewal – like the largely 'paper' processes of UNCED, where NGOs played a high profile role [*Willetts, 1996*]. Official accounts stress constructive relationships built around Rio, yet Shiva [*1993*] suggests that the business community were 'partners' [*Rowell, 1996*] while diverse NGOs were brought in only to *seem* inclusive. For the GEF Participants' Assembly in New Delhi 1998, rules were similarly loosened to allow in hundreds of enthusiastic women's and other groups and avoid the 'bummer' (personal communication from GEF secretariat, 1998) if only the usual 40-odd showed up.

Despite abiding cynicism, NGOs felt vindicated when the Independent Evaluation of the Pilot Phase [*GEF, 1994a*] echoed their critique, not least that GEF alienates the very stakeholders who could make it successful. Hard-pressed, defensive GEF secretariat staff must legally serve many masters already: government departments represented in the council, the conferences of the parties (COPs) to the CBD and FCCC and, *de facto*, IAs' governing bodies. Yet also now they thrive on NGO input, to the extent that new council members were shocked (personal communication, Nov. by 'civil society' access to their consensus building 1997).[15]

NGOs as GEF Supporters

As campaigning organisations NGOs can mobilise support – 'promoting and sustaining a favorable policy environment' (GEF Project Information Document)[16] – for tender institutions. Linked into environmental epistemic communities, some NGOs offer political sway besides technical expertise. Given scarcity of governmental attention to issues tackled by GEF, civil servants value NGO help promoting their institutions. A World Bank 'partnership brief' tells how relations between 'IIEC [the International Institute for Energy Efficiency] and the Bank during the late 1980s [were] more adversarial than co-operative ... [but] began to change with the advent of financing from the GEF ... [now] both the Bank and the IIEC ... are enthusiastic about the future of the relationship,' and other NGO 'stakeholders' engage in such 'strategic inter-dependence and mutual satisfaction'. While unharnessed NGO experts are fierce detractors, as allies, their energies and constituencies can be used.

Another tale indicates how NGOs have supported GEF: during

restructuring in 1993, eight influential US-based NGOs signed a letter asking Bob Dole to delay refinancing of GEF until evaluation of the pilot phase was complete. Restructuring negotiations collapsed in Cartagena at the end of that year, almost fatally. By the time of the second replenishment of the GEF in late 1997, however, the US held out against commitment until a critical monitoring and evaluation (M&E) report was complete, while NGOs stressed GEF's learning to be better. Seventeen major US NGOs signed a letter to 'key committee chairmen' in Congress supporting the full $100 million appropriation recommended in 1998; though lacking a real 'seat at the table' (GEF–NGO Network, 1998), they felt GEF was worth preserving. That the US contribution was agreed with minor delay cannot be attributed only to NGO efforts, but officials' near obsequiousness at the next council meeting suggests their strength.

As a dissipative non-linear institutional system functioning in a highly politicised environment, with constant throughputs of staff, finance and directives, the GEF depends on diversified support of institutional and personal allies. People increasingly move around the 'GEF family': Mohammed El-Ashry, secretariat CEO and council co-chair, is one of several staff to have moved from the non-governmental sector to the GEF/World Bank, and NGO people appear in (usually donor) government delegations. Connected at many levels, NGO staff may be freer to speak and act informally than the environmental community within the World Bank.

As GEF's guidelines grow more demanding, implementers value outside assistance;[17] holders of the purse strings are willing to ease NGO access in return. Whatever their priorities, environmental organisations with constructive attitudes now find a guarded welcome in the inter-governmental system. Their 'outreach efforts have contributed significantly to mobilising broader constituencies to support the GEF process' [GEF–NGO central focal point, 1997]: they may now be in position to seek favours in return.

Establishment of a GEF–NGO Network and Formal Consultations

Having taken on the international financial institutions and engaged in 'big fights' to 'create the political space' for NGO inputs, a few have really used that space (interviews, Nov. 1997). Achim Steiner at IUCN, as 'global focal point', took on co-ordination of GEF-interested NGOs. Described by Steiner as the 'prototype of self-organised networks of NGOs on no money', it has 13 regional focal points (RFPs) who mostly 'fell into' the job or were 'in the right place at the right time' (personal communication, Aug. 1998). They are 'not GEF's representatives on Earth' (interview, May 1997). Some have been more dynamic than others; all are to propagate a newsletter, documents, policy moves, even GEF job vacancies, and to feed back news and views.

Despite recent decline in interest and enthusiasm, the network's efforts ensured that NGOs from around the world have, since February 1995, participated in council's twice-yearly meetings. At any one time five representatives are allowed into the room to make statements. As an *ad hoc* group the NGOs are responsible for their own selection (rather than making recommendations to a CEO decision), inviting arguments over whether consistency and experience should have priority over rotation of travel and speaking opportunities. Ongoing failure to democratise the system even for election of RFPs opens the network to criticism; like other young organisations both GEF and its NGO network remain 'ad-hocracies'where the role of individuals is pivotal.

Superficially, disagreements within the network relate to wealth differentials and accountability for finance. Some stress the need for accountability and finance; others fear co-option and resist formalising fluid alliances. Meetings preparatory to the GEF–NGO consultations over 1997–98 were dominated by these issues. In June 1998, three RFPs declared their network to be 'functioning at a sub-optimal level … in need of reform' (GEF–NGO Network Newsletter, Vol.7, 1998). Recommendations included raising NGO interest in the GEF, increasing the number of RFPs and improving communications.[18] By early 1995, the network had more or less collapsed.

It was with help from the US representative[19] and others that council was in 1995 persuaded to finance travel for NGO representatives from recipient countries to attend consultations.[20] These representatives have faced down an attempt by council to restrict paper submissions to those 'under cover of a letter signed by the CEO of the sponsoring organisation' (interview, April 1998). Such achievements may be unprecedented – opening up a global institution to its critics,[21] or a stark public relations exercise – ensuring that GEF's tame civil society is 'global' in appearance.

The friendly relationship between NGOs and the GEF was generally supported in council by the US, UK and other donor governments, and challenged by recipients including Brazil and Indonesia. On the donor side, France, resentful perhaps of US-based NGOs' dominance, recently still objected to the presence of NGO observers at council meetings. Recipient governments' antipathy may be linked to NGOs' often critical stance towards national policies. 'Clients' wary of domestic harassment translated to the international arena through GEF have elsewhere complained to the World Bank that it consults too many country-level NGOs without their approval (Bretton Woods Update; April/June 1998).

When NGOs annoy, questions can be raised about their legitimacy. Due to scarcities of time and resources, the process by which consensus is established in the GEF–NGO 'community' (similarly to the council:

through regional discussions and a private planning session the day before formal consultations) is not particularly transparent, nor is the process by which Southern NGO representatives are selected for all expenses paid trips to Washington, DC. TNC and IUCN finance visitors from Southern NGOs with whom they have 'good relationships' (interview, Nov. 1997), and opacity in the selection of RFPs[22] suggests the network may be a self-selecting clique – like 'the network' for jobs in the World Bank.[23]

Those criticising GEF's transparency and accountability face similar problems of finance, time management and politically sensitive elite decision-making. Taking on the role of insiders, NGO staff play similar games to those on a World Bank wage. Whether they play purely for sectional interests remains to be seen; first, they must learn the rules.

Access to Information

Despite the availability of documents on GEF activities, awareness of GEF remains slight – even in government departments and NGOs that could benefit.[24] Official documents often say more about what *should* be happening than what actually *is*, but GEF's early documents were less useful; derived from negotiated text, politically rather than practically neat, even the secretariat had difficulty translating 'GEFese' into English. The private sector large and small is ignorant or wary of the GEF; it is self-appointed representatives of 'the public' – mainly lawyers and economists working for NGOs – who seek access to these public goods.

Besides official documents, informal updates and analytic advice provided through the web of RFPs, IUCN and Climate Network Europe produced a handbook advising NGOs on GEF policy-making processes and finance [*CNE, 1996; IUCN, 1997*]. Another guide, on biodiversity and international waters, aims to be 'short and sweet' [*IUCN, 1997*]. Yet culture and language are problems both for GEF and its attendant NGOs. Conserving nature in areas remaining free of consumerist development can affect peoples who do not speak the national language, let alone one of the three languages of GEF.[25] Even if everyone could read, the costs of translation would be prohibitive.[26]

Active members of the GEF–NGO network usually realise that GEF's central decision-making processes are beyond their reach [*Gupta, 1995*]. None apparently knew of the Senior Advisory Panel's existence[27] until 1998, and minutes of council meetings and the closed, contentious GEFOP (which recommended decisions to council) were inaccessible – even to staff of the IAs (interview, Nov. 1997).[28] NGOs also realise that without personal experience of processes, people and language, little can be understood of how GEF works (interview, Nov. 1997). Some therefore help others, performing 'outreach' for which the secretariat has lacked resources.

Yet NGOs still pressure the GEF to provide more useful information to those who might run effective projects 'on the ground'. Though there is an NGO 'information kiosk' on the WWW, it is of little use to over half the world's human population who have never even used a telephone. A kit to prepare applications for the new medium-sized grants (MSGs) is being distributed and the World Bank in 1997 joined with Fundacion Ecologica Universal (FEU) of Buenos Aires to develop a project for briefing recipient country NGOs about MSGs. Contacts for this were established by an NGO visit to the Bank's headquarters, because its Buenos Aires office would not let enquirers through the door (interview, Nov. 1997). Communications continued by e-mail; for all the 'country-driven' rhetoric, participation in GEF seems to need personal and electronic routes to its heart.

Access to Finance

'Mainstreaming NGO participation' in the GEF now involves NGOs co-ordinating ever more projects, even some to be run by governments.[29] NGOs had, according to the GEF's draft 1997 Annual Report, been the source of 137 full-size project ideas submitted to the UNDP, 30 to UNEP and 81 to the World Bank. Uniquely among IGO financiers, nearly US$100 million, or 18 per cent of the total GEF allocation went to NGOs; 16 out of a total 97 projects were conducted entirely by NGOs. Of these, six were international and ten local or partnerships including international NGOs.

From the beginning, GEF has assisted recipient country NGOs through a small grants programme (SGP), demonstrating commitment to environmental protection from the 'bottom-up'. By the end of 1997 nearly a thousand grants of between US$50,000 (national) and $250,000 (regional) had been approved for NGOs and community groups.[30] The SGP is described as 'very sexy' in UNDP from where it is run (administratively as one project), yet receives only around 0.5 per cent of GEF money (interview, Oct. 1997).

In 1997 a GEF–NGO working group finalised an 'expedited pathway, bypassing council (grants up to $750,000 need the approval only of the CEO) for medium-sized grants (MSGs): up to $1 million accessible to NGOs which had 'proved themselves' at this level of funding. Only 8 applications had been approved by spring 1998, but the pathway provides opportunities to reward those promoting GEF with donor governments.[31] Emerging problems – bottlenecks in the process, inconsistent eligibility rulings and unofficial ceilings on finance movable through the pathway by IAs – led recently to calls to improve arrangements (GEF–NGO Newsletter, June/July 1998). The US delegation to the Participants' Assembly raised similar concerns, restating the demand for a 'fourth IA' of NGOs dealing direct with the secretariat.

Although that has not (yet?) happened, sometimes non-governmental capacity is built instead of governments'. In Jordan, for example, the entire national park system is in the hands of an NGO, and in parts of Africa donors prefer to work with well established NGOs than to start from scratch with a new environment ministry (interview, Nov. 1997). Sometimes NGOs are set up by governments: known as GoNGOs (governmental NGOs). Costa Rica's famous success in institutionalising conservation is largely thanks to a GoNGO called INBio; meanwhile WWF-India employs 'retired civil servants and military men' (interviews, April 1998).

The relative scarcity of grassroots NGO involvement in full-size GEF projects is linked to IA field staff's inability to provide fast reliable answers on project eligibility [*GEF, 1998a*]. In investment agency hierarchies, big projects are more straightforward to deal with than complex arrangements preferred by NGOs. Often hard-pressed people are wary of investing resources in applications that may be ineligible. Problems have recently been compounded by structural adjustments within the World Bank, although decentralisation may eventually help. In the meantime, small NGOs' best hope of tapping GEF may be through allied BiNGOs. But can privileged insiders really support the needs of the 'uninvited' [*RTS, 1998*]?

Access to Policy

In working groups with GEF institutions, NGO priorities have recently been 'mainstreaming' environmental values in World Bank programmes and simplifying GEF grant procedures, environmentalists wanting GEF to do more for their own organisations and also for their allies outside the 'institutional ecosystems' which feed on official resource flows. Less active NGOs may 'piggy-back' on the labour of those in the working groups, or they may provide political fodder for activists. How effectively the environmental movement as a whole can bridge value gaps depends partly on how the council, secretariat and IAs respond to their demands, and partly on the responsiveness of diverse smaller, usually southern conservation NGOs to efforts made on their behalf. For all the individuals involved, GEF and its NGO network is a learning process; if positive interest can be built and sustained, with learning may come confidence in the scope for change.

The official information document, *Promoting Strategic Partnerships Between the GEF and the NGO Community*,[32] summarises the consensus of an NGO working group on the 'relatively modest' changes they would still like to see. They complain that GEF procedures are incomprehensible, inconsistent, inflexible and slow; that NGOs with commitment to and expertise in a particular area are ignored by the World Bank procurement department who hire in outside consultants; and that there is a contradiction between the GEF's aspiration to assist capability on the ground and the

World Bank's castigation of local NGOs for lack of implementing capacity [*Wells, 1996*]. Seeking greater equality in dealings with the IAs, Randy Curtis (of TNC) and Achim Steiner (of IUCN) in an *ad hoc* working group[33] held meetings with the World Bank's GEF unit, and produced a report, *Partners or Hired Hands?*

Their main recommendations are for the IAs to set up further working groups with NGOs to identify constraints on and opportunities for working together effectively; to reform and streamline documentation, legal frameworks and implementation procedures for participation in the whole of the IAs' project portfolios – not just components associated with GEF. To manage this process they propose national boards (on which NGOs would sit with governments and others) to review ideas before seeking GEF approval. Such decentralisation of function might contribute to the 'country ownership' of GEF initiatives that M&E reports [*GEF, 1998a, 1998b*] emphasise as vital for sustainability; and strengthen GEF–NGO networks in recipient countries.

Meanwhile, other NGOs can be resentful of their colleagues' access to GEF and the co-option that work on funding pathways seems to imply (interviews, 1997–98). Given an apparently rising tide of grassroots hostility to the imposition on fragile communities and ecosystems of even GEF's most participatory, NGO-influenced conservation projects, there may be a new phase in popular responses to the 'immoral' [*DTE, 1998*] GEF after the Participants' Assembly in New Delhi, April 1998. Whether the GEF–NGO community will split again remains to be seen in the light of who speaks for whom, and who actually listens.

NGOs, the GEF and Participatory Networks

An issue uniting NGOs engaged with GEF is dissatisfaction with participation available to 'local communities' and 'indigenous peoples', as well as themselves. Resource scarcity is one cause; others are deeper. Neena Singh, erstwhile South Asia RFP, states:

> Participatory approaches do not address the unequal power structures upon which present management strategies rest. 'Participation' is sought within the present system and those very power structures that have undermined and countered people's power in every possible way … unfortunately empowerment is looked at as 'something which can be given' by the authorities to the people. History and past experiences show that empowerment cannot be 'given' because empowerment of one means loss of power to the other [*Singh, 1998*].

Thus people in GEF may not actually be able to put the first last [*Chambers,*

1997]. Whatever the rhetoric, GEF staff have to meet traditional World Bank requirements of cost-effectiveness: time and effort spent on participation of 'stakeholders' and 'affected communities' are costs rather than investments [*Gupta, 1995*]. The India Ecodevelopment project, with its 'cutting edge' village level micro-planning components, emerged as a battleground at GEF–NGO consultations in 1997 and again in 1998, when the consultation was held in India and some unconsulted local people were able to complain direct. Such popular hostility to GEF reflects problems arising when authoritarian government departments [*Guha, 1997*] are charged with putting participatory strategies into effect.

The GEF's annual Project Implementation Reviews and Project Lessons Study [*GEF, 1998b*] stress the importance of truly broad participation for effective projects. Yet the social scientist in the GEF secretariat works under assumptions that can clash with those of economic, technical and diplomatic experts. As a voice for outsiders on the inside she may be limited by status as well as resources[34] – it has been suggested that the GEF family of institutions is dominated by 'alpha males' (personal communication, April 1998). Participation takes time and money: GEF is required to be quick and 'cost effective'. In this as other trade-offs, GEF operational decisions must meet multiple demands while minimising friction.

One consequence has been the labelling of all non-institutional attendees of GEF meetings as undifferentiated 'NGOs'. Business representatives can find themselves frozen out: a Global Climate Coalition (GCC, opposed to action under the climate convention) representative was apparently 'not made welcome' at an NGO consultation and never returned (interview, Nov. 1997). Other business NGOs with lower profiles certainly engage with the World Bank and also GEF. The director of France's Energy 21 (promoting renewables) sits on GEF's Senior Advisory Panel; the WBCSD is also involved but declared it 'unethical' to co-operate with our study (letter from Tara Lyons, assistant to Bjorn Stigson, WBCSD chairman, to Dr Sonja Boehmer-Christiansen, Hull University, 26 Feb. 1996).

While the traditional private sector is excluded from public GEF meetings, representatives of other avowedly self-interested[35] but globally less favoured groupings have also largely been absent. In November 1997 a representative of America's First Nations spoke – the first indigenous person to do so after six years of GEF operations and nearly three of regular NGO consultations. He gently needled group conscience that the huge diversity of society was being spoken for by a scarcely representative ad-hocracy of globetrotting professionals. As one new RFP[36] stressed outside the following council meeting, few indigenous people can 'grab a passport, kiss the kids good bye and fly out' for arcane discussions about operational programmes and incremental costs. While only the best-resourced NGOs are really able to get 'in the loop' (interview, Nov. 1997) of global processes, another World Bank 'partnership brief' tells how one NGO, the Rockefeller Foundation, has worked with the World Bank for decades: 'a shared vision and like-minded philosophy were invaluable to ... success'.

Most of the world's civil society live in a different world of value from that of Rockefellers and global bankers, and engaging effectively with them requires almost full time attention, a computer plus modem and international travel. When RFPs were given the task by GEF of identifying representatives of the 12 'major groups' listed under Agenda 21 to attend the GEF Participants' Assembly, several questioned their own suitability for such a role. However, despite such occasional humility, few endanger their chance of power just because there is not enough to go round. While maintaining battle lines, NGOs also seek to sustain goodwill. So, besuited in air-conditioned halls, they promote what they see as a better GEF, with more and better M&E of smaller grants more easily arranged. They do not want to rock the boat lest it sink with all their hopes aboard for, according to one NGO campaigner (personal communication, Nov. 1997), while participation improves, the GEF may turn out to be a good thing.

Co-operation, Co-option and Evolution in Political Ecology

If the neo-liberal 'new world order', based around the 'G7 nexus', sustains hegemonic interests of transnational capital through the institutions of this order, then IGOs constitute the 'globalisation of the state [that] can be interpreted as the political counterpart to the internationalisation of capital ... since 1945' [*Gill, 1997*]. Yet while liberal democracy has been a mantra of political movements promoting globalisation, it does not feature at the global level. If this 'global state' lacks anything like a parliament, it may only be groups classed as NGOs that participate in shaping institutions to support wider interests than banks and bureaucracies.

Groups damning capitalist structures as causes of socio-environmental problems remain outside the hegemonic 'terrain of political contestability' [*Gill, 1997*] and wonder if insider environmentalists are participating in a move to political rather than ecological sustainability [*Levy, 1997*]. Another view was put by Sveta Klimova: 'The successful movements in this century have been those which adopted the discourse of inclusion (rights/ citizenship) rather than exclusion (power struggle) ... You cannot be both outside and against the system and using its resources at the same time.'[37]

Environmental NGOs accepting GDP-defined growth, the central article of faith in globalising neo-liberalism as propagandised by the World Bank [*George and Sabelli, 1994*], enter the discourse of inclusion and gain the grace, favour and resources of those managing the new world order. In Levy's words, 'corporate [and, I would add, inter-governmental] adoption of environmental management ... can be viewed as concessions in a Gramscian "war of position", opening up new opportunities for environmentalists to pursue their goals' [*Levy, 1997*]. The biggest NGOs can now define environmentalism to appeal to both the public and the powerful: they adopt the privileged position of go-between. Whether they break Klimova's rule and channel resources to the 'uninvited' – let alone take on the tasks of a parliamentary opposition for the World Bank (personal communication, Nov. 1997) – remains to be seen.

Were participatory democracy to be functional, there might be no call for NGOs to make manifest a movement. In the meantime, whilst challenging its consequences, few can afford to threaten the structures of global political economy if they are to participate in utilising its 'surplus'. Inevitably co-option is a risk: once accustomed to the globalised lifestyle, influence and the perks of participation, it is hard to conceive of a world without such opportunities. Intelligent institutions may then rechannel the energy of a movement's challenge, utilising its technical competence to strengthen their own agenda.

NGOs' claims to stand up for nature or 'the people' can be compromised [*Edwards and Hulme, 1992*], especially when (unelected) NGOs take over previously governmental functions, and voluntary status comes into question as staff and methods from the private sector are imported to deal with demands for efficiency. Usually Northern BiNGO 'insiders' need credibility with other parts of their 'movement', and may even hint at 'rebel' links to make their cultivation worthwhile to dominant interests. NGOs' growing influence in a structurally unequal system may be linked to their representing radicalised outsider rhetoric while renouncing outsider tactics. Insider NGOs therefore walk a political tightrope: they can be seen as servants of 'neo-colonialism', or as agents of the resistance. Which they are may reflect as simple an issue as who makes friends with whom, in what context.

Conclusion: 'Patsies to the Industry', 'Snarling from the Sidelines',[38] *and Networks in Between*

Beyond the 'beltway crowd',[39] some in the environment movement daily confront destruction and demonstrate radical alternatives; setting the pace for change, they look straight through the GEF. Others, allied with governments both North, South and global, try to make of it what they can. Allowing unprecedented transparency and access, GEF seems a 'Trojan pony'[40] for reformist environmental values inside the World Bank. As NGOs press GEF into service of their values, complex inter-relationships evolve with a system striving resiliently to stabilise its critics.

If GEF's innovations are just public relations twists in a long tale of globalising governance, then it could be a triumph of image over substance if the organisations claiming to challenge globalisation's worst consequences fell for its gloss. Yet they may be using the opportunities opened by GEF's contradictory remit to enter some interstices of the system, and shape it to sustain adaptive relations between 'development' and 'conservation'. Some may be green imperialists, others see potential in the new era of public subsidy for a 'Global Che Guevara Pork Barrel Fund'.[41]

All participants in GEF – bureaucratic, scientific, financial, governmental or non-governmental – play a new game: presenting their needs in 'globalised' language. This game, and the political structures sustaining it, mean conservation can take the form of 'green developmentalism' [*Escobar, 1996; McAfee, 1998*], the latest in 'ecological colonialism' [*Sachs, 1993*]. In these new enclosures [*Midnight Notes, 1990*] the natural environment benefits global elites – 'scientific', 'eco'-tourism and 'genetic resources' – at the expense of priceless cultures and low impact livelihoods that disrupt neat calculations and complicate political fixes. Yet perhaps some environmentalists can avoid co-option and act as 'biosphere people' only to support diverse 'ecosystem people': those unable to avoid globalisation's local costs, let alone capitalise on the benefits (quoted by McNeely in *People and Planet*).[42]

Audley [*1997*] argues that a 'good cop, bad cop' division between NGOs compromising in NAFTA negotiations and those opposed to the treaty led to effective neutralisation of the latter group. However, Arts [*1998*] documents NGOs and the CBD and FCCC, concluding that street protests strengthened NGOs involved in negotiations for the latter. GEF too results from work by committed insider environmentalists, and the process of negotiating further compromise therein may develop wider interests of NGOs as outsiders to the global system.[43] Activists may see in GEF an 'entry point' to globalising finance that is largely blocked elsewhere.

Such access might be small but it might also be temporary. As narrow political movements acting through the WTO and some sort of MAI complete 'the constitution of a single global economy' (Jackson, quoted by Renato Ruggiero (WTO), 1997) the last thing they want are scruffy environmentalists running about disenfranchised, demonstrating radical alternatives. Elites adopting and adapting outsiders' rhetoric also recruit their smartest experts; while radicals extend the visible territory of critique, amenable insiders play the game for consultancy, money and influence. While used to defend the global system from attack, they may channel support to the resistance in their 'constituencies', and in return carry their ideas nearer to the heart of power. Promoting systemic openness, even emancipation, they may co-operatively 'increase the edge'[44] in ecologically intelligent social evolution.

'GEF is all about people trying to cross institutional barriers' (interview, Nov. 1998) – the permeability of which remain in flux. Pressure from a diversifying social movement's allied NGOs has been shaping institutional change; further research might show how that change affects the movement – how valued the effects are by whom. With concerted popular if not democratic action in systemic niches revealed, if GEF survives it might be ever more useful; as a Trojan foal, as a pork barrel for professional environmentalists' 'constituency' interests, and as an indicator that no other IGO is honest enough to charge separate bills for 'global' benefits when distributing development's costs ... .

ANNEX 1

SOME ENVIRONMENTAL NGOs INVOLVED IN THE GEF

First, *the Big (often international) NGOs, or BINGOs*: These groups are generally rich with offices in the Washington, DC area.

International Union for the Conservation of Nature – IUCN or World Conservation Union
IUCN was created in 1948 as a 'hybrid organisation' of members, expert commissions and an international secretariat. Linking agencies, states and NGOs, in some fora IUCN is a BINGO, in others an IGO or 'International Quasi Non-Governmental Organisation'. IUCN aspires to 'mobilise knowledge' for conservation[45] and houses the GEF-NGO network's central focal point.

World-Wide Fund for Nature – WWF
WWF-International was founded in 1961 as a fundraising offshoot of IUCN, 'more comprehensive in its approach than any other organisation', running and supporting conservation programmes through policy and education programmes. With 'access to the world's highest decision levels',[46] it claims 'credibility and a global reputation for its science-based and rational approach, working through dialogue and partnership rather than confrontation'.[47]

The Nature Conservancy – TNC[48]
Started in 1951, TNC calls itself 'Nature's Real Estate Agent', and claims 'a unique niche: preserving nature, endangered habitats and species by buying the lands and waters they need to survive ... protect[ing] land through gifts, exchanges ...debt-for-nature swaps[49] and management partnerships ... community development ... training and funding for legally protected areas'.

Environmental Defence Fund – EDF
An environmental advocacy organisation funded mainly by private foundations and donations. Set up in the early 1970s, staffed in 1997 with over 60 scientists, economists, and lawyers, 'EDF has become a leading advocate of economic incentives [for] solving environmental problems ... sit[ting] down with traditional adversaries, including McDonalds, and come up with environmental solutions together'.

World Resources Institute – WRI
A research institute or thinktank 'created in 1982, WRI is dedicated to helping governments and private organisations of all types cope with environmental, resource, and development challenges of global significance'.[50] WRI is funded almost entirely by corporate sponsorship and donations, including from Monsanto, Du Pont, Shell, Philip Morris and individual Rockefellers.

The NGO Networks: link diverse groups under a common agenda. Even if some members are outsiders to the global system, co-ordinators use the strength of numbers inside.

Biodiversity Action Network – BioNET
A network of North American NGOs set up in 1992 to disseminate information and keep biodiversity on the agenda after UNCED, BioNET produced the latest NGO guide to the GEF and houses the North American RFP. BioNET is funded mostly from private US foundations including the Rockefeller and MacArthur, and contracts to governments, IGOs and other NGOs.

Climate Action Network – CAN
CAN, 'a [global] network of NGOs who share a common concern for problems of climate change and wish to co-operate in the development and implementation of … strategies to combat it', was founded in 1989. Initially funded by EDF, later by the Marshall foundation, CAN tries to give a global voice to members across the world, and is facilitated by a network of seven regional focal points. In East Africa, Climate Network Africa houses a GEF-NGO RFP.

Socio-Ecological Union
A network of over 300 NGOs in the former soviet states and the USA, SEU started in 1988 to promote 'heritage, health and openness'. Members are involved in education, research, direct action and providing advice to the World Bank on avoiding ecological resistance. SEU houses the Russian GEF-NGO RFP.

Southern NGOs: The selected groups mentioned here are based in and staffed largely by nationals of GEF recipient countries; they have good connections in the region and globally.

The Third World Network – TWN
Started in 1984, the Third World Network had offices in five countries by 1997. It provides a platform for 'broadly Southern interests and perspectives at international fora', and is run mostly on membership dues. Provides strong 'outsider' critiques.

Centre for Science and Environment – CSE
Based in New Delhi, CSE houses an RFP, and co-ordinated NGOs at the GEF Participants' Assembly in 1998. A research and dissemination organisation financed by government and aid, CSE works towards 'a policy framework for an equitous, participatory and environmentally-sound development'.[51]

ANNEX 2

ACRONYMS

BioNET	Biodiversity Action Network
BINGO	big international NGO
CAN	Climate Action Network
CBD	Convention on Biological Diversity
CEO	chief executive officer
CSE	Centre for Science and Environment
EDF	Environmental Defense Fund
EF!	Earth First!
FCCC	Framework Convention on Climate change
GEF	Global Environment Facility
GoNGO	governmental NGO
G7	group of 7 (Northern) governments
G77	group of (Southern) governments
IA	Implementing Agency
ICFP	International Conservation Financing Program

IGO	inter-governmental organisation
IPCE	International Parliamentary Conferences on the Environment
IUCN	World Conservation Union
MAI	Multilateral Agreement on Investment
M&E	monitoring and evaluation
MSG	medium-sized grants
NAFTA	North American Free Trade Agreement
NGO	non-governmental organisation
OECD	Organisation for Economic Co-operation and Development
PGA	Peoples' Global Action
RFP	regional focal point
SGP	Small Grants Programme
TNC	The Nature Conservancy
TWN	Third World Network
UNCED	United Nations Conference on Environment and Development
UNDP	United Nations Development Programme
UNEP	United Nations Environment Programme
WCMC	World Conservation Monitoring Centre
WWF	World-wide Fund for Nature
WRI	World Resources Institute
WTO	World Trade Organisation

NOTES

1. Much of the information is from primary texts: GEF and NGO publications, meeting documentation and campaigns material. More complex perspectives come mostly from interviews with GEF and NGO actors attending the tenth council meeting and NGO consultation in Washington DC in late 1997, supplemented by some around the eleventh council and first participants' assembly in New Delhi, April 1998. These discussions were, as a rule, unattributable.
2. Chaired by Lord Kennet (personal communication, 1998).
3. Sierra Club, Audubon, Wilderness Society, NRDC, Environmental Policy Institute, National Wildlife Federation, EDF, Izaak Walton League of America, National Parks and Conservation Association, FoE.
4. A motion could only be passed if both 60 per cent of countries represented (the UN model) and countries providing 60 per cent of GEF finance (the Bretton Woods model) agreed. Despite drawn out negotiations over restructuring GEF's governance, the voting system has never been used thanks to 'consensus' negotiated in private under the aegis of El-Ashry (interview, Nov. 1997).
5. At a WWF-US presentation to the World Bank on conservation strategies in November 1997, World Bank staff asked the NGO people what they could most effectively do to help. They were answered fairly feebly – the NGO people apparently more wary of transgressing unwritten rules than those in the institution they sought to influence. Meanwhile, besides some emancipatory thinkers and 'jobsworths', there are biodiversity experts associated with GEF who feel social diversity to be a 'peripheral issue', others who feel nature is best conserved by excluding locals forcibly (interviews, 1997–98).
6. Under 'enabling activities' for the climate change convention, GEF assists governments with databases of greenhouse gas emissions and sinks; for the CBD, GEF assists a clearing house mechanism for biodiversity information exchange, also national biodiversity databases with the help of the Cambridge, UK-based World Conservation Monitoring Centre (WCMC). The World Bank is also investing heavily in its new image as a 'knowledge bank' [*World Development Report, 1998*], supporting massive information processing facilities to use GIS data for monitoring and planning projects. The 'global panopticon' may be a beneficiary of the new 'green developmental' [*McAfee, 1998*] face of the World Bank as 'Knowledge

Bank'; data on resource distribution may be useful to global bio-prospectors, energy investors and so on.

7. Operational Directive 14.70, paragraph 2.

8. In the GEF's Self-Assessment, we learn that council's 'rules ... provide for invitations to outsiders, NGOs in particular, to attend its sessions. That provision [is] without precedent in other international financial institutions...' [El-Ashry, undated].

9. For example, the work of David Pearce and his fellow members of the 'London School' of environmental economists based around CSERGE at UCL and UEA have been influential in the development of the GEF's 'PRINCE' programme for measuring incremental costs.

10. See http://www.agp.org

11. An alliance of NGOs for abolition of the Bretton Woods institutions after 50 years of their existence.

12. The name of a GEF project to broaden sourcing of project ideas.

13. As 'participant observer', also 'social climbing' 'investigative social researcher' [Cassell, 1988] and occasional activist, I have been insider and outsider. Like other 'NGO' people, I used the fact that GEF staff make friendly use of attendant interests, and I believe that moving and learning in diverging communities has helped this study.

14. 1818 H St, Washington, DC is the address of the World Bank headquarters.

15. As GEF may be for the World Bank, the CBD is said to be a 'revolutionising force' in terms of popular participation in UN processes (interviews, Nov. 1997).

16. Para. 36, Hungary Energy Efficiency Co-Financing Fund, WB/IFC.

17. UNEP in particular is keen to gain GEF and outside support for its programmes; UNDP has always been closer to established recipient-country NGOs through country offices, and seeks their support to generate project applications at the national level.

18. Since the departure of Steiner there seems to be declining enthusiasm for the network.

19. Letter from EDF and eight other US-based NGOs, thanking Susan Levine for help raising funds for NGO participation, 17 Jan. 1995.

20. Due to regular disagreements over the interpretation of principles of 'sustainable use' and 'respect for all life forms', NGOs with a strong commitment to animal rights no longer attend. Nor do 'Deep' ecologists who for the most part find the scientistic, elite managerialist approach of the GEF offensive.

21. The WTO, of a similar age to the GEF, is not so open, and new negotiations on global trade are usually conducted in secrecy. Multilateral negotiations on trade and on the environment have been following two largely incompatible paths.

22. One (attractive, sociable) RFP admitted she had 'no idea' why she was chosen – other than that out of two other candidates, 'nobody knew' one, and 'nobody liked' another (interview, Nov. 1997).

23. Every member of the GEF secretariat or World Bank staff questioned said they had found employment through 'the network' (interviews, 1997–98).

24. According to an unpublished study by David Hoyle for the WWF, 1998.

25. English, French and Spanish.

26. Translation costs were a problem around the Participants' Assembly in when representatives of the 164 governments participating in GEF, also NGOs and tribal peoples, arrived in New Delhi wanting their say.

27. Unmentioned in official GEF documents, this panel meets annually – usually in the Watergate Hotel, Washington DC. Individuals are available for consultation by El-Ashry (personal communication, 1997).

28. At first I was told by the secretariat that no such minutes existed.

29. ENDA-TM, of Dakar, Senegal, channelled funds and technical assistance for a climate change project to government departments in Kenya, Zimbabwe, Mali and Ghana.

30. But not the small-scale private sector.

31. The Washington-based Natural Resources Defense Council is among those said to have been rewarded for their lobbying efforts on Capitol Hill, for 'busting a gut' and 'really coming through for GEF' (personal communication, April 1998).

32. GEF/C.7/Inf.8, 29 Feb. 1996.

33. Including also Corinne Schmidt (TNC), Abby Sarmac (IUCN), Carmen Monico (Interaction)

and Lee Zahno (WWF-US), and a lawyer: Scott Overall. Meeting as individuals from July 1996 to May 1997, they claimed 'the Draft reflects perceptions that are widely shared in the NGO community'.

34. It is alleged that GEF commitment to participation is such that the same piece of standard text was moved from project document to project document (interview, Nov. 1997).

35. The term 'self-interested' is not used negatively here. It was suggested by a member of council (personal communication, April 1998) at the Participants' Assembly that no private sector representatives had been formally invited due to official difficulty selecting among *private* interests when *public* good is the goal.

36. Who had tried to get a Lacandon indigenous representative to accompany him to GEF consultations ... .

37. *social-movements@staffmail.wit.ie*, from *sklimova@afb1.ssc.ed.ac.uk*, 25 May 1998: 're: intellectuals versus activists'.

38. Quotes from a World Bank representative on NGOs and the impacts of big dams (interview, Sept. 1997).

39. 'Beltway' is American for 'ringroad'; the 'beltway crowd' have offices inside that of Washington. DC.

40. El-Ashry conceded to Korinna Horta of EDF at the November 1997 consultation that GEF is not worthy of the title 'Trojan horse' for taking environment into the heart of World Bank operations.

41. This term was discussed partly in jest by representatives of two BiNGOs. 'Pork barrel' is American slang for programmes benefiting local constituencies.

42. Jeffrey McNeely, 'Diverse Nature, Diverse Cultures', *People and Planet*, Vol.2, No.3, pp.11–13.

43. One NGO sends someone to GEF only to see that it 'doesn't make anything worse' (interview, Nov. 1997).

44. A saying of chaos magic: a development of pagan craft through anarchic fractals.

45. Together with WWF, IUCN works closely with UNEP, for example on the Global Biodiversity Assessment and the WCMC, both of which have received GEF money.

46. Besides long and close relationships with national governments and also the British royal family, WWF was chaired by Prince Bernhard of the Netherlands who had initiated the Bilderberg Group in the 1950s [*Hartzell, 1997*]; WWF was also represented on the Trilateral Commission in the 1980s.

47. During the pilot GEF, WWF-US played a key role in the NGO response, and staff of WWF-international recently analysed 'root causes of biodiversity loss' for the GEF secretariat, [*Stedman-Edwards, 1998*].

48. TNC can cause confusion given the more common use of the acronym for TransNational Corporation, also because English Nature was once known as The Nature Conservancy.

49. 'Debt for nature swaps' are a contentious strategy, involving Northern interests buying up parts of a Southern country's national debt in exchange for conservation of selected areas of rich biodiversity.

50. El-Ashry, who worked at WRI before moving to the World Bank and then GEF, recently recruited a colleague, Alan Miller, from early days at WRI to help visualise GEF's future directions for climate issues.

51. CSE's director, Anil Agarwal, argued at UNCED with organiser Maurice Strong: the former proposing due 'reparation' for colonialism not enclosure as conservation, the latter, elite global resource management.

REFERENCES

Allam, Magdi (Ecopeace, Egypt); Sheldon Cohen (BioNET, US); Mersie Ejigu (IUCN, US); Liliana Hisas (Fundacion Ecologica Universal, Argentina); Korinna Horta (EDF, US); and Rob Lake (Birdlife International, UK) (1998), *GEF in the 21st Century*, NGO report to GEF Participants Assembly, New Delhi.

Arts, Bas (1998), *The Political Influence of Global NGOs: Case studies on the Climate and Biodiversity Conventions*, Utrecht: International Books.

Audley, John (1997), *Green Politics and Global Trade: NAFTA and the Future of Environmental Politics*, Washington, DC: Georgetown University Press.

Bowles, Ian A. and Glenn T. Prickett (1994), *Reframing the Green Window: An Analysis of the GEF Pilot Phase Approach to Biodiversity and Global Warming and Recommendations for the Operational Phase*, Washington, DC: Conservation International and Natural Resources Defence Council.

Bryant, Raymond L. (1998 forthcoming), 'Power, Knowledge and Political Ecology in the Third World: A Review', *Progress in Physical Geography*.

Cahn, Robert (1985), *An Environmental Agenda for the Future*, Covelo, CA: Island.

Cassell, Joan (1988), 'Relationship of Observer to Observed when Studying Up', in *Studies in Qualitative Methodology*, Vol.1, pp.89–108.

Climate Network Europe and IUCN (1996), *An NGO Guide to the Global Environment Facility (Letters to Nani G. Oruga)*, Brussels and Washington, DC: CAN and IUCN.

Chambers, Robert (1997), *Whose Reality Counts: Putting the First Last*, London: IT Publications.

Chatterjee, Pratap and Mathias Finger (1994), *The Earth Brokers: Power, Politics and World Development*, London: Routledge.

Conca, Ken (1996), 'Environmental NGOs and the UN System', in T.G. Weiss and L. Gordenker (eds.) (1996), *NGOs, the UN and Global Governance*, Boulder, CO and London: Lynne Rienner.

Curtis, R., Schmidt, C., Steiner, A., Sarmac, A., Monico, C., Zahno, L. and S. Overall (1997), *Partners or Hired Hands: Procurement Reform for Effective Collaboration Between NGOs, and Multilateral Institutions – the Case of the GEF*, Washington, DC: TNC and IUCN.

Down to Earth (DTE) (1998), Pull-out section on Global Governance special: 'GEF Comes to Town', March, New Delhi: Centre for Science and Environment (CSE).

Devall, B. (1990), *Simple in Means, Rich in Ends: Practising Deep Ecology*, London: Greenprint.

Earth First! (1998), *Do or Die*, Brighton: South Downs EF!

Edwards, M. and David Hulme (1992), *Making a Difference: NGOs and Development in a Changing World*, London: Earthscan.

EDF (1992), *Global Eco-Management in the Hands of the World Bank?* Washington, DC: EDF.

El-Ashry, Mohammed (undated), *The Global Environment Facility: A Self-Assessment*, Washington, DC: GEF, UNDP, UNEP, World Bank.

Escobar, Arturo (1996), 'Constructing nature: Elements for a Post-Structuralist Political Ecology', R. Peet and M. Watts (eds.) (1996), *Liberation Ecologies: Environment, Development, Social Movements*, London and New York: Routledge.

GEF (1994a), *Independent Evaluation of the Pilot Phase*, Washington, DC: GEF.

GEF (1994b), *Instrument for the Establishment of a Restructured GEF*, Washington, DC: GEF.

GEF (1996), *Promoting Strategic Partnerships between the GEF and the NGO Community*, Washington, DC: GEF/C7/inf.8.

GEF (1998a), *Study of GEF's Overall Performance*, Washington, DC: GEF/A.1/5.

GEF (1998b), *Project Lessons Study*, Washington, DC: GEF/A.1/7.

Global Focal Point (1997, draft), *Strengthening the Effectiveness of the Global Environment Facility: A Funding Proposal to the GEF to Support NGO Input and Outreach*, Washington, DC: IUCN.

George, Susan and Fabrizio Sabelli (1994), *Faith and Credit: the World Bank's Secular Empire*, Harmondsworth: Penguin.

Gill, Stephen (1997), *Gramsci, Modernity and Globalisation*, Leeds: BISA, 15–17 Dec.

Greenpeace International (1992), *The World Bank's Greenwash: Touting Environmentalism while Trashing the Planet*, London: Greenpeace.

Griffen, Jeff (1997), *Biodiversity, International Waters and the GEF: An IUCN Guide to Developing Project Proposals for the Global Environment Facility*, Gland: IUCN.

Guha, Ramachandra (1997), 'The Authoritarian Biologist and the Arrogance of Anti-Humanism: Wildlife Conservation in the Third World', *The Ecologist*, Vol.27, No.1, pp.14–20.

Gupta, Joyeeta (1995), 'The Global Environment Facility in its North South Context', *Environmental Politics*, Vol.4, No.1, pp.19–43.

Harrison, E. B. (1993), 'Going Green: How to Communicate your Company's Environmental Commitment', unlocated: Business One Irwin.

Hartzell, Jamie (1997), *Dangerous Liaisons: A Survey of Known Groupings of Multinational Companies that Influence International Policy*, http://www.tlio.demon.co.uk/wdm.htm.

IUCN-Jeff Griffen (1997), 'Biodiversity, International Waters and the GEF – An IUCN Guide to Developing Project Proposals for the Global Environment Facility', Gland, Switzerland and Cambridge, UK: IUCN–The World Conservation Union.

IUCN, BioNET and Climate Network Europe (1997), *The Global Environment Facility from Rio to New Delhi: a Guide for NGOs*, Gland and Cambridge: IUCN.

Levy, David (1997), 'Environmental Management as Political Sustainability', *Organisation and Environment*, Vol.10, No.2, pp.126–47.

McAfee, Kathy (1998 forthcoming), *Green Developmentalism*....

Midnight Notes Collective (1990), *The New Enclosures*, Jamaica Plain, MA: Midnight Notes.

Peet, Richard and Michael Watts (eds.) (1996), *Liberation Ecologies:Environment, Development, Social Movements*, London and New York: Routledge.

Pernetta, John (1998), 'An Overview of the Global Environment Facility in International Waters with Reference to Marine Capacity Building', *Marine Policy*, Vol.22, No.3, pp.235–46.

Reclaim the Streets (RTS) (1998), *HAHAHA*, London: RTS agit prop.

Rich, Bruce (1994), *Mortgaging the Earth*, London: Earthscan.

Rowell, Andrew (1996), *Green Backlash: Global Subversion of the Environment Movement*, London and New York: Routledge.

Sachs, W. (ed.) (1993), *Global Ecology: A New Arena of Political Conflict*, London: Zed Books.

Sahgal, Bittu (1998), *Running with the Hare and Hunting with the Hounds?* Bombay: E-mail communication to the author, 11 March.

SchNEWS (1998), http://www.schnews.org.uk, Brighton: Justice?

Shiva, Vandana (1993), 'The Greening of the Global Reach', in W. Sachs (1993), *Global Ecology: A New Arena of Political Conflict*, London: Zed Books.

Singh, Neena (1998 Draft), *Wildlife Conservation in India: the Old Order Changeth*, Delhi: CSE.

Sjöberg, Helen (1994), *From Idea to Reality*, Washington, DC: GEF Working Paper No.10.

Sklair, L. (1998), 'As Political Actors', *New Political Economy*, Vol.3 No.2, July, pp.284–7.

Stedman-Edwards, Pamela (1998), *Root Causes of Biodiversity Loss: An Analytical Approach*, Washington, DC: WWF Macroeconomics for Sustainable Development/Office Programme.

Thomas, Caroline (ed.) (1994), *Rio: Unravelling the Consequences*, London and Portland, OR: Frank Cass

Tickell, O. and N. Hildyard (1992), 'Green Dollars, Green Menace', *The Ecologist*, Vol.22, No.3, pp.82–3.

Visvanathan, Shiv (1991), 'Mrs Brundtland's Disenchanted Cosmos', *Alternatives*, Vol.16, No.3, pp.377–84.

Wade, Robert (1997), 'Greening the Bank: The Struggle over the Environment, 1970–1995' Devesh Kapur, John P. Lewis and Richard Webb (eds.), *The World Bank: Its First Half Century, Vol.2: Perspectives*, Washington, DC: Brookings Institution Press.

Walton, John and David Seddon (1994), *Free Markets and Food Riots: the Politics of Global Adjustment*, Cambridge, MA and Oxford: Blackwell.

Wapner, Paul (1996), *Environmental Activism and World Civic Politics*, New York: State University of New York Press.

Weiss, T.G. and L. Gordenker (eds.) (1996), *NGOs, the UN and Global Governance*, Boulder, CO and London: Lynne Rienner.

Wells, Michael P. (March 19th, 1996), 'NGO Participation in World Bank GEF Projects: a Report for the GEF-NGO Working Group', Washington, DC: unpublished, 19 March.

Werksman, Jake (ed.) (1996), *Greening International Institutions* (Law and Sustainable Development Series), London: FIELD and Earthscan.

World Bank (1997, 1998), *World Development Reports*, Washington, DC: World Bank.

WRI (1989), *Natural Endowments: Financing Resource Conservation for Development*, Washington, DC: International Conservation Financing Project.

Yearley, Stephen (1994), 'Social Movements and Environmental Change', in Michael Redclift and Ted Benton (eds.) (1994), *Social Theory and the Global Environment*, London: Routledge.

Young, Zoe and Sonja Boehmer-Christiansen (1998) 'Green Energy Facilitated? The Uncertain Function of the GEF', *Energy and Environment*, Vol.9, No.1, pp.35–59.

The World Trade Organisation, Social Movements and Global Environmental Management

MARC WILLIAMS and LUCY FORD

When examining the role of social movements' attempts to influence international negotiations, most commentators have seen social movement activity within a simple frame and have concentrated on those groups that are engaging directly in the international policy process. Less attention has been given to others that are using different sorts of strategies. In fact, social movements adopt multi-faceted approaches. Two different strategies to effect transformation in the world trading system are explored. On the one hand, social movements, principally NGOs, are lobbying the WTO directly. On the other hand, less institutionalised grassroots movements have taken a more confrontational attitude.

The World Trade Organisation (WTO) has emerged as one of the key institutions of global governance in the international political economy. As a successor to the General Agreement on Tariffs and Trade (GATT) the WTO widens and deepens global regulation of international trade and payments. It extends GATT disciplines into areas previously governed by protectionist devices in the post-war global trade regime, namely agriculture, textiles, and 'new' issues such as intellectual property rights, and in addition subjects investment measures to regulatory control. The WTO's mandate has brought it into conflict with a range of social movement activists representing consumer, development, labour, and environmental interests. In the context of the WTO, environmental managment arises from the intersection of the extension of free trade principles to previously untouched areas of the global economy and the simultaneous emergence of sustainable development as a key principle of global governance. The coincidence of the trade and environment debate

Marc Williams gratefully acknowledges the support of the Economic and Social Research Council (ESRC). The research reported here was funded under the ESRC's Global Economic Institutions Programme, and is part of a project entitled 'Global Economic Institutions and Global Social Movements'.

and the strengthening of the international trade regime has provided the political space in which environmental activists have sought to challenge the liberal ideology of the hegemonic discourse on trade policy.

Recently, scholars have turned their attention to the role of social movements in world politics. Most commentators have restricted their attention to social movements which engage with existing centres of national and international decision-making. Less attention has been given to those social movement actors that use different strategies. In other words, analysis has concentrated on the politics of engagement rather than that of resistance. We explore two different strategies of attempting transformation in the world trading system. On the one hand are groups which attempt to engage in a constructive dialogue with national and international officials. Working within the political system these groups seek to influence the agenda primarily through forms of constructive engagement. As will be shown, such strategies should not be dismissed as conservative, neither should it be assumed that official policy-makers are receptive to such strategies and perceive them as non-threatening. On the other hand, a variety of social movement actors reject any form of accommodation with national or international bureaucracies and attempt to mobilise direct action against the institutions responsible for organising the world trade system. Although lobbying and other activities take place on different levels, nationally and internationally, we concentrate on efforts by social movement actors at the international level. We describe two broad strategies: engagement and rejection.

The WTO Ministerial Meeting in May 1998 highlighted the two fundamentally different approaches adopted by social movement activists towards the organisation. On the one hand, hundreds of activists met at the Palais des Nations (site of some of the WTO meetings) to discuss environmental, labour, gender, and consumer issues. Some also engaged in discussions with trade officials. On the other hand, activists gathered under the banner of the Peoples' Global Action (PGA), organised a peaceful demonstration on the streets of Geneva, after which some activists, not representative of the PGA, found less peaceful means of expressing their frustration by breaking windows and spraying slogans on Swiss banks and fast food restaurants. We chart both approaches to the WTO. It can be argued that the WTO is a crucial aspect of the neo-liberal project, and central to the creation of new forms of control in the era of globalisation. Social movements are frequently portrayed as harbingers of democracy in an elitist international political system, but we question the assumption that a global civil society largely composed of social movements presents a counter to dominant interests.

The first section of the study explores the context within which social movement activity aimed at the WTO is situated. It interrogates conceptions of global governance, discusses the role of social movements in the framework of an alleged global civil society, and situates the WTO as the institutional nexus of the international trade regime. The second explores the activities of groups engaged in what we have termed the politics of influence. These groups have adopted engagement strategies in an attempt to influence the trade and environment debate as well as to promote transparency and accountability within the WTO. The next section turns to groups which have adopted a rejectionist strategy. Their focus too is the WTO, not as an institution to be influenced, but as a symbol of economic globalisation and trade liberalisation which causes ecological degradation and social injustice. This section explores the politics of confrontation adopted by social movements which challenge the power relations at the heart of the global system and seek radical social change. We conclude by asking whether such a politics constitutes a counter-hegemonic force.

Global Governance, the WTO and Global Civil Society

Global Governance and Environmental Management

The concept of global governance is inherently problematic. Like the term 'international order' with which it competes and in some senses has replaced, 'global governance' suggests both a spatial terrain and a form of control. It also implies some form of neutrality in that the global resolves, dissolves, and replaces local antagonisms with a resolution at a higher (therefore better) level. Similarly the concept of governance suggests rules and order as clearly a preferable state to anarchy and disorder.

Before examining the WTO as a pillar of global governance, this section briefly problematises the concepts of globalisation and sustainable development. Both concepts have a lot in common, in that they have been variously defined, often contradictorily, and both have become part of a dominant discourse through which the environment is managed and, more generally, through which the organisation of social relations is reproduced. The dominant definitions of these terms are the ones that have been appropriated by global institutions such as the WTO. Though these terms are constantly disputed and redefined within academic discourse, the dominant definitions have become a 'reality' which has set the terms of debate within the policy-making process.

There has been much debate about globalisation across academic disciplines from sociological, cultural, political and economic perspectives [e.g,. *Featherstone, 1990; Giddens; 1990; Hirst and Thompson, 1996; Jones, 1995; Scholte, 1993; Waters, 1995*]. Our view is that in the practice of international relations and in the institutions of global governance, it is the neo-liberal economic discourse that is invoked. Here globalisation is perceived as 'the movement towards an integrated global market [reinforced by] deregulation, interacting with accelerating changes in communications and computer technology' [*CGG, 1995: 10*]. This process is portrayed as irreversible and as holding the key to solving 'global' problems such as environmental degradation or poverty through market mechanisms coupled with policy formation within global economic and political institutions. Environmental management and policy-making are embedded in this process and have become globalised. The dominant discourse of global environmental politics focuses on 'global' environmental issues needing global solutions. In this sense, globalisation could be seen as a form of externalisation. Portraying environmental problems as "global" removes them from our reach, beyond our control and in need of global responses and global management. Externalisation is further underlined by downplaying the importance of underlying social, economic, political and cultural causes of environmental degradation. The problems are further portrayed as complex and scientific, thereby justifying the technocratic imposition of solutions from the top down. It constitutes a depoliticisation of the issues as power relations are masked by the call for global solutions [*Sachs,1993: 18; Shiva, 1993: 150*].

The concept of sustainable development, like that of globalisation, has been much debated. However, within the dominant discourse, the notion of sustainable development is seen as integral to a new era of economic growth as well as a global policy solution for the problems of environmental degradation and poverty. The Brundtland Commission's Report *Our Common Future* defines sustainable development as 'development that meets the needs of the present without compromising the ability of future generations to meet their own needs', where 'needs' are defined as the essential needs particularly of the world's poor, and 'development' is vaguely defined as the 'progressive transformation of economy and society' [*1987: 43*]. However, development is still contained within the capitalist political economy. Economic growth *per se* is not questioned and, despite reports such as *The Limits to Growth*, natural parameters (critical thresholds) are only barely acknowledged, and the main limitations are the 'present state of technology and social organisation'.

The report by the Trilateral Commission, *Beyond Interdependence*, is a seminal example of the institutionalisation of the dominant discourse. It states that '[G]iven the growth imperative evident in the material poverty of much of human kind, the only reasonable alternative is sustainable development' [*1991: v*]. Its main concern, however, is world order and the policy imperative is how to bring these 'problems' on board without fundamentally rocking the boat. The emphasis remains on global governance within which environmental management has become embedded, and which is the most suitable location for dealing with global problems through global solutions such as sustainable development.

This global consensus on sustainable development is reflected in the Preamble of the Agreement Establishing the WTO. The recognition of environmental concerns by the new trade institution represented a significant shift in the discourse on trade liberalisation. The first GATT Panel ruling on the dolphin/tuna controversy in 1991 ushered in a hotly contested debate on the relationship beteen trade and the environment. Acknowledgement of the salience of sustainable development by the founders of the WTO represented on one hand a success for environmental campaigners, and on the other the ability of dominant interests to retain control of the agenda.

The World Trade Organisation

Among the institutions of global governance the WTO has been a particular focus amongst environmentalists because of growing concern with the transboundary nature of environmental degradation exacerbated through global trade. The WTO was established on 1 January 1995 as the successor to the GATT, replicating but also extending its mandate. As an organisation the WTO has three main dimensions. It is, first, a legal agreement which provides a framework of rules, norms and principles to govern the multilateral trading system. In other words, it is the legal and institutional foundation of the world trading system. Second, it is a forum for multilateral trade negotiations. Multilateral trade agreements specify the principal contractual obligations determining trade negotiations and trade legislation, and the Trade Policy Mechanism facilitates the evolution of trade relations and trade policy. Third, it acts as a centre for the settlement of disputes.

The creation of the WTO transformed the management of world trade in three respects. First, it engineered a shift from trade liberalisation based on tariff concessions (shallow or negative integration) to discussions of domestic policies, institutional practices and regulations (deep or positive integration). Second, it constructed a new agenda expanding the scope (through the inclusion of services, trade related intellectual property rights, and domestic [non-trade] policies), and changing the character of negotiations from a focus on bargaining over products to negotiations over policies that shape the conditions of competition. A third innovation was a movement towards policy harmonisation for example, in the areas of subsidies, trade-related investment measures, and services. This transformation of the institutional basis of the world trading system from the negative integration practised under GATT to the positive integration envisaged in the WTO is illustrative of the impact of globalisation on world trade. Globalisation has been accompanied by a growing discourse of multilateralism.

Trade liberalisation under GATT consisted essentially of tariff-cutting exercises and can be seen as a negative process of restricting barriers to trade. In this process dispute settlement procedures were weak, and the power of the organisation to discipline errant members was severely limited. The WTO not only extends the mandate of the GATT into new areas, but redefines the relationship between national governments and the world trading system through the creation of an effective dispute settlement mechanism, the provision of a trade policy review mechanism, and the development of a set of mandatory codes. The WTO thus provides a higher and sharper profile for trade issues, and as such attracts the attention of a range of actors. Compared with the GATT, the increased scope, permanence and rule-making authority of the WTO has alarmed environmentalists and other civil society actors who fear that the organisation and control of vital national decisions have been gradually and irretrievably displaced from national control to a supranational organisation shrouded in secrecy.

The ability of social movements to influence the world trade agenda through the WTO is constrained by the WTO's organisational chararacteristics. It is principally a forum for intergovernmental negotiations and is not formally open to social movement activists. Negotiations on international trade remain the exclusive responsibility of governments. Moreover, the multilateral trading system resides on a system of rules. The contractural character of the system reinforces the centrality of states within WTO. But although governments are the legitimate representatives within the bargaining process, trade policy is a political process in which special interest groups attempt to influence national policy. In the post-war trading system, advocates of protection and disciples of free trade have sought to gain control over governmental policies. The resulting policy-mix within various states reflects the differential strengths of interest groups and the efforts of lobbyists. Social movement activity aimed at the WTO is thus inserted into a pre-existing political culture. Groups which seek to influence the trade policy debate through a strategy of engagement contend with business and consumer interest groups over a terrain in which the 'problem' of protectionism is inscribed as significant.

Although social movement organisations are excluded from WTO deliberations, the WTO Secretariat maintains informal relations with NGOs. Consultation between the WTO and social movements was facilitated by two decisions taken by the WTO's General Council in July 1996. The *Guidelines for Arrangements on Relations with Non-Governmental Organisations* (WT/L/162; 23 July 1996) reinforced the intergovernmental nature of WTO's deliberations but made some concession to the roles that NGOs can play in the wider public debate on trade and trade-related issues. Secondly, the General Council agreed to de-restrict documents. Under the *Procedures for the Circulation and De-Restriction of WTO Documents* (WT/L/160/Rev.1; 22 July 1996) most WTO documents will be circulated as unrestricted, some will be de-restricted automatically after a sixty day period, others can be de-restricted at the request of a member but others especially those pertaining to important current policy decisions, will remain restricted [*Van Dyke and Weiner, 1996; Weiner and Van Dyke, 1996*]. Furthermore, the WTO Secretariat provides briefings on its work programme and receives representations from NGOs. Apart from these contacts the Secretariat has organised a number of symposia with social movement representatives.

Global Civil Society and Social Movements

Recently a number of analysts have invoked the concept of global civil society as an explanatory tool in international relations. They argue that the growth of transnational networks and the burgeoning of non-state associations across state boundaries provide evidence of the emergence of a global civil society [*Lipschutz, 1992; Macdonald, 1994; Otto, 1996; Shaw, 1994*]. Current and continuing transformation in the structures and functions of the global political economy has transformed the role of the state, and created a space for the development of non-state actors. Crucially, the traditional meaning of sovereignty has changed as a result of the globalisation of finance, production and distribution [*Williams 1996*].

The process of internationalising national economies creates a *de facto* form of transnational governance. The erosion of sovereignty, processes of globalisation and rapid technological change have contributed to the emergence of divergent, non-exclusive political communities. Instead of identifying themselves on the basis of nationality, people begin to view themselves as part of a broader global community such as women, workers, refugees or peasants. These new forms of identity are transnational, regional and global. By linking civil society across national boundaries, social movements are actively shaping and re-shaping international politics. Social movements challenge the constitutive practices of the international system and in particular expose their potential for offering alternatives and for instigating far- reaching social change. Environmental social movements are often cited as an important element of civil society and as representative of a new form of politics [*Wapner, 1997; Lipschutz, 1992*].

The arguments presented here reveal the problematic nature of the term 'global civil society', especially in terms of conceptualising social movement activity. Various normative notions of civil society exist which describe differing relationships of civil society to the state and the market [e.g., *Kumar, 1993; Wood, 1993*]. From our perspective, what is interesting is the globalisation of this term in the overall context of global governance including environmental management.[1] Wapner describes global civil society as 'the domain that exists above the individual and below the state but also across state boundaries, where people voluntarily organise themselves to pursue various aims' [*1997: 66*]. In particular, global civil society is seem as the domain in which NGOs act; indeed NGOs are seen as constitutive of global civil society.

This liberal conception of global civil society is fostered by the inter-state system and the integrated world market. On the other hand, a critical reading of current developments questions the extent to which social movement actors can effect change in the global system. The space for social movement activity is actually demarcated by the hierarchical structure and is not designed to provide space for a radical, counter-hegemonic challenge, but in fact is rather a site for the co-optation of social movements. The guidelines for global environmental governance laid down in Agenda 21 can be seen as a case in point. They called for the invigoration of democracy on the path towards sustainable development, appealing to governments and international institutions to create the mechanisms to incorporate civil society, NGOs, business and industry into the procedures of policy-making, decision-making and implementation, in effect creating new forms of participation at all levels (UN 1992). This is fine in theory but in practice the reality of such participation is the creation of a pseudo-political forum where global civil society becomes co-opted while real decision-making power is transferred to hegemonic organisations which have not been democratised, such as the WTO, World Bank, the Global Environment Facility (GEF) or the Business Council for Sustainable Development (BCSD) [*Chatterjee and Finger 1994*].

From a Gramscian viewpoint hegemony is seen as being located in bourgeois society (civil society) which is not seen as entirely separate from the state/or the inter-state system. Gramsci's enlarged view of the state includes the underpinnings of political structure in civil society [*Cox, 1993: 51*]. In this view, the establishment of an enlarged liberal sphere of global civil society where people can participate in the management of the environment is consistent with the notion that civil society is a mechanism of hegemony, a concession to 'subordinate classes in return for acquiescence in bourgeois leadership, concessions which could lead ultimately to forms of social democracy which preserve capitalism while making it more acceptable to workers and the petty bourgeois' [*1993: 51*]. This further relates to Gramsci's notion of *transformismo*. Here the discourses ouflined above, such as globalisation, sustainable development or global civil society could be seen as strategies for 'assimilating and domesticating potentially dangerous ideas by adjusting them to the policies of the dominant coalition and can thereby obstruct the formation of (class-based) organised opposition to established social and political power' [*1993: 55*]. Thus it becomes problematic to distinguish between top-down hegemony *versus* bottom-up counter-hegemony, or between the separate spheres of state/market/civil society as hegemony is pervasive throughout.

It is argued within a liberal perspective that the increased salience of NGOs serves to democratise otherwise undemocratic global structures and helps to ensure that the concerns of civil society are no longer marginalised. But UNCED (United Nations Conference on Environment and Development) revealed the impact of divisions and unequal distribution of power which have developed within the environmental movement. The well-established NGOs often disassociated themselves from grass-roots organisations at the global forum, with mainstream environmental groups from the North holding most power. Conca claims that the main influence of NGOs was through having presence on national delegations which ' ... amplified the voice of relatively well-heeled, mainstream Northern environmental organisations and, in particular, several of the larger groups that were within the NGO community based in the USA' [*1995: 449*]. Those with the power were the ones most prepared to sacrifice demands for radical change less acceptable to powerful governments and transnational corporations (TNCs). Global civil society is not necessarily a democratising force within global governance. Moreover, differences between civil society actors result in the adoption of different strategies towards key global institutions.

The Politics of Influence – Engaging with the WTO

In what follows we concentrate on that section of the environmental movement that has been lobbying for reform of the rules of the world trading system. These 'reformers' can be differentiated from the 'radical' groups that seek the abolition of the WTO. Of course, such a dichotomy is not always easy to sustain since individuals and groups not only shift positions over time but some organisations may well house a variety of views. It is possible to discern a shift in the relations between 'reformist' environmentalist groups and the WTO from one of incomprehension to the beginnings of accommodation. Some measure of accommodation is discernible between the trade community and environmental groups with offices in Geneva and engaging in lobbying and advocacy activities. At the outset both groups mistrusted the economic arguments put forward by the other side and little real dialogue was possible. Both groups are now aware that the existing knowledge of trade-environment linkages is very tentative and in the past two years both the WTO Secretariat and NGOs like WWF and the IUCN have been prepared to examine the evidence in a manner unlikely to maintain the previous degree of polarisation. Broadly speaking, the reformers have sought to redirect policies and alter institutional procedures in the WTO. Other environmental groups, for example Greenpeace, are less prepared to engage in these discussions.

Reformist environmental NGOs have developed a twofold strategy in their attempts to alter world trade rules. Analysis and research is aimed at changing the way in which the trade and environment nexus is perceived. They have been instrumental in bringing new ideas and norms into the policy debate. A concerted attack on the harmful consequences of the liberal trading system was initiated by environmental groups in the aftermath of the 1991 GATT Panel ruling in the tuna-dolphin dispute between the United States and Mexico. The ensuing debate between advocates of free trade and environmentalists was critical in framing the evolution of the discourse, resulting in the incorporation of environmental issues within the world trading sytem. Policy advocacy requires new information and political support in order to promote the reform agenda. To this end environmental groups like the WWF, and International Institute for Sustainable Development (IISD) have engaged in analysis of trade and environmental issues with the aim of making policy recommendations directed at policy-makers. Lobbying is thus concentrated on gaining political support among the informed public rather than the general public. In Geneva, environmentalists have built up contacts with representatives of national governments and WTO staff. At the national level, environmentalists have established contacts in various government departments. Within pluralist democracies environmentalists have been trying to affect the composition of national trade negotiating teams in order to increase the participation of environmental ministries in trade talks.

Secondly, environmental groups engaged in lobbying the WTO have formed diverse transnational advocacy coalitions. These networks are useful in developing and supporting public campaigns on specific policies. A recent example was the campaign against the Multilateral Agreement on Investment (MAI) linking diverse national and international coalitions. The decision by OECD governments to postpone negotiations on the MAI resulted in part from the activities of these networks. The first and second Ministerial conferences of the WTO provided opportunities for social movement activists to organise workshops on issues of common concern. In the interval between conferences Geneva-based organisations such as the WWF, and the International Centre for Sustainable Development (ICTSD) established in 1995 to co-ordinate Southern NGO activity, provide nodal points for environmental networking.

The changing relations between environmental groups and the WTO can be illustrated through symposia organised by the WTO Secretariat. The first such event, held in June 1994, was marked by friction and did little to promote constructive dialogue. It was apparent at this meeting that the intellectual disagreement between representatives from the environmental groups present and the Secretariat could not be easily bridged. The purpose of the symposium on trade, environment, and development was to facilitate an exchange of views, but animosity between the two groups resulted in a dialogue of the deaf. Moreover, tensions within the environmental movement contributed to a meeting regarded by all participants as a failure. [*GATT, 1994*]. Subsequent symposia, for example those held in September 1996, May 1997, and March 1998, which included representatives of environment, development and consumer groups, were felt to be more constructive. For example, the International Institute for Sustainable Development claimed that the symposium held in May 1997 was a success because for the first time there was actual interaction between NGOs and member states [*IISD, 1997*].

Institutional Venue

Environmental issues arise throughout the WTO's organisational structure but it has been in the Committee on Trade and Environment (CTE) that discussions have centred on the interrelationship between trade and the environment. The CTE is a deliberative rather than a policy-making body which between its first meeting in February 1995 and the First Ministerial Meeting in Singapore in 1996 concentrated on clarifying the relationship between trade and the environment. The terms of reference of the CTE are:

(i)   to identify the relationship between trade measures and sustainable development;

(ii) to make appropriate recommendations on whether the multilateral trading system should be modified;

(iii) to assess the need for rules to enhance the interaction between trade and environment including avoidance of protectionist measures and surveillance of trade measures used for environmental purposes.

Two parameters have guided the CTE's work programme. The WTO's competence for policy co-ordination in this area is limited to trade and those trade-related aspects of environmental policies which may result in trade effects for its members. In other words, the WTO will not become involved in reviewing national environmental priorities, setting environmental standards or developing global policies for the environment. Secondly, in the event of the identification of problems of policy co-ordination to protect the environment, steps taken to resolve them must uphold or safeguard principles of the trading system. The CTE was given two years to fulfil its mandate with a review of its usefulness to be conducted at the Singapore Ministerial Meeting. This review concluded that the CTE should continue to function but, lacking a chairman, it remained moribund for most of 1997. The first Ministerial Conference of the WTO provided the environmental movement with its first opportunity to address the achievements of the WTO in a comprehensive manner.

ENGOs were strongly critical of the failure of the CTE to make any substantive progress in its deliberations [*WWF, 1996b; IISD, 1997*]. Environmentalists argued that the CTE's agenda was very narrow, and failed to meet the task of addressing trade and sustainable development in order to make recommendations on whether modifications of the multilateral trading system are required [*Friends of the Earth, 1996*]. The CTE, instead of addressing the crucial issues on trade and the environment, had been side-tracked into discussions on technical issues. Furthermore, it had only dealt in any detail with three issues: the relationship between WTO rules and trade measures relating to multilateral environmental agreements (MEAs); eco-labelling and WTO rules; and the effects of environmental measures on market access. Moreover, environmental NGOs were sharply critical of the manner in which environmental issues had been shifted to the CTE. Sustainable development touches on the WTO's work programme in a number of ways, and environmental NGOs argue that this should influence WTO policy.

Between the first and second Ministerial Meetings environmental groups continued to criticise the functioning of the CTE. They argued that not only had the CTE failed to make any progress on trade measures relating to MEAs but it had disrupted the existing consensus by apparently extending the WTO's jurisdiction. One interpretation of the CTE's activities suggests that trade measures agreed in MEAs and applied between the parties could still be taken before a WTO Dispute Panel. That is, WTO members could resort to the WTO dispute settlement mechanism to undermine obligations already agreed in MEAs. Since MEAs are an effective means of addressing transboundary global environmental threats, the WTO could undermine them. Continuing uncertainty over WTO rules could deter parties from the use of trade measures in MEAs [*WWF, 1996b: 2*]. In Geneva and national capitals, environmental groups campaigned for a strenthening of the CTE. Whilst national governments were sanguine about the progress of the CTE in December 1996, by May 1998 the so-called Quad countries (The European Union, United States, Japan and Canada) were prepared to admit publicly that the CTE needed to be revitalised. The extent to which this belated recognition of the inadequacies of the CTE arises from a conversion to the arguments made by environmental groups or is the result of an assessment of the costs of inaction is not clear.[2] Whatever the 'truth' clearly the activities of environmental groups in focusing attention on the CTE, monitoring norm implementation ensured the issue remained at the forefront of deliberations.

Furthermore, research and publication, in bringing new sources of information into the public arena, has shifted the terms of discourse between liberal economists and environmentalists. Discussion has moved from a general debate concerning the trade–environment link to discussion of specific issues in the context of trade and sustainable development. These include: problems related to trade in products created through environmentally damaging and unsustainable production processes; the relationship between the multilateral trading system and MEAs; and eco-labelling. Production, process and methods (PPMs) are central to efforts to introduce sustainable development to the global trading system. PPMs refer to the techniques and methods used in the production of a product. The debate arises because the rules of the liberal trading system regulate products but not the processes used to create them [*WWF, 1996a: 7*].

The trade community is opposed to the inclusion of PPMs on grounds of efficiency and the difficulty of ensuring compliance. Given different absorptive capacities and differing environmental values, the attempt to impose global standards will not only shift specialisation away from comparative advantage, it will also impose external values on sovereign states. Moreover, opponents point out the difficulties inherent in devising systems of monitoring and compliance during production processes. On the other hand, environmentalists contend that it is difficult to sustain a distinction between production and products. PPMs are necessary to protect health and the environment. In this view PPMs would assist in the development of more efficient production and stricter environmental standards. A system based on the polluter pays principle would, it is claimed, diminish the necessity for cumbersome monitoring measures.

Environmentalists allege that WTO rules on eco-labelling are unclear. For example, it is not certain whether WTO rules included in the Technical Barriers to Trade Agreement (TBT) and its annexes cover eco-labels based on non-product related PPMs [*IUCN, 1996: 36*]. One aspect of this controversy relates to the fact that it is not clear whether TBT rules apply to standards involving life cycle analysis. Since TBTs refer to product standards and indirectly to PPMs it is not clear whether the rules apply, for example, to the use of pesticides in production even where there is no pesticide residue. They argue that non-product PPMs should be placed on the agenda, and demand the inclusion of eco-labelling practitioners in the negotiations.

Democratising the WTO

The rhetoric of contemporary global governance is infused with demands for participation and democracy. Environmental activists have been campaigning for increased transparency, participation and accountability in the WTO, portraying it as a secretive organisation lacking in accountability. It is argued that civil society organisations have a crucial role to play in making the world trading system more transparent and accountable (Enders, 1996; Esty, 1997). Environmental NGOs with a focus on the deliberations in Geneva argue that access to information and participation in decision-making is vital for democracy, and will also improve the policy outputs of the WTO. Environmentalists are aware that the nature of trade negotiations means that an open-access regime for NGOs is not feasible. Thus their demands for participation and transparency are couched in reformist terms. Proposed reforms maintain the intergovernmental character of the organisation whilst enhancing public scrutiny of the multilateral trading system. Environmentalists claim that the WTO can be reformed in ways which do not impinge on the need for secrecy in bodies like the Trade Policy Review Mechanism. They suggest that membership of the CTE should be expanded to include NGOs. The claim is for observer status rather than full membership. Moreover, they argue that the Dispute Settlement Mechanism should make greater use of independent experts. On the issue of transparency, NGOs are very critical of existing arrangements for the de-restriction of documents. They argue that if crucial documents can be kept restricted until six months after being issued the monitoring functions of NGOs will be handicapped.

Until recently, demands for increased participation have been firmly rejected. Many developing countries are concerned that any moves in this direction will further enhance Northern interests at their expense since the NGOs with the capacity to engage with the policy process will be from the North. Opponents of reform make four main points. First, it is argued that the various groups attempting to lobby the WTO should do so in their home countries. Since trade policy is the result of a domestic political bargain then it is at the national level that environmental, development, business, and consumer interests should attempt to influence policy.

Second, the WTO's negotiations demand a high level of secrecy which cannot be guaranteed if participation is granted to non-state actors. In the process of bargaining, governments frequently have to trade-off one domestic interest against another. Governments would be unable to make progress in multilateral trade negotiations if other actors were involved. Third, the negotiation process in Geneva should not encourage the active involvement of protectionist groups. Any attempt to widen participation in

WTO decision-making to increase social movement participation will inevitably increase the lobbying activities of the business community. Given the competitive advantage business organisations possess over NGOs, any liberalisation in access for NGOs would increase the influence of large corporations. Some governments argue that not only will it be difficult to devise a method of accrediting legitimate NGOs but that many NGOs do not represent a distinct community of interests.

This defence of current practice in the WTO rests on a reassertion of the intergovernmental status of the organisation, and the special features of trade negotiations. Under pressure from US pressure groups, the US government has frequently adopted a sympathetic approach to the issue of representation. A firmer commitment to opening up the WTO to business groups and NGOs was made by the US at the May 1998 Ministerial Meeting. Furthermore, support for increased contact between non-state actors and the WTO was given by Renato Ruggiero, the Director General of the WTO [*WTO, 1998*]. The demand by social movement activists for increased access to the WTO is matched by private interest groups who also would like to increase their influence over trade policy. It is likely that any increase in participation by social movement groups will have been determined less by commitment to a democratic ideal and more by short-term political interests.

Whilst NGOs' demands for participation are unlikely to be met in the near future, it is apparent that governments are attempting to engage in a more open manner with development and environmental organisations. Defenders of the liberal trade order need allies in order to defeat the ever-present supporters of protectionism. Trade officials are concerned with enhancing the legitimacy of the liberalisation project, and to this end are prepared to engage with representatives of civil society in an attempt to widen the public base of support for increased liberalisation.

The Politics of Resistance – The Rejectionist Stance

Whereas the actors discussed above are firmly located within the liberal conception of global civil society, the space of social movements which reject the dominant approach to global environmental management is not so clearly defined. Above we have seen various attempts of social movement actors, principally NGOs, to lobby the WTO directly in their aim to influence international trade negotiations. We are concerned with social movement actors that have an emancipatory intent, seeking to effect a change for the better, though what this change entails and how it is to come about differs from group to group. The relationship between a politics of influence and a politics of resistance is by no means necessarily dichotomous or contradictory, but neither can it be claimed that social movements have somehow orchestrated a two-pronged strategy of accommodation and confrontation. Some literature suggests that NGOs seeking influence become co-opted, leaving more radical groups marginalised [*Chatterjee and Finger, 1994*]. This is not to say that social movements engaging with the WTO do not share a concern for fundamental change. Indeed, during the the WTO/NGO symposium on trade, environment and sustainable development in Geneva in May 1997, many NGOs, especially from the South, openly critiqued the neoliberal ideology of globalisation, trade liberalisation and sustainable development [*IISD, 1997*]. However, their demands and policy recommendations are more likely to be watered down, whether through conviction or self-censorship, through the very process of engaging on the terms of the dominant institutions. The sphere of global civil society where social movements and NGOs are allegedly active is therefore not an uncontested terrain, free of conflicts and power relations. Indeed, NGOs and social movements not only engage each other, but are further confronted with business actors who have also been categorised within the sphere of global civil society, and whose agenda more often than not is at odds with NGOs' interests. Within global civil society there is a variety of viewpoints to be found. However, those at the radical grass-roots end of the spectrum see the very sphere of global civil society as being inimical to their strategies and interests.

This section discusses the less institutionalised grass-roots movements that are taking a confrontational attitude and challenging the WTO and notions of trade liberalisation *per se*. Such 'marginalised' groups have been organising in localities across the globe, fighting against the negative impacts of development. The recognition that these diverse local struggles are structurally connected has brought about a conscious globalisation of resistance. The Peoples' Global Action (PGA) epitomises resistance strategies of these types of movements.

The PGA against the WTO and 'Free Trade'

The PGA presents a radical departure from attempts to lobby the WTO and influence debates. It views the WTO and economic globalisation as factors that are perpetuating a system responsible for social and ecological degradation. As such it does not focus on any single issue but takes a holistic standpoint which explicitly recognises that ecological exploitation and degradation are fundamentally tied up with other forms of exploitation, social, cultural, economic or political.

The Peoples' Global Action against the WTO and 'free trade' held its first annual conference in Geneva in February 1998, inviting from around the world peoples' movements engaged in struggles against the destruction of humanity and the planet. The PGA is not an organisation but sees itself as a global instrument for communication and coordination of resistance to the global market as well as a tool for movements to build up local alternatives and peoples' power [*PGA 1997: 2*].

Inspired by the Zapatista's 'Encuentro' meetings (Mexico, 1996, Spain, 1997) the Conference was initiated and convened by a committee made up of: Central Sandinista de Trabajadores (Nicaragua), Frente Zapatista de Liberacion Nacional (Mexico), Foundation for Independent Analysis, Foundation for an independent Aotearoa (New Zealand), Indigenous Women's Network (North America and Pacific), Karnataka State Farmers' Association (India), Mama 86 (Ukraine), Movement for the Survival of the Ogoni People (Nigeria), Movimento Sem Terra (Brazil), Peasant Movement of the Philippines (KMP) and Play Fair Europe! [*PGA, 1997: 2*].

The committee set out four points of departure to form the basis for discussions: first, a clear rejection of the WTO and other liberalisation fora which are seen as undemocratic and serving only the interests of multinationals and speculators; second, a confrontational attitude rather than fruitless lobbying; third, a call to non-violent civil disobedience and to the construction of local alternatives by local populations; and fourth, decentralisation and autonomy as organisational principles [*PGA, 1997: 2*]. The forum, rather than a concessionary provision of the institutions of global governance, was a space forged from the bottom-up. Of over 300 delegates from 71 countries very few were "mainstream" NGOs and there were no representatives from the WTO or from the transnational corporate sector.

The PGA's bottom-line was a clear rejection of economic globalisation and a call 'to build bridges to connect the different social sectors, peoples and organisations that are already fighting globalisation across the world' [*PGA, 1998*]. A major part of the conference was taken up with drafting the manifesto, which was approached through a variety of issues, including environment, corporate power, gender, peasants, indigenous peoples, trade unions, youth, unemployed, migrants, housing, culture, students and health. The manifesto identified the need to 'develop new structures ... new types of organisations that emphasise that there is no way of solving the problems we are facing without questioning the logic of capitalist globalisation'. It was further stated that these organisations must bypass the dominant approach; they must be 'independent of governmental structures, autonomous from economic powers, and democratic, promoting the people's participation' [*PGA, 1998*]. The PGA's political stance is therefore firmly one of an anarchist, anti-capitalist nature.

The forum was by no means homogeneous, but was a gathering of groups from a diversity of backgrounds, ages and cultures. Unity was acknowledged as being at the same time deeply rooted in diversity. In the words of one activist, the PGA is 'an attempt to build a transnational alliance of people's movements in contrast to the transnational capitalist class' [*PGA, 1998*]. Underlying this position is a sense of transnational solidarity amongst movements, and yet in the past the analysis of social movements and NGOs has often highlighted a division between the interests of the movements in the 'North' and the 'South'. This view was particularly prevalent in relation to the UNCED proceedings as well as in debates about sustainable development. What seems significant about the PGA is that it has managed to bridge this divide. Some commentators attribute this to the idea of globalisation. Vandana Shiva, for example, sees globalisation as forcing people in the North and the South into 'a common condition of exclusion' which is forging a new solidarity [*Madeley, 1998*]. A sense of solidarity was certainly felt at Geneva when it came to identifying the 'common enemy'. It was clear to all, that a holistic approach was needed and that single issue politics was no longer sufficient. As one activist exclaimed: 'We have to start aiming at the head. We have been militants fighting against nuclear power, against housing, sexism. Different tentacles of the monster. You are never really going to do it that way, you really have to aim at the head' [*SchNEWS and Squall, 1998*]. The WTO is perceived as being symbolic of the head of an imminent 'single global economy'.[3] The view was very much that, in the face of globalisation, resistance needs to be globalised too.

However, although the attitude was one of confrontation, it remained unclear what the PGA's position was in terms of engagement or dialogue with the dominant institutions as well as with NGOs that are lobbying these institutions. On the one hand, it was argued that all NGOs (including the 'accommodationalists') should disengage and join the PGA in its peoples' resistance since lobbying undemocratic institutions was seen as unproductive. On the other, it was maintained that engagement with institutions was an imperative in challenging the system as was building dialogue between the 'insiders' and 'outsiders'.[4]

The politics of influence are more likely an example of co-optation than a strategy for radical social change, given that their demands already accept the parameters of debate or become diluted in the process. The PGA, on the other hand, rejects the dominant discourse and the dominant institutions and calls for more far-reaching change that could not be implemented through the institutions of global governance, thus requiring a by-passing and eventual dismantling of such institutions and the system they stand for. Although the PGA involves many people from across the globe, it has not received much media coverage. The first conference was not reported in the press, apart from one local newspaper in Geneva, and news coverage of the peaceful march in May 1998 in Geneva focused almost exclusively on the eruptions of violence. Despite its plea for nonviolence, it is not clear whether or not the PGA condoned that violence. Given the variety of groups acting under the banner of the PGA, it remains to be seen whether the PGA constitutes a force for positive change or whether it will act as a trojan horse for agents provocateurs.

Cox has pointed out that a transformation in world order would require 'fundamental change in social relations and in the national political orders which correspond to national structures of social relations' [1993: 64]. This project cannot take place within global institutions, as they are seen as 'absorbing counter-hegemonic ideas" [1993: 62]. This line of argument complements the view that the liberal notion of global civil society acts as a vehicle of co-optation. However the return to the national level alone is unsatisfactory, especially in the light of global social activism, such as the PGA, which seems to be forging a global consciousness. Although ultimately social movements will return to their individual localities, one of the main aims of the PGA was to build bridges and mutual awareness of the struggles going on around the globe, thus forging new spaces for radical social change to counter the global governance of unaccountable, undemocratic elites.

Conclusion

We have argued that social movements have developed two strategies in respect of the world trading system – engagement and rejection. Those social movement actors engaged in what we term the politics of influence attempt to engage in reasoned debate with the trade community. These organisations are attempting to shift the trade paradigm so that environmental issues are inscribed in a meaningful manner in trade negotiations. As we have seen, their efforts have met with some success. The complacent approach of trade officials has been replaced by one in which the linkages between trade and the environment are recognised as important. Nevertheless, after more than three years of activity, it is clear that the CTE has failed to develop the environmental agenda. The relationship between trade and environment remains contested. We have argued that the ability of environmentalists to challenge the system of world trade rules has been constrained by the institutional context of the WTO and the discourse of free trade. The WTO is an organisation relatively closed to participation by social movement representatives. The tradition of secrecy in trade negotiations, the intergovernmental status of the organisation, and its function as a negotiating forum militate against increased access for social movement activists.

In the face of this evidence, one could conclude that efforts directed at the WTO are misplaced, since effective pressure to reform world trade is most likely to be found in the domestic arena. Such a conclusion would, however, be premature. If it is accepted that with the creation of the WTO the structure of governance in the global trade regime has shifted, with an increase of power to the international organisation, it follows that campaigns directed solely at the national level will fail to capture the entire range of issues. No definite conclusions can be drawn at this stage, but given that environmental issues will continue to assume importance in the multilateral trading system, the environmental movement will remain one of the actors in the contested terrain of trade and environment. President Clinton asserted that 'the WTO for the first time provides a forum where business, labour, environmental, and consumer groups can speak out and help guide the further evolution of the WTO' (*Bridges Weekly Trade News Digest*, 1998]. It is not yet clear how this will be translated into practice. The inclusion of business groups weakens the potential influence of social movement actors.

The rejectionist approach begins from the assumption that environmental management has become globalised as part of an overall process of building global governance. It is perceived as a technocratic problem-solving approach which is not concerned with the eradication of environmental degradation as mediated through social, economic or political relations, but with the smooth functioning of the system. The discourses of globalisation and sustainable development are seen as fundamentally tied up with this process. Moreover, claims that the agenda-setting process have become democratised through the emergence of a global civil society are further thrown into question, and this liberally conceived sphere is rejected as a site for radical social change. It merely waters down the dominant approach and obscures the reality of environmental governance and management. Though some social movements may, by lobbying and raising public awareness, be instrumental in getting issues into the arena, it remains questionable to what extent they actually exert influence in determining the agenda. A radical challenge goes deeper; it is not just about influencing the agenda but about fundamentally altering the system and building a new agenda that reflects the interests of the people and the planet. However, in terms of modes of engagement, it is not just a question of whether to engage or not to engage. Gauging the success of either mode is a matter of time. At present the powerful institutions of global governance attach little value to the role of social movements, be they reformist or revolutionary.

NOTES

1   Eschle [*1996*] analyses the extrapolation of the concept of civil society on to the global level, pointing to the conceptual problems, in particular the construction of bounded spheres of civil society/market/state and an implicit univeralism that is Eurocentric at heart.
2.   It is feared that continuing conflict over the environment will spill over into other areas of the WTO's work programme.
3.   Renato Ruggiero, Director General of the WTO, exclaimed at the Singapore Ministerial Meeting in December 1996, in the context of the MAI (Multilateral Agreement of Investment), that 'we are writing the constitution of a single global economy' [*Nova and Sforza-Roderick, 1997: 5*].
4.   This was a dialogue between two delegates during an open session. It was never taken up as an issue for wider debate.

REFERENCES

Bridges Weekly Trade News Digest (May 1998), 'Clinton endoreses Call for High Level WTO Meeting on Trade-Environmenta and Calls for WTO Openness', Vol.2, No.18, May.
Charnovitz, S. and J. Wickham (1995), 'NGOs and the Original International Trade Regime', *Journal of World Trade,* Oct.
Chatterjee, P. and M. Finger (1994), *The Earth Brokers,* London:Routledge.
CGG (Commission on Global Governance) (1995), *Our Global Neighbourhood,* Oxford: Oxford University Press.
Conca, K. (1995) 'Greening the UN: Environmental Organisations and the UN System', in T.G. Weiss and L Gordenker (eds.), *NGOs, the UN and Global Governance,* pp.103–20.
Cox, R.W. (1993), 'Gramsci, Hegemony and International Relations: An Essay in Method', in S. Gill (ed., *Gramsci, Historical Materialism and International Relations,* Cambridge: Cambridge University Press, pp. 49-66.
Dalton, R.J. (1994), *The Green Rainbow: Environmental Groups in Western Europe,* New Haven, CT: Yale University Press.
Enders, A. (1996), 'Openness and the WTO', a draft IISD paper, Winnipeg.
Eschle, C. (1996) 'Globalising Civil Society? Social Movements and the Challenge of Global Politics from Below', Paper for the Second European Conference on Social Movements, Vitoria-Gasteiz, Spain.
Esteva, G. and M.S. Prakash (1994), 'From Global to Local Thinking', *The Ecologist,* Vol.24, No5, pp.162–3.
Esty, D. (1997) *Why the WTO needs Environmental NGOs,* Geneva: International Centre for Trade and Sustainable Development.
Featherstone, M. (ed.) (1990), *Global Culture: Nationalism, Globalisation and Modernity,* London: Sage.
GATT (1994), *Report on the GATT Symposium on Trade, Environment, and Sustainable Development,* GATT Document TE 008, 28 July 1994, Geneva.
Giddens, A. (1990), *The Consequences of Modernity,* Cambridge:Polity Press.
Hildyard, N., Sexton, S. and A. Kerski (1995), 'Who are the Realists?' *The Ecologist* Vol.25, No.4, pp.130–33.
Hirst, P. and G. Thompson (1996), *Globalisation in Question: The International Economy and Possibilities of Governance,* Cambridge: Polity.
IUCN (1996), *The "Trade and Environment" Agenda: Survey of Major Issues and Proposals: From Marrakesh to Singapore,* Bonn: IUCN, Dec.
IISD (International Institute for Sustainable Development) (1997), *Earth Negotiations Bulletin,* Vol.5, No.1.
Jones, R.J.B. (1995), *Globalisation and Interdependence in the International Political Economy,* London: Pinter.
Laferrière, E. (1994), 'Environmentalism and the Global Divide', *Environmental Politics,* Vol.3, No.1, pp.91–113.

Kumar, K. (1993), 'Civil Society: An Inquiry into the Usefulness of an Historical Term', *British Journal of Sociology*, Vol.44, No.3, pp.375–95.

Lipschutz, R.D. (1992), 'Reconstructing World Politics: The Emergence of Global Civil Society', *Millennium* Vol.21, No.3, pp.389–420.

MacDonald, L. (1994), 'Globalising Civil Society: Interpreting International NGOs in Central America, *Millennium*, Vol.23, No.2, pp.267–86.

MacNeill, J. *et al.* (1991), *Beyond Interdependence: The Meshing of the World's Economy and the Earth's Ecology*, New York: Oxford University Press.

Madeley, J. (1998), 'Globalisation under attack ... or not', Third World Network, Panos Feature. See also http://www.twnside.org.sg.

Meadows, D.H. *et. al.* (1972), *The Limits to Growth*, London: Pan Books.

Melluci, A. (1989), *Nomads of the Present*, London: Hutchinson.

Meyer, C.A. (1995) 'Opportunism and NGOs: Entrepeneurship and Green North–South Transfers', *World Development* Vol.23, No.8, pp.1277-1289.

Nova, S. and M. Sforza-Roderick (1997), 'Multilateral Agreement on Investment: "The Constitution of a Single Global Economy"', *The Ecologist*, Vol.27, No.1, p.5.

Otto, D. (1996), 'Nongovernmental Organisations in the United Nations System – The Emerging Role of International Civil Society', *Human Rights Quarterly*, Vol.18, No.1, pp.107–41.

PGA (1997), *PGA Bulletin*, No.0, Nov./Dec.

PGA (1998), 'Draft Manifesto of the Peoples' Global Action against "Free Trade" and the WTO', PGA.

Sachs, W. (1993,) *Global Ecology: A New Arena of Political Conflict*, London: Zed Books.

Saurin, J. (1993), 'Global Environmental Degradation: Modernity and Environmental Knowledge', *Environmental Politics*, Vol.2, No.4 (Special Issue), pp.46–64.

SchNEWS and Squall (1998), *Special Report on the United Colours of People's Global Action*, Brighton: Justice?.

Scholte, J.A. (1993), *The International Relations of Social Change*, Buckingham: Open University Press.

Shaw, M. (1994) 'Civil Society and Global Politics: Beyond a Social Movements Approach', *Millennium*, Vol.23, No.1, pp.647–67.

Shiva, V. (1993), 'The Greening of Global Reach', in Sachs [*1993: 149–56*].

Sklair, L. (1994), 'Global Sociology and Global Environmental Change', in M. Redclift and T. Benton (eds), *Social Theory and the Global Environment*, London: Routledge, pp.205–27.

UN (1992), *Agenda 21*, Geneva:United Nations.

Van Dyke, L.B. and J.B. Weiner (1996.) *An Introduction to the WTO Decision on Document Restriction*, Geneva: International Centre for Trade and Sustainable Development/Center for International Environmental Law.

Wapner, P. (1997), 'Governance in Global Civil Society', in Oran Young, *Global Governance: Drawing Insights from the Environmental Experience*, Cambridge, MA: MIT Press, pp.65–84.

Waters, M. (1995), *Globalisation*, London: Routledge.

Weiner, J.B. and L.B. Van Dyke (1996), *A Handbook for Obtaining Documents From the World Trade Organization*, Geneva: International Centre for Trade and Sustainable Development/Center for International Environmental Law.

Williams, M. (1996), 'Rethinking Sovereignty', in G. Youngs and E. Koffman (eds), *Globalisation: Theories and Processes*, London: Pinter, pp.109–22.

WCED (World Commission on Environment and Development) (1987), *Our Common Future*, Oxford: Oxford University Press.

Wood, E. (1990), 'The Uses and Abuses of "Civil Society"', in R. Miliband *et al.*, *The Socialist Register 1990*, pp.60–84.

WTO (1998), 'Ruggiero Announces Enhanced WTO Plan for Cooperation with NGOs', Press Release 107 (17 July).

WWF (1996a), *Expert Panel on Trade and Sustainable Development: Report of First Meeting*, Geneva, Nov.

WWF (1996b), *The WTO Committte on Trade and the Environment – Is It Serious?* Geneva, Dec.

Acting Globally, Thinking Locally? Prospects for a Global Environmental Movement

CHRISTOPHER ROOTES

Because understanding of global environmental problems is very limited except amongst the most highly educated populations of the most industrialised countries, it is not surprising that the latter should dominate environmental movement action on global issues, and that other, less highly educated people should be involved principally in local environmental campaigns. However, the success of local campaigns depends increasingly on the actions of non-local actors, and solutions even to local environmental problems demand transnational organisation. Effective transnational environmental movement organisations, however, are neither democratically accountable nor simply universalist in their assumptions. The prospects of a genuinely global environmental movement may nevertheless be improved by education.

In this era of globalisation, the local is less and less autonomous of actions and developments elsewhere, and the nation state, so often and so recently the agent of the suppression of the particularities of local cultures, languages and political systems, itself appears increasingly subordinated to supranational political institutions and agreements. We are increasingly aware of global environmental problems, and yet most of the environmental movement action we witness and in which we participate is intensely local. My concern here is to examine the character of local environmental action and to show how it is shaped and its outcome determined by actions and inaction at non-local levels. I then consider whether there is or can be a global environmental movement before going on to consider the implications of some recent actions involving Greenpeace.

This is a revised version of papers presented at the Second European Conference on Social Movements, Vitoria-Gasteiz, September 1996 and the 25th Joint Sessions of the European Consortium for Political Research, Bern, February 1997. The author wishes to thank Brian Doherty for helpful comments.

I. Thinking Globally?

It is all too apparent that most people in most countries experience some difficulty in thinking globally about environmental problems. There is, moreover, significant crossnational variation in the salience of environmental concern and in the balance of the forms of such concern.

In Britain, the most nearly universal forms of environmental concern are about the preservation of landscape and countryside and about pollution. Other kinds of environmental concern are less common and have more differentiated socio-demographic profiles [*Witherspoon and Martin, 1993*]: it is especially the less well-educated and women who voice concern over nuclear power and hazardous wastes; scientific, technical and medical professionals exhibit *less* concern than average about pollution and waste. Global green awareness is disproportionately found among the middle-aged and the highly educated.

It would appear that the kinds of concern people have about the environment are, to a significant degree, a function of their knowledge. The International Social Survey Programme in 1991–92 devised a battery of 12 environmental knowledge questions which required simple true or false answers, together with a battery of six questions designed to measure perception of environmental threat. Witherspoon [*1994*] presents the results of the 1993 survey in Britain. Levels of knowledge rose monotonically with educational qualifications, but levels of concern were more generally high. Only 20 per cent knew that the statement that 'the greenhouse effect is caused by a hole in the earth's atmosphere' was false, but 51 per cent thought the 'greenhouse effect' posed an 'extremely' or 'very' dangerous threat to the environment. Interestingly, the most scientifically knowledgeable respondents appeared, at first sight, to be less concerned than average about the threat to themselves and their families posed by environmental dangers[1] *and yet* they were more likely to be politically active on environmental issues. The explanation lies in part in the fact that it is those whose perceptions of nature are most romantic and those whose views of the environment are most pessimistic who voice greatest concern about environmental threats to themselves, their families and the environment; yet romanticism about nature correlates only modestly –and environmental pessimism does not correlate at all – with support for green policies. When their lesser tendency to both romanticism and pessimism about the environment was discounted, the more knowledgeable actually appeared also to be more concerned about environmental hazards [*1994: 122*] as well as most supportive of environmental policies and most likely to be active in environmental movements.

The pattern observable in Britain is also reflected in crossnational comparisons. In both southern and eastern Europe, although large majorities profess concern about the environment, their environmental consciousness is more likely than in northern Europe to take the form of 'personal complaint' rather than 'global concern' [*Hofrichter and Reif, 1990*], and levels of practical environmentalism are, by comparison with northern Europe, relatively low [*Rootes, 1997b*]. Rüdig [*1995*] reports cross-nationally comparative data for knowledge and concern about global warming. At first glance, the pattern of the results is paradoxical: in 1993 about one third of Southern Europeans had not even heard of global warming, yet their levels of concern about it were relatively high (all above the EU average). In Denmark and the Netherlands, however, the pattern was reversed: levels of knowledge were high but concern was relatively low. This paradoxical finding is consistent with British evidence of patterns of anxieties about various potential hazards.

What this suggests is that there is an inverse relationship between knowledge and anxiety but a positive one between knowledge and practical environmental concern. People who are confident in the knowledge that they understand an environmental problem are less likely to be so diffusely and disablingly worried about it that they feel unable to do anything practical to contribute to its mitigation. 'Scientific knowledge probably leads people to adopt a less apocalyptic view of nature, but it is positively associated with environmental concern and activism ...' [*Witherspoon, 1994: 135*]. The confidence of the scientifically and technologically educated may be misplaced, but this finding is nevertheless entirely consistent with the long-accumulated political sociological evidence that knowledge is positively correlated with a sense of personal efficacy, and it may help explain why those countries where environmental problems are objectively greatest and 'personal complaint' environmental concern is predominant are not places in which concerted action to redress such problems is widespread.[2]

It appears that there is a fairly close association between the knowledge people have of environmental problems and the kinds of concerns they evince about them. The connection would seem to be (principally but not exclusively)[3] education: the more highly educated have an enhanced cognitive capacity to comprehend complex environmental issues, to assess risks in relation thereto, and to conceive of practical remedial action, either individual or collective. The British data [*Witherspoon and Martin, 1993*] confirm this: the simpler and less sophisticated forms of environmental concern were most likely to be found among the less well-educated whilst attitudes approximating to a global ecological worldview were more likely to be found among the higher educated.[4]

In order better to understand why different kinds of concern should be so unevenly socially distributed, it may help to consider the intrinsic character of the issues. Issues such as air and water pollution are, like the conservation of the countryside, almost universal concerns because they appear to be relatively simple and visible problems of which most people may have direct experience and of which there is, accordingly, widespread comprehension. By contrast, nuclear waste, the depletion of the ozone layer, and global warming are complex issues beyond the practical experience of most people and on which there is no consensus of scientific opinion; even environmentalists and students of green politics do not reliably understand the differences between global warming and the depletion of the ozone layer [e.g., *Scharf, 1994: 110*], let alone comprehend the processes involved.

Upon closer inspection, even an apparently simple issue like air pollution is very much more complicated. The air pollution of which lay people are most aware and which, because it is most visible, is most likely to be the subject of complaint – particulate fallout – is probably less dangerous than any of several common forms of less visible air pollution, including nitrous oxide, carbon monoxide and ground-level ozone.

To most people, the most serious pollution problems are effectively invisible. They have no direct personal experience or knowledge of the depletion of the ozone layer, of global warming or of nuclear wastes. Moreover, since on all these issues the scientific community is divided, it would be unrealistic to expect otherwise of lay people. As a result, however, most people only 'know' about these issues so much as they believe of what they are told by the mass media. Since most journalists have only scant understanding, and most media little capacity for or commitment to the discursive examination of such complex and disputed issues, media coverage tends to be of events rather than processes, a series of spectacles and sensations with little attempt to deal consistently – or at all – with chronic and endemic environmental problems. As a result, what the public are told is all too little, and public opinion on environmental matters all too often takes the form of panics and scares rather than approximating to anything resembling discursive knowledge. All this conduces to a great deal of anxiety, much confusion, but relatively little practical action.

The environmental concerns that are most likely to become public issues capable of mobilising significant numbers of ordinary citizens are those which:

• affect them or, especially, their children;
• are intelligible by them;
• derive from and/or can be accommodated to popular values;
• are matters about which people are, or believe themselves to be, knowledgeable;

• are questions that people believe are capable of being addressed effectively.

This is one reason why NIMBY protests loom so large among environmental contentions; the backyard, at least, is familiar territory. People who, for one reason or another, are unable to think globally may yet be able to act locally.

II. Acting Locally …

Local environmental protests are no novelty in Britain, but they appear in recent years to have become increasingly frequent and prominent. Nowhere is this more apparent than in those areas of the southeast of England which have, since the early 1980s, come under increasing pressure of economic development and the associated transport infrastructure. Kent, formerly described as 'the garden of England', is, with the advent of greatly increased cross-Channel traffic even before the construction of the Channel Tunnel, now more often referred to as 'the Gateway to Europe'. Some local protests have been relatively successful; the route of the proposed fast rail link between London and the Channel Tunnel was changed several times in response to a series of vociferous and well-orchestrated local campaigns. Nevertheless, the limitations of local environmental action are well illustrated by several recent environmental controversies in Kent.

West Wood Oasis Village

One controversy surrounds the proposal of the Rank Leisure Group to build an 'oasis village' consisting of 400 forest lodges, 350 waterfront villas, 90 studios, a village centre, an artificial lake, a country club and a nine-hole golf course in West Wood, an area of ancient broadleaf woodland enclosed by the coniferous plantations of Lyminge Forest, near Folkestone. West Wood has long been popular with local walkers and picnickers but was severely damaged in the great storm of 1987. The proposed development promised the creation of at least a thousand new jobs in an area of chronically high unemployment and so had the backing of Kent County Council, but the site lies within the North Downs Area of Outstanding Natural Beauty, and an earlier proposal by CenterParcs to develop a woodland holiday and leisure centre in the same area had been thwarted by objections from environmentalists associated with the Kent Trust for Nature Conservation.

Rank, sensitive to the potential for local environmentalist opposition, went to considerable lengths to involve the Trust's officers – as well as local councillors – in consultations before it submitted its formal application. The 'planning gain' offered as a side benefit of the development was a promise to invest in the regeneration of a large area of surrounding woodland as a 'community forest' to compensate local people for the loss of the amenity of access to West Wood. Despite vocal opposition from local residents and some Canterbury environmentalists, the proposal was granted planning permission by the local district council and, after a public inquiry, by the (national) Secretary of State for the Environment. The protesters did not accept the decision, and the 500-member Save Lyminge Forest Action Group brought an action in the High Court for judicial review of the decision.[5]

Thus far the story might simply be held to demonstrate the impotence of local environmental movements in the face of concerted pressure from an assiduous transnational corporation and regional and national governments hungry for economic development, qualified only by the unusual recourse of a well-organised local movement to the national courts. But the story is given an added wrinkle by the news, only weeks before the court hearing, that Rank would in any case delay a final decision on the development pending clear evidence of the financial viability of another such development recently completed in the west of England. That announcement was linked to concerns about Rank's overall cash flow and its need to satisfy the demands of its shareholders for rising dividend income. Thus it is possible that, whatever the outcome of the judicial review, the development will be deferred or abandoned not because of local protests but because of the financial management considerations of a transnational corporation. In that event, even in what would undoubtedly be represented as a 'victory' for local opposition, the overwhelming dependence of the outcomes of local contention upon the actions and inaction of non-local actors would be further demonstrated.

Richborough power station and Orimulsion

A second controversy surrounds the burning of orimulsion, a bitumen-based fuel imported from Venezuela, at the Richborough power station near Sandwich. This was opposed by environmentalists because, when burned, orimulsion emits toxic heavy metals including vanadium. However, it became a public issue only when sulphurous emissions from the plant caused damage to the paintwork of cars stored in an importer's yard nearby. Attempts by Kent County Council's Environment Unit to investigate the issue were stonewalled by the power station's operator, PowerGen, which simply referred to its licence from the Pollution Inspectorate and its (temporary) exemption from limitations on emissions of sulphur dioxide (because the fuel was experimental and the area was considered to have a low overall 'pollution load'). Local Conservative MPs weighed in to defend

PowerGen from what they alleged were the employment-threatening anti-industry intrusions of environmentalists.

The issue was taken up by the Canterbury Greenpeace local support group but it in turn was stymied by its inability to establish dialogue with the company, to secure the support of local or national politicians, or to interest the general public in a problem which, to most of them, was invisible. Greenpeace UK did not take up the issue, and although Friends of the Earth (FoE) nationally has campaigned against the burning of orimulsion in general and at power stations in Cheshire and in Wales, neither it nor the almost moribund local FoE group picked up the Richborough issue. It was only after local protesters had effectively abandoned the field that remedial action seemed possible when Prudential, the major life assurance and pensions group, threatened legal action to secure compensation for the damage allegedly caused by pollutants from the power station to the nearby farmland which Prudential owns. In the event, shortly thereafter, PowerGen announced the closure of the station for 'economic reasons', citing the oversupply of electricity in a region which has no other non-nuclear power stations.

In addition to showing, again, the impotence of local environmental protests in the face of powerful vested interests, this case demonstrates a special difficulty of local environmental protests when the issue is rather less obvious than the loss of a local amenity or the transformation of the landscape. Air pollution may be a matter of nearly universal concern, but the air pollution of which lay people are most aware and which, because it is most visible, is most likely to be the subject of complaint – particulate fallout – is almost certainly less dangerous than the less visible airborne pollution of heavy metals from power station chimneys. It is only when the damage is all too evidently done – when there are demonstrable effects upon property or upon public health – that the local public, let alone national politicians, are capable of being interested in the issue.

Thruxted Mill

A third controversy concerns an animal waste rendering plant, Thruxted Mill, operated by Canterbury Mills in the Kent countryside between Canterbury and Ashford. Local people have for many years complained that the plant causes intolerable pollution in the form of noxious odours and by its practice of disposing of the effluent created by its treatment of animal carcasses by spreading it over surrounding fields. In 1995 the company was convicted and fined for a serious breach of pollution control regulations after local protesters, concerned about the threat to public health, revealed that trees were dying in woodland adjoining the fields over which the effluent was spread. After remedial action and the installation of some new equipment, the plant was in 1996 certified as complying with regulations. However, local people continued to complain about the smell and to worry about possible contamination of groundwater. Indeed, the issue had long been a principal concern of the local parish council, but it was hampered by two considerations: the concern of the local MP and the local district council was muted by worries that the plant's closure might entail the closure of a nearby abattoir with the possible loss of 300 jobs; secondly, because the plant is located in a rural area over five miles (eight kilometres) from the nearest town, Canterbury, it is invisible to all but the few hundred people who live in close proximity to it, people who, in turn, are difficult to mobilise because of the rural character of the area and whose concerns are difficult to communicate to the larger concentrations of people living in Canterbury and in Ashford.

So the matter might have rested were it not for the European Commission's insistence that Britain should embark on a mass cull of cattle in the attempt to eradicate BSE ('mad cow disease'). Ashford had already acquired some notoriety in 1985 as the site of the first confirmed case of BSE and now, according to a local neurologist, it was the centre of an unprecedented local cluster of CJD, the human form of encephalitis allegedly contractible from exposure to tissue from BSE-infected cattle. The massive increase in the numbers of cattle required to be culled in accordance with the EC decision exposed the limits of the UK's capacity effectively to dispose of such a large number of carcasses and brought the spotlight to bear upon the animal waste rendering industry.

One Sunday in the summer of 1996, the national BBC Radio 4 lunchtime news programme, 'The World This Weekend', led with a long story about Thruxted Mill, locals' complaints and anxieties about the plant, its relatively outdated technology and primitive disposal practices, and a neurologist's concerns about the possibility that prions, the infective agent from cattle infected with BSE, might leach into an aquifer and thence, via the nearby Mid Kent Water pumping station, into the district's water supply. Because this is the only large-scale rendering plant in the region, an immediate consequence of the increased cattle cull was an increase in the numbers of carcasses processed at the plant and in the volume of effluent discharged. Suspicions were aired that the EC-inspired anxiety of national government to find means of disposing of ever larger numbers of cattle entailed a relaxation of local pollution control standards.

During the following week, several national newspapers picked up the issue and it became a standard item in the Canterbury and Ashford local press. It transpired that the quantity of effluent from the plant exceeded the absorption capacity of the surrounding land and Canterbury City Council was asked to permit its discharge onto farmland in a neighbouring parish.

This it declined to do on the grounds that it had been advised that the underlying chalk, which the company and its defenders described as 'the finest natural filter', was known to contain fissures which might permit effluent to enter directly into the aquifer. The issue continued to rumble on in the local – and, apparently, in the German – press[6] and protest meetings continued to be well attended. Canterbury Mills duly appealed to the Secretary of State for the Environment against Canterbury City Council's failure to determine the company's application for planning permission within the statutory period of eight weeks, and a public inquiry was held in Canterbury in February 1997.

What is interesting about this case is that it once again shows how environmental protest, so long as it remains purely local, is largely ineffective. It also shows how the actions of a transnational body – in this case the EC – may change the policy of national government so that the nature and context of local action is transformed, with the result that local protesters who hitherto had to be content with letters to and brief reports in local newspapers suddenly had access to national print media and radio and to regional television. Thus is the dependent status of local protest confirmed.

III. From the Local to the Global

Local action may be dependent upon action or inaction at other levels, but that is not to say that it is always ineffective. One important effect of local action may to be educate those involved into more nearly global ways of seeing environmental problems. Studies of local disputes over waste management [*Rootes, 1997c*] suggest that the experience of involvement in NIMBY campaigns against the siting of waste treatment facilities is a profoundly educational one for many of those involved; not only do they learn more about the nature of waste and the technologies for its treatment and disposal, but they become sensitised to issues such as the energy involved in the transportation of waste and the possibilities of smaller scale and more local means of waste management. US evidence on the public reaction to toxic waste contamination reaches similar conclusions. Although the campaign against toxic waste began as NIMBY protests, in the course of the struggle protesters developed a broader understanding and critique of industrial practice and thus the 'movement for environmental justice' was born [*Szasz, 1994*, esp. Ch.4]. Local concerns thus came to be identified with global issues and local campaigns with the global phenomenon and so were seen to be in *everybody's* backyard [*Masterson-Allen and Brown, 1990; cf. Krauss, 1988*]. Indeed, another US study suggests that such broadening of the issues may be a condition of success. Walsh *et al.* [*1993*] conclude that the success of campaigns against the siting of waste facilities depends less upon the static characteristics of communities than upon the early framing of the issues of protest as wider issues of environmental management capable of appealing to a broader public rather than as simple NIMBY protests.

Local action may, nevertheless, often appear futile and the ability to sustain it heavily dependent upon the knowledge, skills, energy and charm of a handful of individuals. It is all too easily overwhelmed by the intrusions of better-resourced national actors and, as a consequence, local actors are obliged to avoid prematurely raising the stakes or committing themselves to courses of action which it is beyond their means to sustain. Yet, if in order to avoid taking on too much, local action operates entirely within the system whose effects it seeks to oppose, its ultimate effectiveness is again open to question. This suggests that no truly radical environmental action – that is to say, radical in the sense of going to the root of the problem – can remain purely local; in order to be effective, it is compelled to attempt to raise itself to the national – or even transnational – level (see Gould, Schnaiberg and Weinberg [1996]. Indeed, without national media coverage, many local protests operate below the threshold of even local visibility.

These difficulties of local environmental action suggest the need for a higher level of interest articulation which may be achieved by a political party or by a social movement organisation operating at the national or transnational level.

However, as the Kent cases demonstrate, it is not simply a question of local protests being linked and collectively mobilised at ever higher levels of aggregation until, ultimately, they are addressed to the global level. Global – or, at least, transnational – actions and events have repercussions at local level which may either crush or enormously enhance the opportunities of local environmental protesters. The global, the national, the regional and the local constantly and increasingly interpenetrate; indeed, it is the meaning of globalisation that there are ever fewer arena of contention whose parameters are purely national, regional or local. In none of the cases outlined above have national or transnational movement organisations become involved. Thus, at the level of action, the autonomy of local environmental movements is preserved. Yet the fate of local protests depends ever more upon the caprice of the action or inaction of more powerful non-local actors. As Vidich and Bensman [1958] remarked 40 years ago in their classic study, *Small Town in Mass Society*, the trouble with studying power at local level is that the most consequential decisions governing the fates of people in local communities are taken elsewhere, in the boardrooms of great corporations or in the chambers of legislatures or public bureaucracies. As it was with American small towns, so it is with local environmental movements.

IV. Acting Globally?

Policy-makers increasingly recognise that environmental problems are not conveniently contained by national political boundaries and so the realm of international agreements and co-operation has greatly expanded. So too has the global reach of transnational corporations and agencies for economic development such as the World Bank whose capacity for impact upon the environment is unprecedented. Local and even national environmental movements appear unequal to the task of contesting the environmental impact of the policies and actions of such global actors. What then are the prospects for the development of competent global environmental movements?

Sklair is pessimistic. Genuinely transnational movements – non-national, people-to-people movements – can indeed be created but they 'tend to be quite bureaucratic organisations liable to all the problems globally that Piven and Cloward identify nationally' [*Sklair, 1995: 509, n.4; 1994*]; the burdens of maintaining, servicing and financing the organisation are such that, far from advancing the cause by concerted action, such social movement organisations are actually a brake upon the more spontaneous and punctual local actions by which real victories might be achieved. Sklair draws parallels with the labour movement and its unequal struggle with transnational capital. It is not difficult to understand why the development of increasingly transnational capital should have comfortably outpaced the development of a transnational labour movement; capitalists and their servants are infinitely better provided with the resources (material, intellectual, cultural, linguistic) which make transnational action possible and effective than are workers and their collective organisations.

Yet the analogy with the labour movement may be misleading. The disproportion of resources is not so severe in the case of the contest between capital and environmentalists. Environmentalists may lack the material resources of great corporations but, because they are themselves drawn disproportionately from the ranks of the highly educated, the professionally and technically skilled and the affluent, they are less markedly disadvantaged with respect to intellectual, cultural and linguistic resources. Modern media of mass communication and information technology diminish the disparities yet further. On the whole, it appears that it is environmentalists who have made greater, more creative and more effective use of these new technologies than the corporations they oppose. Greenpeace's comprehensive rout of Shell over Brent Spar is simply the most spectacular example. Thus Sklair may well be right to be pessimistic about the prospects for effective transnational *poor people's* environmental movements, but he seems to underestimate the possibilities of – and, indeed, the results already achieved by – environmental organisations which at least strive to promote transnational action.

It is a moot point whether we can speak of a global environmental movement in the present tense. Certainly, there are no truly global environmental movement organisations; Greenpeace may be more transnational than most – and certainly more so than are less centralised and less hierarchical organisations such as Friends of the Earth – but its reach is greatest in the relatively rich, industrialised countries of the first world and it is unevenly spread even there. I shall now consider two recent cases, both involving Greenpeace, to illustrate some of the issues with which advocates and students of global or merely transnational environmental movements must reckon.

Greenpeace and Brent Spar

The first is the case of Shell Petroleum's thwarted attempt at deep sea disposal of the Brent Spar drilling platform. In this case, a multinational corporation acting with the approval of the national government concerned and in accordance both with international agreements and best scientific advice, was outmanoeuvred by a relatively modest, albeit spectacular, campaign of direct action by a multinational team of protesters acting in the name of a transnational campaigning organisation adept at the creation and management of news events. Media coverage of the Brent Spar occupation gained global publicity for Greenpeace and in turn stimulated boycotts, not organised by Greenpeace, of Shell's products in countries not originally involved or directly affected.

In this case, a powerful multinational oil company was defeated by a comparatively modestly resourced campaign and by the autonomous sympathetic responses to the news coverage of it. Neither national law nor international agreement nor scientific advice was able to counter or contain the campaign of an organisation which is not formally democratically accountable even to its own supporters. Greenpeace subsequently admitted that its estimate of the pollutant material contained in the Brent Spar platform was seriously exaggerated but this scarcely dented its credibility. As earlier surveys [e.g., *Milbrath, 1984*] have demonstrated, when it comes to environmental issues, people trust environmental organisations more than national governments or corporations.

Greenpeace and French Nuclear Weapons Tests in the South Pacific

The second case is that of the Greenpeace campaign against the French nuclear tests in the South Pacific. Much more logistically demanding and expensive of resources than the Brent Spar campaign, it gained Greenpeace enormous publicity and prestige and sparked an international boycott of

French goods which Greenpeace neither organised nor approved. This boycott directly damaged the market for French agricultural produce in northern Europe as well as the South Pacific, and indirectly, amongst other effects, it depressed the market in Britain for English apples (and apples imported from countries other than France) whose prices were substantially undercut by the glut of French apples diverted from markets where the boycott was more widespread than it was in Britain.

   In this case, Greenpeace contributed powerfully to the embarrassment of a democratically-elected national government and contrived to bring international pressure to bear upon it, but it also unleashed forces which it could not control and which threatened to have devastating effects upon parties quite other than the intended objects of pressure. Not only does this demonstrate the vulnerability even of governments of powerful democratic states to the actions of international campaigning organisations acting outside their borders and sometimes with negligible support within them, but it demonstrates too the virtual impossibility of controlling either the course or the consequences of sympathetic protests or of isolating them to the intended victim.

Implications

These cases raise a series of interesting questions. Are multinational corporations more vulnerable to challenge by transnational social movements than Sklair suggests? Greenpeace does not conform to the stereotype of the new social movements, but its demonstrable successes have led to increasing adoption of its tactics and style by other environmental movement organisations.[7] What does this imply for the theory of new social movements of which democratic mass participation has hitherto been regarded as a hallmark?

Thinking Globally, Acting Locally

Greenpeace has long encouraged its local support groups to confine themselves to locally publicising and raising funds for its national and international campaigns, and explicitly prohibits local groups from using the Greenpeace name in any autonomous local action. It is often a condition of success of local campaigns (particularly in countries as centralised as Britain and France) that they gain the endorsement of national organisations or attract the sustained attention of national mass media. Yet, as Canterbury Greenpeace activists discovered, Greenpeace UK does not endorse or give support to locally originated campaigns. This produced a crisis within Greenpeace UK that was fully reflected in the Canterbury group. Unwilling to confine themselves to the circumscribed role of fund-raising and publicity for Greenpeace's national and international campaigns, members of the Canterbury group embarked on limited local campaigns of their own, notably against the use of orimulsion at Richborough power station, but were frustrated by their inability to make any headway on the issue. This failure was instrumental in the group's increasing disaffiliation from Greenpeace UK and its conversion into a local anti-roads protest group. The problem of which this local instance was symptomatic was recognised by Greenpeace UK in 1995 when, in response to declining numbers of active supporters and stagnating levels of donations, it announced that, in order to 'empower' local supporters, it intended to relax the expectation that local support groups would confine themselves to fundraising and publicity. Given Greenpeace's reliance on the funds raised by local supporters, it is not surprising that there has been no visible evidence of any change in practice.

The experience of active Greenpeace supporters is especially interesting because it is they, as supporters of the leading contender for the status of a genuinely transnational environmental movement organisation more actively and practically committed than most to the perception of the truly global character of environmental problems, who are likely most acutely to experience the tensions between thinking globally and acting locally. The experience of the Canterbury group suggests that the more seriously the injunction to 'think globally, act locally' is taken, the greater is the frustration of movement activists at the gulf between the grandeur of their aspirations and the extreme modesty of what they can actually achieve at local level.

Greenpeace's organisational form reflects a considered pragmatic response to the constraints of effective campaigning action at the transnational level. Effective action at national, let alone transnational, level necessitates organisation and a degree of elite autonomy. At anything approaching a global level, internally democratic social movement organisation is impractical given the need for speed of response and the obstacles to effective communication amongst the members of a multi-national constituency. The complexities of issues and of decision-making at a global level thus dictate that decisions migrate ineluctably into the hands of elites. In the absence of a democratic global polity (and who seriously believes *that* is an imminent prospect?), this is a level at which a democratically accountable political party is impossible. It is small consolation, given the criticism of the 'democratic deficit' within the European Union, that the political actors which have most vigorously promoted global environmental agreements are the democratically elected governments of the EU itself.

If Greenpeace's organisation is undemocratic, the democratic accountability of national governments in environmental matters is increasingly questionable and the corporations which complain of Greenpeace's bullying have even fewer such credentials. Apologists for transnational corporations argue that they are accountable through the market: if people do not like or trust them, nobody will buy their products; they must, via the medium of advertising, persuade people to buy. A no less compelling argument can be made in defence of Greenpeace. If people do not support or approve of Greenpeace actions, they will not donate the considerable sums of money necessary to maintain Greenpeace campaigns. Moreover, it is precisely the democracy of the marketplace that Greenpeace action has often provoked; it was, above all, a consumer boycott of its products in Germany that persuaded Shell to abandon its attempt to dump the Brent Spar platform at sea.

V. Acting Globally, Thinking Locally?

If the Europeanisation, even the globalisation, of environmental movements is one message that can be drawn from these recent episodes, another is the persistence of national differences: the German, French and British publics reacted quite differently in each case. Indeed, in Britain the salience of both these issues was dwarfed by protests against the export of live animals, an issue that is greeted with incomprehension verging on incredulity in many other EU countries. The national peculiarities of environmental movements clearly testify to the persistent impact of national cultures and political structures and bear the imprint of national politics [cf. *Rootes, 1995, 1997a; Faucher, 1998*].

Environmentalists may be enjoined to 'think globally, act locally' but, because political thinking, no less than political action, is contextualised by the peculiarities of national cultures and institutions, citizens of different states will tend to think differently even when attempting to think globally. It is apparent that when would-be global movement actors do attempt to think globally, they are apt to do so in terms heavily freighted with the assumptions of the cultures from which they originate [*Bramble and Porter 1992; Yearley 1996: 92, 137*].

However, if no environmental movement organisation yet convincingly unites environmentalists of the first and third worlds, there is, if we employ a not too restrictive definition of the environmental 'movement' [e.g., *Diani 1992; Rootes 1997b*], a network of contacts and shared concerns that embraces at least the elites of environmental movement activists of North and South. Environmentalists from North and South may start from different perspectives, with different stocks of experience, and have different priorities, but it is said that at Rio the North learned from the South and that the contacts thus initiated have made at least the beginnings of a global environmental movement a reality. Nevertheless, organisations such as Greenpeace may aspire to create a transnational environmental consciousness, and they may, as a result of increasing contacts with activists from cultures other than those of the North, be increasingly sensitive to differences of perspective and balances of interest, but their attempts to create a transnational environmental consciousness continue to be received and translated into policy and action through the filters of national or regional cultures and institutions.

VI. Beyond Environmental Movements?

The erosion of the sovereignty of nation states which most commentators believe to be the inevitable accompaniment of economic globalisation and new communications technology may not, however, be an unmixed blessing for internationally-minded environmentalists. In the absence of effective mechanisms for democratic control in a global political system, the erosion of the sovereignty of nation states completes the disenfranchisement of the poorest and weakest at the same time as it enormously enhances the opportunities and power of elites.

It has been suggested that all environmental action is irremediably local. In the sense of policy delivery, that is true, but the more important truth is that the most consequential decisions and action both against and in defence of the environment have been taken at elite level. The myth of direct democracy that informs so much of the environmental movement – and the injunction to empower local communities – is a moral ideal rather than a practical strategy. Empowered local communities may, after all, make environmental decisions with little or no regard to the consequences for others living beyond those communities. As efforts to clean up Europe's river systems have demonstrated, environmental problems transcend political boundaries but, even where supranational political fora exist to facilitate the discussion of such problems, gaining agreement and effective policy implementation is, given the diversity of perspectives and interests involved, extremely difficult.[8] Without such translocal political arrangements, concerted action to protect and improve the environment would be quite impossible. The more sophisticated and less fundamentalist recommendation that environmental policy decisions should be taken 'at the appropriate level' founders upon the difficulty of deciding in any democratic way *who* should determine what is the appropriate level.

Normal democratic processes do not reliably suffice to get the matters of greatest concern to the least advantaged sections of populations onto the agenda even in the most democratic states. Because ordinary citizens do not have sufficient knowledge or understanding of environmental issues, they cannot be relied upon to bring pressure for the amelioration of those environmental hazards which are actually (rather than merely apparently) most threatening to them or to others. Less visible and more complex environmental problems are not likely to be raised as public issues from below.

Almost everywhere it is elite pressures and action rather than mass, popular pressure that have been the agents of new environmental regulation. If governments, especially in Europe, have been prepared to grapple with such complex issues, it is less because they have responded to the demands of democratic majorities than because they have succumbed to the arguments (and sometimes the threats) of non-elected elites – the scientific community or environmental NGOs. It is remarkable that so much international agreement has been achieved so quickly, but it is difficult to imagine that it could have been done had not the governing elites of the hegemonic powers been receptive to the arguments of scientific elites and NGOs, or, at least, to the blandishments of representatives of governments which were so receptive. When the history of the negotiations which produced these agreements comes to be written, it is more likely to be a history of the interactions among elites than one of popular mobilisation.

The success of NGOs in raising environmental issues raises new questions of accountability. Environmental movement organisations are rarely democratically accountable, even to their members and supporters; Greenpeace makes no pretence of being so. NGOs cannot hope to match the resources of governments, and it is questionable whether, even when they harvest the goodwill of the scientific community, they will always come up with the right answers, simply because they, like governments, have preconceptions and vested interests which mean they cannot be neutral receptors of the best science. To the extent that environmental movement organisations mobilise large numbers of people who are driven by sentiment rather than proper understanding of the issues, they may unwittingly force governments into action and agreements that are not only sub-optimal from a scientific point of view but even counterproductive.[9]

Too much of the discussion of environmental politics has assumed that the pressure for environmental justice flows from below. It is clear that it can only fitfully do so because the less well-educated and less resourceful mass of the populations of all nations have neither the knowledge nor the means to mount an effective challenge to established concentrations of political and economic power. Environmental movement organisations may compensate to some degree, but their own understanding of the issues and their own democratic credentials are questionable. The radical question this raises is whether it may be necessary for elites to impose upon reluctant masses the solutions to pressing environmental problems which those elites believe to be necessary. It is only the relative lack of salience of the most complex environmental problems and the costs of addressing them that has so far obscured the starkness of this scenario.

Greater responsiveness of elites to democratic pressure is no guarantee that environmental justice will be more securely entrenched. In some countries, the ideology of material progress through economic development is so endemic that, when it becomes clear that international environmental agreements impose real economic costs, a powerful backlash is to be expected. Australia, for example, declared itself opposed to the inclusion of carbon dioxide emissions targets in the protocols to the climate change convention negotiated at Kyoto because, Australian delegates argued, to implement such targets would seriously inhibit national economic development and so would threaten employment. It is probable that the Australian Labor government was prepared to risk international isolation[10] on this issue because the domestic political calendar meant it would have been suicidal to have entered an election committed to measures which threatened to curtail already elusive economic growth; its conservative successor is even more unqualifiedly committed to economic growth. The net result is that, on the climate change issue, Australian environmental NGOs have been completely marginalised. What has already happened in Australia for rather special reasons might well be a portent of things to come elsewhere. If governing elites begin to be more responsive to the (inevitably short-term) economic concerns of the governed, then international environmental agreements will become more elusive and their implementation even more erratic.

The democratic solution is to invest in the education of mass publics so that they might be better able to understand the issues and to take a responsible part in environmental politics. At present, this seems a pious hope. Global environmental problems are not only relatively inaccessible to most people, they are largely unintelligible by them. Popular comprehension of global warming is still at the level of seeing proof of the greenhouse effect in every spell of unusually warm weather – and disconfirmation in every severe cold snap. Such issues as this, where there is no scientific consensus and less popular comprehension, are especially susceptible to media simplification and misrepresentation and so are more likely to produce panics and alarms than an informed public opinion capable of being effectively mobilised.

As a result, the issues retreat from the democratic arena to that of elite decision-making, and become a balancing act between scientists and politicians. In his pessimistic prognosis for an effective democratic global environmental movement, Sklair [*1995: 498*] cites Michels on the likelihood that revolutionary goals will be subordinated to bureaucratic means. But Michels was not the unremitting pessimist that most commentators have painted him. He believed that the inescapable price of the organisation of democratic mass parties was an unequal distribution of power within them, but he did not suppose that the *degree* of that inequality was immutable. On the contrary, he suggested that, with increased levels of education, a larger proportion of the citizenry would be capable of effective political participation and he identified the social education of the working class as an urgent task in order to combat the oligarchical tendencies of the working class movement [*Michels, (1911) 1959: 406–7*]. That, it seems to me, displayed fair prescience about the surge of aspirations to democratic participation that has been the general experience of advanced western societies during the past three decades. So it may yet be with the environmental movement. The highly educated are everywhere an increasing proportion of the population, and a more educated – and, especially, a better scientifically and technologically educated – population may be better able both to understand environmental issues and to sustain democratic organisations capable of addressing them.

NOTES

1. See the similar finding in the US by Ladd and Laska [*1991*].
2. But see Kousis (in this volume) for evidence that *local* resistance to environmental degradation is widespread in Greece, Spain and Portugal; the fact that it is not well connected to effective national environmental movement organisations is most likely explained by peculiarities of the ways in which political opportunities and political culture have been structured by past experience of authoritarian rule and the circumstances of the transition to democracy.
3. Moreover, 'green political activists seem to have a worldview or ideology that links their environmental activism with resistance to a preoccupation with economic growth, and with sympathy for strong welfare provision. Thus … green political activism … is much more likely to be found among people who have a coherent ideology linking social and environmental problems and solutions' [*Witherspoon 1994: 128*]. Support for green policies even at some personal cost 'depends not only upon knowledge but upon social values … Those who place a high value on the welfare of others and on a collective approach to solving social problems are more likely to be willing to support environmental policies than those who do not' [*1994: 135*]. This, incidentally, runs counter to arguments [e.g., *Rüdig 1990*] that there is a new 'ecological cleavage' in mass publics. It is not necessary to denigrate the seriousness or novelty of environmental issues to suggest that they appear to add a new dimension to the old collectivist-welfarist versus individualist cleavage.
4. This may help to explain why the correlation between post-materialism and support for Green parties is generally only modest [*Rüdig, 1990: 14; Franklin and Rüdig 1991, 1995*]: amongst the people who vote for Green parties and support environmental movements, as well as highly educated 'post-materialist' ecologists who are not so much fearful for their own security as concerned about global environmental problems whose effects are more remote, there are people, usually less well educated, who are motivated principally by fear of the threats that pollution and nuclear waste pose to their own material security.
5. On the background to and early stages of this development, see David [*1997*]. My account of this and the other local cases discussed here also draws on reports in the local press, especially the *Kentish Gazette*.

6. 'Local feeling runs high at animal plant meeting', *Kentish Gazette*, 19 Sept. 1996.
7. On Greenpeace, see Eyerman and Jamison [*1989*], Dalton [*1994*], Rucht [*1995*], Wapner [*1996: Ch.3*]. Shaiko [*1993*] (implicitly, in his description of Greenpeace USA) and Dalton provide evidence that even a deliberately transnational organisation such as Greenpeace cannot escape the imprint of local circumstances upon its organisation, strategies and orientations.
8. See De Jong and Leroy [*1996*] on Dutch – German boundary problems.
9. The bio-diversity convention may be a case in point.
10. Australia was not, of course, entirely isolated. In the months before Kyoto, Australian representatives made strenuous efforts to orchestrate resistance to the imposition of CO_2 reduction targets, and Australia's stance was shared, at least initially, by the United States, Canada and Japan. Australia does have a special case in that it is a relatively energy-efficient processor of its own primary produce, especially minerals, but special cases are, of course, legion.

REFERENCES

Bramble, B. and G. Porter (1992), 'Non-Governmental Organizations and the Making of US International Environmental Policy', in A. Hurrell and B. Kingsbury (eds.), *The International Politics of the Environment*, Oxford: Clarendon Press.
Dalton, R. (1994), *The Green Rainbow*, New Haven, CT and London: Yale University Press.
David, M. (1997), 'Local Environmental Movements', Ph.D. thesis, Department of Sociology, University of Kent at Canterbury.
De Jong, D. and P. Leroy, (1996), 'Conflicting Constructions of Nature in Transboundary Policy on Nature Conservation and Nature Development', paper presented to the international conference on 'The Environment in the 21st Century: Environment, Long-Term Governance and Democracy', Abbaye de Fontevraud, 8–11 Sept.
Diani, M. (1992), 'The Concept of Social Movement', *Sociological Review,* Vol.40, pp.1–25.
Eyerman, R. and A. Jamison (1989), 'Environmental Knowledge as an Organizational Weapon: The Case of Greenpeace', *Social Science Information,* Vol.2.
Faucher, F. (1998), 'Manger vert: Choix alimentaires et identité politique chez les écologistes français et britannique', *Revue Française de Science Politique*, Vol.48, Nos.3–4, pp.436–56.
Franklin, M. and W. Rüdig (1991), 'The Greening of Europe: Ecological Voting in the 1989 European Elections', *Stratchclyde Papers on Government and Politics*, No.82, Department of Government, University of Strathclyde, Glasgow.
Franklin, M. and W. Rüdig (1995), 'On the Durability of Green Politics: Evidence from the 1989 European Election Study', *Comparative Political Studies*, Vol.28, pp.409–39.
Gould, K.A., Schnaiberg, A. and A.S. Weinberg (1996), *Local Environmental Struggles*, Cambridge: Cambridge University Press.
Hofrichter, J. and K. Reif (1990), 'Evolution of Environmental Attitudes in the European Community', *Scandinavian Political Studies,* Vol.13, pp.119–46.
Krauss, C. (1988), 'Grass-Root Consumer Protest and Toxic Wastes: Developing a Critical Political View', *Community Development Journal*, Vol.23, No.4, pp.258–65.
Ladd, Anthony E. and Shirley Laska (1991), 'Opposition to Solid Waste Incineration', *Sociological Inquiry*, Vol.16, No.3, pp.299–313.
Masterson-Allen, S. and P. Brown (1990), 'Public Reaction to Toxic Waste Contamination: Analysis of a Social Movement', *International Journal of Health Services*, Vol.20, No.3, pp.485–500.
Michels, R. (1959 [original 1911]), *Political Parties: A Sociological Study of the Oligarchical Tendencies of Modern Democracy*, New York: Dover.
Milbrath, L. (1984), *Environmentalists: Vanguard for a New Society,* Albany, NY: State University of New York Press.
Rootes, C.A. (1995), 'Environmental Consciousness, Institutional Structures and Political Competition in the Formation and Development of Green Parties', in D. Richardson and C. Rootes (eds.), *The Green Challenge: The Development of Green Parties in Europe*, London and NY: Routledge.

Rootes, C.A. (1997a) 'Shaping Collective Action: Structure, Contingency and Knowledge' pp.81–104 in R. Edmondson (ed.), *The Political Context of Collective Action*, London: Routledge.

Rootes, C.A. (1997b), 'Environmental Movements and Green Parties in Western and Eastern Europe', in M. Redclift and G. Woodgate (eds.), *International Handbook of Environmental Sociology*, Cheltenham and Northampton, MA: Edward Elgar, pp.319–48.

Rootes, C.A. (1997c), 'From Resistance to Empowerment: The Struggle Over Waste Management and its Implications for Environmental Education', in N. Russell *et a.l* (eds.), *Technology, the Environment and Us*, London: GSE, Imperial College, pp.30–39.

Rucht, D. (1995), 'Ecological Protest as Calculated Law-Breaking: Greenpeace and Earth First! in Comparative Perspective', in W. Rüdig (ed.), *Green Politics Three*, Edinburgh University Press, pp.66–89.

Rüdig, W. (1990), Explaining Green Party Development', *Stratchclyde Papers on Government and Politics*, No.71, Department of Government, University of Stratchclyde.

Rüdig, W. (1995) 'Public Opinion and Global Warming: A Comparative Analysis', *Strathclyde papers on Government and Politics* No. 101, Glasgow: Department of Government, University of Strathclyde.

Scharf, T. (1994), *The German Greens: Challenging the Consensus*, Oxford and Providence, RI: Berg.

Shaiko, R.G. (1993), 'Greenpeace USA: Something Old, New, Borrowed', *The Annals of the American Academy of Political and Social Science*, Vol.528, pp.88–100.

Sklair, L. (1994), 'Global Sociology and Global Environmental Change', in M. Redclift and T. Benton (eds.), *Social Theory and the Global Environment*, London: Routledge.

Sklair, L. (1995), 'Social Movements and Global Capitalism', *Sociology*, Vol.29, pp.495–512.

Szasz, A. (1994), *EcoPopulism: Toxic Waste and the Movement for Environmental Justice*, Minneapolis, MN: University of Minnesota Press.

Vidich, A.J. and J. Bensman (1958), *Small Town in Mass Society*, Princeton, NJ: Princeton University Press.

Walsh, E., Warland, R. and D. Clayton Smith (1993), 'Backyard NIMBYS and Incinerator Sitings: Implications for Social Movement Theory', *Social Problems*, Vol.40, No1.

Wapner, P. (1996), *Environmental Activism and World Civic Politics*, Albany, NY: State University of New York Press.

Witherspoon, S. (1994), 'The Greening of Britain: Romance and Rationality', in R. Jowell *et al.*, (eds.), *British Social Attitudes: The 11th Report*, Aldershot: Dartmouth, pp.107–39.

Witherspoon, S. and J. Martin (1993), 'Environmental Attitudes and Activism in Britain', JUSST Working Paper No.20, Oxford: SCPR and Nuffield College.

Yearley, S. (1996), *Sociology, Environmentalism, Globalization*, London: Sage.

Notes on Contributors

Karl-Werner Brand is Professor of Social Studies of Science in the Interdisciplinary Institute for Science Studies (IIWW), University of Erlangen-Nuremberg, and Head of the Münchner Projektgruppe für Sozialforschung (MPS), Research Unit 'Society and Environment', München, Germany.

JoAnn Carmin received her Ph.D. from the Department of City and Regional Planning, University of North Carolina at Chapel Hill, USA. Her research focuses on local environment mobilisation and community organisations in the United States and Eastern Europe.

Mario Diani is Professor of Sociology in the Department of Government at Strathclyde University, Glasgow, Scotland.

Paolo R. Donati is a researcher and consultant at TESI, Milan, Italy.

Lucy Ford is a research student at the Centre for the Comparative Study of Culture, Development and Environment, University of Sussex, England.

Jeff Haynes is Reader in Politics at London Guildhall University, England.

Manuel Jiménez is a research officer at the Instituto Juan March, Madrid, Spain.

Maria Kousis is Associate Professor in the Department of Sociology, School of Social Sciences, University of Crete, Rethimno, Greece.

Christopher Rootes is Director of the Centre for the Study of Social and Political Movements and Senior Lecturer in Sociology at the University of Kent at Canterbury, England.

Jochen Roose is a research assistant at the Wissenschaftszentrum Berlin für Sozialforschung (WZB), Germany.

Dieter Rucht is Professor of Sociology at the University of Kent at Canterbury, England.

David Schlosberg is an Assistant Professor in the Department of Political Science, Northern Arizona University, Flagstaff, USA.

Hein-Anton van der Heijden is a lecturer in Political Science at the University of Amsterdam, The Netherlands.

Derek Wall is an Honorary Research Fellow in the Centre for the Study of Social and Political Movements, University of Kent at Canterbury, England.

Marc Williams is Professor of International Relations, University of New South Wales, Australia. He was previously Director of the Centre for the Comparative Study of Culture, Development and the Environment, University of Sussex, England.

Zoe Young is a doctoral candidate in the Department of Geography, University of Hull.

Index

316   ENVIRONMENTAL MOVEMENTS: LOCAL, NATIONAL, GLOBAL

Books of Related Interest

Dilemmas of Transition

The Environment, Democracy and Economic Reform in East Central Europe

Susan Baker, *University of Wales, Cardiff* and
Petr Jehlicka, *Charles University, Prague* (Eds)

This volume explores the impact of the twin process of democratisation and marketisation on the environment in East Central Europe. Three environmental matters are investigated: how the twin processes of change have affected (1) the physical environment (2) the expression of environmental interest and (3) the effectiveness of environmental management policies. The book also examines the role of the European Union because of the influence it exercises on environmental policy in East Central Europe. It finds that political and economic instability and external pressures have displaced environmental considerations from centre stage. This has meant a failure within East Central Europe to realise a more far-reaching and more sustainable approach towards the management of transition.

224 pages 1998
0 7146 4764 0 cloth
0 7146 4310 6 paper
A special issue of the journal Environmental Politics

FRANK CASS PUBLISHERS
Newbury House, 900 Eastern Avenue, Newbury Park, Ilford, Essex IG2 7HH
Tel: +44 (0)181 599 8866 Fax: +44 (0)181 599 0984 E-mail: info@frankcass.com
NORTH AMERICA
5804 NE Hassalo Street, Portland, OR 97213 3644, USA
Tel: 1 800 944 6190 Fax: 503 280 8832 E-mail cass@isbs.com
Website: www.frankcass.com

Ecology and Democracy

Freya Mathews, *LaTrobe University* (Ed)

' ... this is as good a collection as I have seen on this topic.'
Ethics

What is the optimal political framework for environmental
reform - reform on a scale commensurate with the global
ecological crisis? In particular, how adequate are liberal forms of
parliamentary democracy to the challenge posed by this crisis?
These are the questions pondered by the contributors to this
volume. Exploration of the possibilities of democracy gives rise
to certain common themes. These include the relation between
ecological morality and political structures or procedures and the
question of the structure of decision-making and distribution of
information in political systems. The idea of 'democracy without
traditional boundaries' is discussed as a key both to
environmentalism in an age of global ecology and to the
revitalisation of democracy itself in a world of increasingly
protean constituencies and mutable, indeed soluble, boundaries.

248 pages 1996
0 7146 4252 5 paper
A special issue of the journal Environmental Politics

FRANK CASS PUBLISHERS
Newbury House, 900 Eastern Avenue, Newbury Park, Ilford, Essex IG2 7HH
Tel: +44 (0)181 599 8866 Fax: +44 (0)181 599 0984 E-mail: info@frankcass.com
NORTH AMERICA
5804 NE Hassalo Street, Portland, OR 97213 3644, USA
Tel: 1 800 944 6190 Fax: 503 280 8832 E-mail cass@isbs.com
Website: www.frankcass.com

Rio: Unravelling the Consequences

Caroline Thomas, *Southampton University* (Ed)

This interdisciplinary collection suggests that at the most
fundamental level, the causes of environmental degradation have
not been tackled. The intellectual debate inside and outside
UNCED has been dominated by powerful entrenched interests
which marginalise rival interpretations of the crisis and block
possible alternative ways forward. The crisis is therefore being
tackled by a continuation of the very policies that have largely
caused it in the first place.

244 pages 1994; repr. 1997
0 7146 4110 3 paper
A special issue of the journal Environmental Politics

FRANK CASS PUBLISHERS
Newbury House, 900 Eastern Avenue, Newbury Park, Ilford, Essex IG2 7HH
Tel: +44 (0)181 599 8866 Fax: +44 (0)181 599 0984 E-mail: info@frankcass.com
NORTH AMERICA
5804 NE Hassalo Street, Portland, OR 97213 3644, USA
Tel: 1 800 944 6190 Fax: 503 280 8832 E-mail cass@isbs.com
Website: www.frankcass.com

Sustainable Development in Western Europe

Coming to Terms with Agenda 21

Tim O'Riordan and Heather Voisey, *both at the University of East Anglia* (Eds)

' an important text for students of contemporary development strategies and interested parties alike.'
Simon Kenton, Environmental, Education and Information

The transition to sustainable development will test government and democracy in a fundamentally radical way. This series of essays looks at three elements of sustainable development in terms of the institutional challenge they pose, and from the viewpoint of five European Union Member States.

192 pages 1997
0 7146 4830 2 cloth
0 7146 4376 9 paper
A special issue of the journal Environmental Politics

FRANK CASS PUBLISHERS
Newbury House, 900 Eastern Avenue, Newbury Park, Ilford, Essex IG2 7HH
Tel: +44 (0)181 599 8866 Fax: +44 (0)181 599 0984 E-mail: info@frankcass.com
NORTH AMERICA
5804 NE Hassalo Street, Portland, OR 97213 3644, USA
Tel: 1 800 944 6190 Fax: 503 280 8832 E-mail cass@isbs.com
Website: www.frankcass.com